本书由浙江大学侨福建设基金资助出版

2011年国家社会科学基金青年项目“中日韩自贸区竞争与反倾销规则协调研究”阶段性成果

倾销：反倾销法抑或竞争法

DUMPING: ANTIDUMPING LAW OR COMPETITION LAW

毕莹 著

知识产权出版社
全国百佳图书出版单位

内容提要

本书从历史渊源出发，跟随反倾销制度的发展，探究其长久以来“不证自明”之前提的真实性——“倾销有害”，在明确其与竞争法的相关性后，结合传统的和新的“重度使用反倾销者”两方面实践，以比较的方法全面探讨将“倾销”置于竞争法而非反倾销法之下的优势，同时梳理及剖析反对该取代的主要理由。最终得出：以世界贸易组织《反倾销协议》为基准的各国反倾销规则应最终为日益发展并相互融合的各国竞争规则以及有关掠夺性价格歧视的国际统一竞争协议所取代。为逐步达到该目标，更多的可行性方案应自双边和区域展开。

责任编辑： 彭小华　　**责任出版：** 卢运霞
执行编辑： 雷春丽　　**封面设计：** 睿思视界

图书在版编目（CIP）数据

倾销：反倾销法抑或竞争法：英文/毕莹著．—北京：知识产权出版社，2011.10

ISBN 978-7-5130-0863-1

Ⅰ.①倾…　Ⅱ.①毕…　Ⅲ.①反倾销法-研究-英文②反不正当竞争-经济法-研究-英文　Ⅳ.①D912.290.4

中国版本图书馆 CIP 数据核字（2011）第 202034 号

倾销：反倾销法抑或竞争法

QINGXIAO：FANQINGXIAOFA YIHUO JINGZHENGFA

毕莹　著

出版发行： 知识产权出版社	
社　　址： 北京市海淀区马甸南村1号	**邮　　编：** 100088
网　　址： http://www.ipph.cn	**邮　　箱：** bjb@cnipr.com
发行电话： 010-82000860 转 8101/8102	**传　　真：** 010-82005070/82000893
责编电话： 010-82000860 转 8107	**责编邮箱：** leichunli@cnipr.com
印　　刷： 知识产权出版社电子制印中心	**经　　销：** 新华书店及相关销售网点
开　　本： 880mm×1230mm　1/32	**印　　张：** 13.625
版　　次： 2011年11月第1版	**印　　次：** 2011年11月第1次印刷
字　　数： 387千字	**定　　价：** 35.00元

ISBN 978-7-5130-0863-1/D·1330（3747）

Acknowledgement

I'm deeply indebted to my supervisors Professor Michiaki Abe and Professor Caslav Pejovic for their patience, kind advice and support. I also owe my thanks to Professor M. Sornarajah for his great encouragement and inspiration.

I would also like to express my deepest gratitude to Professor Steven Van Uytsel, for his great encouragement from the very beginning, his efforts to find for me various useful materials, and his kind offer to help whenever I need to clarify my thinking.

Special thanks to my senior Yuanjie for helping me to clarify my thinking on reorganizing my book and on various specific issues. And also special thanks to my colleague Lilou for learning and exchanging experiences with me, and for her kind comfort during my hardest time. Thanks to my colleagues Lim Tai Ching, Simon Vande Walle and Chonticha Sae-Lim for helping me to clarify and check specific issues of the book.

And also, I would like to thank my grandfather, my parents, and my husband Xiang Rong, for their continued love, support and encouragement. I would like to specially dedicate this book to my dearest grandfather, who unfortunately has passed away during its editing. May your soul rest in peace in heaven!

Abstract

With the proliferation of antidumping laws as well as that of antidumping actions all around the world, the antidumping rules' increasingly potential for protectionist abuse has been criticized in almost all of the current literature. Among them, most scholars are of the opinion that the misuse of antidumping is mainly due to its arbitrary and biased rules and procedures. Recently, an increasing number of scholars started to rethink the fundamental basis for the existence of the whole antidumping system. They pointed out that antidumping rules are established on several false premises, having no justification from competition perspective, and anti-competitive in many respects. Hence, antidumping law should be substituted by competition law (the so-called "substitution" debate).

Through reexamining "dumping" as a private business conduct which might be also subject to competition law, this book also attempts to contribute to the debate of integrating antidumping with competition. This book begins with the process of reconsidering the self-evident premise of antidumping law, i. e. , why dumping is harmful. After confirming its linkage with competition law, the book continues to examine and consider the advantages of putting dumping under competition rules instead of antidumping rules from three perspectives, as well as two major objections against the substitution. In examining the various arguments, this book not only focuses on the traditional heavy users of antidumping, the U. S. and the EU, but also calls for more research to be done to those developing countries as the new heavy users of antidumping. And in this aspect, this book aims at contributing to the current debate by achieving a specific examination on China, one of the new heavy users of antidumping that is unknown to the world.

Based on all of the analyses and examinations from both traditional and new heavy users of antidumping, this book concludes by suggesting that domestic antidumping rules and the WTO Antidumping Agreement should be substituted by harmonized domestic competition rules and the international competition agreement on predatory price discrimination in future. In order to achieve it, this book also calls for more efforts to be made in bilateral and regional areas, as well as a workable proposal to reform current antidumping rules in a way to be substituted by competition rules.

Introduction

1. Background Information

With the proliferation of antidumping laws as well as that of antidumping actions all around the world, the antidumping rules' increasingly potential for protectionist abuse has been criticized in almost all of the current literature. ❶ Hence, thousands of pages with various proposals have been brought up with the same purpose to reform the antidumping system. Among them, most scholars are of the opinion that the misuse of antidumping is mainly due to its arbitrary and biased rules and procedures, so efforts must be continuously done to make it more stringent and transparent, less arbitrary and abusive. ❷ However, years of efforts devoted to the above perspective seem to suggest that there are no substantial improvements, and many

---

❶ *See more*, Spencer Weber Waller, *Bringing Globalism Home: Lessons from Antitrust and Beyond*, Loyola University Chicago Law Journal, 2000, Vol. 32, p. 113; Ian Wooton & Maurizio Zanardi, *Trade and Competition Policy: Antidumping versus Anti-trust*, 2002, pp. 1, 13, http://homepages. strath. ac. uk/ ~ hbs03116/Research/Trade%20and %20Competition %20Policy%20Final. pdf, last visited May 24, 2009; Gunnar Niels, *What is Antidumping Policy Really About?* Journal of Economic Surveys, 2002, Vol. 14, pp. 467, 485, http://www. blackwell – synergy. com/links/doi/10. 1111/1467 – 6419. 00118, last visited September 21, 2011; Brink Lindsey & Daniel J. Ikenson, *Antidumping Exposed : the Devilish Details of Unfair Trade Law*, Cato Institute, 2003, p. viii.

❷ *See, e. g.*, Aradhna Aggrawal, *the WTO Antidumping Code: Issues for Review in Post – Doha Negotiations*, Working Paper No. 99, 2003, pp. 1 – 54, http://www. icrier. org/pdf/WP99. pdf, last visited May 3, 2011.

of the practices that have been identified as leading to significant protectionist biases remain untouched. ❶

Recently, an increasing number of scholars started to rethink the fundamental basis for the existence of the whole antidumping system. They pointed out that antidumping rules are established on several false premises, having no justification from the perspective of competition, and anti-competitive in many respects. ❷ Hence, they are arguing that further fine-tuning and refining of antidumping policy is not the answer to prevent its misuse, the antidote is competition policy. Efforts should be directed at integrating antidumping with competition. ❸

---

❶ *See, e. g.*, Bernard M. Hoekman & Petros C. Mavroidis, *Antitrust – Based Remedies and Dumping in International Trade*, Policy Research Working Paper No. 1347, the World Bank, 1994, pp. 1, 7, http://www - wds. worldbank. org/servlet/WDSContentServer/WDSP/IB/1994/08/01/000009265 _3970716141633/Rendered/PDF /multi0page. pdf, last visited May 3, 2011.

❷ "One would be hard pressed to find a scholar steeped in competition law and policy that supports current antidumping rules. Most would prefer their outright replacement with a competition – based regime that could address any serious instance of dumping that actually harms consumers and the process of competition." *See* Spencer Weber Waller, *Bringing Globalism Home: Lessons from Antitrust and Beyond*, Loyola University Chicago Law Journal, 2000, Vol. 32, p. 113

❸ *See more*, Martyn D. Taylor, *International Competition Law: A New Dimension for the WTO?* Cambridge Univ. Press Inc. 2006, pp. 260 – 285; Andreas Knorr, *Antidumping Rules vs. Competition Rules*, Institution for World Economics and International Management, 2004, pp. 1 – 19, http://www. iwim. uni – bremen. de/publikationen/pdf/W031. pdf, last visited May 3, 2011; J. Michael Finger & Andrei Zlate, *Antidumping: Prospects for Discipline from Doha Negotiations*, Working Papers in Economics, 2005, pp. 1 – 38, http://escholarship. bc. edu/cgi/viewcontent. cgi?article = 1184&context = econ_papers, last visited May 3, 2011; Claude Barfield, *Antidumping: Time to: (1) Go Back to Basics; and (2) Politicize the Final Outcome; or (3) Substitute Safeguards for Antidumping Actions*, Paper Prepared for the Centennial of Antidumping Legislation and Implementation Symposium, 2004, pp. 1 – 40, http://fordschool. umich. edu/rsie/Conferences/ADSym/Barfield. pdf, last visited May 3, 2011.

My research focuses on the interaction between competition law and trade law.❶ Through examining antidumping law, one of the most controversial trade rules, from the perspective of competition law, this book attempts to contribute to the debate of integrating antidumping with competition, or rather, the so-called "substitution" debate.

The debate of antidumping versus competition hasn't drawn much attention until the 1970s. And since the mid-1980s, the lively debate has flourished as to whether and how competition standards should be substituted for antidumping rules.❷ Although this issue is relatively new, it is very significant.❸ The research on this issue can not only contribute to the discussion of protectionist abuse of antidumping, but also to that of globalization of competition law, one of the most important discussions of the present age. Among the various issues under the umbrella of the uniform of competition law, the harmonization between competition law and trade law is undoubtedly taking up an

---

❶ It is understood that the terms "antitrust" and "competition" can be used similarly or differently to each other, here in this book, they are considered to have the same meaning.

❷ Gunnar Niels, *What is Antidumping Policy Really About*? Journal of Economic Surveys, 2002, Vol. 14, pp. 467, 479, http://www.blackwell-synergy.com/links/doi/10.1111/1467-6419.00118, last visited September 21, 2011.

❸ For example, Lloyd deemed that the point of view, which re-examines dumping from the point of view of a form of business conduct that might be subject to competition law, is relatively new but it is causing a fundamental rethinking of the economics of antidumping actions. *See* P. J. Lloyd, *Antidumping and Competition Law*, in Patrick F. J Macrory *et al.*, eds., *II The World Trade Organization: Legal, Economic and Political Analysis*, Springer 2005, p. 69.

essential place. [1] The "antidumping" issue therein is viewed as the threshold for competition law to penetrate into trade area. [2]

In the area of academic research, this issue has been drawing increasing attention of both trade scholars and competition scholars, not only in developed countries, but also in developing countries. [3]In the

---

[1] During the early 1990s, the demand for international competition policy spread to other Uruguay round agreement – on safeguards, services, intellectual property rights, trade-related investment measures, and to the plurilateral agreement on government procurement. *See* Patrick A. Messerlin, Competition Policy and Antidumping Reform: An Exercise in Transition, in JJ. Schott ed. , *the World Treading System: Challenges Ahead*, Washington DC: Institute for International Economics, 1996, p. 219, http://www. iie. com/publications/chapters_preview/66/13iie2350. pdf, last visited May 24, 2009.

[2] Ralf Boscheck considered: "to thoroughly assess the preconditions for an international coordination of competition – related trade issues, it is inevitable, initially at least, to focus on one salient concern. Antidumping provides the most critical case in point. " *See* Ralf Boscheck, *the Governance of Global Market Relations: the Case of Substituting Antitrust for Antidumping*, World Competition, 2001, p. 53.

[3] This issue has incurred a hot discussion among the scholars of developed countries. For example, there are many discussions in the Brookings Trade Forum, including Antidumping and Antitrust: What Problems Does Each Address; Possible Instances of Predatory Pricing in Recent U. S. Antidumping Cases; Economic Impact of Canadian Antidumping Law; The European Community's Experience etc. *See* Robert Z. Lawrence, *Brookings Trade Forum* ed. , Brookings Institution Press 1998, pp. 1 – 434. Besides, there are also increasing discussions among developing countries. *See, e. g.* , Aradhna Aggarwal, Anti Dumping Law and Practice: An Indian Perspective, *Indian Council for Research on International Economic Relations*, 2002, pp. 1 – 68, http://www. icrier. org/pdf/antiDump. pdf, last visited May 3, 2011; Merle Holden, *Anti Dumping: A Reaction to Trade Liberalisation or Anti Competitive?* South African Journal of Economics, 2002, Vol. 5, pp. 912, 918, http: onlinelibrary Wiley. com/doi/10. 1111/J. 1813 – 6982. 2002. tb00051. x/pdf, last visited September 21, 2011; Anamelia Soccal Seyffarth, *The Link between Competition Policy and Antidumping Policy*, George Washington University, School of Business and Public Management, Institute of Brazilian Issues Minerva Program, 2000, pp. 1 – 49, http://www. gwu. edu/ ~ ibi/minerva/Fall2000/Anamelia. Seyffarth. pdf, last visited May 3, 2011.

area of international practice, there have already existed some real cases and is a tendency in both bilateral and regional areas to substitute antidumping law by competition law. ❶ The WTO also set up the Working Group on the Interaction between Trade and Competition Policy(WGTCP), where various opinions on the substitution of competition law for antidumping law have been brought up by various countries. ❷

2. Current Literature

As a relatively new issue, there is only one monograph on antitrust and antidumping in regional area in 1994. ❸ There are no monographs that are devoted to discussing this issue in the multilateral trade, let alone a clear and comprehensive summary of the various arguments for

---

❶ It is examined that, the first one is the experience of the United States. Similarly, when the European Economic Community was created in the late 1950s, it learned the American lesson well. Besides, recently, New Zealand and Australia concluded a free trade agreement in 1983, which included the elimination of antidumping rules for trans-Tasman trade and the replacement of the dumping rules with true competition provisions. Canada and Chile also eliminated antidumping rules in their free trade agreement even though their economies are structurally quite different and separated by thousands of miles. Moreover, the principal South American free trade area, has pursued a similar path in eliminating antidumping duties for trade within the bloc. Discussion is also existed in NAFTA. In Asia, China and Hong Kong Area, China and Macau Area, have decided not to use antidumping between them. Similar practice happened in South Africa Union.

❷ Through examining all of the working documents of the WGTCP from the year 1997 to 2004, it is found that the relationship between the two has induced the hottest discussion in WGTCP around 1998.

❸ *See* Gabrielle Marceau, *Antidumping and Anti-trust Issues in Free-trade Areas*, Oxford Univ. Press Inc. 1994.

or against the "substitution". ❶

Regarding the articles and papers addressing using antitrust to repeal or reform antidumping, before the 1980s, there were relatively fewer discussions. ❷ Since the 1990s, the scholars have paid more attention to this issue, examined it from various perspectives, and tried to present their own opinions towards whether antidumping should be substituted by competition law, and if so, how to make it realized in

---

❶ For such books as focusing on global competition law, the relation between trade law and competition law and so on, the issue of substituting antidumping by competition is often taken as a small part, and discussed very generally and briefly. *See*, *e. g.*, Richard Dale, *Antidumping Law in a Liberal Trade Order*, The Macmillan Press Ltd. 1980, pp. 20 – 22; P. J. Lloyd, Antidumping and Competition Law, in Patrick F. J Macrory *et al.*, eds., *II The World Trade Organization: Legal, Economic and Political Analysis*, Springer 2005, pp. 67 – 82; Kevin C. Kennedy, *Competition Law and the World Trade Organization: the Limits of Multilateralism*, London: Sweet & Maxwell, 2001; Roland Weinrauch, *Competition Law in the WTO: the Rationale for a Framework Agreement*, Wien: NWV Neuer Wissenschaftlicher Verlag, 2004.

❷ In my research, only one paper has been found which discusses about whether antidumping act belongs to anti-trust law or trade law. *See* Comment, *The Antidumping Act – Tariff or Antitrust Law?* The Yale Law Journal, 1965, Vol. 74, pp. 707 – 724.

practice.❶ A few scholars not only discussed the substitution in general, but also examined the relationship between antidumping law and

---

❶ *See more*, Peter D. Ehrenhaft, *Is Interface of Antidumping and Antitrust Laws Possible?* George Washington International Law Review, 2002, Vol. 34, pp. 363 – 400; Gary Hufbauer, *Trade and Antitrust: Is Rapprochement Desirable? Is It Possible? Antitrust and Antidumping: Forever Separate Tables*, New York Law School Law Review, 2003, Vol. 47, pp. 141 – 148; Patrick A. Messerlin, *Should Antidumping Rules be Replaced by National or International Competition Rules*, The Swiss Review of International Economic Relations, 1994, Vol. 49, pp. 351 – 371; Ralf Boscheck, *The Governance of Global Market Relations: the Case of Substituting Antitrust for Antidumping*, World Competition, 2001, Vol. 24, pp. 41 – 64; Spencer Weber Waller, *Bringing Globalism Home: Lessons from Antitrust and Beyond* Loyola University Chicago Law Journal, 2000, Vol. 32, pp. 113 – 136; José Tavares De Araujo Jr., *Legal and Economic Interfaces between Antidumping and Competition Policy*, CEPAL – SERIE Comercio Internacional, 2001, pp. 1 – 26, http://www. eclac. cl/publicaciones/xml/0/9040/lcl1685i. pdf, last visited September 21, 2011; Rodney de C. Grey, *the Relationship Between Antidumping Policy and Competition*, Positive Agenda and Future Trade Negotiations, Geneva, UN, 2000, pp. 413 – 437, http://ctrc. sice. oas. org/geograph/compol/Articles/Grey_AD_1999. doc, last visited May 3, 2011; Bernard M. Hoekman & Petros C. Mavroidis, *Anti-trust-Based Remedies and Dumping in International Trade*, Policy Research Working paper No. 1347, the World Bank, 1994, pp. 1 – 29, http://www – wds. worldbank. org/servlet/WDSContentServer/WDSP/IB/1994/08/01/000009265_3970716141633/Rendered/PDF/multi0page. pdf, last visited May 3, 2011; Merle Holden, *Antidumping: A Reaction to Trade Liberalisation or Anti-competitive?* South African Journal of Economics, 2002, Vol. 5, pp. 912 – 931, http://onlielibrary wiley. com/doi/10. 1111/J. 1813 – 6982. 2002. tb00051. x/pdf, last visited September 21, 2011; Andreas Knorr, *Antidumping Rules vs. Competition Rules*, Institution for World Economics and International Management, 2004, pp. 1 – 19, http://www. iwim. uni – bremen. de/publikationen/pdf/W031. pdf, last visited September 21, 2011; Robert A. Lipstein, Using Anti-trust Principles to Reform Antidumping Law, in E. Graham and J. D. Richardson eds., *Global Competition Policy*, Washington DC: Institute for International Economics, pp. 405 – 438, http://www. iie. com/publications/chapters_preview/56/13ie1664. pdf, last visited May 24, 2009; Patrick A. Messerlin, *Competition Policy and Antidumping Reform: An Exercise in Transition*, in J. J. Schott ed., *the World Trading System: Challenges Ahead*, Washington DC: Institute for International Economics, pp. 219 – 261, http://www. iie. com/publications/chapters_preview/66/13iie2350. pdf, last visited May 24, 2009; Gunnar Niels, *What is Antidumping Policy Really About?* Journal of Economic Surveys, 2002, pp. 467 – 492, http://www. blackwell – synergy. com/links/doi/10. 1111/1467 – 6419. 00118, last visited September 21, 2009; Ian Wooton & Maurizio Zanardi, *Trade and Competition Policy: Antidumping versus Anti-trust*, University of Glasgow and CEPR discussion paper in Economics, 2002, pp. 1 – 31, http://homepages. strath. ac. uk/ ~ hbs03116/Research/Trade% 20and%20Competition%20Policy%20Final. pdf, last visited May 24, 2009; Patrick A. Messerlin, *Antidumping Regulations or Procartel Law? The EC Chemical Cases*, International Trade Working Paper 0397, the World Bank, 1990, pp. 1 – 51, http://www-wds. worldbank. org/servlet/WDSContentServer/WDSP/IB/1990/04/01/000009265 _ 3960929174031/Rendered/PDF/multi0page. pdf, last visited May 24, 2009.

competition law within a typical country or a typical regional area. [1]

Nevertheless, the aforementioned discussion seems rather fragmented. it lacks a general agreement on the desired level of competition and the core concepts, not to talk about the basic definitions, instruments and enforcement policy of competition rules. [2] More efforts should be done to perfect the basic framework of the debate, to conduct a comprehensive summary based on which various arguments for or against the substitution could be examined, and to enrich the relevant research with the most recent state practices. This way this book aims to generate some useful ideas on the substitution debate.

---

[1] *See more*, Aradhna Aggarwal, Antidumping Law and Practice: An Indian Perspective, *Indian Council for Research on International Economic Relations*, 2002, pp. 1 – 68, http://www.icrier.org/pdf/antiDump.pdf, last visited May 24, 2009; Bernard Hoekman, Free Trade and Deep Integration: Antidumping and Anti-trust in Regional Agreements, *the World Bank Development Research Group International Trade*, 1998, pp. 1 – 42, http://www-wds.worldbank.org/servlet/WDSContentServer/WDSP/IB/1998/07/01/000009265_3980928162543/Rendered/PDF/multi0page.pdf, last visited May 24, 2009; Anamelia Soccal Seyffarth, *the Link between Competition Policy and Antidumping Policy*, George Washington University, School of Business and Public Management, Institute of Brazilian Issues Minerva Program, 2000, pp. 1 – 49, http://www.gwu.edu/~ibi/minerva/Fall2000/Anamelia.Seyffarth.pdf, last visited May 24, 2009; J. Luis Guasch & Sarath Rajapatirana, *Antidumping and Competition Policies in Latin America and Caribbean: Total Strangers or Soul Mates?* 1998, pp. 1 – 26, http://www.worldbank.org/html/dec/Publications/Workpapers/WPS1900series/wps1958/wps1958.pdf, last visited May 24, 2009.

[2] Patrick A. Messerlin, *Should Antidumping Rules be Replaced by National or International Competition Rules*, the Swiss Review of International Economic Relations, 1994, Vol. 49, pp. 351, 352.

3. The Ideas of this Book

3.1 The Aim of this Book

The debate of antidumping versus competition is very broad and can be approached from various perspectives. This book aims at contributing to the debate by reexamining "dumping" as a private business conduct that might also be subject to competition law, to explore whether putting dumping under competition rules instead of antidumping rules can be less vulnerable to protectionist abuse.

This book considers that the actual linkage between antidumping law and competition law is "dumping", the business conduct of low-price selling. It is due to the growing criticism on the protectionist abuse of antidumping that there are an increasing number of scholars arguing for substituting antidumping by competition. Hence, the key point to argue for or against the substitution should be, whether using competition rules instead of antidumping rules to deal with dumping, can be less subject to protectionism, or in other words, more consistent with the modern spirit of free trade and fair competition. This is deemed to be the essential criterion applied to examine the substitution debate.

3.2 The Scope of this Book

In terms of the scope of this book, two points need to be noted. The first one is that, since the protectionist abuse of antidumping has already been criticized in almost all of the literature, this book shall not take efforts to argue whether antidumping law is abused for protectionist or not. Instead, the criticism of protectionist abuse shall be briefly dealt with and taken as the premise for the discussion of the substitution debate hereinafter.

The second one is that, it is neither the intention nor can be possibly achieved to examine all of issues of both antidumping law and competition law in this book. Only relevant issues will be referred to. For instance, antidumping law links with competition law maily in the area of price discrimination and predatory pricing. Therefore, apart from the basic principles of competition, administrative enforcements, and legal remedies etc. that relate to all areas within competition law, other issues such as merger, vertical agreements, and horizontal agreements etc. are not within the scope of this book.

3.3 The Research Objects of this Book

The substitution of antidumping law by competition law is a global issue. A better approach than the impossible mission of examining all countries in only hundreds of pages would be, to choose appropriate research objects. In this book, the United States (the U. S.) and the European Union (EU) are chosen as the main research objects for three main reasons.

The first reason links with the essential criterion aforementioned. The discussion of the substitution debate increases along with the criticism on the protectionist abuse of antidumping. Hence, where antidumping rules are more heavily used, where the protectionist abuse of such is relatively more striking, and the examination hereon are much more significant and typical. As the traditional heavy users of antidumping, the U. S. and the EU are deemed to be main research objects.

The second reason is that the U. S. and the EU stand out as two basic models of both antidumping law and competition law for the other countries in the world. The U. S. is among the earliest countries to legislate antidumping law. Moreover, the U. S. antidumping law has provided the basic model for the multilateral antidumping agreement and thereby has great influence on the subsequent national legislations. In terms of competition law, the U. S. and the EU are considered as two significant models learned and copied by most of the other countries.

The third reason is their influence power in the political reality. It goes without saying that in modern multilateral world, the standpoints of the U. S. and the EU are vital to any international issues. Whether to keep antidumping and competition separately forever or to substitute one by the other, monitoring the changes in the attitudes especially that of the U. S. , the strongest opponent against the replace of antidumping law by competition law, is of primary importance to find the answer.

Apart from the U. S. and the EU, this book also calls for more attention to be paid to the most recent state practices. Starting from the mid-1990s, a new feature of antidumping actions has appeared. Developing countries, such as India, Brazil, South Africa, even China, who used to be the main targets of antidumping actions, have become the new heavy users of antidumping. Furthermore, the number of antidumping actions filed by the new users has gradually outnumbered those of the traditional heavy users (maily the U. S. and the EU). Taken into account the essential criterion in this book, new heavy users should also be examined.

Concerning these new heavy users of antidumping, do they have any viewpoints or strategic purposes other than those of traditional heavy users? Furthermore, most of the new heavy users such as Brazil, India, South Africa, and China have newly established competition laws, the perfection of which are understandable far from that of the sophicated the U. S. or the EU. Whether their competition rules on price discrimination and predatory pricing can be equally qualified to be less protectionist abuse than antidumping rules? For the above considerations, exploring into the relationship between antidumping and competition in each of these new users is also indispensible before the final conclusion of substitution can be reached.

From the political perspective, this new factor might have some influence on certain traditional users' enthusiasm for antidumping actions, bring the issue of antidumping on negotiation table again, and thus draw more attention to the debate of antidumping versus competition.

To sum up, the research objects of this book can be divided into two categories: the U. S. and the EU, representatives of the traditional heavy users of antidumping, is on one hand; and Brazil, India, South Africa, China, representatives of the new heavy users of antidumping, is on the other hand. The final conclusion towards this global debate shall be based on the examination of the typical countries in both categories.

3.4 The Structure of this Book

In light of the essential criterion aformentioned, the basic clue of this book is that, in discussing substituting one set of rules by the other, the first thing needs to be conducted is whether the two sets of rules have the same regulating content, then the advantages and disadvantages of substituting one by the other should be examined. Based on all of the above analysis, the viewpoints towards whether one should be substituted by the other shall be brought up in the end.

To be more specific, in this book, the primary issue is to reconsider the self-evident premise of antidumping law, i. e., why dumping is harmful. This is still a controversial and unclear issue in the current literature. Through examining various economic theories on dumping, tracing back to the birth of antidumping law, and following the evolvement from domestic antidumping law to international antidumping agreement, it is considered in this book that the original and supposed goal of antidumping law is to deal with international price discrimination and to condemn predatory dumping, which is also regulated under competition law.

After confirming that the original and supposed goal of antidumping is to deal with predatory dumping, which can also be addressed by competition law through predatory price discrimination, the following issue is whether putting dumping under competition rules instead of antidumping rules can be less vulnerable to "protectionist abuse". This book tries to conduct a comprehensive analysis from three perspectives. Firstly, the basic elements of the two sets of rules on low-price selling will be compared and evaluated one by one. Secondly, the two sets of rules will be placed against the background of modern free trade world, so as to analyse their relationship with the basic trade and competition principles respectively. Thirdly, the typical cases as well as empirical studies indicating the interaction of the two sets of rules in practice will be observed.

The above examination suggests that competition rules are more appropriate than antidumping rules in detecting dumping, without being abused by protectionists. However, legal, institutional and political difficulties have been among the main obstacles so far to actually replace antidumping with competition law. Among them, two major objections against the substitution are "alleged different objectives of antidumping" and "the lack of international competition law". In this book, the main arguments against "substitution" will be summarized, clarified and criticized.

Apart from examining the above various arguments of the substitution debate in the U. S. and the EU, the traditional heavy users of antidumping, India, Brazil, South Africa, China and the other new heavy users are also within the discussion, with a specific survey done in China. Can the examination of the new heavy users provide anything new from the U. S. and the EU? Whether the results support the "substitution", or instead, against it? Such issues will also be inspected. The viewpoint of this book towards the substitution debate will be based thereon.

In order to achieve this, the book is developed into 7 chapters as follows:

Chapter I points out the problems of antidumping law, i. e. protectionist abuse, and justifies the reason why it is time to go back to basics to reexamine dumping;

Chapter II reexamines the justification to condemn dumping in economic theories as well as the evolvement of antidumping rules;

Chapter III tries to identify the common standards on the relate-to-dumping issue, i. e. predatory price discrimination, from analyzing the economic theories and the competition rules;

Chapter IV scrutinizes the central issue of whether competition is more appropriated than antidumping in addressing dumping from three perspectives;

Chapter V considers two major difficulties of substituting antidumping by competition;

Besides centered on the traditional users of antidumping to discuss this debate in the above four chapters, Chapter VI tries to find what experience can be learned from the new users of antidumping. This book especially focuses on the linkage of antidumping rules and competition rules in one typical new user–China, the number one target of antidumping actions in the world, which has just begun to use antidumping actions in an increasing way but simultaneously devoted itself to promoting competition legislation.

Based on all of the above analyses and examinations from both traditional and new heavy users of antidumping, in Chapter VII, this book will come to its final viewpoint towards the main issue: under which rules should dumping be addressed, competition rules or antidumping rules?

4. The Contribution of this Book

Combined with the other literature, this book is also devoted to clarifying the basic framework for the substitution debate. Based on all pieces of information available, applying research methods including historical analysis, economic analysis, comparative analysis, normative analysis and positive analysis, this book attempts to provide with a comprehensive summary of the various arguments for or against the substitution, analyse and form its own viewpoint in logic reasoning.

In examining the various arguments, this book tries to call for more research work, which should not only be continuingly done on the traditional countries like the U. S. and the EU, but should also turn to those new heavy users of antidumping. In order to achieve so, this book aims at contributing to the current debate by conducting a specific survey on China, one of the new heavy users which are unknown to the world.

Contents

Chapter I Time to Reexamine Dumping: Antidumping Law or Competition Law

1. 1 Overview of Antidumping Law

1. 1. 1 The Etymology of "Dumping"

As a word in dictionary, "dumping" seems to have a long history. Some scholars have tried to trace its original use, but there exists no consistent recognition. It is said that the term originates from the Old Icelandic word "thumpa", which means to thump or hit somebody; later "dump" came to be a temporary depot for munitions. [1]

Jackson relates that Adam Smith was the first to use the word dumping, although they may have been more closely related to today's subsidies. [2] Likewise, Viner refers to discussions by Alexander Hamilton in 1791 about foreign-country dumping so as to under sell competitors in other countries thus to "frustrate the first efforts to introduce [a business] ...into another by temporary sacrifices, recompensed, perhaps by extraordinary indemnifications of the government of such country..." [3]

---

[1] Gabrielle Marceau, *Antidumping and Anti-trust Issues in Free-trade Areas*, Oxford Univ. Press Inc, 1994, p. 7.

[2] John H. Jackson & Edwin A. Vermulst, *Antidumping Law and Practice: a Comparative Study*, in John H. Jackson &, Harvester Wheatsheaf, 1990, p. 5.

[3] Jacob Viner, *Dumping: A Problem in International Trade* , the Univ. of Chicago Press, 1923, p. 37.

1.1.2 Legislative Development of Antidumping: Domestic to International

As a term in law, "dumping" was first introduced by the Section 73 of US Wilson Tariff Act of 1894, whereas the first antidumping regulation was enacted in Canada by the Customs Act of 1904. [1] Followed were a number of national antidumping rules[2], including New Zealand in 1905, Australia in 1906, South Africa in 1914, the U. S. in 1916, and the United Kingdom in 1921 etc. [3] The EU adopted its antidumping law in 1968. [4]

Antidumping was not set forth as a multilateral agreement until the GATT 1947. The relevant rules therein were further re-defined during the Kennedy Round in 1967 and the Tokyo Round in 1979. [5] The

---

[1] The fact that, the Wilson Tariff Act which was adopted in 1894 and which indeed was the world's first antidumping law has been largely ignored by the literature on the topic which, more often than not, considers Canada's 1904 Customs Act the world's first antidumping regulation. *See* Andreas Knorr, *Antidumping Rules vs. Competition Rules*, Institution for World Economics and International Management, 2004, pp. 1, 5, http://www.iwim.uni-bremen.de/publikationen/pdf/W031.pdf, last visited May 24, 2009.

[2] Richard Dale, *Anti-dumping Law in a Liberal Trade Order*, The Macmillan Press Ltd. 1980, p. 12.

[3] *See, e. g.*, Maurizio Zanardi, *Antidumping: A Problem in International Trade*, Center Discussion Paper series, No. 2005 - 85, 2005, pp. 1, 5, http://papers.ssrn.com/sol3/papers.cfm?abstract_id=800406#PaperDownload, last visited May 24, 2009; Gunnar Niels, *What is Antidumping Policy Really About?* Journal of Economic Surveys, 2002, Vol. 14. pp. 467, 468, http://www.blackwell-synergy.com/links/doi/10.1111/1467-6419.00118, last visited September 21, 2011.

[4] Patrick A. Messerlin & Geoffrey Reed, *Antidumping Policies in the United States and the European Community*, the Economic Journal, 1995, Vol, 105, pp. 1565, 1566, http://www.jstor.org/stable/2235118?seq=1, last visited May 24, 2009.

[5] Michael J. Trebilcock & Robert Howse, *the Regulation of International Trade*, 2nd Edition, Routledge, 1999, pp. 167 - 171.

WTO, established in 1995 as a result of the Uruguay Round, has transformed antidumping rules from general guidelines to what is now essentially a quite specific international legal system, i. e. the WTO Antidumping Agreement (ADA). ❶

The WTO ADA sets up a standard for antidumping measures to be taken by WTO members and requires members to implement all possible general or specific measures to ensure that their laws, regulations and administrative procedures conform to it. ❷ Due to the uniform requirement of the WTO ADA, although the nuts and bolts of antidumping rules may vary from countries to countries, the basic objective and methodology are by and large the same. ❸

1. 2 The Proliferation of Antidumping laws and Actions

1. 2. 1 The Proliferation of Antidumping laws

Antidumping law did not draw much attention of either the politicians or the legislators at the beginning. It only became a major issue in international trade during the 1970s and the 1980s, as it gradually took the place of other trade barriers that were being dismantled in the

❶ Agreement on Implementation of Article VI of the General Agreement on Tariffs and Trade 1994 (hereinafter referred to as "WTO ADA"), http://www. wto. org/english/docs_e/legal_e/19 - adp. doc, last visited May 24, 2009.

❷ According to WTO ADA, Article 18. 4: Each Member shall take all necessary steps, of a general or particular character, to ensure, not later than the date of entry into force of the WTO Agreement for it, the conformity of its laws, regulations and administrative procedures with the provisions of this Agreement as they may apply for the Member in question.

❸ The basic requirements for condemning dumping will be introduced in detail in chapter II, 2. 3. 3.

context of the GATT and several other trade liberalization initiatives. ❶ After World War II, antidumping law achieved widespread international tolerance following its inclusion within the GATT. ❷

With the reduction of tariff and other trade obstacles, antidumping laws grew significantly. Beginning in the 1950s, antidumping started to acquire a world wide status, with countries adopting antidumping laws at an increasing pace. In 1979, there were less than 10 countries having their antidumping laws. By 1998, that reached about 60. ❸ The total number jumped to more than 120 countries by the end of 2005. ❹ Almost 90% of total world imports have entered countries in which antidumping laws are in place. ❺

1.2.2 The Proliferation of Antidumping Actions

With the proliferation of antidumping laws, followed is the proliferation of antidumping actions. There were 1 558 antidumping investigations initiated globally in the 1980s (an average of 156 per year), doubling the number in the 1970s. In the 1990s, the investigations

---

❶ Gunnar Niels, *What is Antidumping Policy Really About?* Journal of Economic Surveys, 2002, Vol. 14, pp. 467, 469, http://www.blackwell-synergy.com/links/doi/10.1111/1467-6419.00118, last visited September 21, 2011.

❷ Martyn D. Taylor, *International Competition Law: A New Dimension for the WTO?* Cambridge Univ. Press Inc. 2006, p. 262.

❸ Gunnar Niels, *What is Antidumping Policy Really About?* Journal of Economic Surveys, 2002, Vol. 14, pp. 467, 470, http://www.blackwell-synergy.com/links/doi/10.1111/1467-6419.00118, last visited September 21, 2011.

❹ 李文锋、郑乐："我国对外贸易摩擦高发的成因及对策"，载《中国经济时报》，2006 年 12 月 8 日，http://jjsb.cet.com.cn/searchArticle.aspx? keyword = 我国对外贸易摩擦高发, last visited September 21, 2011.

❺ Aradhna Aggarwal, *Antidumping Law and Practice: An Indian Perspective*, Indian Council for Research on International Economic Relations, 2002, p. 1, http://www.icrier.org/pdf/antiDump.pdf, last visited September 21, 2011.

went up to 2 483 (an average of 248 per year), which is far more than that in the previous 40 years. ❶ From 2000 to June of 2010, 2 499 new antidumping initiations were recorded (about 250 per year). ❷

The WTO Secretariat reported that during the period 1 July to 31 December 2008, the number of initiations of new antidumping investigations showed a 17% increase compared with the corresponding period of 2007. On a yearly basis, there were 208 initiations of new antidumping investigations in 2008, as compared to 163 in 2007 and 202 in 2006. ❸ Meanwhile, the proportion of affirmative outcomes to the investigations initiated has increased markedly. Prior to the 1970s, only 5% of antidumping investigations led to affirmative outcomes. In contrast, current statistics show that about half of the investigations worldwide wound up with affirmative measures. ❹

Within the WTO framework, antidumping measures evidently outnumber countervailing measures and safeguards, the other two types of trade remedies. Countervailing duties are allowed to be imposed on

---

❶ *See*, e. g., Brink Lindsey & Dan Ikenson, *Coming Home to Roost: Proliferating Antidumping Laws and the Growing Threat to U. S. Exports*, Trade Policy Analysis, 2001, Vol. 14, pp. 1, 31, http://www.freetrade.org/pubs/pas/tpa-014.pdf, last visited September 21, 2011.

❷ The most recent statistics *see* http://www.wto.org/english/tratop_e/adp_e/ad_init_exp_country_e.xls, last visited May 3, 2011. For the purpose of these tables, as to all of the following statistics of WTO each antidumping initiation and antidumping measure reported covers one product imported from one country.

❸ *WTO Secretariat Reports Increase in New Anti-dumping Investigations*, WTO Press 556, May 7, 2009, http://www.wto.org/english/news_e/pres09_e/pr556_e.htm, last visited May 3, 2011.

❹ 王林生、张汉林:《反倾销热点剖析》,人民出版社2004年版,第2页。

subsidized imports that are found to be damaging domestic producers. ❶ Safeguards are applied by countries to restrict imports of a product temporarily to protect a specific domestic industry from an increase in the import which is causing serious injury to the industry. ❷ Antidumping investigations are more widely initiated than the other two. From 1995 to June of 2010, the number of antidumping initiations reached 3 752, compared with countervailing initiations totally 250 during the same period, and 216 safeguard initiations from 1995 to October of 2010. ❸

1.2.3 New Features of Antidumping Application

Underneath the dramatic growth in the number of antidumping cases, there are two noticeable aspects in modern antidumping application.

1.2.3.1 Developing Countries Became the New users of Antidumping Actions

The first noticeable aspect is that antidumping users have been changing gradually, with more developing countries becoming the main users. An analysis conducted by Finger et al. constructed an index of initiations relative to imports/exports during the period of 1995 to 1999, showing that developing countries were the most common

---

❶ Agreement on Subsidies and Countervailing Measures, http://www.wto.org/english/docs_e/legal_e/24-scm.doc, last visited May 24, 2009.

❷ Agreement on Safeguard, http://www.wto.org/english/docs_e/legal_e/25-safeg.doc, last visted May 24, 2009.

❸ Sources from WTO Statistics: the most recent statistics on Antidumping Measure, *see* http://www.wto.org/english/tratop_e/adp_e/ad_init_exp_country_e.xls, last visited May 3, 2011; On Subsidies and Countervailing Measures, *see* http://www.wto.org/english/tratop_e/scm_e/cvd_init_exp_country_e.xls; On Safeguard Measure, *see* http://www.wto.org/english/tratop_e/safeg_e/safeg_stattab1_e.xls, last visited May 3, 2011.

users of antidumping in relative terms. ❶

Prior to 1995, the major antidumping actions were mainly taken by developed countries, with the U. S., the EU, Canada and Australia as the main initiators, accounting for more than 95% of the investigations in the 1980s. Japan used to be the most targeted country. ❷ Later on, the situation changed. Antidumping actions have been not only taken between developed countries, but also between developed and developing countries, even among developing countries. Furthermore, apart from the traditional users of antidumping law such as the U. S. and the EU, counries such as Brazil, India and South Africa, Mexico, Argentina, whose exports had been the principal targets of antidumping complaints in the past, have become the new heaviest users. China took the place of Japan to be and remained as the most targeted country until now. ❸ After entered into WTO in 2001, China has also started to use antidumping in an increasing way.

1. 2. 3. 2 Targeted Industries of Antidumping Actoins Became Concentrated

Besides the fact that developing countries have joined the

---

❶ J. Michael Finger *et al.*, *Antidumping As Safeguard Policy*, Working Paper No. 2730, the World Bank, 2000, pp. 1 – 21, http://www.fordschool.umich.edu/rsie/Conferences/CGP/Oct2000Papers/Finger.pdf, last visited May 3, 2011.

❷ Thomas J. Prusa & Susan Skeath, *the Economic and Strategic Motives for Antidumping Filings*, Working Paper No. 8424, NBER, 2001, pp. 1, 5, http://www.nber.org/papers/w8424.pdf, last visited May 3, 2011.

❸ From 1995 – 2008, China was subject to antidumping measures in 479 cases, including 66 cases by the U. S., 60 by the EU, 90 by India, 40 by Argentina, 33 by Turkey, 16 by South Africa, 21 by Brazil, 15 by Mexico and so on. The most recent statistics *see* http://www.wto.org/english/tratop_e/adp_e/ad_meas_rep_exp_e.xls, last visited May 3, 2011.

antidumping user club, the second noticeable aspect is that the targeted industries of antidumping actions also became concentrated. There is a large degree of concentration on a few sectors, though a broad range of industries are also affected. In the WTO ever since 1995, about 80% of all antidumping measures have fallen into five categories: base metals (35%), chemicals (19%), plastics (12%), machinery and electrical goods (8%), and textiles (7%). ❶ The major affected industries, i. e. steel and chemicals are capital-intensive and have large fixed costs. The U. S. steel industry is a case in point. Over half of the antidumping investigations in America were initiated by its steel industry, although steel only accounted for 2% of the total import value of the country. ❷

1.3 The Problem of Antidumping Law

1.3.1 "Protectionist Abuse" Criticism

Noticing the proliferation of antidumping laws and actions, as well as the new features thereof, we might consider that, as one of the trade remedies, antidumping laws were supposed to be used as an exception in the trade liberalization, whereas the reality is that there are so many antidumping actions per day. Are there really so many harmful dumping cases? Such striking trends certainly raise the specter that countries are using antidumping laws for reasons other than

---

❶ Sources from WTO Statistics on Antidumping Sectoral: the most recent statistics, *see* http://www.wto.org/english/tratop_e/adp_e/ad_sect_distrib_init_rep_member_e.xls, last visited May 3, 2011.

❷ 王林生、张汉林:《反倾销热点剖析》,人民出版社 2004 年版,第 12 页。

condemning "harmful dumping". ❶

Antidumping law has received increasingly more criticism. Over the last 25 years, thousands of pages have been written about antidumping. One remarkable feature of this vast literature is that-at least within the academic community-most authors would share Michael Finger's view that "antidumping is a trouble-making diplomacy, stupid economics and unprincipled law". ❷ The major criticism on antidumping rules is their increasing potential for protectionist abuse. ❸

---

❶ Thomas J. Prusa & Susan Skeath, *Retaliation as an Explanation for the Proliferation of Antidumping*, Conference paper, 2002, pp. 1, 8, http://www.tulane.edu/~dnelson/PolTransConv/Prusa.pdf, last visited May 3, 2011.

❷ José Tavares De Araujo Jr., *Legal and Economic Interfaces between Antidumping and Competition Policy*, CEPAL - SERIE Comercio Internacional, 2001, pp. 1, 9, http://www.eclac.cl/publicaciones/xml/0/9040/lcl1685i.pdf, last visited September 21, 2011.

❸ Antidumping rules' increasing potential for protectionist abuse has been criticized in almost all of the current literature. For example, Spencer pointed out that "More typically, [antidumping] these laws represent a seemingly neutral set of rules that permit a highly damaging disguised form of protectionism." *See* Spencer Weber Waller, *Bringing Globalism Home: Lessons from Antitrust and Beyond*, Loyola University Chicago Law Journal, 2000, Vol. 32, p. 113. Ian Wooton and Maurizio Zanardi considered that "the criteria for proving dumping and consequent injury allow firms around the world to seek (and obtain) protection from the AD procedures. Industries at large have been granted protection through the numerous petitions they have filed in some countries. In this way, AD duties have become a substitute for tariff protection as trade liberalization as progressed or have been pursued on pure protectionist grounds by some of the traditional users of AD (for example EU and US)." *See* Ian Wooton & Maurizio Zanardi, *Trade and Competition Policy: Anti-dumping versus Anti-trust*, University of Glasgow and CEPR Discussion Paper in Economics, 2002, pp. 1, 13, http://homepages.strath.ac.uk/~hbs03116/Research/Trade%20and%20Competition%20Policy%20Final.pdf, last visited May 24, 2009. (to page 10)

Antidumping rules have been acting more like a protector of domestic industries rather than an opponent of unfair trade practice. For instance, Lindsey Brink and Ikenson Daniel J. in their book described that: "they penalize foreign producers for engaging in commercial practices that are perfectly legal and unexceptionable when engaged in by

---

(from page 9) Gunnar Niels recognized that: "in recent years, the use of antidumping policy has grown significantly, and in fact has become one of the most important instruments of trade policy in many countries. At the same time, antidumping law enforcement has been subject to controversy, particularly because of its perceived protectionist and anticompetitive effects." *See* Gunnar Niels, *What is Antidumping Policy Really About*? Journal of Economic Surveys, 2002, Vol. 14, p. 467, http://www.blackwell-synergy.com/links/doi/10.1111/1467-6419.00118, last visited September 21, 2011.

Besides the scholars, even some of the politicians got the same feeling. For example, Kenneth Dam, deputy Treasure secretary of the present Bush Administration, noted: "The focus of protectionist arguments in the United States has turned away from direct calls for protection to an emphasis on 'fairness'. [...] Despite this smiling fair trade face, the antidumping proceeding always has been and is increasingly a protectionist device, as various Congresses have amended the underlying statute to make the proceeding and remedy more effective. This darker face of antidumping proceeding is so well known inside the Washington Beltway that it has become a trite joke among trade lawyers that antidumping is the protectionist's weapon of choice."

The similar view has been expressed by Alan Greenspan, former chairman of the Federal Reserve Board, pointed out the historical roots of this joke: "Generation after generation has experienced episodes in which the technologically obsolescent endeavored to undermine progress, often appealing to the very real short-term costs of adjusting to a changing economic environment. From the Luddites to the Smoots and the Hawleys, competitive forces were under attack. [...] Administrative protection in the form of antidumping suits and countervailing duties is a case in point. While these forms of protection have often been imposed under the label of promoting 'fair trade', oftentimes they are just simple guises for inhibiting competition."

Both of the above statements *see* José Tavares De Araujo Jr., *Legal and Economic Interfaces between Antidumping and Competition Policy*, CEPAL - SERIE Comercio Internacional (2001), 1, 10, http://www.eclac.cl/publicaciones/xml/0/9040/lcl1685i.pdf, last visited May 3, 2011.

domestic companies...In other words, antidumping laws discriminate against imports, and that is the essence of protectionism. "❶

With trade liberalization promoted, tariff and non-tariff barriers reduced all around the world, antidumping law is increasingly acting as the protective instrument substituting for them. Furthermore, due to its unfounded and easily applying system, it is favored and frequently applied all around the world, hence abused for protectionism.

1.3.2 Tariff – Like Barrier

The guiding economic premise of the modern trade policy that underlies the entire GATT-WTO system is free trade, or liberal trade. ❷ By exploiting the law of comparative advantage, liberal trade policies permit the unrestricted cross-border flow of the highest quality goods and services at the lowest prices, thereby increasing total world wealth. ❸ In order to achieve so, multilateral trade negotiations sponsored by the GATT-WTO are continuously progressing on the reduction of tariffs and non-tariff barriers to trade. The liberal trade policy thereby creates export opportunities and spurs international

---

❶ Brink Lindsey & Daniel J. Ikenson, *Antidumping Exposed : the Devilish Details of Unfair Trade Law*, Cato Institute 2003, p. viii.

❷ Wolf has explained free trade in the following terms: In a liberal economic system, government does not thwart private parties in their attempts to enter voluntary transactions, and taxes are stable, predictable, and nonprohibitive. The General Agreement on Tariffs and Trade (GATT) is liberal in this sense...Interventions [by governments] in liberal exchange across frontiers to make trade fair may be the political price of liberalism, but such interventions are themselves its antibook. *See* Martin Wolf, Why Trade Liberalization is A Good Idea, in The Uruguay Round, in J. Michael Finger & Andrzej Olechowski, eds., *A Handbook on the Multilateral Trade Organisation*, Annual Report 6, World Bank 1996.

❸ Kevin C. Kennedy, Competition Law and the World Trade Organization: the Limits of Multilateralism, London: Sweet & Maxwell, 2001, p. 3.

competition among businesses. [1]

In the realization of trade liberalization, tariff and non-tariff barriers-the traditional instruments for protection-were tremendously reduced all around the world, whereas antidumping is turning to play the role of a tarifflike barrier instead to protect domestic industries, especially in developing countries, the so-called new heavy users of antidumping as introduced aforementioned.

Trade liberalization contributes to the proliferation use of antidumping by developing countries in two respects. The first one lies in that, the international organizations that favor trade liberalization have been devoting themselves to encourage the enforcement of antidumping laws. For instance, membership in the GATT-WTO is accompanied by implementation of antidumping laws. Similarly, the IMF and the World Bank have, in the past, included the enactment or drafting of antidumping legislation as a condition for the release of loans. [2] With their increasing role in world trade arising from their pursuit of trade liberalization, developing countries are exporting their goods besides importing. This leads to a change in the composition of traded goods and more conflicts in international trade, hence resulting in using antidumping rules in a large-scale. [3]

---

[1] Kevin C. Kennedy, *Competition Law and the World Trade Organization: the Limits of Multilateralism*, London: Sweet & Maxwell, 2001, p. 3.

[2] It was illustrated that the World Bank offered technical and legal advice to many countries even if economists within the World Bank voiced their opposition; the IMF approved a credit for Pakistan in 2000 subject to the enactment of a new AD law. *See* Ian Wooton & Maurizio Zanardi, *Trade and Competition Policy: Anti-dumping versus Anti-trust*, University of Glasgow and CEPR Discussion Paper in Economics, 2002, pp. 1, 6, http://homepages.strath.ac.uk/~hbs03116/Research/Trade% 20and% 20Competition% 20Policy % 20Final.pdf, last visited May 24, 2009.

[3] *Ibid.*

The second important respect is that ever since the Uruguay Round of WTO 1995, the large-scale reduction of tariff and increase of market access have incurred the use of antidumping policy as protector. ❶ Antidumping rules are applied as another protectionist weapon substituted for tariff to a great extent. The empirical study done by Lindsey and Ikenson (2001), showing average tariffs and definitive antidumping measures for the new users, suggested that a process of substitution of definitive antidumping measures in place of tariffs as non-traditional countries move along the trade liberalization path. ❷

Take India for instance, before 1991, trade protection was quite severe. In order to achieve self-development, most of the domestic industries were under the protection measures such as import control and high tariff. Ever since 1991, India enhanced the market openness, dismantled import certification and reduced tariff. ❸ During 1990 and 1991, the highest tariff ratio in India reached 355%. That was lessened to 85% around 1993 and 1994, 65% from 1994 to 1995. Tariff reduction became even faster after the implementation of the Uruguay Round 1995. With tariff reduction as well as the repeal of other import

---

❶ Welber Barral *et al.*, *the Use of Antidumping in Brazil, China, India and South Afric – Rule, Trends and Causes*, Kommerskollegium National Board of Trade, 2005, pp. 1, 4, http://www.tralac.org/pdf/Antidumping_in_4_Developing_Countries.pdf, last visited May 3, 2011.

❷ Brink Lindsey & Dan Ikenson, *Coming Home to Roost: Proliferating Antidumping Laws and the Growing Threat to U. S. Exports*, Trade Policy Analysis, 2001, pp. 1 – 35, http://www.freetrade.org/pubs/pas/tpa – 014.pdf, last visited May 3, 2011.

❸ Welber Barral *et al.*, *the Use of Antidumping in Brazil, China, India and South Africa – Rule, Trends and Causes*, Kommerskollegium National Board of Trade, 2005, pp. 1, 35, http://www.tralac.org/pdf/Antidumping_in_4_Developing_Countries.pdf, last visited May 3, 2011.

restrictions, i. e. quantity restriction, antidumping actions have increased in India since 1992. ❶ 153 antidumping investigations have been initiated from 1992 to 2003. Now India has become one of the most active users of antidumping in the world. ❷

1. 3. 3 "Attractive Features" for Protectionism

Appropriate and controllable protective instruments are necessary for promoting and achieving free trade, but the easily applied system makes antidumping far from qualifying this role. Antidumping's extraordinarily attractive for protection seeking industries and for governments inclined to provide protection. It is now abused for protectionism in large scale, which is deemed to be seriously against the spirit of modern trade policy.

Finger summarized that several aspects could explain antidumping's popularity for protectionists, including:

I. The rhetoric of antidumping, which accuses foreigners of unfairness or of predatory pricing designed to drive domestic competitors out of the industry, provides a vehicle for building a political case for protection.

II. In practice, antidumping laws set up special procedures which discriminate against foreign firms and easily allow the authorities to find dumping against foreign firms when similar or identical practices by domestic firms would not be considered unfair or predatory under domestic competition laws.

---

❶ Welber Barral *et al.*, *the Use of Antidumping in Brazil, China, India and South Africa – Rule, Trends and Causes*, Kommerskollegium National Board of Trade, 2005, pp. 36 – 38, http://www.tralac.org/pdf/Antidumping_in_4_Developing_Countries.pdf, last visited May 3, 2011, pp. 36 – 38.

❷ *Ibid.*, pp. 1, 35.

III. The investigation process itself tends to curb imports. Exporters bear significant legal and administrative costs and importers face the uncertainty of having to pay backdated antidumping duties once an investigation is completed.

IV. The action is unilateral. GATT/WTO rules require no compensation, allow no retaliation.

V. It also allows the petitioning industry to excuse its own ineffectiveness vis-a-vis foreign competitors.

VI. Particular exporters could be picked out. GATT/WTO does not require multilateral application.

VII. Antidumping and VERs [voluntary export restraints] proved to be effective complements; i. e., the threat of formal action under the antidumping law provides leverage to force an exporter to accept a VER. [1]

---

[1] J. Michael Finger, *Should Developing Countries Introduce Antidumping*? Working Paper, 1992, http://siteresources. worldbank. org/INTRANETTRADE/Resources/WBI - Training/MFinger_antidumping_eng. DOC, last visited May 7, 2009.

The aspects aforementioned were repeated in more literature. ❶ It is because of such "attractive features" that antidumping rules are likely to be chosen by vested groups as protection weapon after the disfavor of tariff and non-tariff barriers in modern trade world. Antidumping is thereby widely criticized and reform is called for.

1.4 "Antidotes" to Prevent Protectionist Abuse

Due to the antidumping rules' enormous potential for protectionist abuse, the politicians, economists and lawyers have all participated in the ongoing debate on dumping with a zeal that is somewhat unprecedented even in respect of a trade issue. ❷ Various reform proposals from various perspectives have been brought up. These proposals can be

---

❶ *See*, *e. g*, André Sapir also gave the similar summary of the popularity of antidumping. "Antidumping has become the main instrument for dealing with troublesome imports" due to its attractive features: Particular exporters can be singled out since GATT/WTO rules do not require multilateral application; the action is unilateral, with no compensation nor re-negotiation required by GATT/WTO rules; the injury test for antidumping action tends to be softer than the injury test for safeguard action under Article XIX; the rhetoric of foreign unfairness provides a vehicle for building a political case for protection; and the investigation process itself tends to curb imports because of the administrative costs and uncertainty borne by traders. *See* André Sapir, *Some Ideas for Reforming the Community Anti-dumping Instrument*, Working Paper, 2006, p. 1, http://trade. ec. europa. eu/doclib/docs/2006/august/tradoc_129815. pdf, last visited September 21, 2011. Similarly, Niels also pointed out three reasons for the easily initiated and proved antidumping system, including the competition of imports just as all competition in general, always hurts some competitors; Antidumping laws require only slightly more than *de minimis* injury; the proof of injury only requires dumping is a cause of injury, not the cause, so it is very difficult to distinguish between injury from dumping and injury caused by other factors. *See* Gunnar Niels, *What is Antidumping Policy Really About*? Journal of Economic Surveys, 2002, pp. 467, 469, http://www. blackwell-synergy. com/links/doi/10. 1111/1467-6419. 00118, last visited September 21, 2011.

❷ Raj Krishna, *Antidumping in Law and Practice*, Working Paper, 1999, p. 1, http://www. sice. oas. org/geograph/antidumping/krishna. pdf, last visited May 24, 2009.

categorized into two kinds. One is to further refine antidumping rules and the other argues for reforming antidumping in a way to be substituted by competition. [1]

1.4.1 Further Refining

One of the proposals calls for further refining of antidumping rules. Most trade scholars are of the opinion that the misuse of antidumping is mainly due to its arbitrary and biased rules and procedures, so efforts must be continuously done to make it more stringent and transparent, less arbitrary and abusive. [2] They are arguing that:

I. Prices are adjusted for the "level of trade";

II. Dumping margins can be inflated due to certain averaging techniques for price comparison;

III. Antidumping authorities often treat home and foreign prices asymmetrically by deducting certain sales costs from the dumper's export price but not from his home market price;

---

[1] In terms of dealing with the protectionist abuse of antidumping, there is also a calling for substituting antidumping by safeguard measure, *see*, *e. g.*, Claude Barfield, *Antidumping: Time to: (1) Go Back to Basics; and (2) Politicize the Final Outcome; or (3) Substitute Safeguards for Antidumping Actions*, Paper Prepared for the Centennial of Antidumping Legislation and Implementation Symposium, 2004, pp. 1 – 40, http://fordschool.umich.edu/rsie/Conferences/ADSym/Barfield.pdf, last visited September 21, 2011. However, on one hand, compared with the other two, this perspective is not so widely discussed; on the other hand, since the discussion of substituting antidumping by safeguard also involves the examination of the objective of antidumping, which links with the discussion of substituting antidumping by competition, in this book, the relation between antidumping and safeguard is considered as part of the discussion of substituting antidumping by competition and therefore will be examined in detail in Chapter V.

[2] *See*, *e. g.*, Aradhna Aggrawal, *the WTO Antidumping Code: Issues for Review in Post – Doha Negotiations*, Working Paper, 2003, No. 99, pp. 1 – 54, http://www.icrier.org/pdf/WP99.pdf, last visited September 21, 2011.

IV. The basis for comparing prices is not always adequately taken;

V. The use of substitute countries in cases where the imports originate from a presumed non-market economy also may lead to arbitrary price comparison. ❶

For the reasons aforementioned, various suggestions for refining antidumping rules have been brought up. ❷

1.4.2 Reform by Competition

The second kind is of the opinion that further fine-tuning and refining is not the answer to prevent its abuse, the antidote is competition policy. To argue for reforing antidumping by competition is actually to question the fundamental premise for the existence of the whole antidumping system. The debate of antidumping versus competition policy can be traced back to the early 1970s. And since the mid 1980s, the lively debate has flourished as to whether and how competition standards should

---

❶ *See, e.g.*, Gunnar Niels, *What is Antidumping Policy Really About?* Journal of Economic Surveys, 2002, Vol. 14, pp. 467, 469, http://www.blackwell-synergy.com/links/doi/10.1111/1467-6419.00118, last visited September 21, 2011; Maurizio Zanardi, *Antidumping: A Problem in International Trade*, Center Discussion Paper Series, 2005, No. 2005-85, pp. 1, 5, http://papers.ssrn.com/sol3/papers.cfm?abstract_id=800406#PaperDownload, last visited May 24, 2009.

❷ *See, e.g.*, Tara Gingerich, Comment, *Why the WTO Should Require the Application of the Evidentiary Threshold Requirement in Antidumping Investigations*, American University Law Review, 1998, Vol. 48; Elizabeth L. Gunn, Note, *Eliminating the Protectionist Free Ride: the Need for Cost Redistribution in Antidumping Cases*, Boston College International and Comparative Law Review, 2005, Vol. 28; Jennifer Karen King, Notes, *In Need of Enlightenment: the International Trade Commission's Misguided Analysis in Sunset Reviews*, William & Mary Law Review, 2002, Vol. 43; Joseph A. Laroski, Jr., *NMES: A Love Story Nonmarket and Market Economy Status Under U. S. Antidumping Law*, Law and Policy in International Business, 1999, Vol. 30; Steven Thuesen, Note, *Sustainable Production Agriculture in the Face of Foreign Commodity Dumping: Achieving Effective Antidumping and Countervailing Duty Determinations*, North Dakota Law Review, 2001, Vol. 77.

be substituted for antidumping rules. [1]

Why dumping is harmful? Why do we need the whole antidumping system? A number of commentators, in the past have suggested that antidumping rules and duties for perceived international trade "wrongs" are based on fundamental misconceptions that need to be corrected. [2] Even the observers of the international relations who remain attached to motives on which these trade laws are based are becoming increasingly conscious that these trade laws do not achieve these goals, and in addition that they have undesirable and perverse effects. [3] They claim that antidumping rules are established on several false premises, having no justification from competition perspective, and are anti-competitive in many respects. Efforts should be directed at integrating antidumping

---

[1] Gunnar Niels, *What is Antidumping Policy Really About*? Journal of Economic Surveys, 2002, Vol. 14, pp. 467, 479, http://www.blackwell-synergy.com/links/doi/10.1111/1467-6419.00118, last visited September 21, 2011.

[2] John H. Jackson & Edwin A Vermulst, *Antidumping Law and Practice: a Comparative Study*, Harvester Wheatsheaf, 1990, p. 16.

[3] Patrick A. Messerlin, *Should Antidumping Rules be Replaced by National or International Competition Rules*, The Swiss Review of International Economic Relations, 1994, Vol. 49, pp. 351, 352.

policy with competition policy. [1]

1.5 Antidumping: Time to Go Back to Basics

Combined with the other literature, this book suggests that it is time to go to the basics, to reexamine dumping as a private business conduct which might be also subject to competition law, and to explore whether regulating dumping under competition law instead of antidumping law is the antidote to solve the current protectionist abuse problem. There are several reasons for the preference of it to further refining.

Firstly, years of efforts devoted to the perspective of due process seemed suggesting that there were no substantial improvements, and hence could not achieve too much to prevent the system abuse. In the multilateral field, the WTO practice showed that it was really hard to progress. Theoretically speaking, legal security will be reinforced in the matter if stricter rules on antidumping measures are negotiated. Nevertheless, the Uruguay Round experience demonstrated that the negotiations on technical and procedural criteria could have unexpected effects

---

[1] *See, e.g.*, Martyn D. Taylor, *International Competition Law: A New Dimension for the WTO?* Cambridge Univ. Press Inc. 2006; P. J. Lloyd, *Anti-dumping and Competition Law*, in Patrick F. J Macrory *et al.*, eds., II The World Trade Organization: Legal, Economic and Political Analysis , Springer 2005; Aradhna Aggarwal, *Antidumping Law and Practice: An Indian Perspective*, Indian Council for Research on International Economic Relations, 2002, p. 1, http://www.icrier.org/pdf/antiDump.pdf, last visited September 21, 2011; Andreas Knorr, *Antidumping Rules vs. Competition Rules*, Institution for World Economics and International Management, 2004, http://www.iwim.uni-bremen.de/publikationen/pdf/W031.pdf, last visited September 21, 2011; J. Michael Finger & Andrei Zlate, *Antidumping: Prospects for Discipline from Doha Negotiations*, Working Papers in Economics, 2005, http://escholarship.bc.edu/cgi/viewcontent.cgi?article=1184&context=econ_papers, last visited September 21, 2011.

especially for the new heavy users, the developing countries. ❶ To a great extent the complexity in procedural requirements benefits traditional users of antidumping measures, whose skilled bureaucrats in the matter are much more capable of accomplishing the provided requirements and challenge the application thereof by other countries. ❷ In fact, few countries except for the U. S. take advantage of these complex procedural rules in disputes before the Dispute Settlement Body. ❸

Years of efforts of the WTO have indicated that, although the new rules constitute an improvement over prior GATT requirements in this respect, they do little to compensate for the fact that antidumping authorities retain substantial discretion in applying regulations and defining criteria. ❹ The use and abuse of antidumping actions has continued unabated, especially in the U. S. and the EU. There is also increased use of antidumping duties even by developing countries. ❺ Many of the practices that have been identified as leading to significant protectionist

---

❶ Welber Barral, *Antidumping Measures: Prospects for Developing Countries*, IRI/UFSC Working Paper No. 01/03 ,2003, pp. 1, 23, http://papers. ssrn. com/sol3/cf_dev/AbsByAuth. cfm? per_id = 337747#show373320, last visited September 21, 2011.

❷ *Ibid.*, p. 24.

❸ The case Guatemala-cement is a key example of the relevance that procedural issues can reach. This also explains the U. S. attachment to the constant revision of the AD Agreement, creating a special rule of interpretation for the antidumping procedure. This standard of review was considered as one of the main victories of the Uruguay Round by the U. S. government, and it will be discussed again in the near future. *See ibid.*

❹ Bernard M. Hoekman & Petros C. Mavroidis, *Antitrust-Based Remedies and Dumping in International Trade*, Policy Research Working Paper No. 1347, the World Bank, 1994, pp. 1, 7, http://www - wds. worldbank. org/servlet/WDSContentServer/WDSP/IB/1994/08/01/000009265 _3970716141633/Rendered/PDF/multi0page. pdf, last visited September 21, 2011.

❺ Mitsuo Matsushita *et al.*, *the World Trade Organization: Law, Practice, and Policy*, Oxford Univ. 2003, p. 307.

biases remain untouched. ❶ Modern antidumping law continues to have a number of significant failings and there are significant political barriers to further reform. ❷

Secondly, examining from the perspective of competition is to question the fundamental justification of antidumping system, which determines the existence of the whole system and sets the criterions for all the other refinements of antidumping rules. Most people confronted the question of "why antidumping law is nessary?" would provide the "correct" answer that dumping is harmful, or dumping is an unfair practice, without the least hesitation, but might lose in thought when further explanation on why dumping is harmful is requested. Neither the legislative history nor the WTO ADA has offered a clear explanation thereon. ❸"Dumping is harmful" seems self-evident and needs no testification in antidumping investigations.

Perhaps dumping is perceived to be unfair, but because the public do not understand hence fail to appreciate how often it results from ordinary

---

❶ For instances, while the antidumping agreement sought to prevent such abuses of antidumping law, the antidumping agreement still leaves administrative decision makers with considerable discretion. The criteria for determining the margin of dumping and material injury, for example, remain imprecise, leaving scope for abuse. Likewise, there are no specific criteria for determining the relevant markets and there is no generally accepted mechanism for examining the causal relationship between the dumped imports and any material injury. These changes to the GATT/WTO rules may have weakened rather than strengthened the discipline on countries taking antidumping actions. P. J. Lloyd, Anti-dumping and Competition Law, in Patrick F. J Macrory et al., eds., *II The World Trade Organization: Legal, Economic and Political Analysis*, Springer 2005, p. 72.

❷ Martyn D. Taylor, *International Competition Law: A New Dimension for the WTO?* Cambridge Univ. Press Inc. 2006, pp. 263 – 264.

❸ Peter D. Ehrenhaft, *Is Interface of Antidumping and Antitrust Laws Possible?* George Washington International Law Review, 2002, Vol. 34. pp. 363, 367.

economic forces and how often one's own nationals thus engage in it. The logical remedy would seem to inform the public about the true nature of dumping, rather than acquiescence in the purported need to counteract it. ❶With antidumping's protectionist abuse became severer, exploring into the fundamental justification should be seriously considered. Just like Messerlin asserted, "This renewed interest [meaning competition-oriented approach] was driven by growing sentiment that antidumping was becoming a back door for protectionism, that it therefore had to be reformed, and that competition policy was the appropriated venue for reform". ❷

Thirdly, with competition policy penetrating into trade areas in the world globalization, the harmonization and coordination of trade policy and competition policy becomes indispensible. During the early 1990s, the demand for international competition policy spread to the other Uruguay round agreement, such as safeguards, services, intellectual property rights, trade-related investment measures, and even to the plurilateral agreement on government procurement. ❸ The "antidumping" issue therein is considered as the threshold for competition law to

---

❶ Alan O. Sykes, Antidumping and Antitrust: What Problems Does Each Address? In Robert Z. Lawerence, ed., *Bookings Trade Forum*, *Bookings Institution*, 1998, p. 38.

❷ Patrick A. Messerlin, Competition Policy and Antidumping Reform: An Exercise in Transition, in J. J. Schott ed., *the World Trading System: Challenges Ahead*, Washington DC: Institute for International Economics, 1996, p. 219, http://www.iie.com/publications/chapters_preview/66/13iie2350.pdf, last visited May 24, 2009.

❸ *Ibid.*

penetrate into trade area. [1] Competition scholars even claim that, "one would be hard pressed to find a scholar steeped in competition law and policy who supports current antidumping rules. Most would prefer their outright replacement with a competition-based regime that could address any serious instance of dumping that actually harms consumers and the process of competition". [2]

Fourthly, the relationship between antidumping and antitrust has been within the focal discussions in domestic field, bilateral and regional area, and the multilateral area ever since 1970s. Academic world, be they trade or competition scholars, in developed countries or from developing

---

[1] Ralf Boscheck considered: "to thoroughly assess the preconditions for an international coordination of competition-related trade issues, it is inevitable, initially at least, to focus on one salient concern. Antidumping provides the most critical case in point." *See* Ralf Boscheck, *the Governance of Global Market Relations: the Case of Substituting Antitrust for Antidumping*, World Competition, 2001, Vol. 24. p. 53.

[2] Spencer Weber Waller, *Bringing Globalism Home: Lessons from Antitrust and Beyond*, Loyola University Chicago Law Journal, 2000, Vol. 32, p. 113.

countries, attachs great attention to this issue. ❶ In practice, there have already existed "substitution" cases and is a tendency in both bilateral and regional areas to repeal antidumping by competition. ❷ In the WTO, various discussions of the "substitution" issue have been conducted by

---

❶ This issue has incurred a hot discussion among the scholars of developed countries. For example, there are many discussions in the Bookings Trade Forum, including Antidumping and Antitrust: What Problems Does Each Address; Possible Instances of Predatory Pricing in Recent U. S. Antidumping Cases; Economic Impact of Canadian Antidumping Law; The European Community's Experience etc. *See* Robert Z. Lawrence, ed. , *Bookings Trade Forum*, Bookings Institution Press, 1998. Besides, there are also increasing discussions among developing countries. *See, e. g.* , Aradhna Aggarwal, *Antidumping Law and Practice: An Indian Perspective*, Indian Council for Research on International Economic Relations, 2002, pp. 1-68, http://www. icrier. org/pdf/antiDump. pdf, last visited September 21, 2011; Merle Holden, *Antidumping: A Reaction to Trade Liberalisation or Anti Competitive?* South African Journal of Economics, 2002, Vol. 5, pp. 912-931, http://onlinelibrary. wiley. com/doi/10. 1111/J. 1813-6982. 2002. tb00051. x/pdf, last visited September 21, 2011. Anamelia Soccal Seyffarth, *the Link between Competition Policy and Antidumping Policy*, George Washington University, School of Business and Public Management, Institute of Brazilian Issues Minerva Program, 2000, pp. 1-49, http://www. gwu. edu/~ibi/minerva/Fall2000/Anamelia. Seyffarth. pdf, last visited September 21, 2011.

❷ It is examined that, the first is the experience of the United States. Similarly, when the European Economic Community was created in the late 1950s, it learned the American lesson well. Besides, recently, New Zealand and Australia concluded a free trade agreement in 1983, which included the elimination of antidumping rules for trans-Tasman trade and the replacement of the dumping rules with true competition provisions. Canada and Chile also eliminated antidumping rules in their free trade agreement even though their economies are structurally quite different and separated by thousands of miles. Mercosur, the principal South American free trade area, has pursued a similar path in eliminating antidumping duties for trade within the bloc. Discussion is also existed in NAFTA. In Asia, China and Hong Kong Area, China and Macau Area, have decided not to use antidumping between them. Similar practice happened in South Africa Union.

the WGTCP. [1]

According to the aforementioned reasons, this book in the following chapters intends to reexamine "dumping" as a private business conduct that might be also subject to competition law, to provide its own viewpoint towards whether putting dumping under competition rules instead of antidumping rules can be less vulnerable to protectionist abuse.

---

[1] By examining all of the working documents of the WGTCP from the year 1997 to 2004, it is found that the relationship between the two has induced the hottest discussion in WGTCP around 1998.

Chapter II Dumping in Economic Theories and Antidumping Law

The primary issue in this book is to reconsider the self-evident premise of antidumping law, i. e., why dumping is harmful. This is still a controversial issue that needs clarification. In order to approach that, various economic theories on dumping, as well as the evolvement of antidumping rules will be observed in this chapter.

2. 1 Dumping in Economic Theories

In line with the development of antidumping rules, various economic theories on dumping have emerged. ❶ The traditional dumping theory by Viner and the modern dumping theory by Willig thereinto, both favoring the efficiency analysis of dumping, are deemed to be two of the most influential theories. ❷

2. 1. 1 The Traditional Dumping Theory of Viner

Viner (1923) was the first to present a comprehensive theoretical

---

❶ The specific summary of various economic theories of dumping, *see* Gunnar Niels, *What is Antidumping Policy Really About*? Journal of Economic Surveys, 2002, Vol. 14, pp. 467 – 492, http://www. blackwell-synergy. com/links/doi/10. 1111/1467-6419. 00118, last visited September 21, 2011.

❷ In this part, we will focus mostly on reviewing the definition, the classification and the effects of dumping, summarizing the traditional justification for condemning dumping, while the criticisms of the classic dumping theory, and discussion of the specific economic analysis shall be avoided according to the purpose of this book.

treatise on dumping. ❶ It was Viner that tracked the legal practice (especially that of the U. S.) and first introduced "dumping", an international (or transnational) price discrimination, into economics. ❷ In the initial part of his book, Viner defined that dumping is "the price-discrimination between national markets". ❸ Such definition was extended afterwards to regard "sales below cost" also as dumping. ❹

Prior to investigate the effects of dumping, Viner classified dumping into various kinds in light of the motives (or the objectives) of the dumper and the degree of continuity of the dumping. ❺ Based on the two-fold classification is the discussion of which kind of dumping is

---

❶ Gunnar Niels, *What is Antidumping Policy Really About*? Journal of Economic Surveys, 2002, Vol. 14, pp. 467, 471, http://www. blackwell-synergy. com/links/doi/10. 1111/1467 - 6419. 00118, last visited September 21, 2011.

❷ For example, Dale pointed out that: "the most widely accepted economic definition of dumping, which was first suggested by the economist Jacob Viner, who was responsible for many contributions to international trade theory, is price discrimination between national markets." *See* Richard Dale, *Anti-dumping Law in a Liberal Trade Order*, the Macmillan Press Ltd. 1980, p. 1.

❸ Jacob Viner, *Dumping: A Problem in International Trade*, the Univ. of Chicago Press, 1923, p. 3.

❹ Gabrielle Marceau, *Antidumping and Anti-trust Issues in Free-trade Areas*, Oxford Univ. Press Inc. 1994, p. 11.

❺ Jacob Viner, *Dumping: A Problem in International Trade*, the Univ. of Chicago Press 1923, p. 23.

harmfull and which is not. [1] In the second chapter of his book, Viner elaborated his classification in three steps. Firstly, Viner illustrated that there are ten kinds of motives (A to J) to dump, namely:

---

[1] In introducing Viner's classification, modern scholars tend to emphasize more on the continuity of dumping than the motives (or the objectives) of the dumper. For example, Dale introduced the time-based distinction of Viner: the importance generally attached to the time factor in assessing welfare effects is reflected in Viner's economic classification of dumping which has been absorbed into the modern literature on the subject. Viner's primary distinction is between sporadic, short-run or intermittent, and long-run or continuous dumping". -Sporadic dumping is "dumping which is occasional and casual, which occurs only in scattered instances and at irregular intervals and which is not the manifestation of a definitely established price-policy on the part of the dumping concern". - Short-run or intermittent dumping "is continued steadily and systematically for a period of limited duration, which is practiced in accordance with a definitely established export policy and which involves the deliberate production of commodities to be dumped". - Long-run dumping "is carried on not merely sporadically nor even intermittently but continuously over a prospectively permanent period. *See* Richard Dale, Antidumping Law in a Liberal Trade Order", the Macmillan Press Ltd. 1980, p. 8.

Sykes pointed that: Viner introduced a distinction that survived for some time in the literature between "sporadic" dumping, "short-run" dumping, and "permanent" dumping - "Sporadic" dumping was extremely short-lived, as for the purpose of disposing of a temporary overstock - "Permanent" dumping is continuous over a period of many years, as perhaps when the home market is protected from competition but export markets are competitive, - "Short-run" dumping: where dumping was "short run" - of significant but not indefinite duration. *See* Alan O. Sykes, Antidumping and Antitrust: What Problems Does Each Address? In Robert Z. Lawerence, ed., Brookings Trade Forum, Brookings Institution 1998, p. 31.

Marceau mentioned: After Viner's work, dumping was traditionally classified according to its duration because of its allegedly different welfare impacts. Dumping was considered to be sporadic, short-run, and intermittent or, long-run and continuous. ...but Viner's classification of dumping practices and their related impact is contested as being too simplistic..." *See* Gabrielle Marceau, *Antidumping and Anti-trust Issues in Free-trade Areas*, Oxford Univ. Press Inc. 1994, p. 15.

A. To dispose of a casual overstock[1];

B. Unintentional[2];

---

[1] More explanation about motive A by Viner: "A producer may find that in a given season sales at the established prices are not running high enough to clear his stocks on hand or in process. The alternative procedures open to him to meet this situation are: (1) to hold over the surplus stocks to another season; (2) to reduce his prices in his standard market in order to increase sales; or (3) to dispose of his surplus stocks in some distant or unimportant market at the best prices obtainable, even if these are lower than the prices current in his standard markets. He may be reluctant to hold his surplus stocks over to another season, because of the carrying and storage charges, the difficulty of financing an over-large inventory, or the danger of deterioration or of change in style to which his products may be subject. He may also be reluctant to reduce his prices in his standard market. It is probable that it will not be practicable to reduce prices on any portion of his sales in this market without making the reductions general to all purchasers, so that any reduction in domestic price will apply to his entire output. In any case, the demand for his product in his standard market may be inelastic, so that a reduction in price, whether partial or general, will not have a substantial effect on sales. A reduction in price once conceded may make a subsequent reestablishment of the original price difficult or even impossible, or may incite cutthroat competition on the part of rival producers; that is, it may 'spoil' his standard market. For any or all of these reasons a producer may choose to unload his surplus stocks at reduced prices in a minor or hitherto uncultivated market." *See* Jacob Viner, *Dumping: A Problem in International Trade*, The Univ. of Chicago Press, 1923, p. 24.

[2] More explanation about motive B by Viner: "Unintentional dumping can take place only when goods are exported speculatively in anticipation of their sale at a profitable price after arrival in the foreign market, or when goods have been shipped to a foreign market by mistake or for some reason delivery cannot be made to the original purchaser. If such goods were shipped with the expectation that they would eventually be sold at prices as high as those current in the home market, but if they must eventually be disposed of at lower prices, unintentional dumping has taken place. Such dumping is most likely to occur under the consignment system, or under the branch warehouse system, where goods are shipped to be sold after arrival in the foreign market. But such dumping cannot be regarded as unintentional if the goods were shipped with the expectation, or with full realization of the imminent probability, that they would realization of the imminent probability, that they would realize upon sale net prices lower than those current in the home market." *See ibid.*, pp. 24 – 25.

C. To maintain connections in a market in which prices are on remaining considerations unacceptable❶;

D. To develop trade connections and buyers' goodwill in a new market ❷ ;

E. To eliminate competition in the market dumped on❸;

F. To forestall the development of competition in the market dumped on❹;

---

❶ More explanation about motive C by Viner: "A producer may find that the prices obtainable in a given market are lower than those at which he can elsewhere dispose of all of his current production, but he may nevertheless meet the prices current in that market to retain his trade connections therewith, if in the long run it affords a valuable outlet for his product. In this case the producer in Willing to sell at a reduced prices only because this will serve to retain for the future a market which temporarily has no attraction for him." *See* Jacob Viner, *Dumping: A Problem in International Trade*, the Univ. of Chicago Press, 1923, p. 25.

❷ More explanation about motive D by Viner: "A producer may for a time sell at reduced prices in a market in which he is endeavoring newly to establish his trade in order to develop therein a demand for his products which will subsequently make possible their sale in that market at prices as high as those current elsewhere." *See ibid.*, p. 26.

❸ More explanation about motive E by Viner: "A concern may sell at dumping pries in a given market in order to eliminate its competitors in that market or to bring them to terms. Such dumping may be directed against the domestic producers of the market dumped on, or against competing exporters from the dumper's own country, or against competing exporters from a third country. It may be intended wholly to crush competitors, or it may have the more modest objective of inducing competitors by the threat of destructive competition to follow the prices quoted by the dumping concern, to share the market with it on specified terms, or otherwise to make their operations in the given market conform to the wishes of the dumping concern. This type of dumping is often termed 'predatory' or 'malignant' dumping. It is the most objectionable form of dumping from the point of view of the country dumped on." *See ibid.*

❹ More explanation about motive F by Viner: " A concern which has a monopoly of its product in the markets in which it operates but fears that competition may appear in certain of its markets if it exacts too high a price may quote lower prices in those markets in which competition is most likely to develop in order to forestall such development." *See ibid.*, p. 27.

G. To retaliate against dumping in the reverse direction[1];

H. To maintain full production from existing plant facilities without cutting domestic prices[2];

I. To obtain the economies of large-scale production without cutting

---

[1] More explanation about motive G by Viner: "If a concern in one country is embarrassed by competition in its home market from products exported to that market by a foreign manufacturer at dumping prices or at unreasonable low prices, it may endeavor to bring such competition to an end by resorting to retaliatory dumping in the principal market of the offending manufacturer. In other words, dumping may not only be used as the offensive instrument of cutthroat competition in international commerce, but it may also be used as a defense against cutthroat competition." *See* Jack Viner *Dumping: A Problem in International Trade*, The Univ. of Chicago Press, 1923, p. 27.

[2] More explanation about motive H by Viner: "If a manufacturer can sell each year in his domestic market a part, but only a part, of his maximum possible output at higher prices than those ruling in outside markets, he may decide to maintain his domestic prices at this higher level and to seek foreign orders at reduced prices for the balance of his potential output in preference to reducing his domestic prices and in preference to operating only to part capacity. By resorting to dumping he may obtain the economies of operation at full capacity without surrendering the profits to be derived from the sale of part of his output in the domestic market at prices above the foreign level. A reduction in the domestic prices may be unprofitable, especially if the domestic demand for his products is inelastic, even in the absence of the possibility of resort to dumping. This case closely resembles Case A as presented above. It differs from Case A in the one particular that in the present case the commodities dumped are not merely surplus stocks which had originally been produced in anticipation of sale at the full prices but are stock deliberately produced in order to be dumped. It is probable that this is the most prevalent type of dumping, but business men who practice it with the purpose of maintaining at the same time high domestic prices and production to full capacity have a readily explicable reluctance to admit it." *See ibid.*, pp. 27 – 28.

domestic prices❶;

J. On purely mercantilistic grounds. ❷

Secondly, instead of applying the predominate classification at that age by dividing dumping into two kinds (i. e. sporadic and permanent) according to its continuity, Viner distinguished three kinds of dumping, including sporadic, short-run or intermittent, and long-run or continuous. ❸ Sporadic dumping refers to dumping which is occasional and causal, occurs only in scattered instances at irregular intervals, and is

---

❶ More explanation about motive I by Viner: "It is possible that a manufacturer may sell abroad at reduced prices in order to increase his sales, without reduction of his domestic prices, to such a rate that it will not only permit him to maintain full production from his existing plant facilities but will enable him to extend his plant so as to obtain the economies of larger-scale production. It is obvious that once the plant has been extended, further dumping will be illustrative of Case H. " *See ibid.*, p. 28.

❷ More explanation about motive J by Viner: "Dumping on purely mercantilistic grounds, that is, dumping which is resorted to only in order to stimulate export trade for the sake of the national advantages to be derived therefrom by the dumper's country, is altogether unlikely to be practiced on purely private initiative. Producers who believe that a country derived some special advantages from exports which are not to be obtained in equal measure from domestic trade are not hard to find, but the producer who will be Willing solely on such grounds to sell abroad at lower prices than he can obtain for all of his output at home must indeed be rare. Mercantilistic considerations often play a part in dumping, however, where governments grants bounties on exports. If dumping results from the grant of an official bounty on exports and the establishment of this bounty by the government has for its object the stimulation of exports, the dumping may be said to be the result of mercantilistic motives. The producer who resorts to dumping always does so with the aim of deriving a personal pecuniary advantage therefrom, but he may often find an effective defense of his practice against protects from agencies of his government or from domestic consumers in an appeal to mercantilistic prejudices. It is probable that in most actual instances of dumping no single motive is dominant but that some combination of the ones listed above, all of them concerned with private profit and not national policy, are operative. " *See* Jack Viner, *Dumping: A Problem in International Trade*, the Univ. of Chicago Press, 1923, pp. 28 – 29.

❸ *Ibid.*, p. 29.

not the manifestation of a definitely established price – policy on the part of the dumping concern. ❶ Short-run or intermittent dumping is used to define such dumping as is continued steadily and systematically for a period of limited duration, which is practiced in accordance with a definitely established export policy, and which involves the deliberate production of commodities to be dumped. ❷ Long-run or continuous dumping describes dumping which is carried on neither sporadically nor even intermittently but continuously over a prospectively permanent period. ❸

Thirdly, Viner linked the classification of the motives of the dumper with that of the continuity of dumping, based on which the effects of each kind of dumping were examined. Viner argued that though there was no rigid relationship between the particular motive and the degree of continuity of dumping, there exists a fundamental link. For all the motives from A to J, motive A and B, dumping to dispose of a casual overstock and unintentional dumping, would normally be sporadic. ❹ Motive C, dumping to maintain trade connections, motive D, dumping to develop trade connections, motive E, dumping to eliminate competition, motive F, dumping to forestall the development of competition and motive G, retaliatory dumping, would normally be short-run, continuing steadily and systematically for a period lasting from several months to years. ❺ Motive H and I, dumping to maintain full production from

---

❶ Jack Viner, *Dumping: A Problem in International Trade*, the Univ. of Chicago Press, 1923, p. 30.

❷ *Ibid.*, p. 31.

❸ *Ibid.*

❹ *Ibid.*

❺ *Ibid.*

existing plant and dumping to make possible the extension of plant, might be either short-run or long-run, depending in each instance on which of these was necessary for the realization of its objective by the dumping concern. [1] For motive J, mercantilistic dumping, would be long-run normally. [2]

Based on the investigation aformentioned, Viner conducted the economic analysis with consumer welfare as his focal element, to observe the effects of the three types of dumping. His essential idea is that, "from the point of view of the importing country as a whole, there is a sound economic case against dumping only when it is reasonable to suppose that it will result in injury to domestic industry greater than the gain to consumers". [3] Accordingly, of the three types of dumping, only the short-run dumping, which may result in serious injury to or even the total elimination of the domestic industry and the gain to the consumer may not be nearly great enough to offset the damage to the domestic industry, should be condemned. [4]

It is clearly impossible to conclude that short-run dumping is harmful only based on its continued steadily and systematically for several months or years. The continuity of dumping should not be considered

---

[1] Jack Viner, *Dumping: A Problem in International Trade*, the Univ. of Chicago Press, 1923, p. 31.

[2] *Ibid.*

[3] *Ibid.*, p. 138.

[4] For the other two types, Viner deemed that casual or sporadic dumping, corresponding to the bargain sale in internal commerce, is relatively unimportant either in its advantages to the consumer or in its injury to the domestic producer. For the long-run dumping, Viner also believed that the advantage of dumping to the consumer in the importing country must be accepted as in the long run more important than the injury to the domestic producer. *See ibid.*, pp. 138 – 144.

seepartely from the motives of dumper therein. In his book, Viner provided with two exemplifications. One is the threat of predatory dumping. Short-run dumping under motives E and F aformentioned is likely to facilitate the acquisition of monopoly control by establishing abnormally high prices afterwards. This is called "predatory pricing". The other is the waste of resources. For the other motives such as C, D and G under this type, Viner believed that even if prices do not rise later, a net loss is likely to arise because dumping leads resources to become idle while waiting for it to stop. ❶

The dumping theory created by Viner is held as classic and has an essential influence on the subsequent literature. ❷ Based on the above analysis, it can be concluded that in the classic dumping theory,

---

❶ Short-run dumping, whatever its objective, may result in serious injury to or even the total elimination of the domestic industry. The gain to the consumer from a short period of abnormally low prices may not be nearly great enough to offset the damage to the domestic industry, including the capital invested therein, the labor which it employs, and the managerial ability which directs it. The dumping will be especially likely to result in a net loss to the importing country if it serves to bring about later the establishment of abnormally high prices, either because it has facilitated the acquisition of monopoly control by the dumper or because the losses incurred by the domestic industry during the continuance of the dumping or the check to its expansion of productive facilities have lessened its ability to serve its market economically or its willingness to engage in active price - competition within its own ranks or with its foreign rivals. *See* Jack Viner, *Dumping: A Problem in International Trade*, the Univ. of Chicago Press, 1923, pp. 140 - 141.

❷ As recognized by Gunnar Niels that: "After Viner there was a long period during which relatively little happened in the field of dumping theory, perhaps because it did not become a major issue in international trade until relatively recently. ... In fact, current antidumping policy still relies strongly on Viner's work. Modern dumping theory, developed since the 1980s and discussed below, has had very little influence on the policy." *See* Gunnar Niels, *What is Antidumping Policy Really About*? Journal of Economic Surveys, 2002, Vol. 14, pp. 467, 472 - 473, http://www.blackwell - synergy.com/links/doi/10.1111/1467 - 6419.00118, last visited September 21, 2011.

dumping refers to the price-discrimination between national markets, and is classified in light of both the motives of dumper and the continuity of dumping. In the evaluation of the effects of dumping, an efficiency analysis is applied to explore whether the consumer welfare weighs much more than the industry interest in each type of dumping. According to Viner, dumping can be regarded as harmful and condemned only in short-run dumping under two circumstances, one is when it is a predatory dumping resulting in monopoly, and the other is when a dumping resulting in the idleness of resources. The second one concerning the idleness of resources was criticized and generally accepted to be incorrect or implausible in the subsequent literature. [1]

---

[1] The second argument has been criticized later by alleging that "Viner misjudged the true costs of resource mis-allocation in the importing country"; "This argument [that dumping will cause a waste of resources in the importing country as it attempts to adjust to the lower price] will appear again below where dumping below cost makes it somewhat more plausible." *See, e.g.*, Richard Dale, *Antidumping Law in a Liberal Trade Order*, the Macmillan Press Ltd. 1980, p. 3; Gabrielle Marceau, *Antidumping and Anti-trust Issues in Free-trade Areas*, Oxford Univ. Press Inc. 1994, p. 15; John H. Jackson & Edwin A. Vermulst, eds., *Antidumping Law and Practice: a Comparative Study*, Harvester Wheatsheaf 1990, pp. 28 – 29.

2.1.2 The Modern Dumping Theory of Willig

There was many an economic theory of dumping after Viner. ❶ Among them, Willg's dumping theory takes an important part in the modern economics. Economists incline to conduct empirical studies by applying Viner's criteria of dumping. ❷ The general idea of Willig is to divide dumping into two main categories, one is non-monopolizing dumping and the other is monopolizing dumping. Based on such classification, he then argued that only monopolizing dumping is harmful and should be

---

❶ Such as summarized by Gunnar Niels, since the early 1980s, several contributors have tried to explain the phenomenon of dumping by other than traditional analysis. For example, Davies and Mcguinness (1982) show that dumping at less than marginal cost may occur in circumstances of uncertainty, of sales-maximizing behavior by managers and of strategic entry deterrence. Effects on consumer surplus are only analyzed for the exporting country, not for the importing country or the global economy as a whole. Brander and Krugman (1983), Staiger and Wolak (1991) and Hartigan (1994) have presented models of dumping as international price discrimination by oligopolistic rivals. Weinstein (1992) extends that Brander and Krugman model. Either (1982), Gruenspecht (1988) and Clarida (1993) have developed models of dumping as selling below cost of production in a world in which the law of one price holds. *See* Gunnar Niels, *What is Antidumping Policy Really About?* Journal of Economic Surveys, 2002, Vol. 14, pp. 467, 473 – 474, http://www.blackwell-synergy.com/links/doi/10.1111/1467-6419.00118, last visited September 21, 2011.

❷ *See more*, Vincent Aussilloux *et al.*, *Antidumping as Anticompetitive Practice: Evidence from the United-States and the European Community*, http://www.ios.neu.edu/iioc2004/papers/s6k3.pdf, last visited May 14, 2009; Merle Holden, *Anti Dumping: A Reaction to Trade Liberalisation or Anti Competitive?* South Aprican Journal of Economics, 2002, Vol. 5, pp. 912-931, http://onlinelibrary.wiley.com/doi/10.1111/J.1813-6982.2002.tb00051.x/pdf, last visited September 21, 2011; Aradhna Aggarwal, *Anti Dumping Law and Practice: An Indian Perspective*, Indian Council for Research on International Economic Relations, 2002, http://www.icrier.org/pdf/antiDump.pdf, last visited September 21, 2011; José Tavares De Araujo Jr., *Legal and Economic Interfaces between Antidumping and Competition Policy*, CEPAL – SERIE Comercio Internacional, 2001, http://www.eclac.cl/publicaciones/xml/0/9040/lcl1685i.pdf, last visited September 21, 2011.

condemned.

Underneath the category of non-monopolizing dumping are three kinds of dumping of different motives, including market-expansion dumping, cyclical dumping and state-trading dumping. Market-expansion dumping is exporting at a lower net price than is charged at home for the purpose of the expanded export sales. [1] Cyclical dumping is the export at usually low prices of goods for which there is substantial excess production

---

[1] More explanation about market-expansion dumping: the motivation behind this behavior is the additional profits that may be earned by pricing exports at a smaller margin above marginal production and transport exports at a smaller margin above marginal production and transport cost than is charged for sales at home. Here the exporting firm can profitably charge a lower make up in the import market because it faces a higher elasticity of demand there with respect to price. The key difference in the price elasticities of demand in the home and export markets may stem from several factors. First, buyer preferences for the good and for the whole category that includes the good may be stronger at home than abroad. Second, the export market may contain a larger variety of alternative goods that are close substitutes for the product in question. Third, the firm may have a smaller share of the importing country's market than its share of the home market, as a consequence of buyer preferences, transportation or other cost differences, protection at home, or relative proximities to other sources of supply and other market opportunities. Then, even though the overall market demands at home and abroad may be equally price elastic, the demands facing the firm will be more price elastic abroad. This situation may lead to "reciprocal dumping," which may lower prices for consumers in both affected countries. Fourth, the behavior of market rivals may be more competitive abroad than at home. *See* Robert D. Willig, Economic Effects of Antidumping Policy, in Robert Z. Lawerence, ed., *Brookings Trade Forum*, Brookings Institution, 1998, pp. 61 – 62.

capacity owing to a downturn in demand. [1] State-trading dumping may arise from the export and state-owned enterprises in economics whose currencies are not freely convertible to those generally employed in international trade. [2]

In respect of the category of monopolizing dumping, there are two kinds of dumping of different motives, i. e., strategic dumping and predatory dumping. Strategic dumping is the term adopted for exporting

---

[1] More explanation about cyclical dumping: The motivation for cyclical dumping arises from the usually low marginal costs or opportunity costs of production that accompany substantial excess production capacity with little or no use apart from the manufacture of the good in question. A contributing factor may also be the unusually intense degree of competition that may arise among rival suppliers who also possess excess capacity. Here, it is more profitable to cut prices in order to generate more sales than to hold prices up, as long as the price does not fall below the level of marginal variable cost. Considerations of employment may be part of the motivation, where the business or social costs of layoffs might be reduced by the additional production that usually low prices could stimulate. The profit or labor-cost motivations for such aggressive marketing are not inconsistent with the possibility that prices may fall below the level of "full cost", which includes the sunk (committed) cost of capacity. The costs of sunk capacity that is in excess supply are not reflected in marginal or opportunity costs, even though such costs do reflect the costs of capacity when capacity is not in excess. Business patterns of this kind are generally thought to be common and rational in domestic contexts in sectors with high fixed costs and cyclical fluctuations in demand. *See* Robert D. Willing, Economic Effects of Antidumping Policy, in Robert Z. Lawerence, ed., *Brooking Trade Forum*, Brooking Institution, 1998, pp. 62 – 63.

[2] More explanation about state-trading dumping: While state-trading dumping may arise for the same reasons as market-expansion, cyclical, or other categories of dumping, the distinguishing motivation in this case is the desire for "hard currency". With a nonconvertible currency, the exporting nation needs to acquire hard currency to finance its own imports from countries in the trading system of the free world. The exporting nation can gain from foreign sales priced below cost-based constructed values owing to the additional benefits derived from the imports made possible by the hard currency that the export provide. Thus incentives to undertake such international sales will reflect the relative scarcity values of different hard currencies to the exporting nations. *See ibid.*, p. 63.

that injures domestic rivals through a strategy that encompasses both the pricing of the exports and restraints protecting the exporters' home market. [1] Predatory-pricing dumping refers to low-priced exporting that is geared to driving rivals out of business in order to obtain monopoly power in the importing market. The exporter's losses from supplying its goods at the low price are expected to be more than recouped later, under the high prices made possibly by the monopoly position resulting from the irreversible exit of the rivals for the importing market. Dumping herein is intended to injury firms indigenous to the importing country, and it acts as a threat to the state of competition in that country's

---

[1] More explanation about strategic dumping: In this scenario, the production of the good in question requires a substantial investment in R&D or other fixed costs, or involves significant learning by doing, which result in significant static or dynamic economics of scale. In the exporters' home market is foreclosed to foreign rivals and if each independent exporter has a substantial share of the home market in relation to the scale economies, then, with other things being equal, the exporters will have a significant cost advantage over any foreign rivals. Furthermore, potential foreign rivals may be deterred from committing to the initial or ongoing investments needed to stay technologically abreast of the exporters, because they recognize the difficulty they would face in trying to recover their investment costs in competition with exporters operating under the advantage conferred by their protected home market. It should be emphasized that the economic logic of strategic dumping limits its applicability to home markets that are sufficiently large in relation to the rest of the relevant world's trading market for the protection of the home market to have a significant impact on the ability of rivals to compete elsewhere. This consideration implies that smaller economies are unlikely to favor strategic dumping. The profitability of strategic dumping stems from the cost advantage enjoyed by exporters because they have access to wider markets than do their foreign rivals. Such exporters need not have intent to monopolize but may simply be operating as rivals with an advantage: that conferred by the foreclosure of their home market to their foreign competitors. Nevertheless, the artificial advantage will distort the competition and create profitable market power. *See* Robert D. Willing, Economic Effects of Antidumping policy, in Robert Z. Lawerence, ed. , *Brooking Trade Forum*, Brooking Institution, 1998, pp. 64 – 65.

markets. [1]

After defining each type of dumping, Willig continue to evaluate the impacts of Non-monopolizing dumping and monopolizing dumping respectively. An efficiency analysis, benefits of consumer exceeding benefits of suppliers, was adopted as his essential criterion. In terms of the market-expansion, cyclical, and state-trading dumping, the purposes of which are not at creating monopoly power, are entirely consistent with robustly competitive conditions in the importing nation's market. Willig concluded that it is possible, but by no means assured that non-monopolizing dumping causes greater aggregate social loss and injury to

---

[1] More explanation about predatory dumping: Cost-based standards are of particular significance for determining whether predatory-pricing dumping is taking place. Predation is often defined in terms of below-cost pricing, and even where a more complex definition is applied, it is important to compare prices and particular and possibly precise cost measures (such as variable, incremental, and marginal costs). How to recognize price predation is discussed later in this paper, but suffice it to say that it is difficult superficially to discern whether a firm is pricing aggressively in order to compete with its rivals or is to induce the exit of its rivals in order to gain a monopolistic position in the market. However, the conventional view is that if the aggressively low prices are below avoidable costs, then predation can be inferred since competition will not drive a firm to make sales that cost it more than it receives in compensation. *See* Robert D. Willing, Economic Effects of Antidumping policy, in Robert E. Lawerence, ed., *Brooking Trade Forum*, Brooking Institution, 1998, pp. 65 – 66.

domestic import-competing suppliers than benefits to domestic buyers. ❶

In terms of the predatory-pricing dumping, it is undoubtedly that such dumping is anti-competitive hence harmful not only to the importing country, but also to the global economy. ❷ Relating to the impacts of Strategic Dumping, Willig concluded that it is harmful not only because that strategic dumping has a number of adverse effects on the importing country, but also because that the negative effects of strategic dumping on the importing nation are likely to outweigh the net benefits to the

---

❶ In discussing the effects of non-monopolizing dumping, Willig stated that: from the perspective of the importing nation, non-monopolizing dumping hurts the interests of domestic producers of import-competing goods and provides domestic buyers (both the final consumers and firms employing the imports as inputs into their own production) with benefits from low prices. Where local producers are perfectly competitive, the benefit to buyers outweighs, in terms of consumers' surplus, any rent or producers' surplus that is lost as a result of the sales of imports at the low dumping price. This is so even though domestic producers may have to scale down –and some may end up having to close down –when dumping brings prices down to levels at which they can no longer compete. The benefits to buyers is larger than the financial damage to perfectly competitive producers, as long as the domestic industry retains its ability to operate as before in the event that conditions were to change, for example, in the event that importers attempts to exercise monopoly power. It is irrelevant for this conclusion whether the low-priced imports are the result of market expansion, cyclical, or state-trading dumping. *See* Robert D. Willing, Economic Effects of Antidumping Policy, in Robert Z. Lawerence, ed. ,*Brooking Trade Forum*, Brooking Institution, 1998, p. 67.

❷ *Ibid.*, pp. 73 – 74.

exporting country from the perspective of the global economy. [1]

It it noticeable that the economic logic of strategic dumping limits its applicability to such home markets as are sufficiently large in relation to the rest of the relevant world's trading market for the protection of the home market to have a significant impact on the ability of rivals to compete elsewhere. This implies that smaller economies are unlikely to favor strategic dumping. [2] An empirical study conducted by Messerlin and

---

[1] From the perspective of importing country welfare, Willig claimed that strategic dumping is likely to have a number of adverse effects on the importing country. First, and most obviously, the restraints protecting the exporters' home market that are intrinsic to strategic dumping limit the export opportunities of the suppliers in the importing country. Second, this constraint on the sales of the domestic suppliers reduces their ability economically to invest in R&D. learning by doing, and human and physical capital and thereby causes them, at best, to operate with higher costs and less desirable products in the markets that are open to them. Third, although these effects in the absolute would diminish the domestic suppliers' profitability, the impact on them is far more severe if they must attempt to compete with the exporting firms that do have access to the protected market. Fourth, the consumers in the importing country may be subject to the exercise of monopoly power by the exporters if the domestic suppliers and other exporters are unable, over time, to compete effectively. Alternatively, even if the domestic suppliers and other exporters are able to offer a measure of competition despite their disadvantages, the resulting oligopoly is unlikely to perform as well for consumers as it would if the domestic suppliers and other exporters were not disadvantaged by the constraints on the markets they can access.

From the perspective of global welfare, Willig claimed that the negative effects of strategic dumping on the importing nation are likely to outweigh the net benefits to the exporting country. This would follow from the general economic proposition that the profits from the exercise of market power in the importing country's market power in the importing country's market are exceeded by the concomitant losses there of consumers' surplus, and here there is the additional net loss to consumers in the exporting nation who are subject to the market power created by the protection of that market. *See* Robert D. Willing, Economic Effects of Antidumping Policy, in Robert Z. Lawerence, ed., *Brooking Trade Forum*, Brooking Institution, 1998, p. 71.

[2] *Ibid.*, p. 64

Reed of antidumping cases handled by the U. S. and the EU authorities revealed that the only country that was in a position to practice strategic dumping was Japan.[1] Accordingly, strategic dumping is deemed to be a special case that cannot be typificated to all circumstances hence set aside hereafter.

2. 1. 3 Generally Recognized Harmful Dumping: Predatory Dumping

Compared Willig' s dumping theory with Viner' s, certain essential similarities that also indicate the link between dumping and price discrimination can be summarized, though differences in their details respectively. Four aspects of similarities deserves notification.

Firstly, both theories viewed dumping as price discrimination, and such definition connects "dumping" to "price discrimination" in competition law.

Secondly, both theories recognized that there does not exist merely "one" harmful dumping. Instead, dumping can be classified into different kinds according to the different motives or objectives, some of which are harmful whereas some are not.

Thirdly, both theories applied efficiency analysis to evaluate the effects of different types of dumping. Both determined the harmfulness of dumping by exploring whether the consumer benefit exceeded the benefit of suppliers.

Fourthly, both theories concern the pro-monopoly effect and generally accept that predatory dumping is harmful.

---

[1] P. J. Lloyd, Antidumping and Competition Law, in Patrick F. J Macrory et al., eds., *II The World Trade Organization: Legal, Economic and Political Analysis*, Springer, 2005, p. 75.

To sum up, both Viner's and Willig's dumping theories, two of the most influential dumping theories favored by economists, only predatory dumping is harmful and needs to be condemned. ❶

2.2 Dumping in the Original Antidumping Law

After a review of dumping theories, we will turn to the development of antidumping law. The justification to condemn dumping is seldom touched, though there are quite a lot discussions on antidumping. ❷ Dumping is often referred to as unfair trade, unfair practice, or unfair competition, whereas there has been no acknowledgment yet on the justification of antidumping law.

Tracing back into its birth and following its evolvement, from the earliest domestic legislations to the current proliferation of laws and actions under the requirement of multilateral agreement, so as to give an overall examination of the development of antidumping, is deemed to be quite

---

❶ *See also*, Kevin C. Kennedy, *Competition Law and the World Trade Organization: the Limits of Multilateralism*, Sweet & Maxwell 2001, p. 235, "Economists generally agree that, in the absence of predatory intent, dumping is essentially harmless for the importing country because the welfare gains for consumers from low-priced imports more than offset any harm to producer welfare in the country of importation."

Michael J. Trebilcock & Robert Howse, *the Regulation of International Trade*, 2nd Edition, Routledge 1999, p. 188. "However, only predatory pricing gives rise to a legitimate economic rationale for prohibiting dumping: when dumping is merely international price discrimination, the export market benefits."

❷ Sykes finds the few comments from European and the U. S. authorities on the justification for antidumping vague and unconvincing. Antidumping policy became entrenched in the United States, and more and more nations took advantage of the opportunity to emulate it without much attention to its premises. *See* Alan O. Sykes, Antidumping and Antitrust: What Problems Does Each Address? In Robert Z. Lawerence, ed., *Brookings Trade Forum*, Brookings Institution, 1998, p. 25.

significant in identifying the true intent of antidumping. This part will place dumping in the original antidumping law, to investigate on the earliest practice of antidumping, with the U. S. as the main focus hereafter. ❶

2. 2. 1 The U. S. 1894 Wilson Act

The U. S. Wilson Tariff Act adopted in 1894 introduced dumping into law for the first time in the world, whereas Canada was generally viewed as the first country to enact antidumping statute. ❷ Such act's coming into being closely related to the Sherman Act.

2. 2. 1. 1 The 1890 Sherman Act: Price Discrimination

As the earliest U. S. federal antitrust law, the 1890 Sherman Act was a child of the industrial revolution. The giant industrial trusts of that era, in addition to their many productive contributions, engaged in a course of conduct to stamp out and swallow up their competitors and exploit their suppliers and customers. The Sherman Act was passed to

---

❶ *See also*, José Tavares De Araujo Jr., *Legal and Economic Interfaces between Antidumping and Competition Policy*, CEPAL – SERIE Comercio Internacional, 2001, pp. 1, 10, http://www.eclac.cl/publicaciones/xml/0/9040/lcl1685i.pdf, last visited September 21, 2011, "one reason for this is that the U. S. has remained a leading international performance in regard to this instrument, as the principal user and the second worldwide target of antidumping investigations during the last decade (see Miranda, Torres and Ruiz, 1998). Another possible explanation stems from the contrast between the scholars' denigration of antidumping and the longstanding commitment to this trade remedy by the U. S. government."

❷ The Canada's 1904 Customs Act was often considered as the world's first AD regulation. *See, e. g.*, Andreas Knorr, *Antidumping Rules vs. Competition Rules*, Institution for World Economics and International Management, 2004, pp. 1, 5, http://www.iwim.uni-bremen.de/publikationen/pdf/W031.pdf, last visited September 21, 2011.

regulate these trusts. [1] The Congress in 1890 passed the Sherman Antitrust Act, under severe penalties, every contract or combination in restraint of interstate or foreign commerce, and every monopolization or attempt to monopolized such commerce. [2]

The Sherman Act is consist of two brief operative paragraphs. In section 1, contracts, combinations, and conspiracies "in restraint of trade" are declared illegal. The phrase "restraint of trade" has been interpreted to cover such hard-core violations as price fixing and market division, and also practices such as exclusive-dealing contracts and joint ventures when they are anticompetitive. In Section 2, it is held as a violation to monopolize, attempt to monopolize, or combine or conspire with others to monopolize trade. [3]

As a special conduct of violation to monopolize, Price discrimination was not initially set forth in the Sherman Act but developed in cases

---

[1] Edward M. Graham & J. David, Richardson eds., *Global Competition Policy*, Institute for International Economics, 1997, p. 235.

[2] Jacob Viner, *Dumping: A Problem in International Trade*, the Univ. of Chicago Press, 1923, p. 239.

[3] Edward M. Graham & J. David, Richardson eds., *Global Competition Policy*, Institute For International Economics, 1997, p. 240.

later on. [1] In several cases "local price-cutting" [2], or the sale or offer for sale of a commodity in one part of the U. S. at prices which were lower, after allowance for differences in cost of transportation, grade, quality, or quantity sold, than the prices charged in other parts of the U. S., with the intent of thereby establishing a monopoly or destroying or injuring the trade or business of another or preventing another from engaging in the same business, was restrained as in violation of the Sherman Act. [3]

The cases concerning price discrimination drew the legislators' attention. In order to address price discrimination in law, the Sherman Act was revised in two directions, one dealing with interstate commerce and the other concerning extra-state commerce.

2. 2. 1. 2 Domestic Area: the Clayton Act and Robinson-Patman Act

Within the states, the Sherman Act was complemented by the Clayton

---

[1] Of those cases, the most famous one is *Standard Oil Case of* 1911. Among the predatory practices alleged in that case was the sale of oil products at low prices in limited geographical areas in order to drive out small competitors – in effect price discrimination. The notable reaction of the Supreme Court to this and other "unnatural" practices was not a flat prohibition, but the broad "rule of reason". In its most fundamental formulation, this rule directs courts first to examine the nature or character of the particular practice to determine whether it is inherently anti-competitive. If the result of this inquiry in inconclusive, the court then looks to the surrounding circumstances to judge whether the practice has the primary "purpose and effect" of eliminating competition and producing the evils of monopoly. *See* Comment, *the Antidumping Act – Tariff or Antitrust Law*? The Yale Law Journal, 1965, Vol. 74, pp. 707, 718.

[2] For the practice of selling at lower prices to buyers in some regional part of a given national market than to buyers in the remainder of that market, the term "local price-cutting" has likewise become customary, especially in American legal usage. *See* Jacob Viner, *Dumping: A Problem in International Trade*, the Univ. of Chicago Press, 1923, p. 240.

[3] Jacob Viner, *Dumping: A Problem in International Trade*, the Univ. of Chicago Press, 1923, p. 239.

Act in 1914 and the Robinson-Patman Act in 1936 as well. The original prohibitions of Clayton Section 2 were designed to prevent predatory price discrimination that may be substantially to lessen competition or tend to create a monopoly in any line of commerce, or to injure, destroy, or prevent competition with any person who either grants or knowingly receives the benefit of such discrimination or with customers of either of them. ❶ A violation of either of these provisions is subject to criminal penalties and also is actionable in a private right of action, where treble damages and injunctive relief are available, and in administrative or federal court actions initiated by the Federal Trade Commission. ❷

The Clayton Act was later on revised and supplemented by the Robinson-Patman Act in 1936, with its specific criterion formed and developed by courts, scholars, as well as administrative officers gradually. ❸ Nevertheless, either the Sherman Actor or the Clayton Act, or the

---

❶ Section 2(a) of the Clayton Act, provides in pertinent part: "It shall be unlawful for any person engaged in commerce, in the course of such commerce, either directly or indirectly, to discriminate in price between different purchasers of commodities of like grade and quality, where either or any of the purchasers involved in such discrimination are in commerce, where such commodities are sold for use, consumption, or resale within the United States [...] and where the effect of such discrimination may be substantially to lessen competition or tend to create a monopoly in any line of commerce, or to injure, destroy, or prevent competition with any person who either grants or knowingly receives the benefit of such discrimination or with customers of either of them." *See* Report of the Panel, *United States – Antidumping Act of* 1916,2000, WT/DS162/R,pp. 1, 3, http://www.wto.org/english/tratop_e/dispu_e/1680da.pdf; http://www.wto.org/english/tratop_e/dispu_e/1680db.pdf, last visited September 21,2011.

❷ *Ibid.*

❸ The modern theories and competition rules on price discrimination and predatory pricing will be examined in detail in chapter III.

supplementary Robinson-Patman Act thereof, did not apply to extra-state commerce, i. e. , cross-border price discrimination. ❶

2. 2. 1. 3 Foreign Import Area: the Wilson Tariff Act

With increasing attention drawn by price discrimination in interstate commerce, the U. S. started to notice that it was also happening in cross-border area, and was principally conducted by Great Britain and Germany at that era. ❷ There were two feasible ways to address this cross-border issue, by extending the jurisdiction of Sherman Act to also include the cross-border unfair competition, or to enact a separate new law dealing with it. The U. S. finally chose the second way, and enacted the first law in the world concerning antidumping called the Wilson Tariff Act 1894.

Similarly to the Clayton Act, it is regarded as unlawful under Wilson Tariff Act if an importer acting as agent or principal to enter into an agreement in the United States with a foreign exporter or with other American importers to import foreign goods at dumping prices with the intent of eliminating American competitors of the foreign producers or of establishing, even as against other foreign producers, a monopoly of the American market for some foreign producers. ❸

---

❶ The Sherman Act denied the extraterritorial application. In the American Banana Co. v. United Fruit Co. case, the supreme Court decision denied the jurisdiction of the U. S. under this Act over acts done in foreign countries, even if done by citizens of the U. S. and even if there were conspiracy in the United States to perform these acts elsewhere, provided that these acts were not in violation of the law of the country where they were committed. The Court stated: "A conspiracy in this country to do acts in another jurisdiction does not draw to itself those acts and make them unlawful if they are permitted by the local law." *See* American Banana Co. v. United Fruit Co. , 213, U. S, 347

❷ Jacob Viner, *Dumping: A Problem in International Trade*, the Univ. of Chicago Press, 1923, pp. 241 – 242.

❸ *Ibid.*, pp. 240 – 241.

To sum up the above analysis, the earliest antidumping in the world came into being as part of competition law to address cross-border price discrimination.

2.2.2 The U.S. 1916 Antidumping Law

The Wilson Tariff Act has its limitation in regulating the international price discrimination.[1] In order to efficiently prevent the severe export cartels of Germany that were threatening around the U.S. after World War I, the 1916 Antidumping Act, as the first formal antidumping law of the U.S., came into force.[2] This Act was under the heading of "Unfair Competition" in Title VIII of the Revenue Act of 1916.[3] And it had remained in force by the end of 4, March, 2003.[4] There were even legal actions taken in light of the 1916 Antidumping Act in the 1990s.[5]

---

[1] For example, if the agreement were concluded in a foreign country, or if a foreign producer were dumping in the United States with predatory intent but without involving an American agent or importer in such unlawful intent, the decision of the Supreme Court in the *United Fruit Co.* case would indicate that the Wilson Act would not provide a remedy. *See* Jacob Viner, *Dumping: A Problem in International Trade*, the Univ. of Chicago Press, 1923, p. 242.

[2] After the outbreak of the war the disclosure of the unfair methods of competition, and above all the practice of predatory dumping, which has supposedly been widely prevalent in the export trade of foreign countries – and especially Germany – led to a widespread demand in the United States for more effective protection to American industries against such unfair foreign competition. *See ibid.*

[3] *See* Report of the Panel, *United States – Antidumping Act of* 1916, 2000, WT/DS162/R, pp. 1, 2, http://www.wto.org/english/tratop_e/dispu_e/1680da.pdf; http://www.wto.org/english/tratop_e/dispu_e/1680db.pdf, last visited September 21. 2011.

[4] According to the judgment of WTO 1916 Antidumping Act Case, the U.S recalled that, on 4 March 2003, legislation repealing the 1916 Act had been introduced in the U.S. House of Representative. *See* WTO, http://www.wto.org/english/news_e/news03_e/dsb_19may03_e.htm, last visited May 24, 2009.

[5] The information of the cases shall be summarized in the following part.

2.2.2.1 *The WTO 1916 Antidumping Act Case*

The nature of the 1916 Antidumping Law has incurred a hot debate in the WTO 1916 *Antidumping Act Case*.[1] In this case, initially the main issue was the violation rather than the determination of the characteristics of the 1916 Act. Nevertheless, since the U.S. defended itself by asserting that the characteristic of this act is antitrust instead of antidumping, hence it should not be judged under the WTO Antidumping Agreement, the relation of the antidumping law and the antitrust law has become the focal issue. In conclusion, the Panel held that the 1916 Antidumping Act violates the WTO Antidumping Agreement without

---

[1] Thc general information of this case is as follows. Since 1997, Japan, E.U, Russian, China and the other countries and areas have imported the steel products to US in proliferation, which made the U.S. steel industry in panic. Therefore, the relevant interest groups started to sue the foreign import dumping. Among those cases, "*Geneva Steel Corp. vs. Ranger Steel Corp.*" and "*Wheeling Pittsburgh vs. Mitsui & co.*" drew much attention. Because in both of the two cases, the U.S. plaintiffs unimaginably sued by referring to the 1916 Antidumping Act, which has been hardly recalled in modern world. As a result, the foreign defendants bore heavy costs and burden of proof. Therefore, in November of 1998, Japan and E.U applied to the Panel Body of WTO, requiring the Panel to judge that the 1916 Antidumping Act is in many aspects violating the WTO Antidumping Agreement. *See* Philip De Keyser, *Exploring WTO Dispute Settlement in US Antidumping Act* 1916: *An Easy Case*? The Jean Monnet Seminar at Harvard Law School ,2001, http://www.jeanmonnetprogram.org/papers/01/013101.rtf, last visited September 21, 2011.

The Panel made the final decision in March of 2000. This panel decision has been appealed to Appellate Body on 28 August, 2000, but the issue on the nature of the 1916 Act has not been reconsidered. *See* Report of Appellate Body, *United States – Antidumping Act Of* 1916, 2000, WT/DS136/AB/R, http://www.worldtradelaw.net/reports/wtoab/us – 1916 act (ab).pdf, last visited September 21, 2011.

addressing the nature of the act. ❶

Although the Panel didn't clearly define the nature of this act, its reasoning suggested that it favored the viewpoint that "antidumping" and "antitrust" were not separate legal concepts at that time, and the two laws were actually part of one single notion of "unfair competition". ❷ Antidumping law was part of antitrust law to deal with transnational price discrimination. ❸

Apart from referring to Panel's opinion, it is also worth reviewing the legislative purpose, specific rules, as well as cases relating to the 1916

---

❶ It is stated that: "We recall that we were requested to review the conformity of the 1916 Act with the provisions of the WTO Agreement, not to address the general issue of the relationship between trade law and anti-trust law." *See* Report of the Panel, *United States – Antidumping Act of* 1916, 2000, WT/DS162/R, pp. 1, 179, http://www.wto.org/english/tratop_e/dispu_e/1680da.pdf; http://www.wto.org/english/tratop_e/dispu_e/1680db.pdf, last visited September 21, 2011.

❷ While referring to the nature of this act, the Panel stated that: "In our opinion, the argument of the United States is only valid if the United States can prove that the historical context and the legislative history of the 1916 Act gave indications that anti-trust and anti-dumping were already separate legal concepts. If the two were not clearly identified but, rather, were still part of one single notion of 'unfair competition', the U.S. argument should be rejected." *See ibid.*, p. 167.

Continuingly, the Panel concluded: "We note that evidence from the historical context of the 1916 Act supports our finding that the 1916 Act transnational price discrimination test corresponds to 'dumping' within the meaning of Article VI. We also note that, at the time of the enactment of the 1916 Act, there would have been no need to give any different meaning to that test in order to make it fall within the scope of US anti-trust law because, at that time, 'dumping' had not yet been conceptually isolated from the body of US anti-trust laws." *See ibid.*, p. 168.

❸ The legislation background of the 1916 Act has also been addressed by Japan in the 1916 *Antidumping Case*, and the U.S. has no objection. Japan claimed that: "the historical context and legislative history of the 1916 Act show that Congress sought to enact an anti-dumping law to address the commercial problem of dumping, i.e. international discrimination." *See ibid.*, pp. 42–48.

Antidumping Act.

2. 2. 2. 2 Legislative Purpose

The 1916 Antidumping Act was enacted to protect against the international price discrimination. The U. S. government officials, legislators and industries feared that the end of World War I would wreak injury on the U. S. companies and industries as foreign companies and industries sought to revive themselves and recapture or increase their former share of the U. S. market through unfair methods of competition, including dumping. Some Senators and Congressmen proposed higher tariffs to fend off the threat, whereas the Wilson Administration advocated free, but fair, trade and proposed antidumping legislation instead. [1]

Such legislative purpose was also indicated in the U. S. congressional subcommittee: "[Antidumping laws are] designed to free US imports from unfair price discrimination practices [by foreign exporters]. "[2] Representative Kitchin, the chairman of the House Committee on Ways and Means and the House sponsor of the 1916 Act, stated that the 1916 Act was "intended to do no more than to impose on importers the same pricing restrictions which had already been imposed on domestic businesses by the Clayton Antitrust Act of 1914. [3]

To sum up, similar to the 1894 Wilson Tariff Act, the 1916 Antidumping Act remained the production of extending the jurisdiction of

---

[1] Report of the Panel, *United States – Antidumping Act of 1916*, 2000, WT/DS162/R, p. 42, http://www.wto.org/english/tratop_e/dispu_e/1680da.pdf; http://www.wto.org/english/tratop_e/dispu_e/1680db.pdf, last visited September 21, 2011.

[2] Michael J. Trebilcock & Robert Howse, *the Regulation of International Trade*, 2nd Edition, Routledge, 1999, p. 177.

[3] Report of the Panel, *United States – Antidumping Act of* 1916, 2000, WT/DS162/R, pp. 1, 52, http://www.wto.org/english/tratop_e/dispu_e/1680da.pdf; http://www.wto.org/english/tratop_e/dispu_e/1680db.pdf, last visited September 21, 2011.

domestic antitrust acts, including the Sherman Act, Clayton Act and the Robinson-Patman Act, to the cross-border competition.

2. 2. 2. 3 Specific Rules

Compared with the Clayton Act article by article, the term "anti-trust-type statute" can be used to describe the 1916 Antidumping Act.[1] It can

---

[1] The Article stated:

It shall be unlawful for any person importing or assisting in importing any articles from any foreign country into the United States, commonly and systematically to import, sell or cause to be imported or sold such articles within the United States at a price substantially less than the actual market value or wholesale price of such articles, at the time of exportation to the United States, in the principal markets of the country of their production, or of other foreign countries to which they are commonly exported after adding to such market value or wholesale price, freight, duty, and other charges and expenses necessarily incident to the importation and sale thereof in the United States: that such act or acts be done with the intent of destroying or injuring an industry in the United States, or of preventing the establishment of an industry in the United States, or of restraining or monopolizing any part of trade and commerce in such articles in the United State.

Any person who violates or combines or conspires with any other person to violate this section is guilty of a misdemeanour, and, on conviction thereof, shall be punished by a fine not exceeding MYM5 000, or imprisonment not exceeding one year, or both, in the discretion of the court. Any person injured in his business or property by reason of any violation of, or combination or conspiracy to violate, this section, may sue therefore in the district court of the United States for the district in which the defendant resides or is found or has an agent, without respect to the amount in controversy, and shall recover threefold the damages sustained, and the cost of the suit, including a reasonable attorney's fee.

The foregoing provisions shall not be construed to deprive the proper State courts of jurisdiction in actions for damages thereunder.

Two of prominent characteristics of this act have been descried in the 1916 Antidumping Act Case. The first one is the intent. It is a condition for criminal or civil liability under the 1916 Act that the importer must have undertaken this price discrimination with "an intent of destroying or injuring an industry in the United States, or of preventing the establishment of an industry in the United States, or of restraining or monopolizing any part of trade and commerce in such articles in the United States. Another characteristic of the 1916 Act is that it provides for a private right of action in a federal district court and the remedy of treble damages for a private complainant, based on the injury sustained by that complainant in its business or property, as well as for criminal penalties in an action brought by the U. S. government. *See* Report of the Panel, *United States – Antidumping Act of 1916*, 2000, WT/DS162/R, pp. 2 – 3, http://www.wto.org/english/tratop_e/dispu_e/1680da.pdf; http://www.wto.org/english/tratop_e/dispu_e/1680db.pdf, last visited September 21, 2011.

be Summarized that the 1916 Antidumping Act resembles antitrust law in eight aspects as follows:

I. The 1916 Act requires a finding of price differences, like the Robinson-Patman Act. The price differences under the 1916 Act, of course, must be "substantial" in amount and undertaken "commonly and systematically", while the Robinson-Patman Act only requires two sales to different buyers at different prices.

II. The 1916 Act requires a finding that the pricing at issue be undertaken with a specific predatory intent. This predatory pricing requirement is similar to that found in Section 2 of the Sherman Act and in so-called primary line cases under the Robinson-Patman Act.

III. The 1916 Act applies to Articles of "like grade and quality", just as that term is used in the Robinson-Patman Act.

IV. Statute of limitations for bringing a lawsuit under the 1916 Act is the same as that under the Clayton Act and the Robinson-Patman Act.

V. The 1916 Act provides for enforcement through either a civil lawsuit brought by a private party before a US court or a criminal prosecution brought by the U. S. Department of Justice. These remedies mirror those available under the anti-trust laws including the Sherman Act, the Clayton Act and the Robinson-Patman Act.

VI. The issue of whether a private party has the requisite standing to bring a 1916 Act lawsuit is determined by reference to anti-trust standing principles.

VII. The 1916 Act authorizes the award of treble damages to a successful private litigant. This remedy is unusual under US civil law, but it is a common remedy for violations of US anti-trust statutes. Indeed, in the third paragraph of the 1916 Act, the U. S. Congress basically replicated the then – existing language of Section 4 of the Clayton Act and

Section 7 of the Sherman Act which authorized treble damages for "any person who shall be injured in his business or property" by reason of any conduct proscribed by US anti-trust laws.

VIII. With regard to its criminal provisions, the 1916 Act is virtually identical to, and specifies the same penalties as, the criminal provisions of the Sherman Act in force in 1916. ❶

To sum up, the 1916 U. S. Antidumping rules followed the US anti-trust law models. This act was also a mere extraterritorial application of the Sherman Act's principles at the time when the Sherman Act was considered not to apply outside the U. S. territory. ❷

---

❶ Report of the Panel, *United States – Antidumping Act of 1916*, 2000, WT/DS162/R, pp. 29 – 38, http://www.wto.org/english/tratop_e/dispu_e/1680da.pdf; http://www.wto.org/english/tratop_e/dispu_e/1680db.pdf, last visited September 21, 2011.

❷ *See also*, Peter D. Ehrenhaft, *Is Interface of Antidumping and Antitrust Laws Possible?* George Washington International Law Review, 2002, Vol. 34, p. 363, n43, "[The 1916 Act] was based on US antitrust law models. It created a private cause of action, permitting treble damages upon showings that a seller had sold merchandise substantially below the actual market value or wholesale price of the goods with the intent to injury a US industry or restrain trade, and even made such practices a crime."

Comment, *The Antidumping Act – Tariff or Antitrust Law?* The Yale Law Journal, 1965, Vol. 74, pp. 707, 714, "An earlier version of the Antidumping Act enacted in 1916 required a finding of specific intent to restrain commerce. The language of that requirement is strikingly similar to that introduced by the Clayton Act just two years previously, and the remedies provided by the 1916 Act – criminal sanctions and private treble damage suits – are also found in the Clayton Act."

Gabrielle Marceau, *Antidumping and Anti-trust Issues in Free-trade Areas*, Oxford Univ. Press Inc. 1994, p. 8, "Essentially, this law was of criminal nature, was enforced in ordinary courts, and required proof of the predatory intent of the exporter – importer; treble damages was possible. It was a form of legislative extraterritorial application of the Sherman Act's principles at the time when the Sherman Act was considered not to apply outside the U. S. territory".

2. 2. 2. 4 Cases

The 1916 Antidumping Act was invoked infrequently hence there were a limited number of judicial interpretations regarding its specific provisions. [1] Since the 1916 Antidumping Act remained in effect until 4, March, 2003, the relevant cases scattered in a wide range from 1916 to

---

[1] It has been summarized in the 1916 *Antidumping Act Case* that, most of those interpretations can be found in the following – final or interlocutory – court decisions referenced by the parties: *In re Japanese Electronic Products Antitrust Litigation*, 388 F. Supp. 565, Judicial Panel on Multidistrict Litigation, 1975 (hereinafter "*In re Japanese Electronic Products I*"); *Zenith Radio Corp. v. Matsushita Electric Industrial Co., Ltd.*, 402 F. Supp. 244, E. D. Pa. 1975 (hereinafter "*Zenith I*"); *Zenith Radio Corp. v. Matsushita Electric Industrial Co., Ltd.*, 402 F. Supp. 251, E. D. Pa. 1975 (hereinafter "*Zenith II*"); *Outboard Marine Corp. v. Pezetel*, 461 F. Supp. 384, D. Del. 1978; *Schwimmer v. Sony Corp. of America*, 471 F. Supp. 793, E. D. N. Y. 1979; *Schwimmer v. Sony Corp. of America*, 637 F.2d 41, 2nd Cir. 1980; *Jewel Foliage Co. v. Uniflora Overseas Florida*, 497 F. Supp. 513, M. D. Fla. 1980; *Zenith Radio Corp. v. Matsushita Electric Industrial Co., Ltd.*, 494 F. Supp. 1190, E. D. Pa. 1980 (hereinafter "*Zenith III*"), affirmed in part and reversed in part, 723 F.2d 319, 3d Cir. 1983, reversed and remanded, 475 US. 574, 106 S. Ct. 1348, 1986, District Court decision affirmed on remand, 807 F. 2d 44, 3d Cir. 1986; *In re Japanese Electronic Products Antitrust Litigation (Zenith Radio Corp. v. Matsushita Electric Industrial Co., Ltd.)*, 723 F.2d 319, 3d Cir. 1983 (hereinafter "*In re Japanese Electronic Products II*"); *Western Concrete Structures Co. v. Mitsui & Co.*, 760 F.2d 1013, 9th Cir. 1985; *Isra Fruit Ltd. v. Agrexco Agr. Export Co.*, 631 F. Supp. 984, S. D. N. Y. 1986; *In re Japanese Electronic Products Antitrust Litigation (Zenith Radio Corp. v. Matsushita Electric Industrial Co., Ltd.)*, 807 F.2d 44, 3d Cir. 1986 (hereinafter "*In re Japanese Electronic Products III*") *Helmac Products Corp. v. Roth (Plastics) Corp.*, 814 F. Supp. 560, E. D. Mich. 1992 (hereinafter "*Helmac I*"); *Helmac Products Corp. v. Roth (Plastics) Corp.*, 814 F. Supp. 581, E. D. Mich. 1993 (hereinafter "*Helmac II*"); *Geneva Steel Company v. Ranger Steel Supply Corp.*, 980 F. Supp. 1209, D. Utah 1997 (hereinafter "*Geneva Steel*"); Wheeling-Pittsburgh Steel Corporation v. Mitsui Co., 35 F. Supp. 2d. 597, S. D. Ohio 1999 (hereinafter "Wheeling – Pittsburgh") *See* Report of the Panel, *United States – Anti-dumping Act of* 1916, 2000, WT/DS162/R, pp. 1, 141, http://www.wto.org/english/tratop_e/dispu_e/1680da.pdf; http://www.wto.org/english/tratop_e/dispu_e/1680db.pdf, last visited September 21, 2011.

1997. The focus hereafter shall be on the period prior to the multilateral antidumping agreement. ❶

The "competition" nature of 1916 Act was indicated in the court's interpretation in most of the cases. To take some cases for instance, *United States v. Cooper Corp*, a 1941 Supreme Court decision construing the Clayton Act, expressly described the 1916 Act and the Clayton Act as "supplemental" to the original, 1890 Sherman Act. ❷ In *Zenith III* case, the court also gave a clear statement on the status of 1916 Act:

The principal lesson which we draw from the legislative history of the 1916 Act, viewed against the historical background of the first [Woodrow] Wilson Administration, is that the statute should be interpreted whenever possible to parallel the "unfair competition" law applicable to domestic commerce. Since the 1916 Antidumping Act is a price discrimination law, it should be read in tandem with the domestic price discrimination law, section 2 of the Clayton Act, which was amended by the Robinson-Patman Act in 1936. And, in order to be faithful to the intention of Congress to subject importers to the "same unfair competition law". We should not interpret the 1916 Act to impose on importers legal strictures which are more rigorous than those applied to domestic enterprises. ❸

---

❶ After the multilateral antidumping agreement, the explanation of the law has been influenced to some extent. One of the examples is in the Wheeling-Pittsburgh case. In this Court's view, the conclusion reached by the district court in Geneval Steel was correct. The court held that the Antidumping Act of 1916 did not require the type of predatory intent defined in [competition law] because the statute 'has a protectionist reach beyond antitrust and traditional predatory price discrimination pleading requirements" *See Report of the Panel*, *United States – Antidumping Act of 1916*, 2000, WT/DS162/R, p. 58, http://www.wto.org/english/tratop_e/dispu_e/1680da.pdf; http://www.wto.org/english/tratop_e/dispu_e/1680db.pdf, last visited September 21, 2011.

❷ *Ibid.*, p. 50.

❸ *Ibid.*, p. 52.

Via an overall review of 1916 U. S. Antidumping Act from the Panel's decision, legislative purpose, specific rules and cases, it can be concluded that this antidumping law is still part of antitrust law, to proect against predatory pricing, i. e. , the international price discrimination that intends to monopolize domestic markets.

2. 2. 3 The U. S. 1921 Antidumping Law

2. 2. 3. 1 The Debate on the Nature of 1921 Antidumping Law

In 1921, by taking some reference to the Canadian Act of 1904, a new Antidumping Act called the U. S. 1921 Antidumping Act was enacted. [1] The basic idea of this Act is that it empowered the Secretary of the Treasury to make public a finding whenever an industry in the United States is being or is likely to be injured, or is prevented from being established, by reason of the importation into the United States of foreign merchandise, and that merchandise of such class or kind is being sold or is likely to be sold in the United States or elsewhere at less than its fair value. If the "purpose price" or the "exporter's sale price" is less than the "foreign market value", there shall be imposed thereon, in addition to the ordinary duties if any, a special dumping-duty in an amount equal to such difference. [2]

Compared with the 1916 Act, there are several striking differences. First, it provided an administrative procedure instead of criminal rules,

---

[1] *See*, e. g. , J. Michael Finger, The Origins and Evolution of Antidumping Regulation, in J. Michael Finger, ed. *Antidumping: How It Works and Who Gets Hurt* , The Univ. of Michigan Press 1993, p. 20, "*the* 1916 *antidumping act had done little to diminish pressure for a Canadian-style antidumping law, so proposals for such a law were soon introduced in Congress*".

[2] Jacob Viner, *Dumping: A Problem in International Trade*, the Univ. of Chicago Press 1923, p. 260.

for the imposition of antidumping duties equal to the margin of dumping. Secondly, it applied dumping-duty as the remedy other than sanctions, penalties, civil liability etc. Thirdly, it empowered the Secretary of the Treasury to impose duties on dumped goods without regard to the dumper's intent. Fourthly, it incorporated a condition that dumped imports should be shown to actually or potentially injure the domestic industry. ❶

With regard to the nature of the 1921 Antidumping Law, there existed a hot debate on it. There were maily three different kinds of viewpoints thereon. The 1921 U. S. Antidumping Act was held as a model during drafting the section on dumping in the Havana Charter and the GATT. Since the specific rules of the 1921 Antidumping Act varied much from antitrust law, some scholars deem that this act should be the "real" first antidumping law of the U. S., which is completely separate from antitrust law. ❷

The second kind of viewponts still insisted that the essential idea of antidumping concerns competition. The foremost proponents hereof, arguing that antidumping statute should be interpreted as an antitrust law aimed at protecting competition, was the United States Department of Justice. Accordingly, it adopted the practice of submitting antidumping

---

❶ This has been introduced in quite a lot literature. *See, e. g.*, *How the GATT Affects U. S. Antidumping and Countervailing – Duty Policy*, Congressional Budget Office, the Congress of the United States, 1994, pp. 1, 21, http://www.cbo.gov/ftpdocs/48xx/doc4848/doc44.pdf, last visited September 21, 2011.

❷ *See, e. g.*, Douglas Irwin, *the Rise of U. S. Antidumping Actions in Historical Perspective*, Working Paper 10582, NBER, 2004, pp. 1, 4, http://www.nber.org/papers/w10582.pdf? new_window = 1, last visited September 21, 2011. "U. S. antidumping law as we currently know it really began with the Antidumping Act of 1921, part of the Emergency Tariff Act of that year."

briefs to the hearings of the United States International Trade Commission on the grounds that the International Trade Commission was the executive agency responsible for advocating the public interest in competition. ❶

Still a group of other scholars described the 1921 Antidumping Act as a "curious hybrid of traditional tariff ideas and price discrimination theories of antitrust law..." and fell somewhere between the Canadian Act of 1904 and the 1916 Antidumping Act. ❷

Observed from the rules liberally, the 1921 Act actually abandoned many features of 1916 Act that were typically antitrust law style, such as requiring a finding of specific intent to restrain commerce, providing criminal sanctions and private treble damage suits and etc. All of these features were replaced by a duty as a means of curbing dumping. It could be taken as a prima facie evidence that the 1921 Act deviated from the antitrust law substantially. Nevertheless, except for the changes of rules, this book attempts to review other relevant elements. This includes the purpose for the changes of rules, relevant cases etc., to explore whether the justification of antidumping varied and separated from the original price discrimination.

2. 2. 3. 2 Purpose for the Changes of Rules

The issue of why the U. S. decided to change these rules shall be investigated first. Is it due to separate antidumping from antitrust? The relevant documents seemed to suggest that these changes were actually in all likelihood merely designed to avoid the practical difficulties of securing jurisdiction over foreign producers and of proving predatory intent

---

❶ Richard Dale, *Antidumping Law in a Liberal Trade Order*, the Macmillan Press Ltd. 1980, p. 56.

❷ *Ibid.*

under the earlier act. [1]

The 1916 Antidumping Act was in nature criminal, and it was comparatively more difficult to prove the intent of price discrimination in the international area than in the domestic area, thereby there were only a few cases of 1916 Act, let alone won the cases. According to the official document, the U. S. government realized the 1916 Antidumping Act was ineffective by stating that, "The history of the period, legislative and otherwise, show that Congress felt the existing act would prove inadequate to halt an expected massive dumping campaign by European cartels designed to destroy a number of fledgling American industries and to monopolize[d] American markets". [2]

Due to the ineffectiveness and inadequacy of the antidumping provision in the Revenue Act of 1916, the U. S. took 1904 Canadian Antidumping Law into account and enacted the 1921 Antidumping Act. [3] Similar evidence can also be accessed in the report of the Ways and Means Committee, where a "re-evaluation of the basic policy issues involved in antidumping legislation" would be "premature" was recorded. [4]

Taken the purpose for the changes of the rules into account, it seems that the nature of this Act has remained, or at least such changes in rules have nothing to do with the re-consideration or re-evaluation of the

---

[1] Comment, *the Antidumping Act – Tariff or Antitrust Law?* The Yale Law Journal, 1965, Vol. 74, pp. 707, 714.

[2] *Ibid.*

[3] Jacob Viner, *Dumping: A Problem in International Trade*, the Univ. of Chicago Press 1923, p. 259.

[4] Comment, *the Antidumping Act – Tariff or Antitrust Law?* The Yale Law Journal, 1965, Vol. 74, pp. 707, 715.

policy and philosophy of dumping regulation.

2. 2. 3. 3 Statements of the United States Department of Justice

In addition to examine the purpose for the changes of rules, since this act has empowered administrative officers instead of the court to deal with dumping, how the United States Department of Justice and the United States International Trade Commission (USITC) interpreted this Act also deserves further research. ❶ In the following part, the interpretation of the United States Department of Justice shall be observed first.

In terms of the nature of this new antidumping act, the Department of Justice based its interpretation on three distinct grounds. First, it argued that according to well-established legal principles that anti-dumping statute, like the Robinson-Patman Act, should be construed so far as possible in a way which does not derogate from the pro-competitive principles underlying the anti-trust provisions of the Sherman Act. ❷

Secondly, the Department of Justice submitted that the legislative history of the 1921 Act supports the application of an anti-competitive injury

---

❶ The United States Department of Justice is in charge of competition issues, and the United States International Trade Commission is in charge of antidumping issues. The 1921 Antidumping had been in effect before the year 1979. When first adopted in 1921, the statute was administered entirely by the Treasury Department. Subsequently, the Congress shifted to "the Tariff Commission" (later on the name was changed into "the United States International Trade Commission" according to Trade Act of 1974) the take of determining the requisite injury to the domestic industry and confined the Treasury's role to investigating the existence and magnitude of dumping. *See* Peter D. Ehrenhaft, *Is Interface of Antidumping and Antitrust Laws Possible?* George Washington International Law Review, 2002, Vol. 34, pp. 363, 376.

❷ In this context it cites with approval the statement by the court of appeals in Anheuser-Busch to the effect that "Section 2(a) ...[Of the Robinson-Patman act]...must be read in conformity with the public policy of preserving competition...it is not concerned with the mere shift of business between competitors." *See* Richard Dale, *Antidumping Law in a Liberal Trade Order*, the Macmillan Press Ltd. 1980, p. 56.

standard. Dale in his book gave two instances. The first one is that the Tariff commission's (the predecessor of USITC) 1919 Report to the Congress, which provided the basis of the 1921 Act, criticized the Canadian antidumping legislation for not taking account of whether foreign or domestic monopoly might be involved. The second one is that both the House report on the Bill and the Bill's protagonists in the Senate indicated that the purpose of the new antidumping legislation was essentially the same as the 1916 Act, which is to prevent a competitor from "selling goods for less than cost...for the purpose of destroying an industry in this country". According to of the aforementioned arguments, it seems that the objective of the 1921 Act is not to broaden the earlier legislation but to increase its effectiveness by providing for civil rather than criminal remedies and by dispensing with the requirement of proof of specific intent to injure an American industry. [1]

Thirdly, the Department of Justice found support for its pro-competitive interpretation of the anti-dumping law in the injury determinations of the USITC. In the *Chromic Acid from Australia*[2], the USITC applied an anticompetitive test in the injury determination. [3] Concerning such interpretation, the Department of Justice concluded that Section 2 of the Clayton Act of 1914 bans such [discriminatory] predatory price-cutting,

---

[1] The Department of Justice considered that: "Nevertheless, it is now well-recognised that the anti-price discrimination and antidumping statutes were not so artfully drafted as to provide any cut and dried solution to the problem of how to prohibit truly injurious price discriminations without stultifying competition and denying consumers the obvious benefits of lower prices. That task had to be accomplished by careful examination of the factual context of each challenged pricing action, in order to ascertain its intent and the likelihood that it will seriously injure the ability of rival firms to compete in the future." *See ibid.*, p. 57.

[2] Chromic Acid from Australia, 29 Fed. Reg. 2919, 1964.

[3] Specific introduction shall be in the following part.

as do the antidumping acts of 1916 and 1921, which are modeled after the Clayton Act provisions. ❶

2. 2. 3. 4 Statements of the USITC

If the interpretation of the Department of Justice can be considered as strong evidence to prove the nature of 1921 Antidumping Act is competition law, the interpretation of the International Trade Commission is relatviely not so consistent. So far as the "injury to what" question is concerned, the 1921 act merely provides that "the USITC shall determine... whether an industry in the United States in being or is likely to be injured".

Although not in all of the cases the "injury standard" was stated to follow the anti-competitive test, there did have cases clearly applying the anti-competitive test. Prominently among these cases is the *Titanium Dioxide determination*❷, which was considered the first explicit reference to an anticompetitive effect test. ❸ In this case, a positive-injury determination was made based on three aspects, including a significant margin of under-selling; resulting price depression in a major American Market, and consequential capture by the importer of a major share of that market. An anticompetitive effect test was clearly established in the

---

❶ Richard Dale, *Antidumping Law in a Liberal Trade Order*, the Macmillan Press Ltd. 1980, p. 57.

❷ Titanium Dioxide determination, 711, 28 Fed. Reg. 10467, 1963.

❸ Comment, *the Antidumping Act – Tariff or Antitrust Law*? The Yale Law Journal, 1965, Vol. 74, pp. 707, 711.

injury determination. [1]

In the *Chromic Acid from Australia* Case afterwards[2], the USITC not only mentioned but also explicitly relied on what it considered an anti-competitive effect to find injury. The USITC cited *the Titanium case* with approval and phrased its positive injury determination in terms of the anti-competitive effect on the domestic industry. [3]

A more favorable evidence for an anti-trust interpretation of the anti-dumping act might be found in the *Vinyl Clad Fence Fabric from Canada* where the USITC cited with approval a Senate Finance Committee Report that so-called "technical dumping" is not anti-competitive, hence

---

[1] The USITC stated: "It is evident that Congress did not consider sales at less than fair value as being *malum perse*: such sales are condemned in the act only when they have anti-competitive effect and it is only then that such sales may be equated with the concept of 'unfair competition'". *See* Richard Dale, *Antidumping Law in a Liberal Trade Order*, the Macmillan Press Ltd., 1980, p. 58.

[2] Chromic Acid from Australia, 29 Fed. Reg. 2919, 1964. In this case, dumped imports were increasing rapidly and had appropriated 1.4% of the national market and 14% of the West Coast market. This industry was particularly cost sensitive, and although the domestic producers had cut prices, they were still undersold by a significant margin. A price war had begun which continued to the time of the investigation. *See* Comment, *the Antidumping Act – Tariff or Antitrust Law*? The Yale Law Journal, 1965, Vol. 74, pp. 707, 712.

[3] The USITC considered that: "When chromic acid purchased from Australia at less than fair value is sold in the United States at a price significantly lower than all domestic manufacturers' wholesale prices of the like product in the United States market for such product, and where the evidence indicates that as a result of such underselling there is a rapid penetration of a major market area with a subsequent capture of a major 'share' of that market by the importer...such sales of the imported product are anti-competitive." *See* The Titanium case, 29 Fed. Reg. 2919, 1964.

not unfair; it is pro-competitive in effect. ❶ The USITC went on to conclude that in this case, the imports have not had an anticompetitive price advantage over the prices of articles sold by United States producers in the domestic market and this would not be condemned within the meaning of the Antidumping Act of 1921. ❷

To sum up the above analysis from the purpose for the changes of rules, as well as the application of the 1921 U. S. Antidumping Act, it is found that the purpose for changes is actually a response to the effectiveness of coping with international predatory pricing, rather than reflecting a complete shift from the antitrust philosophy of the earlier legislation to an outright tariff approach. ❸ In addition, the pro-competition test is still applied in practice, though the emphasis of dumping proof has been transferred from the "intent" in the 1916 Act to the "injury" in the 1921 Act.

---

❶ "The antidumping act does not proscribe transactions; which involve selling an imported product at a price which is not lower than that needed to make the product competitive in the United States market... such so-called 'technical dumping' is not anti-competitive, hence not unfair; it is pro-competitive in effect." *See* Richard Dale, *Antidumping Law in a Liberal Trade Order* , the Macmillan Press Ltd. , 1980, p. 58.

❷ "The imports have not had an anticompetitive price advantage over the prices of articles sold by United States producers in the domestic market and that such sales therefore do not fall within the ambit of discriminatory sales which might adversely affect domestic competition and thereby cause injury to an industry in the United States within the meaning of the Antidumping Act of 1921, as amended." This is the clearest advocacy of an "injury to competition" standard but it was applied here only to a well-established exemption rule and not to the substantive question of injury, nor has such a standard been followed in subsequent investigations, *See ibid.*

❸ It had been introduced in the journal that similar opinion has been expressed in US. Tariff Commn', 1919 Report on Dumping and Unfair Foreign Competition in the United States. *See* Comment, *the Antidumping Act – Tariff or Antitrust Law?* The Yale Law Journal , 1965, Vol. 74, pp. 707, 714.

The changes of specific rules continued in the antidumping enactments, such as the 1930 Antidumping Act, and the GATT-WTO Antidumping agreement afterwards, resulting in broadening the scope and simplifying the operation of antidumping law. [1] Such changes in rules make antidumping gradually deviated from competition in texts, but their intention is not to assign antidumping goals different from the original one. Correspondingly, this book considers that the justification of antidumping remains to be the protection against international predatory price discrimination.

2.2.4 Antidumping laws in Other Countries

2.2.4.1 The 1904 Canada Antidumping Provisions

An overall investigation into other countries forms the same conclusion. Canada was deemed to be the first country addressing dumping in law. Different from the U. S. antidumping rules, antidumping provisions in Canada started from an apparently different operation, putting

---

[1] The Tariff Act of 1930 allows for the collection of antidumping duties once the Treasury Department had established that goods were being sold in the U. S. market at less than fair value and were injurious to the U. S. industry. The Trade Act of 1974 changed the administrative determination of less than fair value to ensure that products are not sold below cost, rather than just less than home-market sales. It also established time limits for dumping determinations. The Trade Agreements Act of 1979 replealed the 1921 Act, amended the Tariff Act of 1930 to comply with the new GATT code (procedures to apply antidumping duties), and switched the administrative jurisdiction from Treasure to Commerce. The legislative history of the U. S. antidumping laws, *See* Greg Mastel, *American Trade Laws After the Uruguay Round*, M. E. Sharpe. Inc., 1996, pp. 186 – 187.

antidumping law under the customs tariff act. [1] Later on the antidumping law of Canada became the "fashion" for other countries at that era such as South Africa[2], New Zealand, Australia, Great Britain etc. [3] Scholars considered that Canada adopted a law aimed at dumping practices without any relation to competition law and price discrimination therein. [4] A further exploration into the motive of antidumping legislation in Canada, the purpose to condemn predatory price discrimination can still be attained.

Regarding the legislative purpose, according to Canadian Scholars, the legislative initiative responded independently to similar specific developments, i. e. competitive pressure from the United States. It was the pressure on Canada's steel industry from the U. S. Steel that provided the main impetus to the Canadian Bill. [5] Therefore, Canada enacted antidumping legislation to protect its fledgling steel industry against

---

[1] *See*, *e. g.*, Terence P. Stewart, *the GATT Uruguay Round, A Negotiation History Volume II: commentary*, Kluwer Law and Taxation Publishers, 1993, p. 1398, "Canada was the first country to address the dumping problem through direct and specific legislation." Michael J. Trebilcock & Robert Howse, *the Regulation of International Trade*, 2nd Edition, Routledge, 1999, p. 172, "Canada amended its Customs Tariff in 1904 to provide for antidumping duties and in so doing became the first country in the world to establish an antidumping regime."

[2] South African shall be taken as "new users" comparing to "traditional users" in the following chapter.

[3] Patrick A. Messerlin, *Should Antidumping Rules be Replaced by National or International Competition Rules*, the Swiss Review of International Economic Relations, 1994, Vol. 49, pp. 351, 355.

[4] *Ibid.*, p. 354.

[5] Dan Ciuriak, *Antidumping at* 100 *Years and Counting: A Canadian Perspective*, Prepared for "A Centennial of Antidumping Legislation and Implementation" Symposium, 2005, pp. 1, 3, http://www. fordschool. umich. edu/rsie/Conferences/ADSym/Ciuriak. pdf, last visited September 21, 2011.

predatory behaviour by powerful the U. S. steel makers. [1]

2. 2. 4. 2 Antidumping Law: New Zealand, Australia and Great Britain

In terms of New Zealand, the motive for antidumping legislation was also driven by the pressure of predatory dumping from the U. S. In 1905, New Zealand, in response to complaints from domestic and British manufacturers of agricultural implements that an American harvester trust was attempting to monopolize the New Zealand market by systematic price-cutting to New Zealand purchasers, enacted the Agricultural Implement Manufacture, Importation, and sale act. [2]

The initial motive for antidumping legislation in Australia was also to act against import predatory dumping. Plowman stated that the pressure came from the International Harvester trust that was preparing to introduce US and Canadian agricultural machinery into the Australian market; this was viewed as threatening to wipe out the nascent Australian manufacturing sector, which was centered around agricultural machinery at the time. [3] In Australia, antidumping law was originally put under the competition law. In 1906, Australia enacted a law which was aimed chiefly at the suppression of monopolies, but which also contained

---

[1] Martyn D. Taylor, *International Competition Law: A New Dimension for the WTO?* Cambridge Univ. Press Inc. 2006, p. 261. Jacob Viner also gave the same reason that Canada's first antidumping legislation was a response to the U. S. steel Corporation's practice of selling its exports at prices substantially below its domestic prices. *See* Jacob Viner, *Dumping: A Problem in International Trade*, the Univ. of Chicago Press, 1923, p. 192.

[2] *Ibid.*, p. 204.

[3] Dan Ciuriak, *Antidumping at* 100 *Years and Counting: A Canadian Perspective*, Prepared for "A Centennial of Anti-dumping Legislation and Implementation" Symposium, 2005, pp. 1, 3, http://www.fordschool.umich.edu/rsie/Conferences/ADSym/Ciuriak.pdf, last visited September 21, 2011.

provisions dealing with dumping.[1] Australia's original Industries Preservation Act of 1906 sought to protect key Australia Industries from "unfair competition".[2]

The British Antidumping Law was enacted in 1921.[3] The motive of establishing antidumping law in Great Britain was to great extent to cope with import cartel from German. Countries other than Germany were known to resort to dumping practices, but German actions received the greatest scrutiny, particularly as political tensions increased in the Pre-world War I period.[4] Therefore, at the Paris Conference of the Allies in 1916, Great Britain's delegation put forth a proposal calling for multinational efforts in the post-war period against unfair competition on the part of Germany, including dumping.[5] From the draft process, an intention of regarding dumping as one mode of unfair competition can be suggested. British delegation at the Paris Conference of the Allies in 1916 called for joint action to be taken after the war by the Allies to protect their interests against German "economic aggression resulting from dumping or any other mode of unfair competition".[6]

---

[1] Jacob Viner, *Dumping: A Problem in International Trade*, the Univ. of Chicago Press, 1923, p. 206.

[2] The text reads: "Unfair competition has in all cases reference to competition with those Australian industries, the preservation of which...is advantageous to the commonwealth, having due regard to the interests of producers, workers, and consumers." *See* Terence P. Stewart, *the GATT Uruguay Round, A Negotiation History Volume II: commentary*, Kluwer Law and Taxation Publishers, 1993, p. 1399.

[3] *Ibid.*, p. 1401.

[4] *Ibid.*, p. 1391.

[5] *Ibid.*, p. 1400.

[6] Jacob Viner, *Dumping: A Problem in International Trade*, the Univ. of Chicago Press, 1923, p. 216.

2.2.5 Antidumping: Anti Cross-border Predatory Price Discrimination

Through an overall examinination into the earliest practice of the U.S, Canada, New Zealand, Australia, Great Britain etc., it is found that antidumping was originally part of antitrust law, to deal with the import price discrimination. In order to cope with the international predatory price discrimination more efficiently, antidumping law experienced from the "intent" test to "injury" test, as well as from the civil or criminal "liability" to the "competitive tariff", a device for protecting competitive return against an import threat to them. ❶ Neverthelss, the purpose for all of these changes has nothing to do with broadening the original goal of antidumping law. Antidumping Law is still and should be aimed at anti cross-border predatory price discrimination.

2.3 Dumping in the International Antidumping Agreement

2.3.1 GATT/ WTO: Standardizing Antidumping Law

With the significant changes of the rules, antidumping also gradually fell from competition area into the trade law area. This transition in legal area was formally identified by regulating the antidumping law under the GATT in 1947. In the early twentieth century, while nations dealt

---

❶ As mentioned by Sykes, To be sure dumping was perceived to makes things difficult for domestic competitors and often thought to cause prices to fall below comfortable levels, even if it was not ordinarily a threat to the survival of domestic industries. Antidumping law, then, was perhaps understood as a device much akin to the Democrats "competitive tariff", a device for protecting competitive return against an important threat to them. *See* Alan O. Sykes, Antidumping and Antitrust: What Problems Does Each Address? In Robert Z. Lawerence, ed., *Brookings Trade Forum*, Brookings Institution, 1998, p. 22.

with their concerns on unfair trade pratices unilaterally, an effort commenced to deal with dumping through a multinational forum. ❶ In November 1945, the U. S. issued a pamphlet entitled *Proposals for Expansion of World Trade and Employment*, including some rules for international trade and an outline for an International Trade Organization (ITO). ❷

In the *Proposals*, the U. S. suggested that one function of the ITO be to formulate "a general definition of circumstances under which antidumping and countervailing duties may properly be applied to products imported from other members". ❸ Largely at the insistence of the U. S., one of the areas addressed in the original General Agreement was unfair trade in the form of dumping and subsidized exports. ❹ The result of the negoations in the antidumping duty area was Article VI of the GATT. ❺

The rules in GATT were further re-defined in the Kennedy Round in 1967 and the Tokyo Round that closed in 1979. ❻ And later on, the rules were specified into the specific international agreement, i. e., the WTO ADA, during the trade negotiation of the Uruguay Round in 1995. Similar to the WTO countervailing agreement, the WTO ADA is categorized as one of the instruments of the trade remedies against unfair

---

❶ Terence P. Stewart, *the GATT Uruguay Round, A Negotiation History Volume II: commentary*, Kluwer Law and Taxation Publishers, 1993, p. 1404.

❷ *Ibid.*, p. 1405.

❸ *Ibid.*

❹ *Ibid.*

❺ *Ibid.*, p. 1408.

❻ The specific negotiation history, *See ibid.*, pp. 1417 – 1461.

trade in the WTO. ❶

According to Article 18. 4 of the WTO ADA, Antidumping Agreement is aimed at setting up a standard for antidumping measures to be taken by WTO members and requires members to implement all possible general or specific measures to ensure that their laws, regulations and administrative procedures conform to it. ❷ Accordingly, as to the purpose of internationalization, it is not for condemning the harmful dumping universally, but to restrain national antidumping actions. ❸

2. 3. 2 Basic Common Requirements on Dumping

Due to the uniform requirement of the WTO ADA, although the nuts and bolts of antidumping rules may vary among different countries, the basic requirements on dumping are by and large the same. In order to condemn a dumping, there are three elements in the requirements, including proof of "dumped imports", "material injury" to a domestic industry, as well as a causal link between the two, to prove an antidumping case. ❹

In antidumping investigations, most efforts are devoted to the proof of "dumped imports", comparing with the other two elements. According

---

❶ The specific negotiation history, *See* Terence P. Stewart, *the GATT Uruguay Round, A Negotiation History Volume II: commentary*, Kluwer Law and Taxation Publishers, 1993, pp. 1462 – 1691.

❷ According to WTO ADA, Article 18. 4: Each Member shall take all necessary steps, of a general or particular character, to ensure, not later than the date of entry into force of the WTO Agreement for it, the conformity of its laws, regulations and administrative procedures with the provisions of this Agreement as they may apply for the Member in question.

❸ Gunnar Niels, *What is Antidumping Policy Really About*? Journal of Economic Surveys, 2002, Vol. 14, pp. 467, 469, http://www. blackwell-synergy. com/links/doi/10. 1111/1467 – 6419. 00118, last visited September 21, 2011.

❹ WTO ADA, Article 7.

to WTO ADA's definition, dumping occurs if a product is sold for export at a price below its normal value, i. e. when "the export price of a product exported from one country to another is less than the comparable price for the like product when destined for consumption in the exporting country". [1] Here normal value refers to the comparable price in the exporting country. [2] If it does not apply, normal value could be drawn from export price to a third country, or a price constructed by the "cost of production in the country of origin plus a reasonable amount for administrative, selling and general costs and for profits". [3] The difference between the export price and normal value is "the margin of dumping". Although the methodology is seemingly simple from theoretical point of view, it is very complicated in practice. [4]

After determining there exists "dumping", WTO members must make a determination of material injury or threat thereof to a domestic industry or material retardation of the establishement of a domestic industry. [5] In determining whether material injury exists, national antidumping authorities are required to consider "all relevant economic factors and indices having a bearing on the state of the industry, including actual and potential decline in sales, profits, output, market share, productivity, return on investments, or utilization of capacity; factors affecting domestic prices; the magnitude of the margin of dumping; actual and potential

---

[1] WTO ADA, Article 2.

[2] *Ibid.*

[3] *Ibid.*

[4] The specific explanation of how dumping margin is calculated, *See* Brink Lindsey & Daniel J. Ikenson, *Antidumping Exposed : the Devilish Details of Unfair Trade Law*, Cato Institute, 2003, pp. 1 – 16.

[5] WTO ADA, Article 3.

negative effects on cash flow, inventories, employment, wages, growth, ability to raise capital or investments". [1] In determining whether a threat of material injury exists, national antidumping authorities are required to consider specific factors. [2] However, the term "material injury" and "material retardation" are not defined in the WTO ADA. [3] Hence the national antidumping authorities have broad discretion to determine the existence of material injury or a threat of material injury. Furthermore, national antidumping authorities may calculate injuries when more than one exporting country is involved and exporters from all of the exporting coutires are engaged in dumping. [4] This also causes the easy determination of injury.

Before certain antidumping measure is taken, a casual link between dumping and injury must be established. National antidumping authorities must take into consideration all of the relevant factors causing matieral injury to a domestic injury, including those other than dumping, such as domestic competition, deline of demand, change of consumers' preference, restrictive business practices etc., in assessing injury to a domestic industry and the injury caused by those other factors must not be attributed to the dumped imports. [5] The above casual link is comparatively loose and it can be easily proved in practice. Actually in the Kenndey Round of trade negotiation in 1967, it contained a provision requiring that in determining the causation between a dumping and an

---

[1] WTO ADA, Article 3.4.

[2] WTO ADA, Article 3.7.

[3] Mitsuo Matsushita *et al.*, *the World Trade Organization: Law, Practice, and Policy*, Oxford Univ., 2003, p. 323.

[4] WTO ADA, Article 3.3.

[5] WTO ADA, Article 3.5.

injury, there should be evidence to show that dumping was demonostrably the major cause of the injury. However, it is considered as too strict, so this provision was replaced by the current stipulation ever since the 1979 Tokyo Round. ❶

In an antidumping investigation, after the determination of the above three elements, there are thrce possible outcomes. Definitive measure, as one of the outcomes, normally leads to an antidumping duty. A member country can impose antidumping duties against the dumped goods to the value of the dumping margin, and the antidumping duty to be imposed on the dumped product should be no more than the dumping margin. ❷ Termination, also one of the outcomes, occurs when any of the three mentioned essentials fails to be proved or the case is withdrawn by the complainant. ❸ Price undertaking, the third outcome, is agreed upon by the exporter and authorities to revise the exporting prices or to cease exports to the area at the dumped prices, rather than imposition of antidumping duties. ❹

2.3.3 "Dumping is Harmful": Self-evident Premise

Although the WTO ADA is quite specific in rules, it remains silent on the objective of antidumping law, or the justification to condemn dumping. It is well-known that dumping is an "unfair" practice or "unfair" trade, but why dumping is unfair? As to countervailing law, when a foreign seller has an advantage conferred by government subsidies rather than the market, it involves less doubt as to the element of

---

❶ Mitsuo Matsushita *et al.*, *the World Trade Organization: Law, Practice, and Policy*, Oxford Univ., 2003, p. 326.

❷ WTO ADA, Article 7.

❸ WTO ADA, Article 9.

❹ WTO ADA, Article 8.

"unfairness", but dumping is another story. [1]

Why price difference or price below constructed value is harmful without referring to how this price difference or price below constructed value happened? It has stipulated in the Agreement that dumping itself is not prohibited under the WTO Agreement, and there must be proof of "dumped imports", "material injury" to a domestic industry, and a causal link between the two in order to prove an antidumping case. It seems that there are two kinds of dumping, one is injurious dumping, the other is non-injurious dumping, and the law only regulates the former one. Neverthelss, it still does not explain why dumping is harmful, or why we need the law against dumping. Before making efforts to the investigation as well as the determination of the injurious dumping, the primary important issue is to answer the justification of condemning dumping.

To sum up, it seems that for a long time, "dumping is harmful" or "dumping is unfair" is taken as a premise for antidumping law which needs no proof. This has also been recognized by some scholars, like Ehrenhaft stated that: "...Nor the GATT or the WTO Agreements on the subject set forth any clear explanation of why the practice of "dumping" is considered "unfair" so as to warrant remedial measures. Rather the "unfairness" of the practice appears to have seemed self-evident to legislators and trade negotiators... " [2]

---

[1] Alan O. Sykes, Antidumping and Antitrust: What Problems Does Each Address? In Robert Z. Lawerence, ed. ,*Brookings Trade Forum* , Brookings Institution, 1998, p. 37.

[2] Peter D. Ehrenhaft, *Is Interface of Antidumping and Antitrust Laws Possible?* George Washington International Law Review , 2002, Vol. 34, pp. 363, 367.

2. 4 Summary

In this chapter, through examining economic theories, as well as the evolvement of antidumping laws, it is found that, in economic theories, the traditional dumping theory by Viner and the modern dumping theory by Willig, are deemed to be two of thc most influential theories. Although there are quite a few differences in details, such as differences in motives, dumping types etc. , both of them apply the efficiency approach in analyzing dumping, and are of the opinion that dumping is kind of transnational price discrimination, only predatory dumping is generally held as harmful.

In respect of antidumping laws, a journey back to their birth and following its evolvement indicates that, antidumping is originally part of antitrust law, to act against the import price discrimination. It is for dealing with these foreign conducts more efficiently that antidumping rules were changed and gradually distinctive from antitrust rules. This was formally identified by regulating the antidumping law under the GATT in 1947, and later on specifying it into the specific international agreement, i. e. , the WTO ADA in 1995. With regards to the requirements on dumping, due to the uniform requirement of the WTO ADA, the basic requirements on dumping in different countries are by and large the same, including price calculation, injury, as well as the causation between the two.

Nevertheless, neither the change of special rules nor that of legal areas can be the evidence to assert that the justification of antidumping is no longer to condemn predatory dumping. The purpose for creating international antidumping agreement in WTO is simply for unifying domestic rules. Most countries adopted antidumping subsequently merely because they need to follow the requirements of WTO. Correspondingly for a long time, "dumping is harmful or unfair" became a premise that needs no proving. In short, none of the changes are aimed to condemn dumping for others than the original and supposed reason of predatory price discrimination.

Chapter III Predatory Price Discrimination in Economic Theories and Competition Law

In Chapter II, the examination of economic theories as well as legislative history suggests that the original and supposed goal of antidumping is to deal with international price discrimination and to condemn predatory dumping. This chapter will continue to examine alike economic theories as well as modern competition rules concerning predatory price discrimination, prior to identifying whether competition law is better than antidumping law in addressing predatory price discrimination.

3. 1 Predatory Price Discrimination in Economic Theories

3. 1. 1 Price Discrimination: Primary-line and Secondary-line Competition

For economists, price discrimination is not a phenomenon confined to firms with dominant market power and is as such not anti-competitive. Price discrimination usually occurs in two forms. One is when identical products are sold at different prices under identical cost conditions, or non-identical but similar goods are sold at prices which are in different ratios to their marginal costs. The other one is when identical units of a product are sold at a common price under different cost conditions. [1]

There are three economic conditions under which profitable price discrimination may occur, i. e. , monopoly power, existence of two or more markets, and the elasticity of demand for the product. [2] Economists also attempt to approach price discrimination by means of classification. According to the British Economist Arthur C. Pigou, it is conventional in economy to distinguish between first-degree, second-degree and third-degree price discrimination according to whether individual units of the product or service are priced separately, successive blocks of units are so priced or units are sold in identifiable markets to which differentiated

---

[1] *See more*, Richard Dale, *Antidumping Law in a Liberal Trade Order*, The Macmillan Press Ltd. , 1980, pp. 20 – 22; Gabrielle Marceau, *Antidumping and Anti-trust Issues in Free-trade Areas*, Oxford Univ. Press Inc. , 1994, pp. 11 – 13; John H. Jackson & Edwin A. Vermulst, eds. , *Antidumping Law and Practice: a Comparative Study*, Harvester Wheatsheaf, 1990, pp. 24 – 26; Roger J. Van den Bergh & Peter D. Camesasca, *European Competition Law and Economics: A Comparative Perspective* , Intersentia-Hart, 2001, pp. 262 – 263.

[2] To be more specific, first, the seller of the product, or service, whose price is being differentiated must possess monopoly power in the sense that the price receives is responsive to the amount he sells. Secondly, the total market for the product must be separable into two or more sub-markets, which means that the sub-markets must be identifiable and that the product in question cannot, either physically or economically, be transferred between them. Finally, the elasticity of demand for the product, measured at the level of output that would prevail under simple , i. e. non-discriminatory, monopoly, must differ between the sub-markets. *See, e. g.* , Richard Dale, *Antidumping Law in a Liberal Trade Order* , The Macmillan Press Ltd. , 1980, p. 20; Roger J. Van den Bergh & Peter D. Camesasca, *European Competition Law and Economics: A Comparative Perspective* , Intersentia-Hart, 2001, p. 263.

prices apply. [1]

Price discrimination is not viewed with any negative implications in economics. For instance, sporadic price discrimination, is the characteristic of adjustment of competitive markets toward equilibrium. [2] The central concern of competition law is the competitive effects of price discrimination, to focus on the anti-competitive price discrimination by firms with market power. Since price discrimination can be either pro-competitive or anti-competitive in the eyes of economists, the concern should be placed on the differentiation of whether it is deemed to be anticompetitive.

In order to achieve so, two levels of competition are distinguished. The first one is the primary-line competition, i. e. competition between the discriminating monopolist and his rivals in the same line of business; and the second one is the secondary-line competition, i. e. competition between the discriminating monopolist's customers (who may,

---

[1] Briefly speaking, first degree price discrimination occurs when each single unit of output is sold at the highest possible price Whereas first degree price discrimination is mainly a theoretical case, both second and third degree price discrimination regularly occur in practice since they require less information about demand. Second degree price discrimination takes place when a firm sells different units of output for different prices, even though every individual buying the same amount of the goods pays the same price. Third degree price discrimination occurs when a firm segregates consumers into distinctive groups characterized by different elastics of demand which are explained by exogenous criteria such as location, age, sex, or occupation. While discriminatory pricing is generally of the third-degree variety and it is on this practice that attention is focused here, both within the domestic and dumping contexts. *See*, *e. g.* , Richard Dale, *Antidumping Law in a Liberal Trade Order* , the Macmillan Press Ltd. , 1980, pp. 20 – 21; Roger J. Van den Bergh & Peter D. Camesasca, *European Competition Law and Economics: A Comparative Perspective*, Intersentia-Hart, 2001, pp. 264 – 265.

[2] Roger J. Van den Bergh & Peter D. Camesasca, *European Competition Law and Economics: A Comparative Perspective*, Intersentia-Hart, 2001, p. 263.

for instance, be retailers) and their business rivals. [1]

Antidumping law, with foreign conductors and their domestic competitors as its main concern, links with competition law mostly in the primary-line competition. Relating to the anti-competitive effects of the primary-line competition, modern economic theories consider that there can be no presumption that price discrimination is injurious, and price discrimination can only be considered as anti-competitive in the extreme case when it is a predatory pricing. [2] The competitive effects of the secondary-line competition are much more complicated. [3]

3.1.2 Predatory Pricing

After reviewing economic theories of price discrimination, predatory pricing will be examined with a focus on its primary-line anti-competitive effects, so as to link it with antidumping law. In general, predatory pricing constitutes a type of behaviour where prices are too low to the extent that the competitive process itself is damaged. A dominant firm, called the predator, incurs short-term losses in a particular market in order to induce the exit or deter the entry of a rival firm, called the prey, so that super-normal profits can be earned in the future,

---

[1] Richard Dale, *Antidumping Law in a Liberal Trade Order*, the Macmillan Press Ltd., 1980, pp. 23 - 27.

[2] *Ibid.*, pp. 23 - 26.

[3] *Ibid.*, pp. 26 - 27.

either in the same market or in other markets. ❶

There are several factors impacting on the profitability of predatory pricing, including: chances that losses can be made good by future gains are higher if demand is inelastic; if the price war is of short duration and the price reductions relatively small; if the predator is able to gain additional market share; and if entry barriers are high. ❷

In the discussion of predatory pricing, there are two levels of debate among economic scholars. The first one focuses on the issue of "whether predatory pricing is a rationale strategy", the second one pays more attention to the issue of "how to create an optimal legal rule for predatory pricing". ❸

3. 1. 2. 1 Debate I: Rational or Irrational Strategy

In this debate, the Chicago School argues that predatory pricing is irrational from mainly three aspects. First, a dominant firm cutting prices below costs will lose money in the short run, even though it may hope to drive rivals out of business and increase its power to control prices afterwards. Second, even if the predator succeeds in driving the target firm out of the market, in the absence of barriers to entry a monopolist will

---

❶ The stylized story goes as follows. A dominant firm active in many geographical markets or selling many brands of a differentiated product sets a price below cost in one geographical market where its actions are constrained by a fringe of small competitors or cuts the price for one brand which faces competition, while holding a price above cost in other markets. Small competitors that are not sustained by their operations in other markets suffer losses in the short run and exit in the long run. After the elimination of the target firms the dominant firm inherits a monopoly, restricts output, increases prices, and earns economic profits. *See* Roger J. Van den Bergh & Peter D. Camesasca, *European Competition Law and Economics: A Comparative Perspective*, Intersentia-Hart, 2001, p. 262.

❷ *Ibid.*, p. 286.

❸ *Ibid.*, p. 287.

not be able to earn super-competitive profits. Third, even if because of the existence of entry barriers, the strict condition of recoupment is satisfied, predatory pricing is not necessarily the most profitable alternative. ❶

On the contrary, the Game Theory considers predatory pricing as a rational strategy. They described three models of predatory pricing: deep pocket models, including capital market imperfections, signaling models and reputation models. The contribution to competition policy from these models is to recognize the strategic and dynamic nature of predation. They lead to the important insight that the traditional Chicago analysis is only correct under conditions of perfect information. ❷

This book is not purported to argue for or against the above economic theories, whereas a brief conclusion can be made thereon: since there is no definite answer in economic theories for whether the predatory pricing is rational or irrational, it is necessary to regulate and further examine predatory pricing in law.

3. 1. 2. 2 Debate II: Competitive Price or Predatory Pricing

The focal point in this debate is towards an optimal and effective means to identify between a very competitive price and predatory pricing. Various tests of identifying harmful predatory pricing have been brought forward, including price-cost tests, performance tests, rule of reason tests and structural tests.

A great number of scholars suggested an approach which uses the relationship of the dominant firm's prices to its costs as the primary tool for identifying predatory pricing. The representative test was short-run

---

❶ Roger J. Van den Bergh & Peter D. Camesasca, *European Competition Law and Economics: A Comparative Perspective*, Intersentia-Hart, 2001, pp. 287 – 290.

❷ *Ibid.*, pp. 290 – 296.

costbased rules brought forward by the Harvard law professors Areeda and Turner in 1975. ❶ Later on, Posner proposed long-term cost-based rules. ❷ Other similar tests, such as the output expansion by Williamson❸,

---

❶ Short-run cost-based rules by Areeda and Turner of Harvard: pricing below short-run marginal cost should be unlawful, and that short-run marginal cost can be approximated by short-run variable cost. *See* Phillip Areeda & Donald F. Turner, *Predatory Pricing and Related Practices under Section* 2 *of the Sherman Act*, Harvard Law Review, 1974, Vol. 88, pp. 697, 697 – 733, http://scholar. google. com/scholar? hl = zh – CN&lr = &q = info: U79X – gD – nAEJ: scholar. google. com/&output = viewport, last visited September 21, 2011.

❷ Long-term cost-based rules by Posner: the long-run marginal costs were a better measure because some equally or more efficient competitors , i. e. more efficient in having lower long-run marginal costs, will lack the ability, or the will, to sustain losses in the short run. For practical reasons, he also substituted marginal by variable costs. He would consider the intent of the predator and would request the plaintiff to make an initial showing that the market was predisposed to effective predatory pricing. *See* Richard A. Posner, *Antitrust Law: An Economic Perspective* , St. Paul, Minnesota, 1981.

❸ Output expansion rules by Williamson: condemns any marginal-cost-based rules because they ignore the possibility that (1) a firm may build an infrastructure in view of further needs to reduce the variable costs of expanding production or (2) that it may produce at high output in consideration of a potential entry in the market of a competitor. He recommended an average costs test, but would admit exceptions for promotional prices of non-durable consumer goods for a brief period of time. Standards fully allocated costs are close to those of antidumping laws, but most would argue that the threat of expanding output on entry is not credible, so it would not deter entry. *See* Oliver Williamson, *Predatory Pricing: A Strategic and Welfare Analysis*, Yale Law Journal, 1977, Vol. 87, pp. 284, 284 – 340.

or rules governing price rises by Baumol[1], attempted to address the long-term evaluation in different ways by observing the predators' performance after the exit of a rival from the relevant market.

All of the aforementioned tests were criticized as achieving rough justice by relying mainly on cost-price relations and not taking into account the broader economic and strategic aspects.[2] Consequently, much broader tests such as rule of reason tests and structural tests were proposed. Rule of reason tests by Scherer, proposed a wide inquiry into many factors surrounding the predator's conduct including the alleged predator's intent and the actual consequences of low-priced sales.[3] Such broad test by taking every piece of evidence available might not be practically evaluated by competition authorities and therefore might

---

[1] Rules governing price rises by Baumol, who also refuses to rely only on the relationship between prices and costs, concentrates on price increase after the successful predation, i. e., after the new entrant has been driven out of the market. He advocates legislation requiring any price to last five years after the predation. He would not prohibit price-cutting in response to new entry but would force enterprises to select viable prices-unrealistic in that legal intervention takes place after the competitor has been driven out of the market, by which time it may be unable to undertake legal action (it may, however, have a deterrent effect). Secondly, the maintenance of a price for five years is impossible to control in any other manner than retrospectively, i. e. once a competitor which may have been efficient has been eliminated. *See* William Baumol, *Quasi performance of price reductions: a policy for prevention of predatory pricing*, Yale Law Review, 1979, Vol. 89, pp. 1 – 26.

[2] *See*, *e. g.*, Herbert Hovenkamp, *Post-Chicago Antitrust: A Review and Critique*, Columbia Business Law Review, 2001, Vol. 2001, pp. 257 – 337.

[3] The rule of reason test by Scherer: long-run welfare can sometimes be maximized with a dominant firm's prices either above or below marginal costs. He would look at the relative efficiency of the enterprises in the market, the minimum efficient scale, the monopolist's effect on other enterprises, and the subsequent prices. *See* F. M. Scherer, *Predatory pricing and the Sherman Act: A comment*, Harvard Law Review, 1976, Vol. 89, pp. 869 – 890.

further result in legal uncertainty. [1]

By applying structural analysis of the relevant market as a first screen and then moving on to the second screen by incorporating price-cost tests, structural tests, such as the two-tier rules by Joskow and Klevorick, consequently limit investigation to markets where favorable conditions for a successful predatory campaign exist in order to minimize the costs of enforcement errors. [2]

3.2 Overview of Competition Law

We will turn to competition principles and laws. This part shall overview the basic competition principles and the section of Price Discrimination and Predatory Pricing in competition laws first.

---

[1] *See*, *e. g.*, Luis Miguel Hinojosa Martinez, *Predatory Pricing Literature Under European Competition Law*: *The AKZO Case*, Legal Issues of European Integration, 1993, Vol. 2, pp. 95 – 128.

[2] the Two-tier rules by Joskow and Klevorick: market structure determines whether predation is a possible strategy. When predation is alleged, the market structure should firstly be analysed according to three components: short-run monopoly power, conditions of entry, and "dynamic effects of competitors and entrants". Short-run monopoly would be measured by the predator's market share and the elasticity of the demand for its products. Conditions of entry refer to the speed with which potential competition becomes real competition. They would look at capital requirements, consumers' loyalties, the quality of information. The dynamic of the market is determined by rapid growth or decline. Where predation would not cause a competitor to quit or deter entry, any cut in price would be tolerated. The second phase of his enquiry would be a "pricing rule of reason" test in which the intent would be a relevant though not a necessary factor. Prices below the average variable would be deemed predatory , one exception being where the alleged predator can show that closure of the firm was more costly, which would affect the opportunity costs. Price between average variable and average total costs would be presumed predatory , except depressed prices; prices above total costs would be presumed non-predatory unless they change within two years. *See* Paul Joskow & Alvin Klevorick, *A Framework for Analysing Predatory Pricing Policy*, Yale Law Journal , 1979, Vol. 89, pp. 213 – 270.

3.2.1 Consensus on the Basic Competition Principles

Questioning the fundamental objectives or justifications of antidumping law from the perspective of competition policy has not incurred such a hot discussion until the 1970s, and is gradually becoming much more important. From the aspect of antidumping law, the reason for this trend could be the proliferation of antidumping laws and actions, which give a rise to severe protectionist abuse. While from the aspect of antitrust law, the reason should be the increasing consensus on the main objectives of competition policy, accompanied with the gradually globalization of competition law that penetrates into the trade area. This part would like to give a brief review of the various different objectives of competition policy evolved in historical development, and then point out the common main objectives of competition policy acknowledged in recent two decades.

Generally speaking, competition policy includes the set of measures and instruments used by governments that establish the conditions of competition. [1] Differing from competition law, which is taken as only one component of competition policy, competition policy exists in almost all of the countries. [2] Although not all countries have a formal, codified

---

[1] Roland Weinrauch, *Competition Law in the WTO: the Rationale for a Framework Agreement*, Wien: NWV Neuer Wissenschaftlicher Verlag, 2004, p. 18.

[2] Competition policy includes the set of measures and instruments used by governments that establish the conditions of competition. Thus, competition law is only one component of competition policy. Other components are, for instance, deregulation and privatization activities, firm-specific subsidy programs, market access programs etc. as opposed to competition law, the priority of competition policy is to create preconditions which shall assure the effective functioning of competition, rather than the punishment of violations of the rules. See *Ibid.*, p. 18.

competition policy, but all have informal competition conventions. [1]

As to the objectives of competition policy, for hundreds of years, countries design various competition policies and laws which are influenced by varying economic, social and cultural needs and interests. [2] Modern competition laws are greatly influenced by economic efficiency approach. [3] While among those different objectives, only certain major themes stand out and are shared by the majority of countries. [4]

As summarized by Roland, the objectives of competition policy can be categorized into mainly four kinds, namely:

First, at the very basic level, the most common of these objectives is the maintenance of the competitive process or of a healthy degree of rivalry among firms in markets for good and services. Scopes which are associated with this objective are freedom of choice, access to markets, contractual freedom and freedom of individual action.

---

[1] Edward M. Graham & J. David, Richardson eds. , *Global Competition Policy*, Institute For International Economics, 1997, p. 7. According to some empirical analysis, more than seventy countries, comprising 98% of world output and 99% of world trade, have now adopted some form of antitrust policy. *See* Patricia Isela Hansen, *Antitrust In the Global Market: Rethinking "Reasonable Expectations"*, Southern California Law Review, 1999, Vol. 72, pp. 1601, 1612.

[2] Roland Weinrauch, *Competition Law in the WTO: the Rationale for a Framework Agreement* , Wien : NWV Neuer Wissenschaftlicher Verlag, 2004, p. 24.

[3] Competition policy has had, and sometimes still has, different objectives, including decentralization of economic power, the protection small firms, and fairness. Only more recently has efficiency instead of fairness arguably become the main objective of competition in most countries. US competition policy especially has gone through an important learning process. *See* Gunnar Niels, *What is Antidumping Policy Really About?* Journal of Economic Surveys, 2002, Vol. 14, pp. 467, 481, http://www. blackwell - synergy. com/links/doi/10. 1111/ 1467 -6419. 00118, last visited September 21, 2011.

[4] Roland Weinrauch, *Competition Law in the WTO: the Rationale for a Framework Agreement*, Wien : NWV Neuer Wissenschaftlicher Verlag, 2004, p. 25.

The second main goal of competition policy is the promotion of allocative and dynamic efficiency. While during the last two decades achievement of economic efficiency has been regarded as a means to maximize consumer welfare.

The third core objective of competition policy is the promotion of trade and integration within an economic union or a free trade area.

The fourth kind is very broad, which involves many supplementary objectives of competition policy. It includes ensuring fairness and equity in marketplace transactions; promoting democratic values, such as economic pluralism and the dispersion of socio-economic power; preserving and promoting the development of a market economy – especially important for economies in transition and developing countries; facilitating economic liberalization, including privatization, deregulation and the reduction of external trade barriers and minimizing the need for more intrusive forms of regulation in a free market economy. Additionally, competition policy may consider the effects that business practices, e.g., mergers, may have on employment, local communities and regional development. [1]

According to the different economic, social, and political considerations, different countries may give different weight to the listed four kinds of objectives at different periods of time. Take the U.S. and the EU for example. The U.S. competition policy has a strong orientation towards consumer welfare. [2] In the U.S., the congressional, judicial, and the economic scholarly debates about the purposes of antitrust laws have shown the variation over time. During the period of Sherman Act,

---

[1] Roland Weinrauch, *Competition Law in the WTO: the Rationale for a Framework Agreement*, Wien: NWV Neuer Wissenschaftlicher Verlag, 2004, pp. 25 – 27.

[2] *Ibid.*, p. 27.

as well as the Clayton and Federal Trade Commission Acts, the harm to consumers from practices that stiffly competition has been given much emphasis, although scholars also suggest that it was also concerned about the welfare of small businesses. The consumer welfare is strongly supported by the Chicago school, which argued for a purely economic construction of the law. ❶

While during the period of the Robinson-Patman Act, under the rolc of non-economic considerations, the protection of smaller wholesalers and retailers gained a weight in antitrust laws. After the Robinson-Patman Act, the congress started to concern for the protection of small competitors as well as the competitive process, judicial statements about the law also openly embraced the other values of antitrust. ❷

As to the EU, competition policy has a unique function. In the EU, the most important objective of competition policy is the promotion of

---

❶ Bork stated in his famous book "The Paradox Antitrust" that: "the argument of this book, of course, is that competition must be understood as the maximization of consumer welfare or, if you prefer, economic efficiency. *See* Robert H. Bork, *the Paradox Antitrust: a Policy at War with Itself*, the Free Press, 1993, p. 427.

❷ *See, e. g.*, Alan O. Sykes, Antidumping and Antitrust: What Problems Does Each Address? in Robert Z. Lawerence, ed., *Brookings Trade Forum*, Brookings Institution, 1998, p. 10.

market integration. [1] Competition policy plays a decisive role within the European Union because the creation of a single market without internal frontiers in goods, persons, services and capital is impossible as long as the isolation of national markets can be maintained effectively by restrictive business practices or by State aid policies which give competition advantages to the national industries. [2] While subordinated to that, the second fundamental objective of the EC competition policy is alleged to achieve a competitive environment[3], as well as the consideration for

---

[1] "Article 2 provided that the community shall have as its task, by establishing a common market and progressively approximating the economic policies of Member States, to promote throughout the Community a harmonious development of economic activities, a continuous and balanced expansion, an increase in stability, an accelerated raising of the standard of living and closer relations between the States belonging to it." *See* Mario Marques Mendes, *Antitrust in a World of Interrelated Economies: the Interplay Between Antitrust and Trade Policies in the U. S. and the EEC*, Etudes Europeennes, 1991, p. 74. "One of the main objectives of the European competition policy has been market integration and the formation of a unified European market." *See* Olivier Bertrand & Marc Ivaldi, *European Competition Policy in International Markets*, A Contribution for the BRUEGEL's Project on Europe and the Global Economy, 2006, pp. 1, 9, http://www.intertic.org/Conference/Toulouse.pdf, last visited September 21, 2011.

[2] Roland Weinrauch, Competition Law in the WTO: the Rationale for a Framework Agreement, Wien: NWV Neuer Wissenschaftlicher Verlag, 2004, p. 28.

[3] The achievement of a competitive environment was, therefore, singled out as one of the main goals of EEC competition policy. In the words of the Commission, "the second fundamental objective of the Community's competition policy must be to ensure that at all stages of the common market's development there exists the right amount of competition in order for the Treaty's requirements to be met and its aims attained." *See* Mario Marques Mendes, *Antitrust in a World of Interrelated Economies: the Interplay Between Antitrust and Trade Policies in the U. S. and the EEC*, Etudes Europeennes, 1991, p. 75.

the small and medium sized businesses. ❶

Just like the U. S. and the EU, different countries may give different weight to the listed four kinds of objectives at different periods, nevertheless, with harmonization and convergence of antitrust laws, competition rules become more similar, which should remove conflicts related to antitrust goals and interpretations. ❷ Furthermore, consensus breaks down across countries. Ever since the last two decades, there is more convergence of objectives between countries which have well-developed competition laws and policies. ❸

There are two points concerning the consensus. The first one is that competition policy is to protect competition from private and public business restraints that adversely interfere with the competitive process, and that the competitive process should be protected not to promote

---

❶ Another objective of EC competition policy is the protection of small and medium sized businesses which has been recognized in the interpretation of abuses of dominant position prohibited by Article 82 of the EC Treaty. *See* Roland Weinrauch, *Competition Law in the WTO: the Rationale for a Framework Agreement* , Wien : NWV Neuer Wissenschaftlicher Verlag, 2004, pp. 27 – 28.

❷ Olivier Bertrand & Marc Ivaldi, *European Competition Policy in International Markets*, A Contribution for the BRUEGEL' s Project on Europe And The Global Economy, 2006, pp. 1, 30, http://www. intertic. org/Conference/Toulouse. pdf, last visited September 21, 2011.

❸ Roland Weinrauch, *Competition Law in the WTO: the Rationale for a Framework Agreement* , Wien : NWV Neuer Wissenschaftlicher Verlag, 2004, p. 28.

competition for the competitor's sake but to achieve other goals. [1]

The second one is that the basic elements of the objectives of competition policy are consisted of three points, i. e., economic efficiency, consumer protection, and market integration. [2] Of the three, market integration is unique in that it received consensus mostly among bilateral or regional areas such as the EU. The key points of consensus have

---

[1] Kennedy has pointed out in his book that "Antitrust law...focuses on the maintenance of open markets, the promotion of competition, and the maximization of consumer welfare". *See* Kevin C. Kennedy, *Competition Law and the World Trade Organization: the Limits of Multilateralism*, Sweet & Maxwell, 2001, p. 235.

Talyor also recognized that: "competition law gives pre-eminence to considerations of economic efficiency... Competition is viewed as a means of disciplining firms, reducing their market po-wer, and thus ensuring that the market forces of supply and demand operate more effectively and efficiently in allocating global resources...Competition law seeks to lessen power imbalances between firms to ensure that all firms have an equal opportunity to compete on their merits. Competition law also prevents producers from using certain business practices to capture additional wealth from consumers...Indeed, competition laws are commonly drafted so as to favour the interests of end consumers over the interests of producers." *See* Martyn D. Taylor, *International Competition Law: A New Dimension for the WTO?* Cambridge Univ. Press Inc., 2006, p. 264.

[2] Roland considered that consequently, it seems to be difficult to define certain objectives for an international competition law agreement. However, more and more convergence of objectives between countries has been noted within the last decade. Therefore, I think that certain common main objectives, such as economic efficiency, market integration and consumer welfare could be defined for an international agreement, while it may be advisable to pursue other minor goals through separate government policies. *See* Roland Weinrauch, *Competition Law in the WTO: the Rationale for a Framework Agreement*, Wien: NWV Neuer Wissenschaftlicher Verlag, 2004, p. 30.

been recognized among major countries. [1]

3. 2. 2 Predatory Price Discrimination

In general, competition law consists four sections, including horizontal restraints, vertical restraints, abuse of a dominant position, i. e. , unlawful monopolization, merger and acquisition. [2] Horizontal agreements are implicit or explicit arrangements between companies which compete with identical or similar products in the same market at the same stage of production. [3] Vertical market restraints refer to the

---

[1] OECD Publication in 1984 defined the major goal of competition policy in this way: "competition policy has as its central economic goal the preservation and promotion of the competitive process, a process which encourages efficiency in the production and allocation of goods and services, and over time, through its effects on innovation and adjustment to technological change, a dynamic process of sustained economic growth. In conditions of effective competition, rivals have equal opportunities to compete for business on the basis and equality of their outputs, and resource deployment follows market success in meeting consumers' demand at the lowest possible cost." *See* OECD, *Competition and Trade Policies: Their Interaction*, OECD Publications, 1984, p. 86.

[2] This is analyzed in many competition books.

[3] "Horizontal agreements are implicit or explicit arrangements between companies which compete with identical or similar products in the same market at the same stage of production. Hard core cartels in most countries *per se* prohibited like price-fixing, bid rigging, market division or customer allocation & by their nature imply positive effects and apply a rule of reason. like set product standards, reduce risk, create better products or methods of distribution or improve limited exemptions." *See* Roland Weinrauch, *Competition Law in the WTO: the Rationale for a Framework Agreement*, Wien : NWV Neuer Wissenschaftlicher Verlag, 2004, pp. 30 – 31.

explicit agreements between operators at different stages of the value-added chain. [1] Merger and acquisition deal with enterprises that combine in different ways. [2] Price discrimination and predatory pricing fall within the anti-competitive firm behavior of abuse of a dominant position. [3]

Abuse of dominant position is an anti-competitive practice employed by a firm to maintain or achieve a dominant position in the market. Vertical or horizontal actions against competitors, such as exclusive dealing, excessive pricing, price discrimination, tie-ins, refusals to deal,

---

[1] "Vertical market restraints refer to explicit agreements between operators at different stages of the value-added chain. Such arrangements are often the subject of specific provisions of national competition legislation, or are dealt with under a rule-or-reason or case-by-case approach. Like resale price maintenance agreements restrictions on the price to be charged by downstream firms, exclusive distribution agreements (distributors are assigned exclusively within a geographic area, over particular types of clients, or over specific products), exclusive dealing agreements restrictions on the source of supplies for particular inputs used by firms, quantity forcing (downstream to deal a supplier refuses to sell to parties wishing to buy), discriminatory pricing a supplier charges different parties different prices under similar circumstances, predatory pricing suppliers sell at a low price in order to drive competitors out of business or loyalty rebates a dominant supplier offers discounts to certain parties on the condition that they do not sell someone else's products." *See ibid.*, pp. 32 – 33.

[2] "Enterprises combine in different ways. For example, one company puchases outstanding securities or operating assets from another company or two firms exchange securities to form one firm as result of an agreement or takeover. Any transaction in which two independent companies are combined into one and therefore, one of the companies is strengthened while the other one is eliminated is labeled a merger. Three different categories of mergers can be distinguished: Horizontal, vertical and conglomerate mergers." *See ibid.*, p. 33.

[3] This has been generally recognized, For example, in Model Law on Competition, both predatory behavior and discriminatory are "Act or behaviour considered as abuse" under the category of "Acts or behaviour constituting an abuse of a dominant position of market power". *See* UNCTAD, *Model Law on Competition*, *Article* 4 (*II*), http://www.unctad.org/en/docs/tdrbpconf5d7.en.pdf., last visited September 21, 2011.

predatory pricing, or raising rivals' costs may be regarded as abuses. ❶

3.3 Predatory Price Discrimination in Competition Law

This part shall concentrate on the U.S. and the EU, two basic models, to further elaborate modern competition rules and cases of predatory price discrimination. ❷ Linking with the issue of dumping, this part attempts to identify whether there are any common basic standards on predatory price discrimination among different countries, whereas a comprehensive analysis into specific rules and cases shall be omitted.

3.3.1 Competition Rules and Cases in the U.S.

3.3.1.1 Rules

In the U.S., the relevant federal provisions on predatory price discrimination can be found in three acts. A general approach to this issue is contained in the Sherman Act, with a more specific Clayton Act and its amendment Robinson-Patman Act.

As introduced in Chapter II, the Sherman Act did not apply to price discrimination directly, but condemned monopolization or the attempt to monopolize any part of commerce among the U.S. States in Section 2. ❸ The offence thereunder involved two elements: the establishment of monopoly power of the alleged predator in the relevant market, and the

---

❶ Roland Weinrauch, *Competition Law in the WTO: the Rationale for a Framework Agreement*, Wien: NWV Neuer Wissenschaftlicher Verlag, 2004, pp. 34 – 35.

❷ In terms of price discrimination and predatory pricing, in Europe it is regulated on the Community level and within the Member States legislation, similar to the U.S. antitrust legislation on the federal and state level. However, it is beyond the scope of this book to scrutinize each EU Member State as well as each of the State legislation of the U.S.

❸ U.S.C.A. Title 15, Section 1 – 7.

willful acquisition of that power as distinguished from growth as a consequence of a superior product, business acumen or historic accident. [1] Pertaining to the abuse of dominant position, predatory pricing was also regulated thereunder.

Price discrimination was specified in the Section 2(a) of the Clayton Act, and amended by the Robinson-Patman Act afterwards. The relevant article was that:

It shall be unlawful for any person engaged in commerce, in the course of such commerce, either directly or indirectly, to discriminate in price between different purchasers of commodities of like grade and quality, where either or any of the purchasers involved in such discrimination are in commerce, where such commodities are sold for use, consumption ,or resale...and where the effect of such discrimination may be substantially to lessen competition or tend to create a monopoly in any line of commerce, or to injure, destroy, or prevent competition with any person who either grants or knowingly receives the benefit of such discrimination, or with customers of either of them. [2]

3. 3. 1. 2 Cases

The judicial statements of the U. S. have gradually developed and specified with the years, and this evolvement followed economic theories in many aspects. Regarding price discrimination, it is not held as unlawful *per se* but must be shown by the U. S. Federal Trade Commission

---

[1] U. S v. Grinnell Corp. 384 U. S 563, 1996, 571.

[2] *Ibid.*

or other enforcement agencies, to have the specified anti-competitive effect. [1] The administrative statements divide the competition into two levels, so as to examine the competitive effects of price discrimination. [2] Moreover, one significant development over the past decades is that the primary-line discrimination under the Clayton Act has been interpreted more harmoniously with predatory pricing under the Sherman Act. [3]

As to predatory pricing, the U. S. Federal Trade Commission requires that market conditions make predatory pricing a rational and plausible strategy for the predator. Attempted monopolization requires: (1) specific intent to control prices or destroy competition; (2) predatory or anti-competitive conduct directed towards that end, and (3) a dangerous probability of successful monopolization. In the third requirement for attempt to monopolize, that of dangerous probability, there is de facto prerequisite for a high threshold of market power. [4] Accordingly,

---

[1] There are three points for defense. Firstly, price differentiation which reflects cost differences is allowable which is called "the cost justification defense"; Secondly, a seller may lower his price selectively to meet the equally low price of a competitor which is called "the meeting competition defense" Thirdly, there is a clause exempting price changes "in response to changing conditions affecting the market for or the marketability of the goods concerned" as might apply, for instance, to perishable goods, seasonal goods and distress sales. *See* Richard Dale, *Antidumping Law in a Liberal Trade Order*, the Macmillan Press Ltd., 1980, p. 45.

[2] In its Geographical pricing memorandum of 1948 the U. S. FTC drew a distinction between competitive effects at the primary and secondary levels and interpreted the law as requiring that the probable injury to competitors of the seller be patent, severe and sustained. *See ibid.*, p. 46.

[3] OECD, *Predatory Pricing*, 1989, pp. 1, 42, http://www.oecd.org/dataoecd/7/54/2375661.pdf, last visited September 21, 2011.

[4] Gabrielle Marceau, *Antidumping and Anti-trust Issues in Free-trade Areas*, Oxford Univ. Press Inc., 1994, p. 262.

there are actually four aspects of requirement in determining a predatory pricing, including market power, intent, predatory conduct, and the probability to destroy competition.

A review of the cases suggests that economic tests have influenced the consideration given to different aspects thereof from period to period. In the U. S. , cases concerning predatory pricing were infrequent until after the passage of the Robinson-Patman Act, with *Utah Pie Case* in 1967 as the first "modern" decision.[1] In 1975, the enforcement climate changed radically with the publication of the Areeda-Turner article. But given the latter effect and the difficulties of cost determination, the courts augmented the Areeda-Turner rule with other factors, including intent and market structure.[2] Chicago analysts gained a noticeable

---

[1] "Discriminatory price cutting by large inter-state sellers injuring small local businesses was virtually *per se* unlawful. The most dramatic example of the strong enforcement efforts by the Federal Trade Commission was the Utah Pie case. The plaintiff sold frozen pies and had over 65 percent of sales in one regional market. Three national firms entered that market and constantly sold at lower prices than in other regional markets. For a period of four years Utah Pie's sales and profits increased considerably but its market share fell to about 45 percent. The Supreme Court held that a firm operating in two or more markets cannot engage in price competition in one of those markets without doing so in all. The Utah Pie decision was criticized heavily for not considering consumers' interest in low prices." *See* Roger J. Van den Bergh & Peter D. Camesasca, *European Competition Law and Economics: A Comparative Perspective* , Intersentia-Hart, 2001, pp. 298 – 299.

[2] "Their rule suggesting the illegality of prices below average variable costs had an immediate and dramatic impact on the courts. In the five years following the publication of the seminal article no plaintiff prevailed. Given the latter effect and the difficulties of cost determination, the courts augmented the Areeda-Turner rule with other factors, including intent and market structure. While there were variations most courts held that a price below average variable costs was presumptively unlawful, while a price above average total costs was conclusively lawful, but the presumption could be rebutted by evidence of intent and market structure." *See* Roger J. Van den Bergh & Peter D. Camesasca, *European Competition Law and Economics: A Comparative Perspective*, Intersentia-Hart, 2001, p. 299.

influence upon American case law on the subject of predatory pricing in the 1980s. In the famous *Matsushita Case* and *Brooke Group Case* as well, the courts favored the strict application of "the prospect of recoupment", a dangerous probability of successful monopolization, to determine predatory pricing, letting the price-cost test by Areeda-Turner a merely ancillary role. [1]

3.3.2 Competition Rules and Cases in the EU

3.3.2.1 Rules

In the EU, the relevant rules on predatory price discrimination are set

---

[1] In the famous Matsushita Case in 1986, the Court first revealed the pivotal role recoupment was to play in predatory pricing analysis. This case is regarding claims by American TV-set manufacturers against competing Japanese companies. Zenith claimed that the Japanese companies conspired and sold their products below costs in the U.S., while selling similar products in Japan at higher than costs levels in order to cross-subsidize the loss sales in the U.S. The Court rejected these claims as economically implausible by emphasizing the recoupment analysis. That is, because the plaintiff was claiming that the predatory pricing along with the conspiracy had been conducted over a period over 20 years, the defendants, even if eventually successful in the attempt to monopolise, would never be able to recover the losses they would need to sustain along the way.

In Brooke Group Case in 1993, the Supreme Court for the first time in over 25 years provided a detailed analysis of the substantive standards to be applied on predatory pricing. The Court firstly equated the standards of the Sherman and the Robinson-Patman Acts, so that a plaintiff firstly must prove that the prices complained of are below an appropriate measure of costs and, secondly, that he needs to demonstrate that the alleged predator had reasonable prospect or that there is the dangerous probability of recouping its investment in below-cost prices, thus hurting competition. As in this case, the Court viewed oligopoly recoupment as highly unlikely and rejected the claim.

See Roger J. Van den Bergh & Peter D. Camesasca, *European Competition Law and Economics: A Comparative Perspective*, Intersentia-Hart, 2001, pp. 299 - 230.

forth in Article 81 and Article 82 of the EC Treaty. ❶ Although there

---

❶ EC Treaty, Article 81 (ex Article 85):

(1) The following shall be prohibited as incompatible with the common market: all agreements between undertakings, decisions by associations of undertakings and concerted practices which may affect trade between Member States and which have as their object or effect the prevention, restriction or distortion of competition within the common market, and in particular those which: (a) directly or indirectly fix purchase or selling prices or any other trading conditions; (b) Limit or control production, markets, technical development, or investment; (c) share markets or sources of supply; (d) apply dissimilar conditions to equivalent transactions with other trading parties, thereby placing them at a competitive disadvantage; (e) make the conclusion of contracts subject to acceptance by the other parties of supplementary obligations which, by their nature or according to commercial usage, have no connection with the subject of such contracts.

(2) Any agreements or decisions prohibited pursuant to this Article shall be automatically void.

(3) The provisions of paragraph 1 may, however, be declared inapplicable in the case of: – any agreement or category of agreements between undertakings; – any decision or category of decisions by associations of undertakings; – any concerted practice or category of concerted practices, which contributes to improving the production or distribution of goods or to promoting technical or economic progress, while allowing consumers a fair share of the resulting benefit, and which does not: (a) impose on the undertakings concerned restrictions which are not indispensable to the attainment of these objectives; (b) afford such undertakings the possibility of eliminating competition in respect of a substantial part of the products in question.

Article 82 (ex Article 86):

Any abuse by one or more undertakings of a dominant position within the common market or in a substantial part of it shall be prohibited as incompatible with the common market insofar as it may affect trade between Member States. Such abuse may, in particular, consist in: (a) directly or indirectly imposing unfair purchase or selling prices or other unfair trading conditions; (b) limiting production, markets or technical development to the prejudice of consumers; (c) applying dissimilar conditions to equivalent transactions with other trading parties, thereby placing them at a competitive disadvantage; (d) making the conclusion of contracts subject to acceptance by the other parties of supplementary obligations which, by their nature or according to commercial usage, have no connection with the subject of such contracts.

have been a number of cases involving collective price discrimination under Article 81, in nearly all these the objection appears to have been based on the collusive prevention of parallel imports rather than on discriminatory pricing *per se*.❶ Even though multi-firm predatory conduct could be also condemned thereunder, the pricing scheme under cartel predation is rather similar as single firm predation under Article 82.❷ Accordingly, only Article 82 shall be scrutinized hereafter.

Article 82 prohibits a firm's conduct which abuses a dominant position within the Community and may affect trade between Member States. It puts forth a non-exhaustive list of examples, two of which could be applied against predatory pricing conduct. Article 82 (a) prohibits "directly or indirectly imposing unfair purchase or selling prices or other

---

❶ For example, In Pittsburgh Corning Europe, the Commission of the EC's complaint was not that a higher price was charged on glass sales to Germany than elsewhere but that the pricing agreements between Pittsburgh Corning Europe and its distributors in Belgium and Holland effectively prevented arbitrage between high and low price countries. Similarly, in Kodak, the segmentation of markets was achieved by an arrangement between Kodak and its European sales subsidiaries under which each subsidiary charged the price prevailing in the member state of the buyer. In Grundig price differentiation between France and other member states was made possible, firstly, by undertaking from Grundig dealers not to sell outside their respective territories; and secondly, by Grundig's French franchisees having exclusive rights to import, or sell in France, goods bearing Grundig's international trade mark. Both the commission and the European court determined that these arrangements aimed at separating markets (rather than price discrimination itself) were objectionable and in breach of Article 85. Similarly, the commission's decisions in three recent cases involving price discrimination under Article 85, Distillers, BMW Belgium, and Kawasaki were based on the view that the pricing arrangements amounted to an export ban. *See* Richard Dale, *Antidumping Law in a Liberal Trade Order*, the Macmillan Press Ltd., 1980, p. 49.

❷ Christian Barthel, *Predatory Pricing Policy under EC and US Law*, Master Book, Faculty of Law, University of Lund, 2002, pp. 1, 21, http://web2.jur.lu.se/Internet/english/essay/Masterth.nsf/0/3C4189D171765812C1256BC9002B6A18/MYMFile/xsmall.pdf?OpenElement, last visited september 21, 2011.

unfair trading conditions", while Article 82 (c) prohibits "applying dissimilar conditions to equivalent transactions with other trading parties, thereby placing them at a competitive disadvantage". The former provision is applicable to predatory pricing conduct involving unreasonable low prices, whereas the latter condemns selective price cuts in the respective markets. [1]

3. 3. 2. 2 Cases

In the EU, compared with the enriched economic literature and considerable cases in the U. S., predatory pricing is a relatively new issue hence the cases are rather limited. In terms of price discrimnination, the EU also follows economic theories to deal with the anti-competitive effects in the primary-line competition by addressing predatory pricing under the unfairness provision of Article 82(a), and the relevant case law did not develop until the 1980s. [2]

Regarding predatory pricing, under Article 82 only a dominant firm can be condemned of predatory pricing behavior. To prove so, the relevant market has to be defined first, followed by assessing the firm's market power, taking into account their share of the market and other factors. [3] The next step is to condemn the abuse conduct of predatory pricing, involving the determination of unreasonable low prices. [4]

---

[1] Christian Barthel, *Predatory Pricing Policy under EC and US Law*, Master Book, Faculty of Law, University of Lund, 2002, p. 24, http://web2. jur. lu. se/Internet/english/essay/Masterth. nsf/0/3C4189D171765812C1256BC9002B6A18/ $ File/xsmall. pdf? Open Element, last visited September 21, 2011.

[2] Roger J. Van den Bergh & Peter D. Camesasca, *European Competition Law and Economics: A Comparative Perspective*, Intersentia-Hart, 2001, p. 262.

[3] OECD, *Abuse of Dominance and Monopolisation*, 1996, pp. 1, 175 – 176, http://www. oecd. org/dataoecd/0/61/2379408. pdf, last visited september 21, 2011.

[4] *Ibid.*, pp. 177 – 180.

Moreover, the injury to competition is required thereunder to condemn the anti-competitive conduct. Accordingly, similar to the U. S. , four aspects of requirement, i. e. market power, intent, predatory conduct, and the probability to destroy competition, should also be investigated in the EU.

Concerning the cases in the EU, the European Court of Justice (ECJ) places much emphasis on the cost-based test, and maintains the reference to intent as another element of its predation test. Taken the AKZO Case for instance, the ECJ addressed the issue of predatory pricing for the first time.[1] Both the *Tetra Pak II Case* and *Compagnie Maritime Belge Case* thereafter suggested that Chicago School has not had the same influence on European competition law. There is no special need to consider whether the company concerned had any

---

[1] In AKZO Case, AKZO, a Dutch producer holding approximately 50% of the organic peroxide market in Europe, engaged in systematic conduct, inter alia below-cost pricing, selective price cuts and threats, aiming to prevent ECS, a small competitor originally operating in the English market of flour additives from expanding in the related plastics submarket. AKZO first threatened ECS to drive them out of the flour additives market and eventually offered large discounts to ECS' customers. ECS claimed an infringement of Article 86 (now Article 82) EC Treaty to the Commission, which found that AKZO had abused its dominant position by offering below-cost prices.

According to the ECJ, prices below Average Variable Costs almost certainly indicative of predatory pricing and are to be considered abusive, since a firm has no interest in setting such prices unless it is to eliminate a rival because each sale entails a loss. Prices that are set above Average Variable Costs but below Average Total Costs are to be considered predatory only if the price is part of a plan for eliminating competition.

See, *e. g.* , Christian Barthel, *Predatory Pricing Policy under EC and US Law*, Master Book, Faculty of Law, University of Lund, 2002, pp. 1, 24, http://web2. jur. lu. se/Internet/english/essay/Masterth. nsf/0/3C4189D171765812C1256BC9002B6A18/MYMFile/xsmall. pdf? Open Element, last visited September 21, 2011.

reasonable prospect of recouping the losses. ❶

3.3.3 Basic Common Requirements on Predatory Price Discrimination

Apart from the U. S. and the EU, the issue of predatory price discrimination is also regulated in many other countries. ❷ A review into the U. S. and the EU etc. shows that certain consensus on Predatory Price Discrimination can be found. As to price discrimination, although the specific regulations vary among different countries, the essential

---

❶ In the Tetra Pak II case 1994, for the commission's finding that Tetra Pak had practiced predatory pricing was specifically challenged by reference to the economic theory accepted in the most recent American case law. Tetra Pak argued that, even if it had priced its products under cost, it could not have been indulging in predatory pricing because it had no reasonable hope of recouping its losses in the long term. The court, however, upheld the Commission's finding without any serious examination of this argument, maintaining that where a producer charged AKZO-type loss-making prices, a breach of Article 82 (then 86) EC Treaty was established ipso facto without any need to consider specifically whether the company concerned had any reasonable prospect of recouping the losses which it had incurred.

In the following Compagnie Maritime Belge Case, various shipping companies abused their dominant position by employing the strategy of "fighting ships". The firms were members of a shipping conference which engaged in a predatory pricing conduct by selectively offering low prices on routes of their rival Grimaldi and Cobelfret, not being a member of the shipping conference, in order to eliminate the competition. Whenever a sailing was announced by the latter, the members of the conference would employ their ships on that route. The freight prices were drastically reduced and different from the ones normally charged, with the sharing of the loss of revenues by the conference members. In this case, the ECJ did not follow the suggestion that there is a need to establish an intention or a possibility of recoupment should be part of the test for abusively low pricing by dominant undertakings.

See, *e. g.*, Roger J. Van den Bergh & Peter D. Camesasca, *European Competition Law and Economics: A Comparative Perspective*, Intersentia-Hart, 2001, pp. 300 – 305.

❷ For the introduction of other countries, for example, Canada, Australia, etc., *See*, *e. g.*, Richard Dale, *Antidumping Law in a Liberal Trade Order*, the Macmillan Press Ltd., 1980, pp. 52 – 53.

idea is the same: abiding by economic theories, competition law considers that price discrimination in the primary-line competition is anti-competitive only when it is proved to be predatory pricing.

In regard to predatory price discrimination, four basic elements can be identified in determining this abusive conduct of dominant market power, including market conditions, intent of monopoly, cost calculation and injury to competition. The relevant competition authorities may attach different emphasis to each element from period to period in different countries. Taken the U. S. for instance, previously it concerned more on the cost calculation, but has turned to a strict recoupment analysis emphasizing the hurt to competition. In the EU, predatory pricing is a relatively new issue and a great attention is paid to the cost calculation.

3. 4 Summary

Modern competition Law is strongly influenced by economic theories, especially the efficiency analysis. As to the competition policy, ever since the last two decades, there has been more convergence of objectives between countries, three basic competition principles thereof can be identified, including protecting competitive process, promoting economic efficiency, and maximization of consumer welfare.

As to the competition rules, price discrimination and predatory pricing are normally within the concern of the anti-competitive firm behavior of abuse of a dominant position. A further exploration into the major countries, including the U. S. , the EU, suggests that a common basic standard can be identified. In terms of price discrimination, competition law considers that price discrimination in the primary-line competition as linking with antidumping laws, is anti-competitive as long as it is proved to be predatory pricing. Relating to the common basic standard of condemning predatory price discrimination, four basic elements can be identified, including market conditions, intent of monopoly, cost calculation and injury to competition.

Chapter IV Dumping: Antidumping Law or Competition Law*

After confirming that the original and supposed objective of antidumping is to deal with predatory dumping, which can also be addressed by competition law through predatory price discrimination, the next issue is to explore whether putting dumping under competition rules instead of antidumping rules can be less vulnerable to "protectionist abuse". This chapter attempts to achieve so from three perspectives. First of all, the basic elements of the two sets of rules on low-price selling will be compared and evaluated. Secondly, we will put the rules against the background of modern free trade world, to analyze their relationship with the modern basic trade and competition principles respectively. Moreover, the typical cases as well as empirical studies will be discussed to see the the interaction of the two sets of rules in practice.

4.1 Less Protectionist Abuse in Competition Law

In order to appraise which law is less susceptible to protectionist, a comprehensive comparison between antidumping rules and competition rules must first be made. In the following part, four basic elements of the two sets of rules, including the objectives, basic substantive rules, basic procedural rules, and the remedies, will be compared and analyzed.

---

* 此部分内容经修改已发表,Biying, *Substituting Antidumping Law with Competition Law: the better option in avoiding Protectionist Abuse*, 载[日]《法政研究》,2009 年第76 卷第3 号, 第447 ~498 页。

4.1.1 Objectives: Less Susceptible to Protectionism

As to the objectives of competition policy, for hundreds of years, countries design various competition policies and laws which are influenced by varying economic, social and cultural needs and interests. ❶ With harmonization and convergence of antitrust laws all around the world, competition rules become more similar, which to some extent remove conflicts related to antitrust goals and interpretations. ❷ Hence, ever since the last two decades, consensus on competition objectives has been reached across countries which have well-developed competition laws and policies. ❸

According to Weinrauch, there are two essential points concerning the consensus. The first one is that competition policy is to protect competition from private and public business restraints that adversely interfere with the competitive process, and that the competitive process should be protected not to promote competition for the competitor's sake but to achieve other goals. ❹ The second one is certain common main objectives, including economic efficiency, market integration and consumer

---

❶ Roland Weinrauch, *Competition Law in the WTO: the Rationale for a Framework Agreement*, Wien: NWV Neuer Wissenschaftlicher Verlag, 2004, p. 24.

❷ Olivier Bertrand & Marc Ivaldi, *European Competition Policy in International Markets*, A Contribution for the BRUEGEL's Project on Europe And The Global Economy, 2006, pp. 1, 30, http://www.intertic.org/Conference/Toulouse.pdf, last visited September 21, 2011.

❸ Roland Weinrauch, *Competition Law in the WTO: the Rationale for a Framework Agreement*, Wien: NWV Neuer Wissenschaftlicher, 2004, p. 28.

❹ *Ibid.*

welfare could be defined.[1] Except for market integration which receives consensus mostly among bilateral or regional areas, such as the EU, the other key points are generally shared among major countries.[2]

---

[1] Roland considered that consequently, it seems to be difficult to define certain objectives for an international competition law agreement. However, more and more convergence of objectives between countries has been noted within the last decade. Therefore, I think that certain common main objectives, such as economic efficiency, market integration and consumer welfare could be defined for an international agreement, while it may be advisable to pursue other minor goals through separate government policies. *See* Roland Weinrauch, *Competition Law in the WTO: the Rationale for a Framework Agreement*, Wien : NWV Neuer Wissenschaftlicher Verlag, 2004, p. 30.

[2] For example, Kennedy pointed out in his book that "Antitrust law...focuses on the maintenance of open markets, the promotion of competition, and the maximization of consumer welfare." *See* Kevin C. Kennedy, *Competition Law and the World Trade Organization: the Limits of Multilateralism*, London: Sweet & Maxwell, 2001, p. 235.

Mario Marques Mendes stated that competition policy teaches that competitive rivalry in the marketplace is the most reliable means, consistent with a free market economy, of achieving three major dynamic objectives: efficiency in the allocation of productive resources through time innovative vigor in the production process, and distribution of products to the consumer at lowest possible prices. Efficiency in the allocation of global resources in thus furthered and prices are lowered towards a global minimum. *See* Mario Marques Mendes, *Antitrust in a World of Interrelated Economies: the Interplay Between Antitrust and Trade Policies in the U. S. and the EEC*, Etudes Europeennes, 1991, p. 149.

Talyor also recognized that: "competition law gives pre-eminence to considerations of economic efficiency... competition is viewed as a means of disciplining firms, reducing their market power, and thus ensuring that the market forces of supply and demand operate more effectively and efficiently in allocating global resources... competition law seeks to lessen power imbalances between firms to ensure that all firms have an equal opportunity to compete on their merits. Competition law also prevents producers from using certain business practices to capture additional wealth from consumers... indeed, competition laws are commonly drafted so as to favour the interests of end consumers over the interests of producers." *See* Martyn D. Taylor, *International Competition Law: a New Dimension Por the WTO?* Cambridge Univ. Press Inc. 2006, p. 264.

OECD Publication in 1984 defined the major goal of competition policy in this way: "competition policy has as its central economic goal the preservation and promotion of the competitive process, a process which encourages efficiency in the production and allocation of goods and services, and over time, through its effects on innovation and adjustment to technological change, a dynamic process of sustained economic growth. In conditions of effective competition, rivals have equal opportunities to compete for business on the basis and equality of their outputs, and resource deployment follows market success in meeting consumers' demand at the lowest possible cost." *See* OECD, *Competition and Trade Policies: Their Interaction*, OECD Publications, 1984, p. 86.

With regard to antidumping rules, international trade economists have traditionally taken a very different view of dumping from international trade officials. [1] From the traditional dumping theory of Viner[2], to the modern dumping theory of Willig[3], most of the international trade economists are of the view that dumping is kind of transnational price discrimination and only predatory dumping is generally recognized as harmful. [4] However, this theory, the original and fundamental justification of antidumping system, which determines the existence of the whole system and sets the criteria for all the other refinements of antidumping rules, has been gradually ignored by international trade officials during the development of modern antidumping rules. The slogan "dumping is

---

[1] P. J. Lloyd, Antidumping and Competition Law, in Patrick F. J *Macrory et al.*, *eds.*, *II The World Trade Organization: Legal, Economic and Political Analysis*, Springer 2005, p. 72.

[2] Jacob Viner, *Dumping: A Problem in International Trade*, the Univ. of Chicago Press, 1923.

[3] Robert D. Willig, Economic Effects of Antidumping Policy, in Robert Z. Lawerence, ed., *Brookings Trade Forum*, Brookings Institution, 1998.

[4] "Economists generally agree that, in the absence of predatory intent, dumping is essentially harmless for the importing country because the welfare gains for consumers from low-priced imports more than offset any harm to producer welfare in the country of importation." *See* Kevin C. Kennedy, Competition Law and the World Trade Organization: the Limits of Multilateralism, Sweet & Maxwell, 2001, p. 235.

"However, only predatory pricing gives rise to a legitimate economic rationale for prohibiting dumping: when dumping is merely international price discrimination, the export market benefits." *See* Michael J. Trebilcock & Robert Howse, *the Regulation of International Trade*, 2nd Edition, Routledge, 1999, p. 188.

harmful or unfair" became a self-evident premise for a long time. [1]

As a consequence, the easily applied system of antidumping, as Taylor described, pretending as a universally accepted fact but actually with no well-founded theoretical basis, is extraordinarily attractive for industries seeking protection, and for governments inclined to provide protection. [2] Such lobbying by producers that are sufficiently concentrated and have sufficient vested interests and resources has a high chance of success given that politically appealing arguments can be made for protection against the so-called "unfair" foreign competition. [3] Hence, antidumping rules are increasingly being abused for protectionism in a large scale.

Comparing the essential objectives of competition law with antidumping law, it is found that, influenced by economic theories, setting up the basic goal of protecting competitive process rather than the individual competitors, aiming at promoting economic efficiency as well as protection of consumer welfare, competition rules can take the overall welfare of the country into consideration, instead of only protecting the welfare of the producers. Hence, it is less vulnerable to be influenced by those domestic firms with vested interests, and thereby is less susceptible to protectionism.

---

[1] Ehrenhaft stated that: "...nor the GATT or the WTO Agreements on the subject set forth any clear explanation of why the practice of 'dumping' is considered 'unfair' so as to warrant remedial measures. Rather the 'unfairness' of the practice appears to have seemed self-evident to legislators and trade negotiators..." *See* Peter D. Ehrenhaft, *Is Interface of Antidumping and Antitrust Laws Possible*? George Washington International Law Review, 2002, Vol. 34, pp. 363, 367.

[2] Martyn D. Taylor, *International Competition Law: A New Dimension for the WTO*? Cambridge Univ. Press Inc. 2006, p. 269.

[3] *Ibid.*

4.1.2 Basic Substantive Rules: Predatory Pricing v. Healthy Competition

The second aspect of the comparative analysis is concerned with basic substantive rules. Regarding competition, there are four common sections of competition field, that is, horizontal restraints, vertical restraints, abuse of a dominant position, i. e., unlawful monopolization, and merger and acquisition. The issue of price discrimination and predatory pricing are mainly within the concerns of abuse of a dominant position, i. e., unlawful monopolization.[1] Unlike other sections under competition field, with respect to price discrimination and predation some consensus has been reached.[2] Modern economic theories suggest that there can be no presumption that price discrimination is injurious. And with regard to the primary-line competition[3] that may link with

---

[1] This has been generally recognized, For example, in Model Law on Competition, both predatory behavior and discriminatory are "Act or behaviour considered as abuse" under the category of "Acts or behaviour constituting an abuse of a dominant position of market power". *See* UNCTAD, *Model Law on Competition*, Article 4 (II), http://www.unctad.org/en/docs/tdrbpconf5d7.en.pdf, last visited September 21, 2011.

[2] *See, e. g.*, Gunnar Niels, *What is Antidumping Policy Really About*? Journal of Economic Surveys, 2002, Vol. 14, pp. 467, 485, http://www.blackwell-synergy.com/links/doi/10.1111/1467-6419.00118, last visited September 21, 2011.

[3] In the consideration of economics, since price discrimination can be either pro-competitive or anti-competitive, the problem is to identify those situations where it is proved to be anticompetitive. In order to achieve this purpose, two levels of competition have been distinguished. The first one is the primary-line competition, that is, competition between the discriminating monopolist and his rivals in the same line of business; and the second one is the secondary-line competition, that is, competition between the discriminating monopolist's customers (who may, for instance, be retailers) and their business rivals. Antidumping law, involving foreign conductors and their domestic competitors, links with competition law only in the primary-line competition, *See* Richard Dale, *Antidumping Law in a Liberal Trade Order*, the Macmillan Press Ltd. 1980, pp. 23-27.

antidumping, price discrimination can only be considered as anti-competitive in the extreme case when it amounts to predatory pricing. [1]

As to modern competition rules, the U. S. and the EU are considered as two basic models referred to and followed by most of the other countries. In the U. S. , the relevant federal provisions on predatory price discrimination are found in three statutes. A general approach to this issue is contained in the Sherman Act, and a more specific one can be found in Clayton Act and its amendment Robinson-Patman Act. [2] In the EU, predatory price discrimination is indicated in EC Treaty, Article 82

---

[1] *Richard Dale, Antidumping Law in a Liberal Trade Order*, the Macmillan Press Ltd. 1980, pp. 23 – 26.

[2] Sherman Act did not stipulate the issue of price discrimination, but in Section 2 it condemns monopolization or the attempt to monopolize any part of commerce among the U. S. States, the issue of predatory pricing is generally governed under this section. *See* U. S. C. A. Title 15, Section 1 – 7. The specific stipulation of price discrimination is in the Section 2(a) of Clayton Act, which is late amended by Robinson-Patman Act to detail and broaden the provisions. The general stipulation is that: it shall be unlawful for any person engaged in commerce, in the course of such commerce, either directly or indirectly, to discriminate in price between different purchasers of commodities of like grade and quality, where either or any of the purchasers involved in such discrimination are in commerce, where such commodities are sold for use, consumption , or resale... and where the effect of such discrimination may be substantially to lessen competition or tend to create a monopoly in any line of commerce, or to injure, destroy, or prevent competition with any person who either grants or knowingly receives the benefit of such discrimination, or with customers of either of them. *See* U. S. v. Grinnell Corp. 384 U. S. 563 ,1996, 571.

(ex Article 86). ❶ Influenced by economic theories, modern competition rules *ad summam*, either in the U. S., the EU, or any other major countries, consider that price discrimination in the primary-line competition is anti-competitive only when it is proven to be predatory pricing. ❷ In the determination of predatory pricing, four common prerequisites can be identified, which include a high threshold of or dominant market power, requisite intent, price-below-cost calculation and injury

---

❶ In the EU, the relevant rules on predatory price discrimination are indicated in EC Treaty, Article 82(ex Article 86), which provides that: "any abuse by one or more undertakings of a dominant position within the common market or in a substantial part of it shall be prohibited as incompatible with the common market insofar as it may affect trade between Member States. Such abuse may, in particular, consist in: (a) directly or indirectly imposing unfair purchase or selling prices or other unfair trading conditions; (b) limiting production, markets or technical development to the prejudice of consumers; (c) applying dissimilar conditions to equivalent transactions with other trading parties, thereby placing them at a competitive disadvantage; (d) making the conclusion of contracts subject to acceptance by the other parties of supplementary obligations which, by their nature or according to commercial usage, have no connection with the subject of such contracts." *See* EC Treaty.

❷ For example, as to the U. S., over the past decade, one significant development is that primary line discrimination under Clayton Act has been interpreted more harmoniously with predatory pricing under Sherman Act. *See* OECD, *Predatory Pricing*, 1989. pp. 1, 42, http://www.oecd.org/dataoecd/7/54/2375661.pdf, last visited September 21, 2011. As to price discrimination, the EU also follows economic theories to deal with the anti-competitive effects in the primary-line competition through addressing predatory pricing under the unfairness provision of Article 82(a). *See* Roger J. Van den Bergh & Peter D. Camesasca, *European Competition Law and Economics: A Comparative Perspective*, Intersentia-Hart, 2001, p. 262.

For the introduction of other countries, for example, Canada, Australia, etc., *See, e. g.*, Richard Dale, *Antidumping Law in a Liberal Trade Order*, the Macmillan Press Ltd. 1980, pp. 52–53.

to competition. [1] Notwithstanding, competition authorities in different countries may choose to emphasize on particular prerequisites in different time periods. [2]

With regard to modern antidumping rules, due to the uniform requirement of the WTO Antidumping Agreement, although the nuts and bolts of them may vary among different countries, the basic requirements on dumping are by and large the same. [3] In order to condemn a dumping, antidumping rules require three fold of proof, including low-price calculation, injury to the domestic industry, as well as a causal link between the two. [4] In the following part, the basic substantive rules of competition and antidum-ping shall be compared and analyzed respectively.

4. 1. 2. 1 Essential Basis

There are five main distinctions between competition and antidumping, in terms of their substantive rules. The first essential distinction

---

[1] For example, Gabrielle Marceau pointed out that: "Attempted monopolization requires: (1) specific intent to control prices or destroy competition; (2) predatory or anti-competitive conduct directed towards that end, and (3) a dangerous probability of successful monopolization. In the third requirement for attempt to monopolize, that of dangerous probability, there is de facto prerequisite for a high threshold of market power." *See* Gabrielle Marceau, *Antidumping and Anti-trust Issues in Free-trade Areas*, Oxford Univ. Press Inc. 1994, p. 262.

[2] In the U. S., previously it focuses on the cost calculation but now turn to a strict recoupment analysis that emphasizing the hurt to competition. For the EU, predatory pricing is a relatively new issue and it emphasizes a lot on the cost calculation.

[3] According to WTO ADA, Article 18.4: Each Member shall take all necessary steps, of a general or particular character, to ensure, not later than the date of entry into force of the WTO Agreement for it, the conformity of its laws, regulations and administrative procedures with the provisions of this Agreement as they may apply for the Member in question.

[4] WTO ADA, Article 7.

lies in the basic notion in the system design. With regard to dumping, economic theories identified complex motives and causes for dumping practices, which indicates that only predatory dumping can be considered problematic and might be sanctioned, and most of the other types of dumping, such as market-expansion dumping, cyclical dumping and etc., are actually accepted as pro-competitive.[1] This notion seems to be totally ignored in the long development of antidumping rules and modern antidumping rules consider nearly all types of dumping as *per se* harmful without any discernment.

While in the consideration of modern competition policy, the assumption of antidumping rules classifying spatial price differentiation of any kind, as *per se* unfair can only be justified if perfect competition serves as the theoretical benchmark for analysis, modern competition policy has long abandoned this model due to its utmost unrealistic assumptions.[2] Instead, modern competition rules acknowledge that price discrimination can either be pro-competitive or anti-competitive. Hence, they are more selective in their application and are more effective at distinguishing between harmful predatory pricing and healthy competitive pricing, between fair and unfair trade practices.

4. 1. 2. 2 Market Power

The second distinction is about whether it is necessary to check market. In the competition context, predatory pricing is generally viewed as

---

[1] *See, e. g.*, Andreas Knorr, *Antidumping Rules vs. Competition Rules*, Institution for World Economics and International Management, 2004, pp. 1, 10, http://www.iwim.uni-bremen.de/publikationen/pdf/W031.pdf, last visited May 3, 2011.

[2] *Ibid.*

one of the abusive conduct of dominant market position, so those foreign firms undertaking such behaviors should have certain requisite degree of market power in the market. [1] Although the relevant thresholds of market power are different among nations, the basic procedure is more or less the same. [2] Specifically speaking, first of all is the definition of the relevant market, which is defined in terms of both product and geography in order to identify those competitors who are actually capable of constraining the behavior. [3] Once the relevant product and geographic

---

[1] Martyn D. Taylor, *International Competition Law: A New Dimension for the WTO?* Cambridge Univ. Press Inc. 2006, p. 277.

[2] *See more* Kevin C. Kennedy, *Competition Law and the World Trade Organization: The Limits of Multilateralism*, London: Sweet & Maxwell, 2001, p. 227 ; Gabrielle Marceau, *Antidumping and Anti-trust Issues in Free-trade Areas*, Oxford Univ. Press Inc. 1994, p. 111; Robert D. Willig, Economic Effects of Antidumping Policy, in Robert Z. Lawerence, ed. , *Brookings Trade Forum*, Brookings Institution, 1998, pp. 74 – 75.

[3] Specific criteria are different among countries. In the EU, e. g, the relevant product market is defined as: all those products and/or services which are regarded as interchangeable or substitutable by the consumer, by reason of the products' characteristics, their prices and their intended use. The relevant geographic market is defined as : the area in which the undertakings concerned are involved in the supply and demand of products or services, in which the conditions of competition are sufficiently homogeneous and which can be distinguished from neighboring areas because the conditions of competition are appreciably different in those areas. The scope of the relevant geographic market starts at the national level and might expand to include the Community-wide level.

In defining the relevant markets, the U. S. , like the EU requires the identification of the firms that are competitors in a given product in a given geographic area. After defining the relevant market, the U. S. and the EU evaluate market shares and consider barriers to market entry. However, the European Commission's market definitions, in the opinion of some commentators, "tend to be more consonant with views of practical business people, less theoretically rigorous than US market definitions. *See* Kevin C. Kennedy, *Competition Law and the World Trade Organization: the Limits of Multilateralism*, London: Sweet & Maxwell, 2001, p. 228.

markets are determined, market share of the firm or firms under review or investigation is determined.[1] Apart from the definition of relevant market and a firm's market share, the number of competitors and their respective market shares, as well as excess capacity in the market and the ease of entry into the market are all factors that are taken into account in determining market power.[2] This indicates that competition sanctions shall never apply to low-price selling by any firm without market power.

By contrast, antidumping rules are applied to markets irrespective of whether or not they have these characteristics.[3] They are simply triggered by a domestic competitor alleging that prices of imports do not

---

[1] In the EU, a 50 percent and sometimes 40 percent market share translates into dominance, especially if the next largest firms lags far behind. The EU takes the view that a dominant position can generally exist when a firm has a market share of 40 – 45 percent, although dominance may exist even if the market share is 20 – 40 percent.

The U. S. , unlike the EU, measures market power and its possible increase microeconomically by considering the relevant factor in the specific context. The supreme court has held, however, that monopoly power could be inferred from a market share of 80 percent. Where barriers to market entry are high, other courts have required less market share for a finding of monopoly power. In the U. S. , courts consistently find that a market share of less than 70 percent is insufficient to establish dominance, and that a market share of less than 40 percent virtually precludes a finding of monopoly.

In Canada, in the context of a predatory pricing investigation, the Predatory pricing enforcement guidelines issued by the Director of investigation and research in 1992 note that "it is unlikely that an alleged predatory with a market share of less than 35% would have the ability to unilaterally affect pricing." *See ibid.*, pp. 229 – 230.

[2] Kevin C. Kennedy, *Competition Law and the World Trade Organization: the Limits of Multilateralism*, London: Sweet & Maxwell, 2001, p. 230.

[3] Robert D. Willig, Economic Effects of Antidumping Policy, in Robert Z. Lawerence, ed. , *Brookings Trade Forum*, Brookings Institution, 1998, p. 75.

cover their full costs or that there is a negative differential in prices.[1] Hence, through setting the requisite degree of market power, competition rules are more selective and efficient than antidumping rules in relieving those harmless, pro-competitive behaviors of firms without market power.

4. 1. 2. 3 Requisite Intent

The third distinction is in requisite intent. The logic of competition rules is that for predatory pricing to occur, a firm with market power must have used its market power with the requisite purpose or intent.[2] Hence, the exemptions of purposes, such as the disposal of such commodities as fresh and living commodities, seasonal commodities and overstocked commodities at reduced prices in accordance with law, can be proven and used as defense in a competition suit. The degrees of emphasis on predatory intent are quite different among countries. Some would require a showing of a specific intent to destroy whilst others would recognize the difficulty of proving this subjective requisite. Instead, they look into the actual market effect on competition and try to reflect or turn this subjective requisite into an objective one, which

---

[1] Gabrielle Marceau, *Antidumping and Anti-trust Issues in Free-trade Areas*, Oxford Univ. Press Inc. 1994, p. 111.

[2] Martyn D. Taylor, *International Competition Law: A New Dimension for the* WTO? Cambridge Univ. Press Inc. 2006, p. 278.

results in setting up various tests on price and cost calculation. [1] Notwithstanding, predatory purpose is still required by the competition laws of many nations. [2]

In this aspect, competition rules also differ from antidumping rules which do not require any intent or purpose. Regardless of why firms sell their products at a lower price, modern antidumping rules are applied to all low-price selling, simply requiring the evidences of price difference as well as consequential injurious effects. [3] The distinction in requisite intent also indicates that competition rules are more selective and efficient than antidumping rules in exempting those low-price behaviors of the firms with the normal meeting, the competition intent.

4. 1. 2. 4 Price Calculation

The fourth difference is price calculation. With regard to competition, the principal focus of predatory pricing is on below-cost sales. A number of scholars have devoted themselves to "create an optimal legal

---

[1] "However, consensus breaks down in the case law and the literature on the issue of predatory intent. Some writers would require a showing of a specific intent to destroy as evidenced by conduct that would not be employed in the normal course of competition. Others reject this view and any requirement of a showing of predatory intent, instead looking to the actual market effect on competition. Under this view, a predatory pricing plaintiff may lose business on pricing grounds because the defendant has engaged in aggressive, but lawful price competition, not because of anti-competitive predatory pricing. Distinguishing between the two has spawned a number of tests that turn on an analysis of below-cost pricing." *See*, *e. g.*, Kevin C. Kennedy, *Competition Law and the World Trade Organization: the Limits of Multilateralism*, London: Sweet & Maxwell 2001, p. 231.

[2] Martyn D. Taylor, *International Competition Law*: A New Dimension for the WTO? Cambridge Univ. Press Inc. 2006, p. 278.

[3] *Ibid.*

rule for predatory pricing"[1], and various tests have been brought forward, including price-cost tests, performance tests, rule of reason tests and structural tests.[2] Common recognition is that "sales below

---

[1] Roger J. Van den Bergh & Peter D. Camesasca, *European Competition Law and Economics: A Comparative Perspective*, Intersentia-Hart, 2001, p. 287.

[2] Short-run cost-based rules by Areeda and Turner of Harvard: pricing below short-run marginal cost should be unlawful, and that short-run marginal cost can be approximated by short-run variable cost. *See* Phillip Areeda & Donald F. Turner, *Predatory Pricing and Related Practices under Section 2 of the Sherman Act*, Harvard Law Review, 1974, Vol. 88, pp. 697 – 733, http://scholar.google.com/scholar?hl = zh – CN&lr = &q = info: U79X – gD – nAEJ: scholar.google.com/&output = viewport, last visited September 21, 2011.

Long-term cost-based rules by Posner: the long-run marginal costs were a better measure because some equally or more efficient competitors (more efficient in having lower long-run marginal costs) will lack the ability, or the will, to sustain losses in the short run. For practical reasons, he also substituted marginal by variable costs. He would consider the intent of the predator and would request the plaintiff to make an initial showing that the market was predisposed to effective predatory pricing. *See* Richard A. Posner, *Antitrust Law: An Economic Perspective*, St. Paul, Minnesota, 1981.

The rule-of-reason test by Scherer: long-run welfare can sometimes be maximized with a dominant firm's prices either above or below marginal costs. He would look at the relative efficiency of the enterprises in the market, the minimum efficient scale, the monopolist's effect on other enterprises, and the subsequent prices. *See* F. M. Scherer, *Predatory pricing and the Sherman Act: A comment*, Harvard Law Review, 1976, Vol. 89, pp. 869 – 890.

The Two-tier rules by Joskow and Klevorick: market structure determines whether predation is a possible strategy. When predation is alleged, the market structure should firstly be analysed according to three components: short-run monopoly power, conditions of entry, and "dynamic effects of competitors and entrants". Short-run monopoly would be measured by the predator's market share and the elasticity of the demand for its products. Conditions of entry refer to the speed with which potential competition becomes real competition. They would look at capital requirements, consumers' loyalties, the quality of information. The dynamic of the market is determined by rapid growth or decline. Where predation would not cause a competitor to quit or deter entry, any cut in price would be tolerated. The second phase of his enquiry would be a "pricing rule of reason" test in which the intent would be a relevant though not a necessary factor. Prices below the average variable would be deemed predatory (one exception being where the alleged predator can show that closure of the firm was more costly, which would affect the opportunity costs). price between average variable and average total costs would be presumed predatory (except depressed prices); prices above total costs would be presumed non-predatory unless they change within two years. *See* Paul Joskow & Alvin Klevorick, *A Framework for Analysing Predatory Pricing Policy*, Yale Law Journal, 1979, Vol. 89, pp. 213 – 270.

cost" is viewed as prima facie evidence of predatory intent and thus an anti-competitive purpose. [1]

Antidumping rules paid less attention to the cost-price relation. The most important thing in antidumping investigation is to simply detect a kind of price difference. According to WTO Antidumping Agreement, dumping occurs if a product is sold for export at a price below its normal value, i. e. when "the export price of a product exported from one country to another is less than the comparable price for the like product when destined for consumption in the exporting country". Here normal value refers to comparable price in the exporting country. [2] There are also other stipulations applied in the event that the above comparable price cannot be considered as normal value. For instance, normal value could be drawn from export price to a third country, or a price constructed by the "cost of production in the country of origin plus a reasonable amount for administrative, selling and general costs and for profits". [3] It is even easier to decide the existence of price difference either involving a third country or constructing a price.

Comparing competition rules and antidumping rules from the aspect of price calculation can also expound that competition rules are much stricter, more careful in conducting a price-below-cost calculation, rather than a simple price-difference calculation. It is less easy for vested interests to start up the investigation and to provide relevant evidences. Hence, competition rules are less subject to protectionism than antidumping rules.

---

[1] Martyn D. Taylor, *International Competition Law: A New Dimension for the WTO?* Cambridge Univ. Press Inc. 2006, p. 278.

[2] WTO ADA, Article 2.

[3] *Ibid.*

4. 1. 2. 5 Injury

The fifth distinction lies in injury. Competition rules differ from antidumping rules in two fold, i. e. , the concept of injury, as well as the chain of causation between the behavior and the injury. ❶ As to the concept of injury, injury to "competition" is the standard used. ❷ Modern competition rules require the injury of predatory pricing to affect competitive process itself. In predatory pricing cases, unreasonable restraint of trade (which can be *per se* in the case of, e. g. , price fixing) or a substantial lessening of competition must be proven. ❸

In contrast with competition rules, injury to consumers of direct competitors is not even required in antidumping investigation. ❹ Antidumping rules stress more on injury to domestic competitors, and antidumping duties are in fact applied in circumstances where they preserve the high profitability or inefficiency of domestic firms, which opens the gates for protectionists. ❺

Differences are also apparent in terms of the causation between the behavior and the injury. Competition rules require a clear evidence of causation and injury. They require a "significant" causal relation

❶ Rodney de C. Grey, *the Relationship Between Antidumping Policy and Competition*, Positive Agenda and Future Trade Negotiations, Geneva, UN, 2000, pp. 436 - 437, http://ctrc.sice.oas.org/geograph/compol/Articles/Grey_AD_1999.doc, last visited September 21, 2011.

❷ Gabrielle Marceau, *Antidumping and Anti-trust Issues in Free-trade Areas*, Oxford Univ. Press Inc. 1994, pp. 113 - 114.

❸ Kevin C. Kennedy, *Competition Law and the World Trade Organization: the Limits of Multilateralism*, London: Sweet & Maxwell, 2001, p. 236.

❹ Gabrielle Marceau, *Antidumping and Anti-trust Issues in Free-trade Areas*, Oxford Univ. Press Inc. 1994, p. 113.

❺ Martyn D. Taylor, *International Competition Law: A New Dimension for the WTO?* Cambridge Univ. Press Inc. 2006, p. 280.

between price discrimination and injury, and they require a "substantial" lessening of competition. ❶ In this respect, losses of sales are not sufficient to prove injury caused by the practices of the other firm. ❷ The anti-competitive conduct must be the cause of the complainant's. For instance, an important defense is available under the Robinson-Patman Act, but unavailable under the antidumping law–the "meeting competition" defense. ❸ In addition, in private antitrust litigation, the claimants must have personally suffered injury. Since healthy competition always involves pressures to lower one's price, a reduction in price does not necessarily indicate an injury to competition. ❹

On the contrary, there is almost no requirement of causation in antidumping cases. ❺ Although in law dumped imports must cause or threaten to cause material injury, in practice there is no need for the petitioners to show that dumped imports are the "sole, principal or even substantial" cause of injury. In fact, an unedifying definition of material injury as "harm which is not inconsequential, inmaterial, or unimportant" is provided. ❻ Hence, even if the quantity of goods imported has not increased, decreases in domestic production which raise the

---

❶ *See, e. g.*, Patrick A. Messerlin, *Should Antidumping Rules be Replaced by National or International Competition Rules*, the Swiss Review of International Economic Relations, 1994, Vol. 49, pp. 351, 360.

❷ Gabrielle Marceau, *Antidumping and Anti-trust Issues in Free-trade Areas*, Oxford Univ. Press Inc. 1994, p. 113.

❸ Kevin C. Kennedy, *Competition Law and the World Trade Organization: the Limits of Multilateralism*, London: Sweet & Maxwell, 2001, p. 236.

❹ Gabrielle Marceau, *Antidumping and Anti-trust Issues in Free-trade Areas*, Oxford Univ. Press Inc. 1994, p. 113.

❺ *Ibid.*

❻ Kevin C. Kennedy, *Competition Law and the World Trade Organization: the Limits of Multilateralism*, London: Sweet & Maxwell, 2001, p. 236.

proportion between foreign and domestic goods up, can be considered as a potential injury. ❶ The loose requirement of the causation between the behavior and the injury also increases the protectionist abuse of anti-dumping rules in practice.

4. 1. 2. 6 *Possible Protectionist Effects: Competition Rules v. Antidumping Rules*

From the above analysis from the perspective of basic substantive rules, it can be seen that in addressing the same type of low-price selling conduct, with regard to antidumping rules, there is no need to examine either into market power or requisite intent allowing for exemption. Moreover, injury can be easily established with a loose chain of causation. The most important or in fact the only prerequisite in condemning dumping is calculation of price difference. Hence, "harmful dumping" can be comparatively easily established. Successful anti-dumping actions are therefore flourishing and being taken advantages by protectionist.

On the contrary, in addressing predatory price discrimination, competition rules are more selective in their application and are more effective at distinguishing between fair and unfair practices. Since low-price selling may have either a pro-competitive or an anti-competitive effect, competition rules are much more sophisticated in distinguishing between healthy competition and harmful predatory conducts, which requires a careful examination of market power, requisite intent, price-below cost calculation, as well as a comparatively strict injury test in each case. As Taylor considered in his book:

---

❶ Gabrielle Marceau, *Antidumping and Anti-trust Issues in Free-trade Areas*, Oxford Univ. Press Inc. 1994, p. 113.

When courts consider predatory pricing cases they typically have difficulty distinguishing between inefficient and unfair "predatory behavior", and efficient and fair "fierce competition". One is to be condemned, [whereas] the other is to be endorsed. Given the difficulty in distinguishing between these two types of conduct, there is an understandable reluctance on the part of courts to conclude that predatory pricing has occurred. Successful predatory pricing actions are therefore extremely rare in competition law unless there is clear evidence of pricing below cost. No such difficulties arise in antidumping actions. ❶

In this respect, competition rules are considered better than antidumping rules, without being abused for protectionism.

However, it is not the intention of this book to argue that competition rules are absolutely immune to protectionism in addressing all of the issues underneath. In fact, in addressing certain issues such as merger and takeover, competition rules can also have protectionist effects. Although consensus on basic competition objectives has been received all around the world in recent decades, there are also many supplementary objectives of competition policy which vary from one country to another. This includes, for example ensuring fairness and equity in marketplace transactions; promoting democratic values and the development of a market economy; facilitating economic liberalization; considering the effects that business practices such as mergers may have on employment, local communities and regional development. ❷ And also, competition policy in some countries is supposed to protect small and medium

---

❶ Martyn D. Taylor, *International Competition Law: A New Dimension for the WTO?* Cambridge Univ. Press Inc. 2006, p. 278.

❷ Roland Weinrauch, *Competition Law in the WTO: the Rationale for a Framework Agreement*, Wien: NWV Neuer Wissenschaftlicher Verlag 2004, p. 27.

sized businesses in certain sectors. [1] Hence, in designing relevant substantive rules as well as in interpreting each specific prerequisite of such rules, those supplementary objectives as above might also open the door for certain domestic vested interests, e. g. , in determining the relevant market in a merger case. [2] Monti in his book also pointed out that several member states within EU have in place legislation that is designed to protect foreign takeovers of national companies, and quite a few cases were given to illustrate such protectionist effects of competition rules. [3] Especially in key sectors of the economy such as gas, electric utilities, banking etc. , the goals of competition on the one hand, and national protectionism on the other, continue to clash despite the best hopes of the original architects and modern leaders. [4]

4. 1. 3 Basic Procedural Rules: Less Discretion in Implementations

This part shall continue to compare and analyze competition rules and antidumping rules from the perspective of procedural rules. With regard to antidumping procedures, the broad discretion of the relevant antidumping authorities is well known as one of the most important causes

---

[1] For example, another objective of EC competition policy is the protection of small and medium sized businesses which has been recognized in the interpretation of abuses or dominant position prohibited by article 82 of the EC treaty. *See ibid.*

[2] *See, e. g.* , Nihat Aktas & Eric De Bodt & Richard Roll, *Is European M & A Regulation Protectionist*? Economic Journal ,2007, Vol. 117, pp. 1096 – 1121.

[3] Giorgio Monti, *EU Competition Law* , Cambridge Univ. Press Inc. 2007, pp. 305 – 307.

[4] Susan Beth Farmer, *Chapter 9 – Competition Policy and Merger Analysis in Deregulated and Newly Competitive Industries*, Competition policy and merger analysis in deregulated and newly competitive industries ,2008, p. 1, http://ssrn. com/abstract = 1138232, last visited September 21, 2011.

for the easy abuse for protectionism purposes. ❶ As the minimum requirement for domestic antidumping rules, WTO ADA is long being criticized for leaving too much discretion for importing countries. ❷ And the issue of discretion in the antidumping law of each country has been documented by numerous authors. ❸

In practice, antidumping actions are normally exclusively prosecuted by government agencies through an administrative process. ❹ Interestingly, the U. S., as the strongest supporter for antidumping in the

---

❶ Just as mentioned in the beginning of this book, most trade scholars are of the opinion that the misuse of antidumping is mainly due to its arbitrary and biased rules and procedures, so efforts must be continuously done to make it more stringent and transparent, less arbitrary and abusive.

❷ While the antidumping agreement sought to prevent such abuses of antidumping law, the antidumping agreement still leaves administrative decision makers with considerable discretion. *See* Martyn D. Taylor, *International Competition Law: A New Dimension for the WTO?* Cambridge Univ. Press Inc. 2006, pp. 270 – 271.

❸ For example, "the rules for price undertakings in the European Union are not well articulated, leaving a considerable discretion to the EU Commission and the Council of Ministers." *See* Bibek Debroy *et al.*, eds., *Antidumping: global abuse of a trade policy instrument*, Academic Foundation, 2007, p. 125; "The Community Authorities appear to have an almost unlimited discretion as to whether to accept undertakings..." *See* Clive Stanbrook & Philip Bentley, *Dumping and subsidies: the law and procedures governing the imposition of anti-dumping and countervailing duties in the European Community*, Kluwer Law International, 1996, p. 141; "These criteria are hardly specified at all and allow for considerable discretion in interpretation." *See* Douglas R. Nelson *et al.*, eds., *the WTO and Antidumping II* Edward Elgar Publishing, 2005, p. 483. *See also* Simon J. Evenett, *the simple analytics of U. S. antidumping orders: Bureaucratic discretion, anti-importer bias, and the Byrd amendment*, European Journal of Political Economy, 2006, Vol. 22, pp. 732 – 749; Daniel J. Ikenson, *Abuse of Discretion: Time to Fix to Administration of the U. S. Antidumping Law*, Trade Policy Analysis, 2005, No. 31, pp. 1 – 27, http://www.freetrade.org/pubs/pas/tpa – 031.pdf, last visited September 21, 2011.

❹ Gabrielle Marceau, *Antidumping and Anti-trust Issues in Free-trade Areas*, Oxford Univ. Press Inc. 1994, p. 115.

world, has received the most criticism on the issue of discretion.[1] With regard to the extensive discretion of the antidumping authorities, generally speaking, it includes:

I. They can "ask for any amount of information, relevant or otherwise, and can demand it practically on the spot"[2];

II. They can "choose to ignore any information a company or industry provides for the flimsiest of reasons"[3];

III. They can "drag on the investigations on endlessly and restart after they have been closed"[4];

IV. They can "choose to use one standard for a case and an entirely different standard for another case involving the same company or industry"[5], and "change standards retroactively with no recourse"[6];

V. They can adjust prices for fairness[7];

VI. They can choose to use "Best Information Available" (BIA) and can "totally disregard better information that is provided by the target of

---

[1] The abuse of discretion over the U. S. antidumping procedures from 1986 to 1993 has been investigated by McGee. These abuses included wholly inadequate due process and natural justice for foreign firms, such as unreasonable tight time frames for the preparation of submissions and unreasonable information requests. Other examples included bias in the calculation of antidumping margins and the arbitrary application of critical antidumping definitions. *See* Robert W. McGee, *the Case to Repeal the Antidumping Laws*, Northwestern Journal of International Law and Business ,1993,Vol. 13,pp. 491 – 561.

[2] *Ibid.,p.* 561.

[3] *Ibid.*

[4] *Ibid.*

[5] *Ibid.*

[6] *Ibid.*

[7] "A fair comparison shall be made between the export price and the normal value". *See* WTO ADA, Article 2 (4).

the investigation"[1];

VII. They can use the prices of substitute countries in cases "where the imports originate from a presumed non-market economy"[2], which is quite arbitrary and biased;

VIII. They have tremendous power to affirm the existence of material injury as well as the causal relationship between dumping and injury, in favor of domestic complaints.[3]

As listed above, antidumping rules offer numerous possibilities for an efficient protection of domestic vested interests.

Compared to antidumping rules, competition rules are much clearer in their objectives, and have stricter, more specific rules in market investigation, cost calculation, injury determination and so on. Hence, the relevant authorities have significantly less discretion than those of antidumping in implementing their respective law. Just as Hoekman claimed that:

Antidumping authorities have much greater discretion than do antitrust authorities in implementing the respective laws. With respect to key issues such as the methodology used to calculate dumping margins, the determination of the "relevant" market , i. e. , how to define the "like" products with which dumped imports are competing and thus injuring, and how to ascertain whether dumped imports have caused material injury current procedures are biased in favor of domestic industry.

---

[1] Robert W. McGee, *the Case to Repeal the Antidumping Laws*, Northwestern Journal of International Law and Business, 1993, Vol. 13, pp. 491, 562.

[2] Gunnar Niels, *What is Antidumping Policy Really About?* Journal of Economic Surveys, 2002, Vol. 14, pp. 467, 479, http://www. blackwell - synergy. com/links/doi/10. 1111/1467 - 6419. 00118, last visited September 21, 2011.

[3] *Ibid.*

This contrasts with antitrust enforcement, where it is much clearer what the objective of the law is and where methodological guidelines have been developed that are applied. ❶

Moreover, compared to antidumping procedures, which is more administrative-based, the whole competition investigation is rather judicial-based. Hence, it is comparatively fair and equal, and can give foreign competitors more chances to defend. Taking the U. S. for instance, the antitrust laws are administered by the Department of Justice, the Federal Trade Commission, State attorneys – general and private parties. The Federal Trade Commission conducts its investigations according to the Administrative Procedure Act, which is a regularized and adjudicatory process. Actions brought by the Department of Justice as well as private litigants are filed in federal district court, with appeal to the U. S. courts of Appeals. ❷ In this respect, it can be also asserted that, competition rules can involve less abuse of discretion hence less protectionist abuse in practice.

4. 1. 4 Remedies: More Effective in Preventing Reoccurrence

Another point worth discussing is remedies. As to antidumping, the normal remedy is the imposition of antidumping duties. Apart from this, an exporter has other limited choices which include accepting price

---

❶ Bernard M. Hoekman & Petros C. Mavroidis, *Antitrust-based Remedies and Dumping in International Trade*, Policy Research Working Paper No. 1347, the World Bank, 1994, pp. 1, 8, http://www – wds. worldbank. org/servlet/WDSContentServer/WDSP/IB/1994/08/01/000009265_3970716141633/Rendered/PDF/multi0page. pdf, last visited September 21, 2011.

❷ Kevin C. Kennedy, *Competition Law and the World Trade Organization: the Limits of Multilateralism*, London: Sweet & Maxwell, 2001, p. 236.

undertaking, increasing its prices, or stop exporting. [1] Whatever the remedy, under antidumping rules, the petitioner receives no compensatory damages for an injury caused by the dumped imports, although if the margin of dumping is sufficiently high, the foreign producer may be forced to exit the domestic market. [2]

With regard to competition, both private and public enforcement can be involved in the process of competition investigation. In the U. S. , the government authorities responsible for antitrust laws include the Department of Justice, the Federal Trade Commission, as well as State attorneys-general. In addition, private parties are very actively in challenging anti-competitive behavior before the courts, where compensatory damages, treble damages and the other civil remedies can be issued. [3] Criminal fines and prison sentences might also be involved depending on specific circumstances. In the EU, the European Commission and the relevant antitrust authorities of the Member States are the primary authorities responsible for issuing various sanctions towards the violation of antitrust law. [4] Moreover, great efforts have been made recently within

---

[1] Gabrielle Marceau, *Antidumping and Anti-trust Issues in Free-trade Areas*, Oxford Univ. Press Inc. 1994, p. 117.

[2] Kevin C. Kennedy, *Competition Law and the World Trade Organization: the Limits of Multilateralism*, London: Sweet & Maxwell, 2001, p. 236.

[3] Eleanor M. Fox, *US and EU Competition Law: A Comparison*, in Edward M. Graham & J. David, Richardson eds. , *Global Competition Policy* , Institute For International Economics, 1997, p. 352.

[4] *Ibid.*, p. 353.

the EU to encourage private actions. [1] Hence, under competition rules, various remedies can be chosen in order to find the most suitable remedy based on the specific circumstances in each case. [2]

Supposing that dumping is viewed as an unfair, *per se* harmful behavior, the essential idea should be the design of relevant remedies to prevent its reoccurrence. However, remedies in the form of imposing antidumping duties, price undertaking and the like, aiming at increasing the price of the "dumped" goods for certain duration, antidumping action does not bear directly on the firms' or their competitive behavior and thereby cannot prevent its reoccurrence effectively. On the contrary, the remedies provided under competition rules, which aim to prohibit the practice with appropriate penalties if the offense continues, would be the appropriate action. From this perspective, it can also be deduced that competition rules are more effective in preventing reoccurrence than antidumping rules. [3]

---

[1] On April 3, 2008, the European Commission issued a "White Paper on Damages Actions for Breach of the EC Antitrust Laws", which recommends various reforms to facilitate private lawsuits for antitrust violations in the national courts of its member states. *See Commission White Paper on Damages Actions for Breach of the EC Antitrust Rules*, EC Competition Policy Newsletter, 2008, http://ec. europa. eu/competition/publications/cpn/cpn2008_2. pdf, last visited September 21, 2011.

[2] Kevin C. Kennedy, *Competition Law and the World Trade Organization: the Limits of Multilateralism*, London: Sweet & Maxwell, 2001, p. 236.

[3] "An issue that has not received attention is whether antidumping duties or price undertakings will be effective in restoring competition even if it is true that there is predatory or strategic dumping. In general, the answer is. antidumping action does not bear directly on the firms' or firms' competitive behavior. It only raises the price of the dumped good for the duration of the action. The appropriate action would be a prohibition of the practice with appropriate penalties if the offense continues." *See also* P. J. Lloyd, Antidumping and Competition Law, in Patrick F. J Macrory et al., eds., *II The World Trade Organization: Legal, Economic and Political Analysis*, Springer 2005, p. 76.

4.2 Competition Law in Line with the Free Trade Framework

After comparing and analyzing the basic elements of antidumping rules and competition rules, the two sets of rules will next be placed against the framework of the modern free trade world.

4.2.1 Integration of Trade and Competition Principles

Traditionally, trade policy focused on facilitating access to markets, reduction of tariffs, and so on, while at the same time maintaining some level of protection for the domestic industries.[1] Compared to this, modern trade policy can be less subject to domestic protectionism. To be more specific, the guiding economic premise of the modern trade policy that underlies the entire GATT-WTO system and is well acknowledged by most of the countries is free trade or liberal trade.[2] By exploiting the principle of comparative advantage,

---

[1] These protective components have been based on the need or desire to shelter, presumably temporarily, incipient domestic industries from more advanced and efficient cost-quality foreign competitors, or they are based on pressures from politically influential interest groups, or on distributional grounds. *See* J. Luis Guasch & Sarath Rajapatirana, *Antidumping and Competition Policies in Latin America and Caribbean: Total Strangers or Soul Mates?* 1998, pp. 1, 3, http://www.worldbank.org/html/dec/Publications/Workpapers/WPS1900 series/wps1958/wps1958.pdf, last visited September 21, 2011.

[2] In a liberal economic system, government does not thwart private parties in their attempts to enter voluntary transactions, and taxes are stable, predictable, and nonprohibitive. The General Agreement on Tariffs and Trade (GATT) is liberal in this sense... Interventions [by governments] in liberal exchange across frontiers to make trade fair may be the political price of liberalism, but such interventions are themselves its antithesis. *See* Martin Wolf, Why Trade Liberalization is A Good Idea, in J. Michael Finger & Andrzej Olechowski, eds., *the Uruguay Round, A Handbook on the Multilateral Trade Organisation*, Annual Report, World Bank, 1996, Vol. 6.

liberal trade policies permit the unrestricted cross-border flow of the highest-quality goods and services at the lowest prices, thereby increasing total world wealth. ❶ In accordance with this, multilateral trade negotiations under GATT/WTO are continuously devoted to the reduction of tariffs and non-tariff trade barriers.

As to competition policy, with more and more of its effects having spilled over borders, it has evolved from the traditional, mostly domestic policy to increasingly international policy in the modern world. ❷ Hence, the proper extension of the competition policy could and should bring the need for some trade policy instruments, and argue for a consistency and at least coordination if not integration between competition policy and trade policy. ❸

With the development of the modern multilateral world, the distinction between competition policy and trade policy has become blurred. The seemingly unrelated policies began to interact with each other. Barcelo in his analysis postulates the validity of free trade theory and its similarity with competition policy. He assumes that "world welfare will be promoted if barriers to trade are reduced and business concerns are encouraged to compete across national

---

❶ Kevin C. Kennedy, *Competition Law and the World Trade Organization: the Limits of Multilateralism*, London: Sweet & Maxwell, 2001, p. 3.

❷ J. David Richardson, the Coming Competition Policy Agenda in the WTO, in Jeffrey J. Schott ed., *Lauching New Global Trade Talks*, Peterson Institute, 1998, p. 1, http://www.iie.com/publications/chapters_preview/61/11ie2660.pdf, last visited September 21, 2011.

❸ J. Luis Guasch & Sarath Rajapatirana, *Antidumping and Competition Policies in Latin America and Caribbean: Total Strangers or Soul Mates?* 1998, pp. 1, 4, http://www.worldbank.org/html/dec/Publications/Workpapers/WPS1900series/wps1958/wps1958.pdf, last visited September 21, 2011.

boundaries". [1]

Furthermore, in the present world, although there are quite a few distinctions between them, the basic objectives of trade liberalization policy and competition policy are becoming consistent with each other. [2] Weinrauch in his book pointed out the consistencies between trade policy and competition policy, especially in terms of sharing certain basic trade and competition principles. These include: I. Both trade liberalization policy and strict enforcement of competition law are able to open national markets and to make them more competitive. They improve the allocation of resources and promote economic efficiency, as well as consumer welfare. II. Both of them are based on principles, such as transparency, non-discrimination and the need for rule-based economic behavior. III. Both reflect the tension between the desirability of long-term benefits and what is politically feasible in the short run. [3]

Noticing the broadly compatible and mutually supportive competition policy and trade policy in the modern free trade world, many efforts have been devoted to the coordination and harmonization of the two. A thorough evaluation of the advantages of using competition rules instead of antidumping rules to deal with dumping cannot be achieved without taking this background into consideration. Hence, the following part will put the two rules against the background of the

---

[1] Mario Marques Mendes, *Antitrust in A World of Interrelated Economies: the Interplay Between Antitrust and Trade Policies in the U. S. and the Eec*, Etudes Europeennes, 1991, p. 149.

[2] *See, e. g.*, Roland Weinrauch, *Competition Law in the WTO: the Rationale for a Framework Agreement*, Wien : NWV Neuer Wissenschaftlicher Verlag, 2004, p. 55.

[3] Ibid., pp. 55 – 56.

modern free trade world, to examine which of the rules are more consistent with modern basic trade principles as well as competition principles. This can also indicate whether putting dumping under competition rules instead of antidumping rules can be better prevent traditional protectionism.

4.2.2 Avoidance of conflict with Basic Trade Principles

The first advantage of competition rules over antidumping rules is that competition rules can avoid seriously undermining the basic modern trade principles supported by the GATT/WTO system. It is summarized that antidumping rules conflict with basic trade principles in three aspects.

4.2.2.1 Conflict with Principle of Free Trade

The first aspect is that, categorized under "trade remedies", antidumping measure acts as a tariff-like barrier leading to protectionist abuse, which is against the guiding economic premise of the modern trade policy that underlies the entire GATT/WTO system, i.e., free trade.

In conformity with the requirements of trade liberalization, many efforts have been devoted to reduce tariff and non-tariff barriers traditionally used for protection all around the world, whereas antidumping is increasingly used as a tariff-like barrier to protect domestic industries. This is clearly against the spirit of free trade. As pointed out by Lloyd, the proliferation of antidumping actions has indicated that antidumping is actually becoming the major restraint on trade. [1]

---

[1] *See*, *e.g.*, P.J. Lloyd, Antidumping and Competition Law, in Patrick F. J Macrory et al., eds., *II The World Trade Organization: Legal, Economic and Political Analysis*, Springer 2005, p.68

4. 2. 2. 2 Conflict with Principle of Non-discrimination

The second aspect is that, antidumping rules allow member states to easily deviate from one of its main principles, i. e. , non-discrimination. [1] Antidumping investigations are discriminatively conducted in two ways. On the one hand, according to the WTO ADA, it does not require multilateral application, therefore antidumping actions can be taken selectively, and particular exporters could be picked out. [2] By means of this, antidumping action actually discriminates among the original import countries. Although Article 9(2) of WTO ADA states that any duty must be imposed on a non-discrimination basis on imports from all sources found to be dumped and causing injury, except on imports from sources from which price undertakings have been accepted[3], it only suggests non-discrimination on that portion of the imports of the product liable for antidumping action. However, implied discrimination exists between the dumped and the non-dumped imports of the product in the ordinary sense of trade discrimination. [4]

On the other hand, in practice, antidumping laws set up special

---

[1] Five principles are of particular importance in understanding both the pre-1994 GATT and the WTO: nondiscrimination, reciprocity, enforceable commitments, transparency, and safety valves. *See* Bernard Hoekman, *the WTO: Functions and Basic Principles*, pp. 41, 42, http://www. terry. uga. edu/ ~ eornelas/Econ4040/WTO – basics. pdf , last visited May 14, 2009.

[2] J. Michael Finger, *Should Developing Countries Introduce Antidumping? Working Paper*, 1992, http:// www. worldbank. org/INTRANETTRADE/Resources/WBI – Training/ MFinger_antidumping_eng. DOC, last visited May 14, 2009.

[3] WTO ADA, Article 9 (2).

[4] P. J. Lloyd, Antidumping and Competition Law, in Patrick F. J Macrory et al. , eds. , *II The World Trade Organization: Legal, Economic and Political Analysis*, Springer 2005, p. 69.

procedures which discriminate against foreign firms and easily allow the authorities to find dumping against them, when similar practices by domestic firms would not be considered unfair or predatory under domestic competition laws.❶ Hence, with similar conducts of low-price selling, conducts of foreign seller are actionable whilst conducts of domestic sellers are not actionable. This is discriminatory in another way.❷ In terms of this kind of discrimination, scholars have argued that the different treatments of low-price selling between antidumping and competition laws actually infringe the obligation of National Treatment of the GATT/WTO, one of the major components

---

❶ J. Michael Finger, *Should Developing Countries Introduce Antidumping?* Working Paper, 1992, http://siteresources. worldbank. org/INTRANETTRADE/Resources/WBI - Training/MFinger_antidumping_eng. DOC, last visited May 7, 2009.

❷ P. J. Lloyd, Antidumping and Competition Law, in Patrick F. J Macrory et al., eds., *II The World Trade Organization: Legal, Economic and Political Analysis*, Springer 2005, p. 69.

of non-discrimination. [1]

4. 2. 2. 3 Conflict with Principle of Reciprocity

The third aspect is that, antidumping rules conflict with the principle of reciprocity, another essential element of modern trade policy. The principle of reciprocity reflects both a desire to limit the scope for free-riding that may arise because of the most-favored nation rule and a desire to obtain "payment" for trade liberalization in the form of

---

[1] The obligation of National Treatment covers any legislation, rights, and obligations whether or not they are mentioned in the GATT/WTO. National treatment: "Imported and locally-produced goods should be treated equally – at least after the foreign goods have entered the market. The same should apply to foreign and domestic services, and to foreign and local trademarks, copyrights and patents. This principle of 'national treatment' (giving others the same treatment as one's own nationals) is also found in all the three main WTO agreements (Article 3 of GATT, Article 17 of GATS and Article 3 of TRIPS), although once again the principle is handled slightly differently in each of these. National treatment only applies once a product, service or item of intellectual property has entered the market. Therefore, charging customs duty on an import is not a violation of national treatment even if locally-produced products are not charged an equivalent tax." *See* WTO, Principles of the Trading System, http://www.wto.org/english/theWTO_e/whatis_e/tif_e/fact2_e.htm, last visited May 14, 2009.

Although the GATT/WTO does not require the treatment of domestic and foreign producers to be the same, what matters is that domestic and foreign goods benefit from equal opportunities on the domestic market. Antidumping laws may authorize a special remedy against imports, but the substantive and procedural rights given to foreigners in the antidumping process must comply with the obligation of National Treatment. However, the comparison of the basic elements of antidumping rules with competition rules on similar low-price selling has clearly indicated that the substantive and procedural standards of antidumping do not provide "equality of opportunities in the importing market". From this perspective, the different treatments of low-price selling under antidumping rules and domestic competition rules are actually against the national treatment that requires that the importing country offer as many opportunities to exporters in the antidumping process as it does for domestic producers in similar situation. *See, e. g.*, Gabrielle Marceau, *Antidumping and Anti-trust Issues in Free-trade Areas*, Oxford Univ. Press Inc. 1994, pp. 103 – 132.

better access to foreign markets. ❶ Obtaining a reduction in foreign import barriers as a quid pro quo for a reduction in domestic trade restrictions gives specific export-oriented domestic interests that will gain from liberalization an incentive to support it in domestic political markets. ❷ A related point is that for a nation to negotiate, it is necessary that the gain from doing so be greater than the gain available from unilateral liberalization. Reciprocal concessions ensure that such gains will materialize. ❸

Antidumping measure conflicts with the principle of reciprocity in that the GATT/WTO rules neither require any compensation nor allow any retaliation. ❹ The only conditions that must be satisfied relate to proof of dumping and injury and, therefore, antidumping actions can be taken unilaterally. Consequently, they breach the reciprocity involved in past tariff negotiations. ❺

---

❶ A rationale for reciprocity can be found in the political-economy literature. To be more specific, the costs of liberalization generally are concentrated in specific industries, which often will be well organized and opposed to reductions in protection. Benefits, although in the aggregate usually greater than costs, accrue to a much larger set of agents, who thus do not have a great individual incentive to organize themselves politically. In such a setting, being able to point to reciprocal, sector-specific export gains may help to sell the liberalization politically. *See* Bernard Hoekman, *the WTO: Functions and Basic Principles*, pp. 41, 43, http://www.terry.uga.edu/~eornelas/Econ4040/WTO-basics.pdf, last visited May 14, 2009.

❷ *Ibid.*

❸ *Ibid.*

❹ J. Michael Finger, *Should Developing Countries Introduce Antidumping?* Working Paper, 1992, http://siteresources.worldbank.org/INTRANETTRADE/Resources/WBI-Training/MFinger_antidumping_eng.DOC, last visited May 7, 2009.

❺ P. J. Lloyd, Antidumping and Competition Law, in Patrick F. J Macrory et al., eds., *II The World Trade Organization: Legal, Economic and Political Analysis*, Springer 2005, p. 69.

4.2.3 Avoidance of Anti-competitive Effects

Compared against the modern multilateral world, the second advantage of competition over antidumping is that competition rules can avoid the anti-competitive effects that antidumping rules may bring about, and thereby refrain from conflicting with basic competition principles in the following five aspects.

4.2.3.1 Conflict with Protection of Competitive Process

The first aspect is that, antidumping, focusing on protecting individual competitors, conflicts with the basic idea of competition policy, which is to protect competitive process in conformity to the economic efficiency. Antidumping law focuses on material injury to individual firms, whereas competition policy is concerned only with the extent to which the relevant conduct harms the competitive process by reducing the level of competition.

Hence, to the extent that antidumping law excludes foreign competition from the domestic market, it may be viewed as anticompetitive.[1] In practice, this anticompetitive influence is great since the antidumping complaints can be easily affirmed and end up with the imposition of antidumping duties.

4.2.3.2 Conflict with Consumer Welfare

The second aspect is that, the protection of domestic industries by imposing antidumping duties, lifting the price of imported goods, is

---

[1] P. J. Lloyd, Antidumping and Competition Law, in Patrick F. J Macrory et al., eds., *II The World Trade Organization: Legal, Economic and Political Analysis*, Springer 2005, p. 69.

always ignored and at the cost of the consumer welfare. ❶ Joseph Stiglitz, a Nobel Prize winner and former chief economist at the World Bank, highlighted the anti-competitive effects of antidumping law: "Perpetuating unfair trade laws [including antidumping law] that are themselves unfair thus imposes substantial burdens on our consumers and on our most efficient exporters while protecting our least efficient import-competing firms." ❷

Some empirical studies of the negative effects on consumers have also been done. For example, one report shows that of about 250 antidumping petitions filed by U. S. steel producers since 1980, around 100 are still enforced 20 years later. At present, they "protect" less than 0. 1 per cent of the U. S. labor force at an estimated 40 per cent

---

❶ This has been mentioned in quite a few literatures: "the primary economic cost of antidumping measures is the increased cost of imports. Consumers have to buy higher-cost domestic goods instead of lower-cost foreign goods." *See* Roland Weinrauch, *Competition Law in the WTO: the Rationale for a Framework Agreement*, Wien : NWV Neuer Wissenschaftlicher Verlag, 2004, p. 60.

"This anticompetitive behavior is the real threat. Dumping of foreign product does not hurt US. consumers; rather, antidumping laws do... Antidumping laws are a form of backdoor protectionism that has been abused by certain U. S. companies with the support of the Commerce Department. This behavior is costly to import-using industries and consumers, and is agitating US trade partners whose markets are sought by US business." *See* Dan Ikenson, *Antidumping Laws Hurt American Consumers*, CATO Institute , 2001, http://www. freetrade. org/node/222, last visited September 21, 2011.

"America imposes dramatic costs on both its own economy and consumers to provide partial, indirect relief to a limited number of domestic industries." *See* Spencer Weber Waller, *Bringing Globalism Home: Lessons from Antitrust and Beyond*, Loyola University Chicago Law Journal, 2000, Vol. 32, pp. 113, 131.

❷ José Tavares De Araujo Jr. , *Legal and Economic Interfaces between Antidumping and Competition Policy*, CEPAL-SERIE Comercio Internacional, 2001, pp. 1, 10, http://www. eclac. cl/publicaciones/xml/0/9040/lcl1685i. pdf, last visited September 21, 2011.

cost-penalty to steel consuming sectors employing more than 50 times as many workers. Similar efforts in the 1980s to protect the U. S. car industry cut consumers' real incomes between USMYM3. 50 and USMYM5. 50 for each dollar of added profit; each job saved cost consumers between USMYM93 000 to USMYM250 000 per year. Comparable figures can be found for most economies delaying adjustments while claiming to benefit from free trade. ❶

In circumstances where the dumped product is a raw material or semi-finished product, the consumers are often the downstream producers rather than the final consumers. Similarly, the use of antidumping rules is also likely to conflict with competition in that, the availability of materials at low prices may enable smaller firms producing finished products to compete more strenuously with large and integrated firms controlling the domestic source of supply, and therefore permitting such dumping is likely to lower prices to all consumers. ❷

4. 2. 3. 3 Facilitation of Collusion or Cross-border Cartels

The third aspect is that, antidumping may facilitate collusion between home and foreign firms. ❸ Antidumping rules are said to offer domestic producers "a specific trade weapon whose threatened use alone may cause international competitors to raise prices or restrain

---

❶ Ralf Boscheck, *the Governance of Global Market Relations: the Case of Substituting Antitrust for Antidumping*, World Competition, 2001, Vol. 24, pp. 41, 54.

❷ Comment, *the Antidumping Act – Tariff or Antitrust Law?* The Yale Law Journal, 1965, Vol. 74, pp. 707, 713.

❸ Ian Wooton & Maurizio Zanardi, *Trade and Competition Policy: Antidumping versus Anti-trust*, *University of Glasgow and CEPR Dicussion Paper in Economics*, 2002, pp. 1, 14, http://homepages. strath. ac. uk/ ~ hbs03116/Research/Trade% 20and% 20Competition% 20Policy%20Final. pdf, last visited May 24, 2009.

sales and effectively agree to collude at the consumers' expense". ❶ In this respect, antidumping rules may also conflict with competition policy.

For instance, apart from the imposition of antidumping duties, the WTO ADA also provides that antidumping proceedings may be concluded if the exporters of the dumped product offer price underta-kings (to voluntarily raise their prices to certain extent so as to ensure that their exports will not injure the relevant domestic producers) which the authorities of the importing country consider acceptable. Such measure allowed by antidumping rules is actually taken as restrains of competitive process and forbidden by antitrust law. ❷ In practice, most antidumping complaints ended up with price undertakings. As an alternative to imposition of antidumping duties, this self-constrained measure may effectively incentivize or force foreign suppliers to legally collude with their domestic competitors, which can be considered as a trigger of dumping with the aim of forming lawful cross-border cartels. ❸

4. 2. 3. 4 Facilitation of Monopoly Power or Domestic Cartels

The fourth aspect is that, through restraining the competition from

---

❶ Ralf Boscheck, *the Governance of Global Market Relations: the Case of Substituting Antitrust for Antidumping*, World Competition, 2001, Vol. 24, pp. 41, 42.

❷ From a legal perspective, antidumping rules allow practices such as price undertakings and quantitative trade restrictions that are forbidden by competition law, and punish certain types of price differentiation that are justifiable under the antitrust rules. *See* José Tavares De Araujo Jr., *Legal and Economic Interfaces between Antidumping and Competition Policy*, CEPAL-SERIE Comercio Internacional, 2001, pp. 1, 5, http://www.eclac.cl/publicaciones/xml/0/9040/lcl1685i.pdf, last visited September 21, 2011.

❸ Andreas Knorr, *Antidumping Rules vs. Competition Rules*, *Institution for World Economics and International Management*, 2004, pp. 1, 13, http://www.iwim.uni-bremen.de/publikationen/pdf/W031.pdf, last visited May 3, 2011.

foreign producers, antidumping rules help to maintain domestic monopoly power or form domestic cartels. In terms of monopoly power, it has been pointed out as early as 1965 that dumping may result in positive and significant advantages to consumers and to society in general in where the product market is dominated by a domestic monopoly. ❶ In terms of domestic cartels, it is also taken as a further danger for competition existing when antidumping laws are used to cartelize domestic market. ❷ The application of antidumping law may conflict with competition policy either through facilitating the domestic monopoly power or helping to form domestic cartels.

This kind of conflict has been detected both in the U. S. and the EU, the heavy traditional users of antidumping. In the U. S., the most recent empirical study has been done on the cases from 1990 to 1999 by Nisha with the main aim to highlight the anti-competitive nature of the U. S. antidumping legislation. ❸ Through investigation, Nisha found that in 73 percent of the cases the AD petition was filed by only one petitioner, that is, by a single firm. This characteristic hints at a lack of competition in the domestic market. Continuously,

---

❶ In such a case the entry of dumped goods in appreciable quantity might force the monopolist to lower his price to a competitive level, or might weaken his position thereby reducing barriers to competing American firms. *See* Comment, *The Antidumping Act – Tariff or Antitrust Law*? The Yale Law Journal, 1965, Vol. 74, pp. 707, 713.

❷ Gunnar Niels, *What is Antidumping Policy Really About*? Journal of Economic Surveys, 2002, Vol. 14, pp. 467, 480, http://www. blackwell – synergy. com/links/doi/10. 1111/1467 –6419. 00118, last visited September 21, 2011.

❸ The chemical industry is the second largest user of the antidumping law after the steel industry. It filed 113 antidumping petitions in the period 1980 – 1999. *See* Nisha Malhotra, *Is Antidumping Legislation a Threat to Competition*: *A Case Study of the U. S. Chemical Industry*, Competitiveness Review, 2006, http://www. econ. ubc. ca/nmalhotra/Research/ChemicalIndustryCompreview1. pdf, last visited September 21, 2011.

Nisha gave three typical cases to illustrate how the single firm used antidumping to maintain its monopoly power, including:

One was in 1995 where four cases were filed (against four different countries) for "Polyvinyl Alcohol". Air Products & Chemicals Inc. filed a petition with ITC and ITA requesting that antidumping duties be imposed against producers of polyvinyl alcohol from Taiwan, the People's Republic of China, the Republic of Korea and Japan.[1] Nisha explained how Air Products & Chemicals Inc. used antidumping to maintain its domestic monopoly power as follows: 1994 saw an increase in the world supply of polyvinyl alcohol, which pushed the prices down. To what extent the injury to the domestic industry was a result of an increase in overall world supply, or from imports from the above four countries is a hanging question. In late 1991, Air products had added a 75-million-pound facility at Pasadena, Texas that might have contributed to the excess supply. In cases such as these, restricting import competition can be interpreted as a bail out for a misinformed investment decision by a domestic industry.[2]

Another was the Aramid Fibre Case, in which antidumping was used for dividing markets between two producers in the world. Actually the world market for Aramid fiber only consists only of two

---

[1] The general background is that the Cases against China, Japan and Taiwan got an affirmative decision. The case against Korea was given a negative decision; ITC decided that the Korean product had a negligible impact on the U. S. industry. Thus, import of Polyvinyl Alcohol from China, Japan and Taiwan would pay antidumping (a 77.4 percent antidumping duty is to be imposed on Japanese products). *See Is Antidumping Legislation a Threat to Competition: A Case Study of the U. S. Chemical Industry*, Competitiveness Review, 2006, http://www.econ.ubc.ca/nmalhotra/Research/ChemicalIndustryCompreview1.pdf, last visited September 21, 2011.

[2] *Ibid.*

producers, giving it a duopolistic structure. The sole domestic producer of Aramid fiber was the petitioner itself, E. I. DuPont. By imposing an antidumping duty on imports from the Netherlands (foreign firm – Akzo/Teijin Twaron) ITC succeeded in discouraging competition in the U. S. market. ❶ This case shows how antidumping helped to divide the international market between the two firms, giving them monopoly power in their own markets.

The third case was where US ITC also made an affirmative final determination in the Coumarin case filed by Rhone-Poulenc. It was the only Coumarin producer in Europe and the U. S. and had also won an AD decision against China under European antidumping laws. China had garnered over 48 percent of the European market while the production of Rhone-Poulenc fell by nearly 60 percent. After the decision imports from China fell significantly, giving Rhone-Poulenc most of the U. S. market. ❷ Nisha concluded that, such cases as above indicated that by granting import protection to domestic markets with single firms, ITC and ITA might be promoting monopolies at the cost of consumer welfare. ❸

In the EU, two of the most famous empirical studies concerning chemical industry were done by Messerlin and Akbar. Messerlin tried to examine the relationship between antidumping and pro-cartel effect

---

❶ *Is Antidumping Legislation a Threat to Competition: A Case Study of the U. S. Chemical Industry*, Competitiveness Review, 2006, http://www.econ.ubc.ca/nmalhotra/Research/ChemicalIndustryComprevieww1.pdf, last visited September 21, 2011.

❷ Nisha Malhotra, *Is Antidumping Legislation a Threat to Competition: A Case Study of the U. S. Chemical Industry*, Competitiveness Review, 2006, http://www.econ.ubc.ca/nmalhotra/Research/ChemicalIndustryCompreview1.pdf, last visited September 21, 2011.

❸ *Ibid.*

by focusing on the chemical cases between 1980 and 1987. ❶ According to his observation, nearly thirty EC anti-cartel cases initiated since 1980 deal with products also involved in almost a hundred antidumping cases. ❷ Amongst PVC and LdPE cartels are the two major "twin cases".

With regard to the product polyvinyl chloride (PVC), in November 1981, the antidumping office of the Commission (DG I) initiated an antidumping proceeding against four East European producers of PVC from 4 East European producers, i. e., Czechoslovakia, East Germany, Hungary and Romania. In September 1982, three of them agreed to price undertakings to terminate the dumping effects of their exports, and the fourth producer from Czech producers also agreed to similar undertakings as the other three in January 1983. ❸ Similarly, in terms of another chemical product polyethylene, antidumping action against four East European producers, i. e., Czechoslovakia, East Germany, Poland and Soviet Union, was taken by DG I in September 1982, and was terminated by four price undertakings in May 1983. ❹ In late 1983, which is only a few months after the

---

❶ Patrick A. Messerlin, *Antidumping Regulations or Procartel Law?* The EC Chemical Cases, International Trade Working Paper 0397, the World Bank, 1990, pp. 1 – 51, http://www-wds. worldbank. org/servlet/WDSContentServer/WDSP/IB/1990/04/01/000009265_3960929174031/Rendered/PDF/multi0page. pdf, last visited September 21, 2011.

❷ *Ibid.*, p. 3.

❸ Patrick A. Messerlin, *Antidumping Regulations or Procartel Law?* The EC Chemical Cases, International Trade Working Paper 0397, the World Bank, 1990, p. 8, http://www – wds. worldbank. org/servlet/WDSContentServer/WDSP/IB/1990/04/01/000009265_3960929174031/Rendered/PDF/multi0page. pdf, last visited September 21, 2011.

❹ *Ibid.*, p. 9.

antidumping investigation terminated, the competition office of the Commission (DG IV) became aware of possible price collusion and started investigation on both the low-density polyethylene (LdPE) market and PVC market. [1] In March and December 1988, DG IV initiated an official anti-cartel proceeding on the constitution of LdPE cartel and PVC cartel respectively, followed by imposing heavy fines on both the EU and non-EU firms involved. [2]

In his paper, Messerlin pointed out that both PVC and LdPE producers referred to antidumping actions at about the same time as they began to organize the collusion. DG IV rulings provided ample evidence that as DG IV acting against "dumped" imports of LdPE and PVC from ECE countries, the complaining EU firms were themselves involved in concerted attempts to fix prices and market share at regular meetings. [3] Together with the other cases, Messerlin concluded that "antidumping procedures have been easy to capture by the same few firms which lodged antidumping complaints in order to enforce cartel agreements" [4], and it help to "impose a high level of protection and are a crucial factor of cartelization". [5]

Based on the Messerlin's work, Akbar continued to examine the

---

[1] Patrick A. Messerlin, *Antidumping Regulations or Procartel Law?* The EC Chemical Cases, International Trade Working Paper 0397, the World Bank, 1990, pp. 9, http://www-wds.worldbank.org/servlet/WDSContentServer/WDSP/IB/1990/04/01/000009265_3960929174031/Rendered/PDF/multi0page.pdf, last visited September 21, 2011.

[2] *Ibid.*

[3] *Ibid.*, pp. 9-46.

[4] *Ibid.*, p. 47.

[5] *Ibid.*

antidumping and antitrust linkage. ❶ In addressing the issue of antidumping facilitating domestic cartels in chemical industry, Akbar gave a specific explanation on the famous Soda Ash Case. The facts of the antidumping case were described as follows:

Over a period from 1982 to the present day, EU producers have been protected from imports of soda ash from major competitors in the US and ECE through the imposition of antidumping duties or equivalence measures...this was an attempt in a couple of cases, they alleged, to eliminate EU production and thereby create a monopoly position for exporters to the EU. The EU commission, with one important exception, agreed to investigate injury and imposed antidumping duties on imports from the US and ECE. Imports of soda ash from the US are already subject to a tariff of 9. 1 percent. ❷

At the same time when these antidumping duties were put in place, an investigation by the EU antitrust authorities concluded that there were a series of anti-competitive and concerted practices taking place in the EU. DG IV alleged that the two main EU producers, Solvay of Belgium and ICI / Brunner Mond of the UK, were at the centre of the conspiracy. ❸ DG IV's analysis of the cartel was fairly clear: ICI / Brunner Mond and Solvay, when faced with the possibility of competition with each other, chose to collude. ❹ As DG IV was imposing fines on the firms alleged to have cartelized the EU market for soda

---

❶ Yusaf H. Akbar, *Global Antitrust: Trade and Competition Linkages*, Ashagate Publishing, 2003.

❷ *Ibid.*, p. 59.

❸ Yusaf H. Akbar, Global Antitrust: *Trade and Competition Linkages*, Ashagate Publishing, 2003.

❹ *Ibid.*, p. 60.

ash, a decision was taken by the EU commission to not renew the antidumping duties on imports from the U. S. which were due for reappraisal and possible renewal. [1]

Here the issue is whether DG I had lifted antidumping duties on US imports in light of the anti-cartel actions? Akbar confirmed this possibility by supporting it with an interpretation of the same case by the GATT/WTO. The soda ash cases were highlighted by the GATT/WTO secretariat in its trade policy Review of 1993: "A recent case in which the EC authorities intervened to restore competitive condition concerns in soda ash, where domestic procedures had sought antidumping protection to defend cartel rents against competing imports. The companies involved were convicted under EC competition law and the antidumping measures repealed in 1990/1991." [2] Based on evidences as such, Akbar demonstrated the possibility of antidumping rules facilitating intra-EU cartel[3], and concluded that where the industry is made up of a small number of large firms, the reduction in competitive supply facilitates domestic collusion. [4]

4. 2. 3. 5 Conflict with Market Integration in Regional Free Trade

The last aspect is that, as aforementioned, competition policy has a special role in bilateral and regional areas, i. e., market integration. Since antidumping defined two markets, domestic and foreign, it is

---

[1] Yusaf H. Akbar, *Global Antitrust: Trade and Competition Linkages*, Ashagate Publishing, 2003. p. 61.

[2] *Ibid.*

[3] In the soda ash case, not only did antidumping shelter high-cost producers from competition, it allowed Solvay and Brunner Mond to orchestrate an intra-EU cartel. When antidumping duties were briefly lifted, the entry of US soda ash imports shook up the cartel by forcing intra-EU shipments of soda ash. *See* Yusaf H. Akbar, Global Antitrust: *Trade and Competition Linkages*, Ashagate Publishing, 2003, p. 71

[4] *Ibid.*, pp. 70 – 73.

considered as a barrier to the market integration since a single market would prevent market segmentation and make price discrimination impossible. ❶ Accordingly, historically, a free trade relationship has involved the elimination of antidumping rules because the partners were creating a new single market in place of the dual or multiple markets of the past in which antidumping rules functioned as a penalty for "unfair" tactics and as a safety valve regulating trade between different economic structures. ❷

Currently, substitution has been and is being achieved in both bilateral and regional areas. The first is the experience of the U. S. ❸ When the European Economic Community was created in the late 1950s, it learned the American lesson well. ❹ New Zealand and Australia concluded a free trade agreement in 1983, which included the elimination of antidumping rules for trans-Tasman trade and the replacement of the dumping rules with true competition provisions. ❺

---

❶ P. J. Lloyd, Antidumping and Competition Law, in Patrick F. J Macrory et al., eds., *II The World Trade Organization: Legal*, Economic and Political Analysis, Springer 2005, p. 77.

❷ Spencer Weber Waller, *Bringing Globalism Home: Lessons from Antitrust and Beyond*, Loyola University Chicago Law Journal, 2000, Vol. 32, pp. 113, 133.

❸ Once the separate colonies created a nation, and not merely a confederation, the newly created states of the Union were constitutionally barred from imposing any form of import or export duties on trade between the American states. *See ibid.*, p. 133.

❹ In the Treaty of Rome, the Member-States were barred after a brief transition period from imposing antidumping or any other form of duties on trade between the Member-States. Price differences between Member-States are dealt with as an abuse of a dominant position under the competition rules rather than as a trade issue. Spencer Weber Waller, *Bringing Globalism Home: Lessons from Antitrust and Beyond*, Loyola University Chicago Law Journal, 2000, Vol. 32, p. 133.

❺ Martyn D. Taylor, *International Competition Law: A New Dimension for the WTO?* Cambridge Univ. Press Inc. 2006, pp. 273 –276.

Canada and Chile also eliminated antidumping rules in their free trade agreement even though their economies are structurally quite different and separated by thousands of miles. ❶ Besides, Mercosur, the principal South American free trade area, has pursued a similar path in eliminatingantidumping duties for trade within the bloc. ❷ Discussion is also ongoing in NAFTA. ❸ In Asia, it has been decided not to use antidumping laws in the China – Hong Kong region, as well as the China – Macau region. Both Article 4 of Mainland and Hong Kong Closer Economic Partnership Arrangement (CEPA-HongKong) and Article 7 of Mainland and Macao Closer Economic Partnership Arrangement (CEPA-Macau) stipulate that antidumping measures should not be used amongst members. ❹ Similar practice takes place in South Africa Union. ❺

4.3 Empirical Evidence Supporting the Substitution by Competition Law

Apart from comparing the basic elements of antidumping rules

❶ Martyn D. Taylor, *International Competition Law: A New Dimension for the WTO?* Cambridge Univ. Press Inc. 2006, pp. 273.

❷ Guasch, J. Luis Guasch & Sarath, Rajapatirana, *Antidumping and Anti-trust Issues in Free-trade Areas*, Oxford Univ. Press Inc. 1994, pp. 310 – 319.

❸ Gabrielle Marceau, *Antidumping and Competition Policies in Latin America and Caribbean: Total Strangers or Soul Mates?* 1998, pp. 1 – 26, http://www.worldbank.org/html/dec/Publications/Workpapers/WPS1900series/wps1958/wps1958.pdf, last visited May 24, 2009.

❹ Welber Barral *et al.*, *the use of Antidumping in Brazil, China, India and South Africa-Rule, Trends and Causes*, Kommerskollegium National Board of Trade, 2005, pp. 1, 32, http://www.tralac.org/pdf/Antidumping_in_4_Developing_Countries.pdf, last visited September 21, 2011.

❺ *Ibid.*, p. 58.

that deal with dumping and competition rules that deal with price discrimination, as well as the relationship of the respective rules with basic trade and competition principles in the modern free trade world, the practical interaction between the two also deserves examination. Based on the current typical cases and the empirical studies in major countries, this part will compare and analyze the two sets of rules from the practical perspective.

4.3.1 Rarely Overlap in Practice: Typical Cases

The application of competition rules was confined to the domestic scene for a long time. However, with the development of international trade and economy, the principle of territoriality proved insufficient to protect from foreign anti-competitive behavior. The U. S. in the 1945 United States v. Aluminium Co. of American (Alcoa) case changed this view. Since then, the Sherman Act became applicable to conduct abroad, if the conduct was intended to and had effects on the U. S. commerce. [1] Similarly, in the EU, the implementation doctrine to broaden the application of its competition rules was developed by the ECJ in the Wood pulp case in 1980s. [2] Following this, more countries started to admit the extraterritorial effect of competition law, and nowadays it is commonly acknowledged around the world. [3]

Due to territorial confinement of competition rules in quite a long time, antidumping rules that deal with dumping and competition rules

---

[1] Roland Weinrauch, *Competition Law in the WTO: the Rationale for a Framework Agreement*, Wien: NWV Neuer Wissenschaftlicher Verlag, 2004, p. 84.

[2] *Ibid.*, p. 80.

[3] As a consequence of this beggar-thy-neighbor policy, countries have started to aggressively enforce their competition laws by giving them extraterritorial reach. *See ibid.*, p. 73.

that deal with price discrimination rarely overlapped in practice. With the extension of their extraterritorial effects, studies in major countries show that there exist practical cases that may indicate the common regulated area of the two rules. These cases can be divided into three categories. The first one refers to those antidumping cases that deal with international predatory price discrimination; the second includes antitrust cases that deal with international predatory price discrimination, which specifically refers to the extraterritorial effect of antitrust law; and the third is such international predatory price discrimination dealt with both in antidumping law and in antitrust law. In the following part, the typical case under each category will be briefly introduced.

4. 3. 1. 1 Kodak-Fuji Dispute

The first category refers to the antidumping cases that deal with international predatory price discrimination. An excellent example of this is found in the dumping dispute between Eastman Kodak and Fuji Film. In 1990s, Fuji has moved to expand its market share around the world and it began dumping in the U. S. market. This dumping successfully forced Kodak to cut prices to defend its market share, decreased profitability and limited the resources the company had to defend other markets. As a result, Eastman Kodak filed a dumping case against Fuji, which was settled in a suspension agreement in August of 1994 allowing Eastman Kodak's market share and profitability to recover in the U. S. market. [1]

The Kodak-Fuji dispute has attracted widespread attention in the international community with respect to both trade and competition

---

[1] Greg Mastel, American Trade Laws After the Uruguay Round, M. E. Sharpe. Inc. 1996, pp. 83 - 84.

policy. ❶ It marks the first time that international antitrust issues have been referred to a WTO tribunal in 1996. ❷ Actually, before the case was brought to WTO, Kodak had resorted to quite a few remedies against Fuji in the U. S. including antidumping measures and 301 Section. ❸ Apart from these, in relation to the main complaints by Kodak towards the alleged anticompetitive trade practices by Fuji, it was suggested that Kodak could have brought the case to the Japanese competition authority or the U. S. antitrust law enforcement agencies

---

❶ Takaaki Kojima, *International Conflicts Over the Extraterritorial Application of Competition Law in a Borderless Economy*, Weather Center for International Affairs, 2001 – 2002, pp. 1, 17 – 18, http://www.wcfia.harvard.edu/fellows/papers/2001 – 02/kojima.pdf, last visited september 21, 2011.

❷ Patricia Isela Hansen, *Antitrust In the Global Market: Rethinking "Reasonable Expectations"*, Southern California Law Review, 1999, Vol. 72, pp. 1601, 1603.

❸ The general background of this WTO suit is that: "In May 1995, Kodak, a US. film maker, filed a complaint with the U. S. Trade Representative (USTR) under Section 301 of the 1974 Trade Act (as amended) alleging that Japan was tolerating anticompetitive practices by Fuji, a Japanese film maker, obstructing Kodak to acquire an appropriate market share in the Japanese consumer photographic film and paper market. The United States requested that Japan enter into bilateral negotiations but Japan rejected bilateral negotiations under Section 301. Japan maintained that Kodak's complaint concerned enforcement of the Antimonopoly Act of Japan and that Kodak could file its complaint directly with the JFTC. In June 1996, the U. S. TR made public the results of its investigation, concluding that the actions of Japan were unreasonable and therefore violated Section 301. At the same time, the U. S. TR also requested consultations with Japan in accordance with the dispute settlement provisions of the World Trade Organization (WTO). Consultations were held under GATT Article XXIII: 1 in July but failed to reach a resolution, while a panel of the WTO was established in October. After two panel meetings in 1997, the panel's report was issued in January 1998, finding that the allegations put forward by the United States under GATT provisions were not proven." *See* Takaaki Kojima, *International Conflicts Over the Extraterritorial Application of Competition Law in a Borderless Economy*, Weather Center for International Affairs, 2001 – 2002, pp. 1, 18, http://www.wcfia.harvard.edu/fellows/papers/2001 – 02/kojima.pdf, last visited September 21, 2011.

before the U. S. government brought the case to the WTO. ❶ Although no antitrust litigations have been actually initiated in the end, the relevant information shows the common regulated area of antidumping rules and competition rules. Some scholars also recognized that in this case, antidumping rules actually acted as an international extension of the Robinson-Patman Act's objective of ensuring a diverse and competitive market for the ultimate benefit of consumers and producers. ❷

4. 3. 1. 2 Wood Pulp Case

The second category refers to those antitrust cases that deal with international predatory price discrimination, which specifically refers to the extraterritorial effect of antitrust law. One of the well-known cases is the wood pulp case 1988 of the EU. ❸In this case, companies from the U. S., Canada, Norway, Portugal and Spain were accused as breaching Article 81 by the Commission of collusion on prices in the European Wood Pulp market in 1984. They tried to defend themselves

❶ "However, with respect to the main complaints by Kodak concerning alleged anti-competitive trade practices by Fuji, Kodak had brought the case to neither the Japanese competition authority nor the U. S. antitrust law enforcement agencies before the U. S. government brought the case to the WTO, although Kodak could have done so if it sought remedies under the competition laws of Japan or the United States. As a matter of fact, in its complaint with the U. S. TR, Kodak stated that it would not request that the U. S. government enforce antitrust laws, and the DOJ did not exercise extraterritorial antitrust jurisdiction." *See*, *e. g.*, Takaaki Kojima, *International Conflicts Over the Extraterritorial Application of Competition Law in a Borderless Economy*, Weather Center for International Affairs, 2001 - 2002, pp. 18 - 19, http://www.wcfia.harvard.edu/fellows/papers/2001 - 02/kojima.pdf, last visited September 21, 2011.

❷ Greg Mastel, *American Trade Laws After the Uruguay Round*, M. E. Sharpe. Inc. 1996, p. 84 .

❸ *Commission Decision of 19 December 1984 Relating to A Proceeding Under Article 85 of the EEC Treaty*, L085 Official Journal, 1985, http://eur - lex.europa.eu/LexUriServ/LexUriServ.do?uri = CELEX:31985D0202:EN:HTML, last visited September 21, 2011.

by claiming that "the EU lacks jurisdiction over them since they are not established within the EU. Many of the defendants had no affiliate within the EU". ❶ The European Court of Justice rejected their claims and exerted its jurisdiction by applying the Implementation doctrine. ❷ This case is quite famous for its extraterritorial application of the EC competition law.

During the investigation of this case, European Commission gave a very specific examination of the market, the undertaking concerned, the pricing system of the firms concerned, and so on. ❸ In observing whether the firms had "knowingly and deliberately concerted with regard to their announced and transaction prices", the setting of low price was examined. The evidences presented in the 60 paragraph of the commission decision are:

Price increases for export of pulp are perhaps premature for the third quarter. Everybody is, however, keen on reaching higher levels as soon as possible... In case the second quarter has not yet been price-fixed, wholly or partly, the low price sellers should try to increase their levels...Everybody seems to be aware of the necessity of increasing the prices as soon as possible but maybe the third quarter is still premature ... Cirnelima from Riocel has admitted that in the Federal Republic of Germany their prices are US MYM 335 to

---

❶ Olivier Bertrand & Marc Ivaldi, *European Competition Policy in International Markets*, A Contribution for the BRUEGEL's Project on Europe And The Global Economy, 2006, pp. 1, 9, http://www.intertic.org/Conference/Toulouse.pdf, last visited September 21, 2011.

❷ *Ibid.*

❸ *Commission Decision of* 19 *December* 1984 *Relating to A Proceeding Under Article* 85 *of the EEC Treaty*, L085 Official Journal, 1985, http://eur-lex.europa.eu/LexUriServ/LexUriServ.do?uri=CELEX:31985D0202:EN:HTML, last visited September 21, 2011.

340. However, no lower prices have been given Jacobson... Unicel will not be spoken of so much in the future as already so much has been sold at ridiculous prices. They are increasing their levels ... They are not prepared to meet the Riocel's prices. ❶

The evidences as such show that through extraterritorial application, antitrust law is used to detect collusive price behaviors, including international predatory price discrimination of the firms. Cases of this kind also indicated the possible overlap of antidumping rules and competition rules. This case is considered by some scholars as the only upheld one case of predatory dumping in the EU. ❷

4. 3. 1. 3 Television and Semiconductor Dispute

The third category includes those behaviors of international predatory price discrimination dealt with both in antidumping law and in antitrust law. The two examples are Television Dispute and Semiconductor Dispute, both of which are between the U. S. and Japan. With regard to Television Dispute, in the late 1950s, Japanese television manufacturers formed a cartel to control production and prices within Japan and began its fierce competition on the U. S. market in the early 1960s, using both dumping and rebates to distributors for televisions sold. ❸ As an issue of international predatory price discrimination, both antidumping law and antitrust law have been involved in

---

❶ *Commission Decision of 19 December 1984 Relating to A Proceeding Under Article 85 of the EEC Treaty*, L085 Official Journal , 1985, http://eur - lex. europa. eu/LexUriServ/LexUriServ. do?uri = CELEX:31985D0202:EN:HTML, last visited September 21, 2011.

❷ Yusaf H. Akbar, *Global Antitrust: Trade and Competition Linkages* , Ashagate Publishing, 2003, p. 28.

❸ Greg Mastel, *American Trade Laws After the Uruguay Round*, M. E. Sharpe. Inc. 1996, pp. 85 - 86.

this dispute. Akbar mentioned in his book that:

Zenith Radio Cop. Inc. , a U. S. manufacturer of television sets applied for an antidumping investigation alleged that Matsushita Electric Industrial of Japan had sold television sets in the U. S. market at prices below Japanese domestic prices in order to eliminate the U. S. competitors... Attempts to sue under antidumping law failed. The remaining firms then sued under U. S. antitrust law alleging predatory pricing...❶

Scholars also alleged that antidumping action in these instances is a direct extension of the U. S. antitrust laws, benefiting both American industry and ultimately American consumers. ❷

Apart from Television Dispute, Japanese dumping of semiconductors seems also an example of predatory pricing aimed at driving the U. S. semiconductor industry out of business and dominating the television industry. In the early 1980s, Japanese companies began to cut the price of memory chips known as DRAMs on the U. S. market. The U. S. producers initiated antidumping action and Japanese companies were imposed with antidumping duties (margin often exceeding 100%). ❸ Besides resorting to antidumping measures, some of U. S. producers also referred to antitrust law. As mentioned in Irwin's paper:

Motorola pondered filing an antidumping petition on 64K DRAMs in early 1982 but lacked industry support. Instead, it asked the

---

❶ Yusaf H. Akbar, *Global Antitrust: Trade and Competition Linkages*, Ashagate Publishing, 2003, p. 37.

❷ Greg Mastel, *American Trade Laws After the Uruguay Round*, M. E. Sharpe. Inc. 1996, p. 86.

❸ *Ibid.*, p. 85.

Department of Commerce to informally monitor Japanese prices... Japanese firms responded by reducing their exports to the United States to forestall an antidumping petition, at which point the Department of Justice launched an antitrust investigation into reports of Japanese collusion to raise prices in the U. S. market. ❶

This case also indicated that antidumping rules and competition rules can and sometimes do jointly regulate the common area-international predatory price discrimination.

4. 3. 2 Antidumping Cases under Competition Criteria

Apart from the typical cases, empirical studies are also of great importance. Just like Niels pointed out that: "A more thorough understanding [of competition versus antidumping] is needed of what would happen if competition standards were applied to antidumping cases. Through this that the overwhelming majority of dumping practices does or does not imply any danger to competition or efficiency can be indicated." ❷ Such empirical studies on the probability of

---

❶ Douglas A. Irwin, The Semiconductor Industry, in Robert Z. Lawerence, ed., *Brookings Trade Forum*, Brookings Institution, 1998, p. 180.

❷ Gunnar Niels, *What is Antidumping Policy Really About*? Journal of Economic Surveys, 2002, Vol. 14, pp. 467, 486, http://www. blackwell - synergy. com/links/doi/10. 1111/1467 - 6419. 00118, last visited September 21, 2011. This has also been required in other papers, for instances, "This leads to an interesting question: How many AD cases would lead to the imposition of sanctions, if antitrust rules had been applied instead?" *See also* Andreas Knorr, *Antidumping Rules vs. Competition Rules*, Institution for World Economics and International Management, 2004, pp. 1, 13, http://www. iwim. uni - bremen. de/publikationen/pdf/W031. pdf, last visited May 3, 2011; "The opposition of international trade economists to the use of antidumping action to counter cross-border price discrimination has been supported by the empirical findings on the pattern of dumping actions." *See* P. J. Lloyd, Antidumping and Competition Law, in Patrick F. J Macrory *et al.*, eds., *II The World Trade Organization: Legal, Economic and Political Analysis*, Springer 2005, p. 75.

predatory or anti-competitive dumping through examining antidumping cases under competition requirements or economic criteria have already been conducted with regard to the traditional heavy users of antidumping laws. As to the U. S. and the EU, during 1980s to 1990s, the most well-known empirical studies were conducted by Shin and Messerlin respectively.

4. 3. 2. 1 Empirical Study by Shin

As to the U. S., Shin (1998) analyzes 282 antidumping investigations in the U. S. between 1980 and 1989 with non-negative outcomes. ❶ She uses the criteria developed in the antitrust literature and analyzes cases of monopolizing or anti-competitive dumping. ❷ Such kind of test is quite influential and is followed by Messerlin and the

---

❶ Hyun Ja Shin, Possible Instances of Predatory Pricing in Recent U. S. Antidumping Cases, in Robert Z. Lawrence, ed., *Brookings Trade Forum*, Brookings Institution Press, 1998, pp. 85 – 86.

❷ Shin's basic idea is that employing cost-based to determine the outcome of antidumping investigations does not seem to be a practical and implementable strategy. A more readily administrable test for harmful dumping is one that searches the market for structural characteristics that should exist for predation to be profitable strategy in the long run. Only if these structural characteristic are found to exist should more complicated calculations be made. In accordance with this test, first of all, those antidumping cases as pertaining to a particular product that were simultaneously applied to the exports of several countries can be easily eliminated. Since if there are multiple exporters from a single country or exporters from several countries, successful coordination both in bearing the initial losses during the predatory period and in the later recoupment of these losses becomes increasingly difficult in a market where they would all be active. After elimination of the cases having the above considerations, the concentration of the market and the industries has been examined in the remaining antidumping cases. In Shin's study, the constructed Herfindahl index was applied to examine the market concentration of the U. S. as well as the foreign seller concentration. Based on the above test, Shin made a conclusion on the possibility of predatory pricing in antidumping cases of the U. S. during certain period. *See ibid.*, pp. 84 – 89.

other scholars in carrying out the similar studies on the EU and other countries. According to her research, an examination of the antidumping investigations initiated in the 1980s indicates that only 39 cases were brought in industries that exhibited substantial domestic and foreign market concentration, which represent 14 percent of the sample which would have to be examined further, seeking for example for the existence of market entry barriers as another necessary precondition for successful predatory practice. ❶

4. 3. 2. 2 Empirical Study by Messerlin

Messerlin (2001) conducted a similar study as Shin for the EU. ❷ His study also only considered the possibility of the existence of the first stage of predatory pricing: the acquisition of a large market share. In his study, of the 658 cases initiated between 1980 and 1999, only 461 can be subjected to his first screen of examination because they are the only ones for which information on foreign market shares in the EC markets in available in the official proceedings. And the examination result of this empirical study showed that, only 2% of 461 cases initiated between 1980 and 1987 are candidates for closer examination on predation grounds. ❸

4. 3. 2. 3 Other Empirical Studies

Besides Shin and Messerlin, later on, the recent antidumping cases

---

❶ Hyun Ja Shin, Possible Instances of Predatory Pricing in Recent U. S. Antidumping Cases, in Robert Z. Lawrence, ed., *Brookings Trade Forum*, Brookings Institution Press, 1998, p. 94.

❷ Jacques H. J. Bourgeois & Patrick A. Messerlin, *the European Community's Experience*, in Robert Z. Lawerence, ed., *Brookings Trade Forum*, Brookings Institution, 1998, pp. 127 – 145.

❸ *Ibid.*

of the U. S. and the EU during the year 1998 to 2002 were also studied by Aussilloux. [1] The analysis of Aussilloux et al. (2001) shows that 25% of the antidumping procedures implemented by the EU between 1994 and 1997 presented risk of market monopolization, and so they were not economically justified. The conclusion was that in many of these cases the procedures themselves may constitute anticompetitive instruments aimed at fighting against the imports. [2] Later on, the empirical study of Aussilloux et al. covering 1998 – 2002 cases shows that 31% of the antidumping procedures introduced by the EU appear to have a theoretical economic foundation in terms of likely anticompetitive effects, and 24% of the procedures engaged by the U. S. during this period have economic foundation in terms of likelihood of anticompetitive effects. [3]

Besides economic scholars, relevant international organizations also paid much attention to this. For example, OECD (1996) also did a survey on "antidumping cases potentially involving monopolizing behavior", focusing on the U. S., Canada, Australia, and the EU mainly during 1980s to 1990s. [4] According to its statistics, the

---

[1] Vincent Aussilloux *et al.*, *Antidumping as Anticompetitive Practice: Evidence from the United-States and the European Community*, pp. 1 – 38, http://www. ios. neu. edu/iioc2004/papers/s6k3. pdf, last visited May 14, 2009.

[2] *Ibid.*, p. 3.

[3] *Ibid.*, p. 16.

[4] *Trade and competition: Frictions after the Uruguay Round*, Working Papers No. 165, OECD Economic Department, 1996, pp. 1 – 34, http://titania. sourceoecd. org/vl = 2289142/cl = 18/nw = 1/rpsv/cgi – bin/wppdf? file = 5lgsjhvj86q5. pdf, last visited September 21, 2011.

antidumping measures imposed by the U. S. (1979 - 1989) totaled 282, with 35 potential monopolizing dumping. The antidumping measures imposed by Canada (1980 - 1991) totaled 92, with no potential monopolizing dumping. The antidumping measures imposed by Australia (1988 - 1991) totaled 20, with 5 potential monopolizing dumping. The antidumping measures imposed by the EU. (1980 - 1989) totaled 270, with 23 potential monopolizing dumping. [1]

Ever since mid-1990s, a new noticeable feature of antidumping actions is that, more and more developing countries such as Mexico, Argentina, Brazil, India, South Africa, and even China, that used to be the main targets of antidumping actions, have become the "new users" of antidumping law, and the number of antidumping actions filed by these countries has gradually outnumbered those of the traditional users. [2] Similar empirical studies have been carried out with regard to some of these countries. For example, Holden investigated the antidumping cases of South Africa (1991 - 1998) and concluded that 3% of the successful applications were likely to have involved

[1] *Trade and competition: Frictions after the Uruguay Round*, Working Papers No. 165, OECD Economic Department, 1996, p. 17, http://titania. sourceoecd. org/vl = 2289142/cl = 18/nw = 1/rpsv/cgi - bin/wppdf? file = 5lgsjhvj86q5. pdf, last visited September 21, 2011.

[2] Take China for example, from 1995 - 2008, China was subject to antidumping measures in 479 cases. Among them, 66 cases were initiated by the U. S., 60 by the EU, 12 by Australia, and 15 by Canada. All of the rest cases (more than 300 cases) were initiated by developing countries, including 90 by India, 40 by Argentina, 33 by Turkey, 16 by South Africa, 21 by Brazil, 15 by Mexico and so on. The most recent Statistics *See* http://www. wto. org/english/tratop_e/adp_e/ad_meas_rep_exp_e. xls, last visited May 3, 2009.

anticompetitive behavior on the part of the foreign suppliers. ❶ Aggarwal applied certain economic criteria of predatory dumping to antidumping investigations in India between 1993 and 2001 and found that they were met in a few cases. ❷

4.4 Dumping: Competition Law instead of Antidumping Law

Whether putting dumping under competition rules, instead of antidumping rules, can be more appropriate, in terms of being less vulnerable to protectionist? This chapter seeks to conduct a comprehensive examination of this "substitution" issue by comparing and analyzing both rules from three perspectives, as discussed above. It is found that compared to antidumping rules, competition rules are more meticulous in each of the basic elements, more consistent with basic modern trade and competition principles, and can be less submitted to protectionist abuse in practical cases.

4.4.1 More Meticulous in Each of the Basic Elements

By comparing and analyzing the above four basic elements of the two rules, it is concluded that competition rules are more meticulous than antidumping rules in dealing with low-price selling without being abused for protectionists.

---

❶ Merle Holden, *Antidumping: A Reaction to Trade Liberalisation or Anti Competitive? South African Journal of Economics*, 2002, pp. 912, 929, http://onlinelibrary.wiley.com/doi/10.1111/j.1813-6982.2002.tb00051.x/pdf, last visited September 21, 2011.

❷ Aradhna Aggarwal, *Antidumping Law and Practice: An Indian Perspective*, Indian Council for Research on International Economic Relations, 2002, pp. 1, 9-20, http://www.icrier.org/pdf/antiDump.pdf, last visited september 21, 2011.

With regard to the objectives, competition rules set up the basic goal of protecting competitive process rather than the individual competitors, aim at promoting economic efficiency as well as protection of consumer welfare, and take the overall welfare of the country into consideration, rather than only protecting the welfare of the producers. Hence, they are less likely to be abused by those domestic firms with vested interests, and thereby are less susceptible to protectionism.

From the perspective of basic substantive rules, in addressing the specific issue of predatory price discrimination, competition laws are more selective in their application and are more effective at distinguishing between fair and unfair trade practices. Since low-price selling may have either a pro-competitive or an anti-competitive effect, competition rules are much more careful and sophisticated in distinguishing between healthy competition and harmful predatory conducts, without being abused for protectionism, as with antidumping rules.

From the perspective of basic procedural rules, antidumping rules offer numerous possibilities for a broad scale of discretion for an efficient protection of domestic vested interests. By contrast, with comparatively clearer objective and stricter methodological guidelines, the enforcement authorities of competition rules have significantly less discretion than the enforcement authorities of antidumping rules in implementing their respective laws. Moreover, as a rather judicial-based procedure, the whole competition investigation is comparatively fair and equal, hence gives foreign competitors more chances to defend.

In respect of remedies, imposition of duties, price undertaking and so on under antidumping law do not bear directly on the firms or firms' competitive behavior. The remedies can only raise the price of the dumped good for the duration of the action to compensate the victims but cannot prohibit the unfair behavior from reoccurring. On the contrary, the remedies provided under competition rules, aimed at the prohibition of such practice with appropriate penalties should the offense continues, would be the more appropriate action.

4.4.2 More Consistent with Basic Modern Trade and Competition Principles

In the modern free trade world, despite quite a few distinctions between them, the basic objectives of trade liberalization policy and competition policy are becoming consistent with each other. Therefore, a thorough evaluation of the advantages of using competition rules rather than antidumping rules to deal with dumping cannot be achieved without taking this background into consideration. Putting the two rules against this background, it is concluded that competition rules are more consistent with basic modern trade and competition principles, and thereby putting the issue of dumping under competition rules can be less subject to traditional protectionism.

In terms of modern basic trade principles, the first advantage of competition rules over antidumping rules is that the former can avoid undermining three of the fundamental principles of GATT/WTO system, including free trade, non-discrimination, as well as reciprocity.

In terms of modern competition policy, the second advantage of competition rules over antidumping rules is that conflict with basic competition principles can be avoided and therefore averting anti-competitive effects in practice in five main aspects, which include ensuring competitive process in conformity with the economic efficiency, maximization of the consumer welfare, avoiding the facilitation of collusion between domestic and foreign producers, avoiding the maintenance of domestic monopoly power or forming domestic cartels, and promoting market integration in bilateral and regional areas.

4.4.3 Less Protectionist Abuse in Practice

Through the examination of practical cases, it is found that although the jurisdictional limit of competition rules has, for a long time accounts for the rare overlap with antidumping rules, with the extension of the extraterritorial effects of competition rules, the two sets of rules became interacted. By summarizing their practical interaction into three categories and briefly illustrating the typical cases under each one, studies indicate that in practice, antidumping rules and competition rules can and do sometimes jointly regulate common area, i. e., international predatory price discrimination. In other words, competition rules, instead of antidumping rules, can and do sometimes deal with international dumping. This overlapping area has been increasingly broadened with the internationalization of competition rules in the modern multilateral world.

Empirical studies on the probability of predatory or anti-competitive dumping through examining antidumping cases under competition requirements or economic criteria have already been conducted mostly with regard to the traditional heavy users of antidumping. The common impression is that the number of antidumping cases would sharply decrease if competition standards were applied. This means, based on comparatively solid economic theories, devoted a lot to the sophisticated operation of detecting harmful low-price selling, as well as conforming to the modern basic trade and competition principles, competition rules, compared to antidumping rules, can better deal with the issue of dumping, without resulting in the proliferation or protectionist abuse to a greater extent.

Based on all of the above examination from three perspectives, it is considered in this book that supposing competition rules and antidumping rules have the same objective in dealing with low-price selling conduct, then putting dumping under competition rules, instead of antidumping rules, can be more appropriate, in terms of competition rules being less vulnerable to protectionism. From this point of view, this book supports substituting antidumping rules by competition rules. However, difficulty remains in current world where not all countries have such well-founded competition rules as those of the U. S. , the EU etc. Especially with regards to developing countries, competition policy and rules are still being under construction.

Chapter V Difficulties of Substitution in Practice

The above chapter suggests that competition rules are more appropriate than antidumping rules in detecting dumping, without being abused by protectionist. However, legal, institutional and political difficulties have been among the main obstacles so far to actually replace antidumping with competition. [1] There are two major objections against the substitution, i. e. "alleged different objectives of antidumping law" and "imperfection of competition law".

5. 1 Difficulties in respect of Antidumping

In respect of antidumping, scholars are arguing that antidumping law and competition law have totally different goals. For instance, Alan Wm. Wolff was strongly against the idea of substitution. He argues that antidumping and compeititon have separate and equally valid objectives. The actual rationale for antidumping law is one that antitrust practitioners should feel good about. Competition law cannot do the essential work which antidumping does. Therefore, there is no reasonable foundation for replacing the antidumping rules with competition laws or modifying them in a way that would make them reflect

---

[1] Gunnar Niels, *What is Antidumping Policy Really About*? Journal of Economic Surveys, 2002, Vol. 14, pp. 467, 485, http://www. blackwell - synergy. com/links/doi/10. 1111/1467 -6419. 00118, last visited september 21, 2011.

competition policy principles. ❶

Even if originally antidumping law was part of antitrust law to deal with cross-border predatory price discrimination, modern antidumping law has different goals that are totally different from competition law. Alan Sykes of the University of Chicago claims that antitrust law and antidumping law come from the same family tree, but the two branches have diverged widely. ❷

The arguments against substitution as forementioned are mainly based on the statements of the U. S. government submitted to the Working Group on the Interaction between Trade and Competition Policy of WTO (WGTCP). We will first give a comprehensive investigation into various opinions concerning the objectives of antidumping stated to WGTCP, so as to identify what are the alleged dissimilar objectives of antidumping law.

A survey of all of the working documents from the year 1997 to 2004 indicates that the relationship between competition law and antidumping law brought forward a hot discussion around 1998. Governments were disputing over two key points: one is the objectives and justifications of antidumping law and competition law respectively, and the other is the identification of the anti-competitive effects of antidumping law as well as the solutions thereto. ❸

---

❶ *See*, e. g. , Alan Wm. Wolff, *Trade and Antitrust: Is Rapprochement Desirable? Is It Possible? The (Notionally) Bridgeable Chasm Between Antitrust and Trade Policy*, New York Law School Law Review, 2003, Vol. 47, pp. 167 – 190.

❷ Alan O. Sykes, *Antidumping and Antitrust: What Problems Does Each Address?* in Robert Z. Lawerence, ed. , *Brookings Trade Forum*Brookings Institution, 1998, p. 42.

❸ Those governments' opinions which focus on the reform of the specific rules from the perspective of due process shall be omitted here for the purpose of this book.

Concerning the objectives of antidumping law, the governments' opinions can be categorized into three kinds. [1] The first kind of viewpoint claims that antidumping law and antitrust law have totally different objective or justification, and thereby there is no linkage between the two, let alone the anti-competitive effects. The second one asserts that antidumping law has or should have the same justification as the competition law, and the right way to cope with its anti-competitive effects is to be reformed by competition policy or repealed by competition law. The third one deems that although antidumping law and competition law have different objectives, antidumping law involves many anti-competitive effects and thereby should be reformed by competition policy and substituted by competition law.

5.1.1 "Maintaining Multilateral World" and "Level Playing Field"

The U.S. is the strongest supporter to the viewpoint that antidumping law and antitrust law have totally different objective or justification. In the communication dated 27 July 1998 to the WTO, the U.S. first stated clearly that the antidumping law and competition law have different objectives and are founded on different principles, and

---

[1] This is one of the so-called "new issues" in the WTO, addressing how domestic and international competition policy instruments, such as antitrust or competition laws, interact with international trade. As a result of the Ministerial Conference in Singapore (1996), the Working Group on the Interaction between Trade and Competition Policy (WGTCP) was established to study various aspects of this issue, with the participation of all WTO Members. However, In July 2004 the General Council of the WTO decided that the interaction between trade and competition policy (in addition to investment, and transparency in government procurement) would no longer form part of the Work Programme set out in the Doha Ministerial Declaration and therefore that no work towards negotiations on any of these issues will take place within the WTO during the Doha Round. *See Interaction Between Trade and Competition Policy*, WTO, http://www.wto.org/english/tratop_e/comp_e/comp_e.htm, last visted May 13, 2009.

they seek to remedy different problems. ❶ It claimed that antidumping law is a trade remedy which WTO members have agreed as necessary to the "maintenance of the multilateral trading system". ❷ A review of antidumping laws and their history prior to GATT also showed that the true motive for the early antidumping laws is a general but undefined concern for "fairness" rather than a concern that foreign "trusts or combine" might monopolize the domestic market. ❸

---

❶ The U. S. stated in the beginning that: "In the view of the United States, this Group cannot gain from any inquiry into the alleged 'anti-competitive effects' of the anti-dumping rules. As many Members have acknowledged, there is no reasonable foundation for replacing the antidumping rules with competition laws or modifying them in a way that would make them reflect competition policy principles. Stated simply, the antidumping rules and competition laws have different objectives and are founded on different principles, and they seek to remedy different problems. If the antidumping rules were eliminated in favor of competition laws or modified to be consistent with competition policy principles, the problems which the antidumping rules seek to remedy would go unaddressed." *See* WT/WGTCP/W/88, Communication from the United States, August, 1998.

❷ The U. S. stated: "Contrary to the assumptions of some economists, the antidumping rules are not intended as a remedy for the predatory pricing practices of firms or as a remedy for any other private anti-competitive practices typically condemned by competitions law. Rather, the antidumping rules are a trade remedy which WTO members have agreed is necessary to the maintenance of the multilateral trading system. Without this and other trade remedies, there could have been no agreement on broader GATT and later WTO packages of market-opening agreements, especially given the imperfections which remain in multilateral trading system." *See ibid.*

❸ The U. S. stated: "A review of antidumping laws and their history prior to GATT 1947, when antidumping remedies were made part of the multilateral trading system, suggests, at the rhetorical level, some link with a concern over the predatory pricing practices of large foreign monopolies. However, a closer examination of the antidumping legislation actually enacted, shows that the true motive for the early antidumping laws was not a concern that foreign 'trusts or combines' might monopolize the domestic market. Rather, it was a general but undefined concern for 'fairness' when domestic firms had to face competition from foreign firms and, more particularly, a response to manufacturing interests seeking to maintain or increase the levels of tariff protection and/or ensure the market 'normalcy' to which they had become accustomed." *See* WT/WGTCP/W/88, Communication from the United States, August 1998.

Accordingly, to achieve this "maintenance" function, by offsetting the injurious dumping, antidumping rules represent an effort to promote "fair trade", meaning maintaining a "level playing field" [1] among producers in different countries by coping with two issues: one is to protect against adverse trade effects that can arise from "market-distortive government industrial policies", and the other is to neutralize inequities that may arise from differences in national economic systems, i. e. "the interaction of different economic systems". [2]

In the communication, the U. S. discussed the specific situations of "market-distortive government industrial polices" and "differences in national economic systems" at large length. In terms of the former, the U. S. argued that although these policies take on many different forms, they provide similar artificial advantages to the benefiting producers. [3] There are four different categories of market-distortive government industrial policies, including:

I. Government's industrial policies which combine limits on domestic competition with market access barriers that keep out foreign competitors. The ability of a country's producers to engage in injurious dumping can arise from a combination of two types of government's

---

[1] "In the international context, where the antidumping rules apply, 'fairness' means a level playing field, with similarly situated producers being treated similarity. In other words, 'fair' trade envisions that producers will use only natural comparative advantages, such as natural resources, a favorable climate, advanced technology, skilled workers, greater efficiency or lower labor costs, and not any artificial advantages." *See ibid.*

[2] "Normally, the ability to engage in injurious dumping can be traced to artificial advantages resulting from either (or both) of two situations, i. e., market-distortive government industrial policies and/or differences in national economic systems. It is these situations that principally give rise to the need for the antidumping rules." *See ibid.*

[3] WT/WGTCP/W/88, Communication from the United States, August 1998.

industrial policies. First, the government may pursue measures designed to result in limited (or no) domestic competition for these producers. Second, it may adopt measures that substantially protect these producers from foreign competition, either through high tariffs or any of a host of possible non-tariff barriers. In the communication, the U. S. listed a number of policies. ❶

II. Domestic price controls, which governments can use in a number of ways to support domestic industries. For instance, a government

---

❶ More explanations on this type: The existence of only *limited domestic competition* may be due to many different types of industrial policies falling under the umbrella of government actions intended to influence the structure of the home market with the aim of affecting the number or type of producers. Examples of these policies include: Government policies limiting the number of producers in a particular industry, such as through the restrictive award of licenses; State monopolies; Government policies favoring a "national champion" firm within an industry; Government policies which divide up and stabilize market shares; and Any of a variety of other government policies which regulate commerce by creating, promoting or tolerating monopolies or oligopolies or by favoring some domestic competitors over other domestic (and foreign) competitors.

Protection against foreign competition, meanwhile, may be due to either high tariffs or any number of non-tariff barriers. Examples of possible non-tariff barriers include: Import charges, quantitative restrictions, import licensing and customs barriers; Standards, testing, labeling and certification, including, for example, the acquiescence of a government in unwarranted regulations sought by industry, a government's unnecessarily restrictive application of sanitary and phytosanitary standards, and a government's refusal to accept foreign manufacturers' self-certification of conformance to home market product standards; Investment barriers, such as limitations on foreign equity participation and on access to government-funded research and development programs, local content and export performance requirements, and restrictions on transferring earnings and capital; State trading rights; Services barriers, such as limits on the range of financial services offered by home market financial institutions, regulation of international data flows and restrictions on the U. S. of foreign data processing; Lack of intellectual property protection, including inadequate patent, copyright and trademark regimes; Government procurement practices such as closed bidding; and Bribery and corruption.

In addition, the ability of a country's producers to engage in injurious dumping can arise from the absence of, or the lack of adequate enforcement of, meaningful national competition laws. *See* WT/WGTCP/W/88, Communication from the United States, August 1998.

sets the domestic price of a product at an artificially high level, while it uses prohibitively high tariffs to prevent foreign producers from undercutting this price, or an artificially low price is set domestically for a product that is an input for one or more finished products. ❶

III. Government subsidization, particularly where market forces do not drive the subsidy recipients to pass on the subsidy benefits to consumers in order to remain competitive in their home market. ❷

IV. State trading arrangements, typically involving commodity

---

❶ More explanations on this type: One scenario, which has many variations, is where a government sets the domestic price of a product at an artificially *high* level, while it uses prohibitively high tariffs to prevent foreign producers from undercutting this price. Here, even though the domestic producers of the product may be inefficient and have relatively high costs, the domestic price is often set high enough for them to reap super-competitive profits. The domestic producers can use this artificial advantage to leverage exports at low prices. A similar scenario can develop when an artificially *low* price is set domestically for a product that is an input for one or more finished products. Here, the domestic producers of the finished products receive the artificial advantage of paying a below-market price for an input. This same advantage is not available to producers of the finished products located in other countries because the input producers, when exporting the input, do not face any price controls, and therefore can sell at a competitive price. Thus, the domestic producers of the finished products can use this advantage over producers of the finished products located in other countries to leverage exports at low prices. *See* WT/WGTCP/W/88, Communication from the United States, August 1998.

❷ More explanations on this type: The government subsidies create an artificial advantage for the recipient domestic producers that is not enjoyed by producers located in other countries, to the extent that they do not receive similar subsidies from their governments. In these circumstances, the government subsidization enables the recipient domestic producers, when exporting, to engage in the low pricing that constitutes dumping. Meanwhile, the same results can occur even when government subsidies finance failing domestic producers. Here, even though the recipient domestic producers may not become more competitive vis-à-vis non-subsidized producers located in other countries, excess capacity in the domestic industry still can be created, and dumping abroad often results. *See ibid.*

products such as agricultural products also can lead directly to injurious dumping. [1]

Regarding the latter, i. e. differences in national economic systems, it was considered in this communication that in many circumstances, the differences between two national economic systems result not just from the prevailing business climate or culture. Instead, these differences also are attributable, to great extent, to the role which the government chooses to play in how business is conducted. [2] Five examples were offered to show how the injurious dumping occurred under this situation:

I. When social and legal arrangements for employment and underemployment differ between countries, with labor being more of a fixed cost in one country and more of a variable cost in another country;

---

[1] More explanations on this type: Although more common in planned economies, state trading arrangements also can be found in market economies. A common scenario involves domestic producers which are not internationally competitive because their cost of production is higher than the world market price for their goods. Here, the domestic producers are allowed to sell goods to a state trading company at prices equal to their costs, and then the state trading company dumps the goods abroad at whatever prices it can obtain. Normally, this price will be the lower world market price, and over time this world market price may even decline if the state trading arrangement induces significant excess production of the goods. Another scenario involves internationally competitive domestic producers which produce goods whose price on the world market can fluctuate significantly from year to year. Here, in order to insulate them from harmful price downturns, the domestic producers are allowed to sell their goods to a state trading company at a predetermined price, which in a particular year may be well above or below the world market price. Dumping takes place in years that the predetermined price is above the world market price if the state trading company subsequently sells the goods abroad at the world market price. *See*WT/WGTCP/W/88, Communication from the United States, August 1998.

[2] *Ibid.*

II. Where the business climates in the exporting and importing countries give rise to differing debt-equity structures and debt burdens.

III. Where government-tolerated relationships among businesses fundamentally vary between the exporting and importing countries;

IV. Where the government has a standing practice of adopting market-stabilization measures and tolerating collusive behaviour among domestic producers once a product market becomes mature, with the result that market shares among domestic producers become stagnant and price competition is eliminated;

V. Where economies that make use of state planning. In these economies, unlike in market economies, the government will issue directives to producers to achieve a certain level of exports. [1]

5.1.2 "Predatory Pricing" and "Monopolizing Dumping"

The second kind of the viewpoints deemed that antidumping law has or should have the same justification as the competition law, and because that, the correct way to cope with its anti-competitive effects is to be reformed by competition policy or repealed by competition law. Countries such as Japan, Korea, Peru, Mexico, Chile, and Hong Kong were the advocates.

Japan is one of the strongest supporters thereof. In the communication dated 21 September 1998, Japan asserted that both competition law and antidumping law deal with predatory pricing. [2] In the following communications dated 28 May 1999, Japan re-emphasized its

---

[1] More explanations on each example *See* WT/WGTCP/W/88, Communication from the United States, August 1998.

[2] WT/WGTCP/W/92, Communication from Japan, September 1998.

viewpoint towards the nature of antidumping law. [1] According to Japan, antidumping law and competition law have the identical objective in different areas: competition law seeks to eliminate predatory pricing in domestic trade, while antidumping law addresses such pricing in international trade. However, they protect different objects. Antidumping law protects competitors whereas competition law safeguards competition. Japan claimed that since there is significant doubt about the economic validity of the criteria for imposing antidumping measures, the possible action of reforms would be to improve the criteria by introducing the perspective of competition policy. [2] This indicates that Japan favored the economic efficiency analysis of antidumping law and its substitution by competition law.

Korea also shared the similar opinion. In the communications dated 30 March 1998, 3 September 1998, and 9 March 2001, by exploring whether antidumping rules are justifiable from an economic perspective, Korea considered that unless predatory intent is confirmed, antidumping regulations do not make any economic sense but merely incur anti-competitive and protective effects. Accordingly, antidumping law

---

[1] In the communication of WT/WGTCP/W/122 dated 28 May 1999, which is titled as "The contribution of competition policy to achieving the objectives of the WTO including the promotion of international trade", Japan claimed that Antidumping measures were originally intended to regulate "predatory pricing" in the international contest just like domestic competition laws do in domestic markets. *See* WT/WGTCP/W/122, Communication from Japan, May 1999. In the communication of WT/WGTCP/W/123 dated 28 May 1999, which is about "response to US view on antidumping", Japan stated that Antidumping measures, as they are currently used, constitute a system for protecting a broad spectrum of domestic industry from price competition. This is, in reality, a result of political pressure and is counter to their essential objectives of competition policy. *See* WT/WGTCP/W/123, Communication from Japan, May 1999.

[2] WT/WGTCP/W/92, Communication from Japan, September 1998.

is not the optimal response to dumping. The best policy is rather to remove the main cause of dumping, i. e. , to break down the monopoly status of firms in the exporting countries. ❶ To support its arguments, Korea cited Willig's dumping theory of dividing dumping practices into monopolizing and non-monopolizing categories. The monopolizing results in reduced welfare of the importing country, but the non-monopolizing may increase the welfare of the importing country. Therefore, antidumping law on non-monopolizing dumping practices may reduce the welfare of the importing country. ❷

Hong Kong also examined antidumping law via the efficiency analysis. It argued that the justification of antidumping law is similar to competition law, hence suggesting limiting the objective of antidumping law to punish only monopolizing dumping. In Hong Kong's statement, the WTO rules on the determination of dumping, injury and causality are so broadly drafted that antidumping measures are often imposed even if international price differentiation is economically justified, such as due to anticipated change in tastes or different elasticity in different economics. ❸ Moreover, dumping neither endangers nor distorts competition in the importing economy, for instance, when the often small market shares of allegedly dumped imports render abuses of market power impossible. ❹ Hong Kong suggested that international price differentiation on its own would not be a pretext for action; and the producer-oriented injury concept should be replaced by a competition-oriented concept focusing on the risks of "monopolizing

---

❶ WT/WGTCP/W/73, Communication from the Republic of Korea, March 1998.
❷ *Ibid.*
❸ WT/WGTCP/W/85, Communication from Hong Kong, China, August 1998.
❹ *Ibid.*

dumping", which have reduced competition and consumer welfare in the importing economies. [1]

Similar analysis and statements can also be found in the communications of Mexico, Peru and Chile to the WTO. That the justification of antidumping law is identical to competition law can be indicated in their suggestions of confining antidumping law to cope with monopolizing or anti-competitive dumping. Mexico considered that dumping has indeed predatory effects or objects when an exporter with market power has the capacity and possibility to: Ⅰ. fix prices below the balancing prices, Ⅱ. displace his competitors and, Ⅲ. recover the losses thus incurred by the subsequent imposition of monopoly prices. [2] Peru recognized that antidumping law is designed to prevent discriminatory pricing policies from being set up as unfair competition practices in the market for which exports are intended, the purpose of competition law is to prevent price discrimination from affecting competition in the market where the customers for good or services compete. [3] Chile considered that antidumping measures may only be applied when the objective conditions in a market make anti-competitive behaviour practicable. [4]

5.1.3 "Predatory Pricing" to "Protection from Foreign Competition"

The third kind of viewpoints argued that antidumping law and competition law have different objectives. It is because antidumping law involves many anti-competitive effects that it should be reformed by

---

[1] WT/WGTCP/W/85, Communication from Hong Kong, China, August 1998.

[2] *Ibid.*

[3] WT/WGTCP/W/74 , Communication from Peru, April 1998.

[4] *Ibid.*

competition policy hence substituted by competition law. This is held by quite a few countries, such as the Australia, New Zealand, the EU and etc.

Taken Australia for instance, in the communication, it did not state clearly what the justification antidumping law and competition law each is. Instead, it pointed out that Australia's experience has highlighted that antidumping and competition matters can intersect. Moreover, conceptually, antidumping matters can be of concern to competition authorities and are an important complement to policies dealing with price discrimination in domestic sector. ❶

With respect to New Zealand, although the earliest antidumping laws were founded on the need to deal with international price predation, this focus has long since been lost. Now antidumping law is viewed as one of the trade policies which protect domestic industries from foreign competition. Thus, competition tends to view antidumping laws as limiting competition by providing a margin of protection for uncompetitive domestic producers. ❷

The EU differed from the other countries under this category in that it concerned much more about the unification of global competition law. Therefore, the EU viewed that although the modern antidumping law and competition law have different objectives and justifications, similarly as stated by the U. S. , the abuse of antidumping law can be prevented by creating the global competition law. Without referring to the earliest history of antidumping law, the EU argued that antidumping law agreement of WTO is aimed at removing the trade-distorting

---

❶ WT/WGTCP/W/98, Communication from Australia, September 1998.

❷ WT/WGTCP/W/81, Communication from New Zealand, August 1998.

effects of dumped imports and to restore effective competition in the market when injury is being caused to a domestic industry. [1] According to the European scholars, under most situations the "trade-distorting effects" refer to market segmentation and closed home market such as so-called NME (non-market economic) countries. [2]

Therefore, in the viewpoint of the EU government, antidumping law and competition apply in different economic, legal and institutional contexts. Competition law prohibits and subjects to strict penalties certain forms of pricing behaviour by firms. Competition law applies in principle within the context of an integrated market, whereas antidumping law applies in an economic setting which is still characterized by border measures and other regulatory obstacles and distortion of trade. [3] Notwithstanding, the EU claimed that it can be expected that so far as countries apply a stricter policy of competition law enforcement, and further progress is made in the integration of markets, the need to have recourse to antidumping action would be reduced over time. [4]

5.1.4 Alleged Different Objectives: "Unfair Trade" and "Quasi Safeguard"

The conducted investigation shows that governments alleged there are three different kinds of objectives of antidumping law. The first

---

[1] WT/WGTCP/W/78, Communication from the European Community and Its Member States, July 1998.

[2] *See*, e.g., Edwin Vermulst, *Competition and antidumping: continued peaceful coexistence?* 1999, pp. 1, 13, http://www.feem.it/NR/rdonlyres/82DF239A-108E-4023-8C71-76A31E05E62D/302/6799.pdf, last visited september 21, 2011.

[3] WT/WGTCP/W/78, Communication from the European Community and Its Member States, July 1998.

[4] *Ibid.*

one conforms to the efficiency analysis, viewing that the objective of antidumping law remains to protect against anti-competitive dumping such as predatory dumping or monopolizing dumping. Japan, Korea etc. are of this viewpoint hence arguing for substituting antidumping by competition.

The second one alleges that antidumping law is purported to protect domestic industries against "unfair" foreign competition resulted from either market-distortive government industrial policies or different economic structures. Countries like the U. S., the EU are of this opinion. Especially the U. S. is strongly against the substitution.

The third one is of the viewpoint that antidumping law is used to protect domestic industries from foreign competition, or in other words, a quasi safeguard measure. The representative countries include Australia, New Zealand etc. That the U. S. argued that part of antidumping's responsiblity is to protect domestic industries from different economic structures is equal to argue that, antidumping should be a quasi safeguard measure. This can be indicated in the interface theory of Jackson. ❶ The interface theory favors the application of antidumping law as buffers, or a "meditative or interface mechanism" between social, economic, and structural differences present in international trade. ❷ Jackson wrote in his book that:

---

❶ The interface theory refers not only to dumping and antidumping, but also refers to many other trade problems facing the international system, and it was first argued by the economist Ethier in economic and mathematical variables that nobody understood, but Jackson and his team made it simple. *See* Gabrielle Marceau, *Antidumping and Anti-trust Issues in Free-trade Areas*, Oxford Univ. Press Inc. 1994, p. 46.

❷ Gabrielle Marceau, *Antidumping and Anti-trust Issues in Free-trade Areas*, Oxford Univ. Press Inc. 1994, p. 46.

As world economic interdependence has increased, it has become more difficult to manage relationships among various economies. This problem is analogous to the difficulties involved in trying to get two computers of different designs to work together. To do so, one needs an "interface" mechanism to mediate between the two computers. Likewise in international economic relations, particularly in trade, some "interface mechanism" may be necessary to allow different economic systems to trade together harmoniously. ❶

Accordingly, a commonly expressed goal of trade policy in connection with "unfair" practices is that of the "level playing field". Unfortunately, it is often very difficult to carry this analogy too far. ❷ The distinction between fair and unfair trade has become increasingly blurred. ❸ What seems "unfair" to members of one society may seem perfectly fair to those of another society. ❹ Therefore, by acting as a crude or blunt instrument to cause different economic systems to share more equitably the burdens of adjusting to shifts of world trade flows, antidumping rules should be viewed as part of the subject of "safeguards" rather than as part of subject of "unfair trade". ❺

---

❶ John H. Jackson, *the World Trading System: Law and Policy of International, Economic Relations*, MIT Press, 1997, p. 248.

❷ *Ibid.*, p. 248.

❸ *Ibid.*, p. 247.

❹ *Ibid.*, p. 248.

❺ Jackson mentioned in his book that: Could it be that the antidumping rules are acting as a crude or blunt instrument to cause different economic systems to share more equitably the burdens of adjusting to shifts of world trade flows? If so, perhaps we should view antidumping rules as part of the subject of "safeguards" rather than as part of subject of "unfair trade". *See* John H. Jackson, *the World Trading System: Law and Policy of International*, Economic Relations, MIT Press 1997, 274.

Similar statement can also be found in other literature supporting interface theory. For instance, Denton deemed that:

This [antidumping law] function would not attempt to cleanse the international system of distortions, but only to subdue protectionist pressure by reducing the "unfairness" of foreign commercial structures. In this light, the international sanctioning of national rules is a "buffer" which ameliorates the effects of structural differences... the interface argument also suggests that maybe national antidumping laws operate a quasi safeguard measure. [1]

To sum up, the first major objection against substitution argues that antidumping has dissimilar objectives to predatory price discrimination. The U. S. is the strongest supporter. "To protect against unfair trade" and "to be used as a quasi safeguard measure" are two major alleged objectives of antidumping.

5. 2 Difficulties in respect of Competition

The second major difficulty lies in competition part. Antidumping advocates always readily point out that competition policy has some problems *per se*. The major objections are two fold, including lack of domestic competition laws to cover predatory price discrimination, as well as lack of international agreement for enforcement.

5. 2. 1 Lack of Domestic Competition Law

Scholars point out that not all of the countries have competition laws to cover predatory price discrimination. For instance, P. J. Lloyd suggested one possible objection to the substitution of action under

---

[1] Gabrielle Marceau, *Antidumping and Anti-trust Issues in Free-trade Areas*, Oxford Univ. Press Inc. 1994, p. 47.

national competition law for action under international law is that some of the countries that have antidumping laws do not have competition laws that cover predatory pricing or price discrimination or other pricing behavior that might produce dumping as measured under international laws. ❶ There is a special concern that few of the new countries that take antidumping actions have effective national competition laws. ❷ Moreover, countries have various competition principles and rules on predatory price discrimination. Although there are relevant national rules, competition standards are far from uniform across countries. ❸

Consequently, domestic competition laws may fail to address anti-competitive conduct for a number of reasons, such as certain anti-competitive conduct may be exempted from the application of national competition laws due to domestic policy considerations or benefits to the national economy, without regard to wider cross-border effects. ❹ National competition laws may address anti-competitive conduct, but may be inadequately enforced for a number of different reasons, including corrupt or inept enforcement agencies, poorly resourced enforcement agencies, or due to differences in enforcement practices between nations. ❺ And national competition laws may fail to address

---

❶ P. J. Lloyd, Antidumping and Competition Law, in Patrick F. J Macrory *et al.*, eds., *II The World Trade Organization: Legal*, Economic and Political Analysis Springer, 2005, p. 78.

❷ *Ibid.*

❸ Gunnar Niels, *What is Antidumping Policy Really About?* Oxford Economic Research Associates, p. 485.

❹ Martyn D. Taylor, *International Competition Law: A New Dimension for the WTO?* Cambridge Univ. Press Inc. 2006, p. 221.

❺ *Ibid.*, p. 222.

certain forms of anti-competitive conduct relative to the globally optimal level of regulation. ❶

5.2.2 Lack of International Agreement for Enforcement

In addition, current competition policy lacks international agreement on enforcement standards, and there is no institutional framework exists for enforcing international competition rules. This is the difficulty in reality for substitution which is well acknowledged.

For instance, Gunnar Niels pointed out in his paper that supranational competition rules would require a new institution enforcement framework. The great advantage of antidumping is that such a framework is already in place. ❷ Ian Wooton and Maurizio Zanardi also stated that, what might be considered the "best" policy on efficiency grounds, a supranational application of competition policies, is not however considered politically feasible. ❸

5.3 Alleged Difficulties Cannot Prevent Substitution

As analyzed, the main objections against "substitution", including alleged different objectives of antidumping, as well as the lack of either domestic or international competition law, have been observed. This book deems that neither "unfair trade" nor "quasi safeguard" is

---

❶ Martyn D. Taylor, *International Competition Law: A New Dimension for the WTO?*, Cambridge Univ. Press Inc. 2006, p. 222.

❷ Gunnar Niels, *What is Antidumping Policy Really About?* Journal of Economic Surveys, 2002, Vol. 14, pp. 467, 486, http://www.blackwell-synergy.com/links/doi/10.1111/1467-6419.00118, last visited September 21, 2011.

❸ *See*, e.g., Ian Wooton & Maurizio Zanardi, *Trade and Competition Policy: Anti-dumping versus Anti-trust*, *University of Glasgow and CEPR Discussion Paper in Economics*, 2002, pp. 1, 13, http://homepages.strath.ac.uk/~hbs03116/Research/Trade%20and%20Competition%20Policy%20Final.pdf, last visited May 24, 2009.

the goal of antidumping. And also, competition law is gradually qualified to substitute antidumping law both in domestic and international levels. All of the alleged difficulties cannot prevent substitution.

5. 3. 1 Neither "Unfair trade" nor "Quasi Safeguard" is the Goal of Antidumping

In order to examine the first major difficulty of substituting antidumping by competition in practice, i. e. , modern antidumping law is alleged to have different goals that are totally different from competition law, the above part started from identifying different objectives and concluded that there are primarily two newly-alleged objectives of antidumping, one is to protect against unfair trade, and the other one is to be used as a quasi safeguard measure to protect domestic competitors. In the following part, this book intends to argue that neither of the alleged objectives can or should be achieved by antidumping.

On one hand, the alleged arguments for "unfair trade" are deceptive and hypocritical, and the broad "unfair trade" should not be the essential goal of antidumping system. On the other hand, antidumping system is not aimed at and cannot qualify a protective mechanism, as a "quasi safeguard" measure, that is controllable and necessary for the modern free trade world. So the goal of antidumping should remain to deal with predatory price discrimination.

5. 3. 1. 1 "Unfair trade" – Deceptive and Hypocritical

The U. S. gave a specific analysis of unfair trade, as the "new goal" of antidumping. In the communication, it explained that:

The focus of the antidumping rules is not competition within a national market, and it is not consumer welfare or allocative efficiency. Rather, consistent with other WTO agreements, the Antidumping Agreement implicitly recognizes that there is an accepted norm for the behaviour of governments in the broad multilateral trade context, i. e. a government should not pursue industrial policies which distort market structures or processes and thereby provide artificial advantages to domestic producers to the detriment of producers in other countries. The Antidumping Agreement also recognizes that there should be a remedy for certain harms caused when different economic systems interact. Competition laws appropriately do not take these matters into consideration. With competition substituted for the antidumping rules, or with the antidumping rules modified to reflect competition policy principles, the injurious effects of the numerous unfair situations described above would go unremedied. [1]

Accordingly, antidumping law is deemed to be a remedy instrument necessary for maintaining a "level playing field", an essential element to fair trade, by offsetting the injurious dumping. Here a tremendously broad view of the "fairness" has been taken by the U. S. to include indirectly addressing the harmful result of market – distortive government industrial policies as well as neutralizing the inequities arising from differences in national economic system.

This book disagrees for three main reasons. First, the comprehensive survey of the economic theories as well as the evolvement of antidumping laws in chapter II indicates that antidumping system is not supposed to deal with the broad unfair trade. In economic theories, efficiency approach favored by most economists suggested that dumping is a kind of transnational price discrimination, and only predatory dumping is generally recognized as harmful.

Moreover, a journey back to its birth time and following its

---

[1] WT/WGTCP/W/88, Communication from the United States, August 1998.

evolvement indicated that, originally antidumping was part of antitrust law, to deal with the import price discrimination. It is for attacking these foreign conducts more efficiently that antidumping rules were changed and gradually deviated from antitrust rules. To create an international antidumping agreement in WTO was just for unifying domestic rules. Most countries adopted antidumping later on merely because they needed to follow the requirements of WTO. Therefore, for a long time, "dumping is harmful or unfair" has been a premise that needs no proving. None of these changes and developments was for condemning dumping for other justifications. The core idea of antidumping system remains condemning dumping, a kind of price discrimination. The antidumping system is not designed to deal with unfair trade, and those listed unfair government policies have no direct relation with the conduct of low-price selling.

Secondly, even though those listed unfair government policies are condemnable or injurious, the correct way should be to address or identify those unfair government policies directly, rather than emphazing on investigating price differences. In its communication, the U. S. government assembled a number of market-distortive government industrial polices, as well as differences in national economic systems. As analyzed above, the latter "differences in national economic systems" is considered as arguments for quasi safeguard measure hence will be discussed in the next part. The former will be analyzed first.

"Market-distortive government industrial polices" include an extraordinarily diverse set of examples: high tariffs; government subsidies; price controls; government limitations on investment; limitations on the number of producers in a particular sector; anticompetitive sanitary and phytosanitary standards; a range of services barriers, including restrictions of provision of financial services, regulation of international data flows and data processing; misuse of standards, testing and certification procedures; permissive policies toward vertical and horizontal restraints of competition; cross-subsidization in multi-product firms. The above list is not complete, but the inescapable conclusion is that nearly every area of domestic public policy can be a cause of antidumping action under this broad interpretation of artificial advantages. [1]

The U. S. considered that antidumping law is to protect domestic industries from foreign competitors by indirectly addressing the above government industrial policies. The Problem is that those unfair government policies have no direct relation with the conduct of low-price selling. Even if they are injurious and condemnable, isn't it more efficient and rational to address or identify them in each case, and target them directly after proving that they exist?

Barfield in his paper conducted a further illustration to each listed policy. [2] For instance, the tariff rates have been set as a result of negotiations by individual nations in the Uruguay Trade Round. If a nation has negotiated high tariffs, so be it; if it breaks the agreement

---

[1] *See also* Claude Barfield, *Antidumping: Time to: (1) Go Back to Basics; And (2) Politicize the Final Outcome; Or (3) Substitute Safeguards for Antidumping Actions*, Paper Prepared for the Centennial of Antidumping Legislation and Implementation Symposium, 2004, pp. 1, 19, http://fordschool.umich.edu/rsie/Conferences/ADSym/Barfield.pdf, last visited September 21, 2011.

[2] Claude Barfield, *Antidumping: Time to: (1) Go Back to Basics; And (2) Politicize the Final Outcome; Or (3) Substitute Safeguards for Antidumping Actions*, Paper Prepared for the Centennial of Antidumping Legislation and Implementation Symposium, 2004, pp. 1, 19, http://fordschool.umich.edu/rsie/Conferences/ADSym/Barfield.pdf, last visited September 21, 2011.

and raises its rates, it must renegotiate rates with all other members of the WTO or face retaliation. [1] Industrial subsidies lead to a similar situation: the WTO has set rules for illegal and legal subsidies, and if a nation believes these rules have been violated, it will bring a case to the WTO – thus obviating the use of national trade remedy systems. [2] Similar comments can be given to the other listed policies. [3] Actually all the policies thereof can and should be addressed in a direct way.

Thirdly, although a mechanism as an indirectly supplement for

---

[1] Claude Barfield, *Antidumping: Time to: (1) Go Back to Basics; And (2) Politicize the Final Outcome; Or (3) Substitute Safeguards for Antidumping Actions*, Paper Prepared for the Centennial of Antidumping Legislation and Implementation Symposium, 2004, p. 20, http://fordschool. umich. edu/rsie/Conferences/ADSym/Barfield. pdf, last visited September 21, 2011.

[2] *Ibid.*

[3] The submission also mentions government policies to limit the number of producers in a sector or limitations on foreign equity participation or ownership in a sector. Two points are relevant in this case: First, like other nations, the United States has long limited investment in certain quite important sectors, such as airlines and telecommunications. It thus comes with ill grace for the U. S. government to take unilateral action against other governments for the same practice. Second, GATT and WTO rules, except in unusual circumstances generally in the services area, do not cover investment issues; thus, there are no legal impediments to governments applying certain restrictions (as the United States has done).

The examples cited relating to rules for competition are also of questionable validity, particularly with regard to cross-subsidization and relaxed limitations on vertical restraints. In the United States and numerous other countries, many firms have multiple product lines, and there is no restriction on cross-subsidization *per se*, absent some other anticompetitive practice by the firms. Thus, companies such as IBM and Texas Instruments for many years produced computers and computer components such as chips, with chips being priced to increase the competitiveness of the final product. In no case did the U. S. government object – nor should it have. Similarly, while U. S. competition policy has changed greatly over the past half-century, current thinking holds that under most conditions vertical restraints of trade are not anti-competitive. To lump these industry practices as evidence of an "artificial" advantage is hypocritical and deceptive. *See ibid.*, pp. 20 – 21.

maintaining fair and free multilateral trade is necessary, antidumping is far from qualified. As analyzed in Chapter I, the proliferation of antidumping cases has suggested that the indirect way to address the broad and blurred "unfair trade" via antidumping, the investigation of which emphasizes on price differences rather than targeting unfair government policies themselves, and the remedy of which is taken the form of removing price differences rather than correcting or condemning the unfair government policies themselves, have accounted a lot for its protectionist abuse.

Accordingly, this book is of the opinion that the alleged arguments for "unfair trade" are deceptive and hypocritical. Antidumping system cannot act as a good protector of such broad "unfair trade". Economists have argued that national legislators introducing legislation providing for antidumping actions and the architects of GATT/WTO understood that the action was essentially protectionist but described it as designed to combat "unfair" trade in order to disguise the intent.[1]

5. 3. 1. 2 "Quasi Safeguard" – Do we Need Two Protective Mechanisms

Apart from "unfair trade", another more persuasive allegation is the so-called "quasi safeguard" measure. Antidumping system is aimed at protecting domestic competitors by neutralizing the inequities arising from differences in national economic system. This book deems that antidumping is not designed to be a mechanism for the protective purpose.

---

[1] For example, Finger described that: "Antidumping is the fox put in charge of the henhouse: trade restrictions certified by GATT. The fox is clever enough not only to eat the hens, but also to convince the farmers that it is the ways things ought to be. Antidumping is ordinary protection with a grand public relations program." *See* P. J. Lloyd, Antidumping and Competition Law, in Patrick F. J Macrory *et al.*, *II The World Trade Organization: Legal, Economic and Political Analysis*, Springer, 2005, p. 73.

First of all, as analyzed, the comprehensive survey of the economic theories as well as the evolvement of antidumping laws in chapter II shows that antidumping system is not supposed to achieve the protective purpose. In modern multilateral free trade world, countries need a protective mechanism against the injury to domestic competitors, but such mechanism has no direct relation with the conduct of low-price selling. The core idea of antidumping system is to investigate and condemn dumping, a kind of price discrimination, whereas the injury investigation is not a decisive factor in imposing antidumping duties. Therefore, antidumping system is not designed and thereby cannot achieve the protective purpose.

Secondly, it is understandable that we need a protective mechanism in the modern multilateral free trade world, but the problem is that, as we already have the safeguard measure that clearly sets "protection" as its essential purpose, why do we need another mechanism that aim at exactly the same protective purpose? The correct instrument for providing temporary protection to inefficient industries is a safeguard measure, not antidumping. [1]

---

[1] *See more*, José Tavares De Araujo Jr., *Legal and Economic Interfaces between Antidumping and Competition Policy*, CEPAL – SERIE Comercio Internacional, 2001, pp. 1, 11, http://www.eclac.cl/publicaciones/xml/0/9040/lcl1685i.pdf, last visited September 21, 2011; Claude Barfield, *Antidumping: Time to: (1) Go Back to Basics; And (2) Politicize the Final Outcome; Or (3) Substitute Safeguards for Antidumping Actions*, Paper Prepared for the Centennial of Antidumping Legislation and Implementation Symposium, 2004, pp. 1, 26 – 32, http://fordschool.umich.edu/rsie/Conferences/ADSym/Barfield.pdf, last visited September 21, 2011; Gabrielle Marceau, *Antidumping and Anti-trust Issues in Free-trade Areas*, Oxford Univ. Press Inc. 1994, p. 46; Michael Finger *et al.*, *Antidumping As Safeguard Policy*, World Bank Working Paper No. 2730, 2000, pp. 1, 10, http://www.fordschool.umich.edu/rsie/Conferences/CGP/Oct2000Papers/Finger.pdf, last visited September 21, 2011.

As a protective mechanism, safeguard has many advantages over antidumping:

Ⅰ. Safeguard actions are much more flexible in both substance and duration. Antidumping duties, once levied, remain in place for at least five years and thus can continue long after the alleged dumping has ended. ❶

Ⅱ. In determining a safeguard action, the relevant authorities can take into account the overall national welfare including consumer and corporate users' interests and other political and diplomatic factors – which cannot be achieved by antidumping. ❷

Ⅲ. Unlike antidumping actions, safeguards introduce pressure for action-forcing results and do not allow industries to drift supinely for years under the cover of government protection. ❸ For safeguard measures, the emphasis is shifted to the readjustment of the industry in the importing country during the period of safeguard. In the case of a surge of cheaper imports of better quality, it would be more reasonable to focus on the disturbance caused to the importing country and allow for reorganization of domestic production and relocation of workers. ❹

Ⅳ. Increased use of safeguard actions would reduce the

---

❶ Claude Barfield, *Antidumping: Time to: (1) Go Back to Basics; And (2) Politicize the Final Outcome; Or (3) Substitute Safeguards for Antidumping Actions*, Paper Prepared for the Centennial of Antidumping Legislation and Implementation Symposium, 2004, pp. 1, 28, http://fordschool.umich.edu/rsie/Conferences/ADSym/Barfield.pdf, last visited September 21, 2011.

❷ *Ibid.*

❸ *Ibid.*

❹ Gabrielle Marceau, *Antidumping and Anti-trust Issues in Free-trade Areas*, Oxford Univ. Press Inc. 1994, p. 49.

inflammatory and often spurious comparisons made between "fair" and "unfair" trade practices. As Jackson stated that, the distinction between fair and unfair trade has become increasingly blurred. ❶ Societies and their economic systems differ so dramatically that what seems "unfair" to members of one society may seem perfectly fair to those of another society. ❷ By setting up protection as its objective clearly and relevant rules to use this protective instrument properly, safeguard can avoid the disputes between fair or unfair trade and therefore is a better than antidumping.

Ⅴ. One of the important differences between antidumping and safeguard actions is that while antidumping measures often target a country, although they are supposed to be imposed in a discriminatory manner without any obligation to compensate, safeguard measures must be imposed without national discrimination and with compensation. ❸ Therefore, as a protective measure, the unselective and reciprocal safeguard is more consistent with the basic trade principle of non-discrimination.

Thirdly, even if we can keep two or more different protective mechanisms as the "pressure valve" to maintain an open trade policy, antidumping has serious weaknesses. Since the modern world views the removal of all of the trade barriers as its essential task, and hence has strict limitations on domestic protection, why does it allow such a loose protective measure as antidumping to be used in such a great scale? The only possible reason that governments prefer antidumping

---

❶ John H. Jackson, *the World Trading System: Law and Policy of International*, Economic Relations, MIT Press, 1997, p. 247.

❷ *Ibid.*, p. 248.

❸ *Ibid.*

in such a great scale is because it is easier to apply, not because it is a better protective policy. [1]

In the modern free trade world, it is critical that the policy process by which the government decides to intervene or not intervene gives voice to those interests that benefit from open trade and would bear the costs of the proposed intervention. [2] There are two basic criteria to value such a protective mechanism. One is whether it can help the government to separate trade interventions that would serve the national economic interests from those that would not; and the other one is even in those instances in which the decision is to restrict imports, whether it can support the politics of openness and liberalization. [3] It seems antidumping fails to satisfy either criterion. It looks at only half of the economic impact on the domestic economy. It gives standing to competitive domestic interests but not to domestic users. Moreover, treating foreign competitors discriminatively and biasedly, it fails to support openness or liberalization. The proliferation of antidumping cases has reinforced that it is not a controllable protective mechanism in the free trade region. On the contrary, antidumping has been largely abused for protectionists and is actually against the basic spirit of modern free trade.

According to the above analysis, it is held in this book that,

---

[1] José Tavares De Araujo Jr., *Legal and Economic Interfaces between Antidumping and Competition Policy*, CEPAL-SERIE Comercio Internacional, 2001, pp. 1, 11, http://www.eclac.cl/publicaciones/xml/0/9040/lcl1685i.pdf, last visited September 21, 2011.

[2] Michael Finger *et al.*, *Antidumping as Safeguard Policy*, World Bank Working Paper No. 2730, 2000, pp. 1, 10, http://www.fordschool.umich.edu/rsie/Conferences/CGP/Oct2000Papers/Finger.pdf, last visited September 21, 2011.

[3] *Ibid.*, p. 10.

antidumping system is not aimed at and cannot qualify as a protective mechanism controllable and necessary for the modern free trade world.

5.3.2 Competition is Gradually Developed to Substitute Antidumping

The second major difficulty of substitution lies in the side of competition. It is argued that, some of the countries lack competition rules on predatory pricing or price discrimination, and few of the new countries that take antidumping action have effective national competition laws. Moreover, competition standards are far from uniform across countries, and there is no international competition agreement up till now.

In the following part, this book favors the opinion that although currently there is no international competition law or problems likewise, all of these cannot be taken as the reasons to prevent the substitution of antidumping by competition in future. Competition is gradually qualified, and the recent development of these factors supports the trend towards substituting antidumping by competition.

5.3.2.1 Development of Domestic Competition Law

Globalization of Competition Law

The statistics show that more than 80 countries now have competition laws. Those with modern laws and strong enforcement agencies are in a position to protect their consumers and their producers from the harm caused by hard core cartels and other anti-competitive activity. [1]

Until 1980 mainly the developed countries had adopted competition laws. From 1981 to 1990 only nine more countries introduced

---

[1] *Draft opening remarks of Mr. Seiichi Kondo Deputy Secretary General Organisation for Economic Co-operation and Development*, Global Forum on Competition, 2001, pp. 1, 3, http://www.oecd.org/dataoecd/0/32/2434223.pdf, last visited September 21, 2011.

competition laws: five of these are developed countries and four are developing countries. By the end of 1990, only 35 countries had adopted a competition law; and from 1991 to 2000, nearly 60 countries adopted a competition law. Most of these are developing countries. ❶

Domestic Competition Rules to Cover Predatory Price Discrimination

In terms of the issue of predatory price discrimination, as examined in Chapter III, it is being generally addressed in competition laws in most of the major countries, such as the U. S., the EU, Canada, Australia, Japan and etc. In the U. S., the relevant federal provisions on predatory price discrimination are to be found in three acts. A general approach to this issue is contained in the Sherman Act, and a more specific one can be found in Clayton Act and its amendment Robinson-Patman Act. In the EU, the relevant rules on predatory price discrimination are set forth in Article 81 and Article 82.

In addition, for the new users of antidumping laws, such as Brazil, India, South Africa, and China, competition laws have been newly established and gradually developed. As a conduct of abuse of dominant position, the issue of predatory price discrimination has been addressed in all of them, and the essential basic requirements are trading the beaten track of the U. S., the EU and the other traditional countries. ❷

In Brazil, the modern era of competition policy began in 1994 with

---

❶ Franz Kronthaler & Johannes Stephan, *Factors Accounting for the Enactment of A Competition Law – Empirical Analysis*, Halle Institute for Economic Research, 2005, pp. 1, 4, http://www.iwh – halle.de/projects/competition_policy/Factors_01.PDF, last visited September 21, 2011.

❷ The development of competition policy and laws in these new users, as well as their considerations towards the substitution of antidumping by competition will be specifically dealt with in the chapter VI. Here it will be introduced briefly.

the enactment of a new law as part of the "Real Plan", a set of policies developed to deal with a period of hyperinflation. [1] The issue of predatory price discrimination, "unreasonably sell products below cost", was regulated in Article 21 thereof, which contains a lengthy but non-exclusive list of acts, including various kinds of horizontal and vertical agreements and unilateral abuses of market power that are considered unlawful if they produce the effects enumerated in Article 20. [2]

In India, competition Law came into being with the passage of the Competition Act by the Parliament and assented to by the President of India on 13th January, 2003. On and from that date, it came to be known as the Competition Act, 2002 (Act 12 of 2003). [3] "Predatory Price", "Cartel", "relevant market" and "relevant product market" have been specifically defined in the new Act whereas these important definitions were not available in the earlier Act. [4]

In South Africa, the Competition Act No. 89, which was adopted in 1998 became effective as of 1 September 1999 ("Competition Act") The Competition Act was amended in 2000, in part to clarify the relationship between general competition law and other regulatory bodies. [5] South

---

[1] *Competition Law and Policy in Brazil*, Policy Brief, OECD, 2005, p. 1, http://www. competitionlaw. cn/upload//temp_08031010189425. pdf, last visited September 21, 2011.

[2] *Brazil – Peer Review of Competition Law and Policy*, OECD, 2005, pp. 1, 18, http://www. oecd. org/dataoecd/12/45/35445196. pdf, last visited September 21, 2011.

[3] *Public Awareness on Competition Law and Policy*, Competition Commission of India B Block, pp. 1, 11, http://www. competition – commission – india. nic. in/speeches_articles_presentations/Public% 20Awareness% 20on% 20Competition% 20Law. pdf, last visited May 13, 2009.

[4] *Ibid.*, p. 13.

[5] *South Africa – Peer Review of Competition Law and Policy*, OECD, 2003, pp. 1, 17, http://www. oecd. org/dataoecd/43/58/34823812. pdf, last visited September 21, 2011.

Africa's law on single-firm conduct is based on abuse of dominance, but it also includes a rule about price discrimination that resembles North American statutes. The Competition Act prohibits some other particular exclusionary acts by dominant firms, including selling below marginal or average variable cost. [1]

In China, the first Chinese competition law, i. e. the Law of the People's Republic of China against Unfair Competition was passed in September, 1993. Article 11 in the Chapter named "Acts of Unfair Competition" therein stipulates that, a business operator shall not, for the purpose of pushing out their competitors, sell their commodities at prices lower than costs. Afterwards, as the core of competition system, Chinese Antimonopoly Law was published in 2007 and came into force in 2008. The issue of low-price selling is regulated in the Article 17 of Chapter named "Abuse of a Dominant Market Position" therein. [2]

Basic Common Standards on Predatory Price Discrimination

Although competition standards are far from uniform across countries, at least with respect to predatory price discrimination some consensus has been reached. The research into major countries in Chapter III indicates that in modern world, the basic elements of competition principles across countries have been commonly shared and the basic common standards on predatory price discrimination can be identified.

As to the competition principles, modern competition Laws are strongly influenced by economic theories, especially efficiency analysis. Although different countries have different objectives of

---

[1] *South Africa – Peer Review of Competition Law and Policy*, OECD, 2003, p. 25, http://www.oecd.org/dataoecd/43/58/34823812.pdf, last visited September 21, 2011.

[2] This will be discussed in length in next chapter.

competition policy, three basic competition principles can be identified, including protecting competitive process, promoting economic efficiency, and maximization of consumer welfare.

As to the rules on predatory price discrimination, a careful examination into the major countries, including the U. S., the EU and so on, indicates that unlike other issues under competition framework such as merger, with respect to price discrimination and predation some consensus has been reached.[1] Price discrimination and predatory pricing are generally within the concern of the anti-competitive firm behavior of abuse of a dominant position.

With respect to price discrimination, although the specific rules vary among different countries, the essential idea is mainly the same: competition laws, in conformity to economic theories, consider that price discrimination in the primary-line competition, which links with antidumping laws, is anti-competitive only when it is proved to be predatory pricing.

With respect to the common basic standard of condemning predatory price discrimination, although different countries have different specific rules on this issue, four basic elements can be identified, including market conditions, intent of monopoly, cost calculation and injury to competition.

Accordingly, unlike what the scholars argued that the competition standards are far from uniform across countries, the basic common standards on predatory price discrimination can be agreed. These can be taken as the basic elements for uniform and are actually easing the

---

[1] *See also* Gunnar Niels, *What is Antidumping Policy Really About*? Journal of Economic Surveys, 2002, Vol. 14, pp. 467, 485, http://www. blackwell - synergy. com/links/doi/10. 1111/1467 - 6419. 00118, last visited September 21, 2011.

difficulties of substituting antidumping by competition in practice.

Lack of Domestic Competition Law Cannot Prevent Substitution

Even if there are no or ineffective national rules on predatory price discrimination, it cannot be used as the excuse to prevent the substitution. The answer to this is to accelerate the legislation and development of relevant competition rule. Just like scholars pointed out, the problem is due to weak and ineffective law and the solution is: make it more effective. ❶

To sum up the above examination, in terms of the domestic level, competition laws have been developed and improved in the new countries that take antidumping actions, and the issue of predatory price discrimination is being addressed in most of the major countries. A research into major countries indicated that in modern world, the basic elements of competition principles across countries have been commonly shared and the basic common standards on predatory price discrimination can be identified. Furthermore, that there are no effective national rules cannot be used as the excuse to prevent the substitution. The answer to this is to accelerate the legislation and development of relevant competition rules.

5. 3. 2. 2 Prospects of International Rules on Predatory Price Discrimination

The efforts towards an international competition law have been continuingly made, though there have been no existing global rules yet. From the League of Nations, the International Trade Organization (ITO), the Havana Charter, the Economic and Social Council Code (ECOSOC), GATT, the United Nations Conference on Trade and

---

❶ Aradhna Aggarwal, *Antidumping Law and Practice: An Indian Perspective*, Indian Council for Research on International Economic Relations, 2002, pp. 1, 68, http://www.icrier.org/pdf/antiDump.pdf, last visited September 21, 2011.

Development (UNCTAD), all of who attempted to create an international agreement on competition law, to the Organization for Economic Cooperation and Development (OECD), the key player attempting to promote the globalization of competition laws, various approaches have been tried though failed in the past. [1]

---

[1] A. Past approaches to the creation of international competition law (5, failed)

I. The League of Nations: inter-war period.

II. The international Trade Organization(ITO) and the Havana Charter – After World War II.

III. The Economic and Social Council Code (ECOSOC) – US rejected by saying that: Differences which presently exist in national policies and practices... are of such magnitude that the proposed international agreement would be neither satisfactory nor effective in accomplishing its purpose...present emphasis should be given not to international organizational machinery but rather to the more fundamental need of further developing effective national programs to deal with restrictive business practices, and of achieving a greater degree of comparability in the policies and practices of all nations in their approach to the subject.

IV. GATT consultation has only been invoked once by the U. S. in 1996.

V. The United Nations Conference on trade and Development (UNCTAD) Restrictive Business Practices Code: taken by developing countries. – THE UNCTAD code provides a good example of the difficulties in negotiating a multilateral code because the key blocs had completely different objectives. – The industrialized nations wanted to establish real competition law, the developing countries attempted the adoption of rules to control multinational corporations and to foster economic development. – The industrialized countries advocated the liberalization of competition policy at this time (Chicago school), and developing countries were dissatisfied with the lacking use of the consultation procedures and insufficient technical assistance provided for the implementation of the Code.

VI. the Organization for Economic Cooperation and Development (OECD) Recommendations: Apart from attempts to create an international agreement on competition law, the OECD has become a key player in attempts to promote the globalization of competition law, particularly, through the successive adoption of recommendations with regard to the cooperation on restrictive business practices or more recently with regard to "hard core" cartels. The OECD also adopted guidelines for multinational enterprises in 1976 which contain many provisions similar to the UNCTAAD Code. The OECD is a forum that promotes "soft" harmonization, whereby harmonization occurs through the informal process of information sharing and discussion and not through the adoption of an international agreement. Due to its limited membership and the soft character of its rules the OECD has not provided a "real" solution to international competition problems. For example, in the U. S. – Japan Economic relations nonbinding OECD recommendations have not shown much prominence, although both countries have been supportive of such rules.

See Roland Weinrauch, *Competition Law in the WTO: the Rationale for a Framework Agreement*, Wien : NWV Neuer Wissenschaftlicher Verlag, 2004, pp. 107 – 111.

Approach I: the Multilateral Competition Agreement

There are now primarily three options proposed for the creation of international competition law. The first option proposes the adoption of international competition rules in the form of a multilateral or plurilateral agreement. It emphasizes the need to impose rules from the top into the legislation of states. Such as the "comprehensive code approach" chosen by the Munich group, a working group of American, European and Japanese academics that prepared the Draft International Antitrust Code (DIAC)[1]; the modest approach – a case for forging the links between competition and trade which has most prominently been argued by Eleanor M Fox.[2]

Approach II: Competition Law in the WTO

The second option concentrates on the use and improvement of existing international rules, like the non-discrimination provisions in WTO agreements, and instruments, like the dispute settlement

---

[1] The DIAC was designed as a GATT Plurilateral Agreement and tried to combine two approaches to international competition law, namely, the "trade Approach" which asks for international competition rules under the viewpoint of promoting international trade and the "intellectual property and unfair trade practices approach" which asks for the amendment of article 10 bis of the Paris Convention by competition rules aiming at a parallel treatment of unfair trade practices and trade restraints. *See* Roland Weinrauch, *Competition Law in the WTO: the Rationale for a Framework Agreement*, Wien : NWV Neuer Wissenschaftlicher Verlag, 2004, p. 112.

[2] Due to differences in national systems the modest approach proceeds on the hypobook that international problems call for some international solution, but that diversity is desirable and should be preserved to the extent that tailored solution can meet the major problems caused by disharmony and lack of unified vision in the world competition/trading system. Therefore, it rather suggests to formulate a narrowly focused agenda in response to specific tensions and opportunities that present themselves in the context of the world competition / trading system. Starting with a vision of freedom of trade in global commerce and linking competition to trade at a constitutional level of generality. *See ibid.*, p. 116.

procedures within the WTO, to deal with competition issues. One proposal suggested by Hong Kong is competition-oriented reforms throughout the whole WTO legal system, including GATT, GATS and its Protocols, TRIPS, the plurilateral agreements etc. [1]

Another "WTO Approach" suggested by Robert E. Hudec is non-violation nullification and impairment. This approach requires legal interpretation by the appellate body on a case-by-case basis or a formal interpretation by WTO General Council. [2] Also Spencer Weber Waller embraces this. He believes that we already live in a world with certain identifiable international competition rules constituting international law, and the current system can already resolve a variety of competition problems such as international customary law or using non-discrimination principle to cope with anti-cartel issues. [3]

Approach III: Bilateral, Regional, or Extraterritorial Enforcement of Competition

The third option suggests the development of international rules from the bottom (convergence or soft harmonization) by means of bilateral and regional cooperation supplemented by effective extraterritorial enforcement of national competition laws. For instance, Harry First suggests choice of law principles. By means of a network of similar rules and values, courts can articulate an international common law of competition which does not succeed by hierarchical imposition but by persuasion. In his opinion, the case-by-case common law process of law development shown by cartel cases will provide the

---

[1] Roland Weinrauch, *Competition Law in the WTO: the Rationale for a Framework Agreement*, Wien: NWV Neuer Wissenschaftlicher Verlag, 2004, p. 128.

[2] *Ibid.*

[3] *Ibid.*

flexibility to work out the necessary solutions for the internationalized economic world. ❶

Phedon Nicolaides suggests that it is only feasible at higher stages of economic integration because the institutional framework established by integrating regional blocs is indispensable for the enforcement of common competition rules. ❷

Currently, the successful practices of substitution have been achieved and made even greater efforts to in both bilateral and regional areas. As introduced in Chapter IV, the first is the experience of the United States. Once the separate colonies created a nation, and not merely a confederation, the newly created states of the Union were constitutionally barred from imposing any form of import or export duties on trade between the American states. ❸

Similarly, when the European Economic Community was created in the late 1950s, it learned the American lesson well. In the Treaty of Rome, the Member-States are barred after a brief transition period from imposing antidumping or any other form of duties on trade between the Member-States. Price differences between Member-States are dealt with as an abuse of a dominant position under the competition rules rather than as a trade issue. ❹

Recently, New Zealand and Australia concluded a free trade agreement in 1983, which included the elimination of antidumping

---

❶ Roland Weinrauch, *Competition Law in the WTO: the Rationale for a Framework Agreement*, Wien : NWV Neuer Wissenschaftlicher Verlag, 2004, p. 125.

❷ *Ibid.*, p. 126.

❸ Spencer Weber Waller, *Bringing Globalism Home: Lessons from Antitrust and Beyond*, Loyola University Chicago Law Journal, 2000. Vol. 32, pp. 113, 133.

❹ *Ibid.*

rules for trans-Tasman trade and the replacement of the dumping rules with true competition provisions. ❶ Canada and Chile also eliminated antidumping rules in their free trade agreement even though their economies are structurally quite different and separated by thousands of miles. ❷

Besides, Mercosur, the principal South American free trade area, has pursued a similar path in eliminating antidumping duties for trade within the bloc. ❸ Discussion is also existed in NAFTA. ❹In Asia, it was agreed not to use antidumping between China and Hong Kong area, and China and Macau area as well. Both Article 4 of Mainland and Hong Kong Closer Economic Partnership Arrangement (CEPA-HongKong) and Article 7 of Mainland and Macao Closer Economic Partnership Arrangement (CEPA-Macau) stipulate that antidumping measures should not be applied between members. ❺ Similar practice took place in South Africa Union. ❻

---

❶ Martyn D. Taylor, *International Competition Law: A New Dimension for the WTO?* Cambridge Univ. Press Inc. 2006, pp. 273 – 276.

❷ *Ibid.*, p. 273.

❸ Guasch, J. Luis & Rajapatirana, Sarath, *Antidumping and Competition Policies in Latin America and Caribbean: Total Strangers or Soul Mates?* 1998, pp. 1 – 26, http://www.worldbank.org/html/dec/Publications/Workpapers/WPS1900series/wps1958/wps1958. pdf, last visited September 21, 2011.

❹ Gabrielle Marceau, *Antidumping and Anti-trust Issues in Free-trade Areas*, Oxford Univ. Press Inc. 1994, pp. 310 – 319.

❺ Welber Barral *et al.*, *The use of Antidumping in Brazil, China, India and South Africa – Rule, Trends and Causes*, Kommerskollegium National Board of Trade, 2005, pp. 1, 32 http://www.tralac.org/pdf/Antidumping_in_4_Developing_Countries. pdf, last visited September 21, 2011.

❻ *Ibid.*, p. 58.

Possibilities of International Rules on Predatory Price Discrimination

Avoiding from commenting on or preferring to each of the above options, two points linking with this book can be got through reviewing the three options. The first one is that the "antidumping" issue is viewed as the threshold for competition law to penetrate into trade area. Just as Ralf Boscheck considered: "to thoroughly assess the preconditions for an international coordination of competition-related trade issues, it is inevitable, initially at least to focus on one salient concern. Antidumping provides the most critical case in point."❶

The second one is that whatever kind of options, the consensus on predatory price discrimination as well as the calling for harmonizing of antidumping and predatory price discrimination can be reached. Such as Fox proposed that consensus might be found among the following substantive principles applicable to transactions with significant transnational effects including bringing their antidumping laws into correspondence with their predation laws in order to encourage sustainable low price competition.❷

Ernst – Ullrich Petersmann suggested that the internationalization should limit to a few substantive principles. Such as:

A generalization of the existing but so far very limited WTO prohibitions of export and import cartels and of undermining WTO market access commitments by restrictive business practices; ... procedures ... and these international competition law principles should become part of an optional plurilateral agreement in terms of Annex IV to the WTO

---

❶ Ralf Boscheck, *the Governance of Global Market Relations: the Case of Substituting Antitrust for Antidumping*, World Competition, 2001, Vol. 24, pp. 41, 53.

❷ Roland Weinrauch, *Competition Law in the WTO: the Rationale for a Framework Agreement*, Wien: NWV Neuer Wissenschaftlicher Verlag, 2004, p. 116.

Agreement. [1]

An incentive to join such an agreement could be, for example, the special treatment of exporting countries with effective competition policies in the context of antidumping proceedings according to article VI GATT. [2]

In the suggestion of Hong Kong, priority should be given to competition-oriented reforms of existing WTO rules and to their producer bias for the protection of import-competing producers without adequate regard to domestic competition and consumer welfare, e. g. , Antidumping and safeguards provisions. [3]

To sum up, in terms of the international level, there are still many difficulties but also prospects for the creation of international competition law. Many efforts have been continuingly made to achieve this ultimate goal. The successful practices of substitution have been achieved and made great efforts to in both bilateral and regional areas. As to the specific issue of predatory price discrimination, the consensus on the basic elements as well as the subordination of antidumping to competition can be got. In other words, international agreement on predatory price discrimination replacing antidumping rules can be reached much easier compared to other sections under competition law.

---

[1] Roland Weinrauch, *Competition Law in the WTO: the Rationale for a Framework Agreement*, Wien : NWV Neuer Wissenschaftlicher Verlag, 2004, p. 119.

[2] *Ibid.*, p. 116.

[3] *Ibid.*, p. 127.

Chapter VI The "Substitution" Debate and the New Users

6. 1 Linkage between Antidumping and Competition

6. 1. 1 Overview of the New Users

The above examination was fcoused on the traditional users of antidumping, including the U. S. and the EU. It suggested that putting dumping under competition law rather than antidumping law can be less vulnerable to protectionist. The alleged difficulties in respect of neither antidumping nor competition can prevent the substitution in future. More efforts should be made to harmonize national competition rules on predatory price discrimination, create an international agreement on predatory price discrimination, and finally substitute antidumping rules by competition rules. Unfortunately, the political reality shows that antidumping is not likely to be abolished soon around the world. Indeed, the subject of antidumping is so politically sensitive in the U. S. that its trade negotiators do not even want to utter the word, let alone put it on the agenda of the next trade round in the WTO. ❶

As introduced in Chapter I, starting from mid-1990s, a new feature of antidumping actions has emerged. Developing countries, such as India, Brazil, South Africa, even China, who used to be the main targets of antidumping actions, have turned to be the new users of antidumping. Furthermore, the number of antidumping actions filed by the new users has gradually outnumbered those of the traditional users, i. e. the U. S., the EU, Australia, and Canada.

Simultaneously, with the assistance of international organizations, competition legislations in developing countries have sprung up like mushrooms. As introduced in Chapter V, as to the new users of antidumping laws, such as Brazil, India, South Africa, and China, competition laws have been newly established and gradually developed. As a conduct of abuse of dominant position, predatory price discrimination is addressed in all of the competition laws thereof, with the basic requirements trading the beaten track of the U. S., the EU etc.

Combined with the "substitution" debate, from the political perspective, this new factor might have some influence on certain traditional users' enthusiasm for antidumping actions, bring the issue of antidumping on negotiation table again, and thus draw more attention

---

❶ Robert E. Litan, *Moving Towards an Open World Economy: the Next Phase*, Brookings, 1999, http://www.brookings.edu/papers/1999/1206globaleconomics_litan.aspx, last visited September 21, 2011. In the U. S., industries that use imported inputs, led by the computer industry and a well-organized group of metal users, have brought increasing pressure on the government to take their interests into account in any decision to restrict imports. *See* J. Michael Finger, *Should Developing Countries Introduce Antidumping?* Working Paper, 1992, http://siteresources.worldbank.org/INTRANETTRADE/Resources/WBI – Training/MFinger_antidumping_eng.DOC, last visited May 7, 2009.

to the debate of antidumping versus competition. Apart from the traditional users, does the examination of the new users also support the "substitution", or instead, against it? A look into the relationship between antidumping and competition in each of these new users is also worth analyzing.

Regarding antidumping laws and practices of the new users, Junji Nakagawa in his book summarized that, in addition to the standard theoretical explanation of antidumping as a response to "unfair trade", there are six other factors relevant to the emergence of the new users. ❶ These factors including:

Ⅰ. For those contracting parties to the GATT other than the traditional users, the overall reduction of trade barriers as a result of the Uruguay Round Negotiation brought about the need for introducing or strengthening protection measures for domestic industries, and antidumping was there, along with safeguards. We may call this antidumping as a pressure or safety valve for trade liberalization. ❷

Ⅱ. Certain domestic industrial sectors in the new users were quite successful in lobbying for antidumping measures. We may call this either antidumping as industrial policy or antidumping with a constituency. ❸

Ⅲ. WTO membership establishes a member's right to institutionalize antidumping laws, which seems to have contributed to the increase in the initiation of antidumping investigations by the new users. In other words, WTO ADA, in itself, has had some catalytic

---

❶ Junji Nakagawa ed., *Antidumping Laws and Practices of the New Users*, Cambridge Univ. Press, 2007, p. 12.

❷ *Ibid.*, p. 12.

❸ *Ibid.*, p. 13.

effect in the proliferation of antidumping laws worldwide. ❶

Ⅳ. Many countries adopt antidumping laws, at least in part, to counter the sanctioning of their exports. Antidumping is used not only to protect against dumped imports, but also to defend their exports against the abuse of antidumping laws abroad. We may call this a tit-for-tat strategy or antidumping as strategic retaliation. ❷

Ⅴ. The traditional users and the new users form "the Antidumping Club", and that the new users were simply admitted to the club. By enacting antidumping legislation and initiating investigations against imports from the traditional users, a new user metaphorically knocked on the door of the club. ❸

Ⅵ. Fluctuations in a country's exchange rate may have affected the user of antidumping at least by a few new users such as Argentina. ❹

Correspondingly, a general impression is that the new users adopted antidumping rules mainly in accordance with the requirements of WTO, and hence there was no much further or deeper exploration into the justification of antidumping law. As to the new users, antidumping law is currently used for protecting domestic industries, retaliation and the like. All of these purposes have nothing to do with the conduct of low-price selling, hence cannot justify why we need to condemn dumping.

With the proliferation of antidumping and its increasing abuse for protectionisim in these new users, the "substitution" debate, i. e. ,

---

❶ Junji Nakagawa ed. , *Antidumping Laws and Practices of The New Users*, Cambridge Univ. Press 2007, p. 13.

❷ *Ibid.*, p. 13.

❸ *Ibid.*, p. 14.

❹ *Ibid.*

the linkage between antidumping and competition in new users has also started to draw more attention. It was argued that such a substitution on the international level would be particularly for the benefit of developing countries. [1] Moreover, relevant studies on the relationship between the two sets of rules have already been conducted in some of the new heavy users, such as Brazil, India, and South Africa etc. The scholars in general also favor the substitution of antidumping by competition, or reforming antidumping to be in consistent with competition rules and principles.

6.1.2 Brazil

Anamélia Soccal Seyffarth in his paper "The Link between Competition Policy and Antidumping Policy" illustrated the Brazilian experience with antidumping policy and introduced that the country also increased the use of the Antidumping Code. It was effective in the time when Brazil did the import tariff reforms (1985 - 1994), because some adjustments in the internal market were still needed. Nowadays, however, the internal producers have to face the international competition. [2] Continuingly, the author deemed that the reduction of protectionism in antidumping measures can be an important force for market contestability by multiplying the number of potential entrants and

---

[1] Roland Weinrauch, *Competition Law in the WTO: the Rationale for a Framework Agreement*, Wien: NWV Neuer Wissenschaftlicher Verlag, 2004, p. 60.

[2] Anamelia Soccal Seyffarth, *the Link between Competition Policy and Antidumping Policy, George Washington University, School of Business and Public Management, Institute of Brazilian Issues Minerva Program*, 2000, pp. 1, 46, http://www.gwu.edu/~ibi/minerva/Fall2000/Anamelia.Seyffarth.pdf, last visited September 21, 2011.

reducing set-up and withdrawal costs. [1] To cope with the protectionism in antidumping measures is to reformulate the antidumping measures from the competition perspective.

Accordingly, some propositions were considered. The first one is to remove antidumping regulation, since international pricing may be a competition problem and as such it should in principle be addressed as a part of competition laws. [2] The second one is to use competition objectives and standards within the WTO to guide the applications of antidumping actions, which would lead to an improvement in the re gulation of antidumping actions and consistency with competition law relating to other anti-competitive behavior. [3] The third one is that the WTO could negotiate amendment of Article to replace the (producer) injury test by a national (or international) economic welfare test, which would obligate countries investigating alleged dumping to offset consumer or user gains against producer losses. [4]

Based on the investigation into the relationship between antidumping and competition in Brazil, the author claimed that from the Brazilian perspective, the most feasible proposition is to allow consi deration of competition policy in the determination of both the dumping margin and injury test. [5]

In addition, studies relating to the anti-competitive effects of

---

[1] Anamelia Soccal Seyffarth, *the Link between Competition Policy and Antidumping Policy*, George Washington University, School of Business and Public Management, Institute of Brazilian Issues Minerva Program, 2000, p. 46, http://www.gwu.edu/~ibi/minerva/Fall2000/Anamelia.Seyffarth.pdf, last visited September 21, 2011.

[2] *Ibid.*, p. 31.

[3] *Ibid.*, p. 32.

[4] *Ibid.*, p. 33.

[5] *Ibid.*, p. 46.

antidumping actions were also conducted. For instance, in terms of anti-competitive practices, a research done by Braga and Silber on the orange juice industry found that antidumping actions were mostly applied to protect orange growers and higher-cost frozen concentrate producers at the expense of the U. S. juice and soft drink processors and distributors linked by marketing arrangements to Brazilian concentrate exporters. Its main effect has probably been to strengthen the oligopoly-oligopsony relationship between Brazilian producers and their US partners, as suggested by their joint defense strategy in the antidumping investigation, further hindering the prospects for competition in the world market for frozen concentrated orange juice. [1]

6. 1. 3 India

Aradhna Aggarwal examined the antidumping policy in India from two perspectives: economic and legal. [2] From the economic perspective, the paper did an empirical study to examine whether predatory behavior was actually present when protection was granted. The analysis was carried out with the aid of four criteria, including the num-

---

[1] Carlos Alberto Primo Braga & Simao Davi Siber, *Brazilian Frozen Concentrated Orange Juice: the Folly of Unfair Trade Cases*, Country Economics Department, the World Bank, 1991, pp. 1 – 46, http://www – wds. worldbank. org/servlet/WDSContentServer/WDSP/IB/1991/05/01/000009265_3961001095824/Rendered/PDF/multi0page. pdf, last visited September 21, 2011.

[2] Aradhna Aggarwal, *Antidumping Law and Practice: An Indian Perspective*, Indian Council for Research on International Economic Relations, 2002, pp. 1 – 68, http://www. icrier. org/pdf/antiDump. pdf. Besides, Aditya Bhattacharjea in his paper "trade and competition policy" also discussed the prevention of abuse of antidumping procedures by replacing them with stricter antitrust standards. And the author believes that India should resist a multilateral agreement on competition at the WTO. *See* Aditya Bhattacharjea, *Trade and Competition Policy*, Working Paper No. 146, *Indian Council For Research on International Economic Relations*, 2004, pp. 1 – 65, http://www. icrier. org/pdf/wp146. pdf, last visited September 21, 2011.

ber of foreign sellers should be small; the share of subject countries should be high in total imports; import penetration should be high; and finally exporters should be enjoying dominant position in their markets. Applying these criteria to antidumping investigations in India between 1993 and 2001, Aradhna Aggarwal found that they were met only in a few cases. [1] Combined with other analyses, it may therefore be concluded that in the majority of the cases antidumping policy cannot be justified on economic grounds. [2]

The anti-competitive effects of antidumping actions in India were also detected. Preliminary evidence presented in the paper suggested that the in India, antidumping actions actually function as the protection of highly concentrated industries. [3] In India, antidumping petitions are often made by a one single domestic producer with a market share of above 90 percent. [4] Dominants producers lobby and litigate antidumping cases. In the process, they incur huge expenditure sacrificing economic efficiency. [5]Moreover, since most cases are in the intermediate products' markets, higher prices may have adverse effects throughout the economy. [6]

---

[1] Aradhna Aggarwal, *Antidumping Law and Practice: An Indian Perspective*, Indian Council for Research on International Economic Relations, 2002, pp. 1, 9 – 20, http://www.icrier.org/pdf/antiDump.pdf, last visited September 21, 2011.

[2] *Ibid.*, p. 66.

[3] *Ibid.*

[4] Welber Barral *et al.*, *the use of Antidumping in Brazil, China, India and South Africa – Rule, Trends and Causes*, Kommerskollegium National Board of Trade, 2005, pp. 1, 4, http://www.tralac.org/pdf/Antidumping_in_4_Developing_Countries.pdf, last visited September 21, 2011.

[5] Aradhna Aggarwal, *Antidumping Law and Practice: An Indian Perspective*, Indian Council for Research on International Economic Relations, 2002, pp. 1, 66, http://www.icrier.org/pdf/antiDump.pdf, last visited September 21, 2011.

[6] *Ibid.*, p. 66.

From the legal perspective, Aradhna Aggarwal focused on legal provisions and discussed in detail the shortcomings in the antidumping code in India, including the manipulation of the law for protectionist purpose, as well as the discretionary powers of the authorities. [1]

Based on the above analysis, the author argued that the first best option for reforming antidumping system would be to abolish anti-dumping altogether. Governments must attempt to dismantle the anti-dumping mechanism and merge it with the competition policy. Although this would be preferable, it may not be feasible in practice to pursue it unilaterally. It could be pursued through bilateral agreement or in the context of plurilateral arrangements. [2] Another option would be to follow a strict predation standard in investigating anti-dumping cases and limit the scope of antidumping to predatory cases only. [3]

6.1.4 South Africa

Compared with Brazil and India, the studies on the linkage between antidumping and competition in South Africa are relevant fewer. Currently, there were only scattered discussions on the probable conflict between competition and antidumping.

In South Africa, traditionally the Department of Trade and Industry was responsible for both trade remedy and competition policy. Only until recently, the Competition Act of 1999 granted the Competition Commission, Competition Tribunal, and Competition Courts as

---

[1] Aradhna Aggarwal, *Antidumping Law and Practice: An Indian Perspective*, Indian Council for Research on International Economic Relations, 2002, pp. 33 – 35, http://www.icrier.org/pdf/antiDump.pdf, last visited September 21, 2011.

[2] *Ibid.*, p. 68.

[3] *Ibid.*

separate bodies that have their own mandate and policy. [1] This separate administration might result in potential inconsistency between competition policy and trade remedy policy. At any rate, both the competition and antidumping authorities remained obliged to report its policies to the Department of Trade and Industry, in order to coordinate policies to be mutually supportive in the end. [2]

Concerning South Africa, Merle Holden conducted a study of the applications for antidumping duties during 1991 to 1998. A striking feature of the successful applications is the extreme concentration among domestic producers. 69% of the applicants were the sole manufacturer of the product in South Africa. [3] This result indicated that antidumping actions may be anti-competitive to great extent by facilitating domestic producers to maintain their domestic monopoly power.

Moreover, through applying the criteria on predatory dumping similar to that of Shin, to all of the antidumping cases during 1991 to 1998 in South Africa, Merle Holden concluded that, only 3% of the successful applications were likely to have involved anticompetitive behavior on the part of the foreign suppliers. [4]

---

[1] OECD, *Competition Law and Policy in South Africa*, An OECD Peer Review, 2003, pp. 1, 46, http://www.oecd.org/dataoecd/52/13/2958714.pdf, last visited September 21, 2011.

[2] Junji Nakagawa ed., *Antidumping Laws and Practices of The New Users*, Cambridge Univ. Press, 2007, p. 209.

[3] Merle Holden, *Antidumping: A Reaction to Trade Liberalisation or Anti-competitive?* 5 *South African Journal of Economics*, 2002, pp. 912, 928, http://onlinelibrary.wiley.com/doi/10.1111/j.1813-6982.2002.tb00051.x/pdf, last visited September 21, 2011.

[4] *Ibid.*, p. 17.

6.1.5 The Other New Users

As to the other new users, J. Luis Guasch and Sarath Rajapatirana conducted a survey of antidumping v. competition in major Latin American countries which included Brazil, Argentina, Chile, and Mexico etc. [1] They concluded that antidumping is by and large anti-competitive. [2] Further fine-tuning and refining of antidumping policy is not the answer to prevent the slippage into protection with the use of this instrument. The antidote is competition policies. [3]

They also argued that the current efforts should be directed toward the implementation of comprehensive competition policies and credible enforcement agencies, which should also be aimed at phasing out most of the trade policy instruments, such as antidumping, countervailing duties and safeguards and their replacement by a broader application of competition policies and of extraterritorial jurisdiction. [4]

The current research relevant to the new heavy users of antidumping is far from enough. Further and deeper research needs to be conducted on them and expanded to more new users. In the following part, this book attempts to conduct a comprehensive examination on antidumping v. competition in China, one of the important new users not investigated yet, so as to broaden the current practical examination on one hand and on the other hand to see what indications can be got

---

[1] J. Luis Guasch & Sarath Rajapatirana, *Antidumping and Competition Policies in Latin America and Caribbean: Total Strangers or Soul Mates?* 1998, pp. 1 – 26, http://www.worldbank.org/html/dec/Publications/Workpapers/WPS1900series/wps1958/wps1958.pdf, last visited September 21, 2011.

[2] *Ibid.*, p. 20.

[3] *Ibid.*, p. 22.

[4] *Ibid.*

from it.

Mentioning antidumping, China is a country in point. As the number one target of antidumping actions in the world, China has just begun to use antidumping actions in an increasing way. From 1997 until 2010, China has already initiated and awarded its final decisions in fifty antidumping cases. ❶ Another sixteen filing cases are still pending. ❷ Simultaneously, China has also devoted itself to promoting competition legislation and enhancing its enforcement. As the core of the competition system, Chinese Antimonopoly Law has recently been published in 2007. ❸ After long being antidumped by other countries, would China decide to use antidumping more, or use the newly established competition to deal with dumping issue instead? This would indicate the position of China towards replacing antidumping by competition, and hence influence the substitution negotiation in reality to certain extent.

6.2 Antidumping Practice in China

6.2.1 Development of Antidumping Legislation

A general introduction of antidumping practice in China will be given in this part, whereas its linkage with competition will be observed in the following part. The legislative history of antidumping in China is not long. Article 30 of the Foreign Trade Law 1994, was the first

---

❶ For convenience of discussion in this paper, the number of antidumping cases is calculated according to the number of targeted products.

❷ http://gpj.mofcom.gov.cn/d/r.html, last visited March 10, 2011.

❸ Chinese Antimonopoly Law was adopted at the 29th session of the Tenth National People's Congress on August 30, 2007 and took effect as of August 1, 2008.

domestic law of China regulating antidumping. [1] As the first implementing regulation of this Article, Antidumping and Anti-subsidy Regulations of the People's Republic of China (Regulation 1997) was promulgated by the State Council on 25 March 1997. China, in anticipation of its eventual accession to the WTO at that time, seems to have drafted this regulation to comply with the rules of the WTO ADA. [2] Though this regulation contained a few articles regulating countervailing duties, most articles dealt with antidumping. [3]

Later on, as China acceded to the WTO on 11 December 2001, in order to bring its domestic antidumping law into conformity with the WTO ADA, the State Council therefore promulgated the Regulations of the People's Republic of China on Antidumping on 26 November 2001, which entered into force on 1 January 2002 (Regulation 2002). Regulation 2002 consisted of six Chapters and 59 Articles,

---

[1] Foreign Trade Law 1994, Article 30 provides that: "Should a well established or fledgling industry at home be in substantial harm or under threat of such harm due to the import of relative goods in under normal value, the State may take any countermeasures to expel or mitigate such harm or threat." 英文译本出自北大法宝网站, http://www.lawinfochina.com/display.aspx? lib = law&id = 664, last visited September 18, 2009.

Please be noticed that, the above Article 30 and the following Chinese legal texts are all tranaslated by the author.

[2] Junji Nakagawa ed., *Antidumping Laws and Practices of The New Users*, Cambridge Univ. Press, 2007, p. 29.

[3] Regulation 1997 consisted of six chapters and 42 articles. Amongst three chapters is dealing with antidumping. Chapter II dealt with dumping and injury (Article 3 to 10); Chapter III dealt with antidumping investigation (Article 11 to 21); Chapter IV dealt with antidumping measures (Article 22 to 35).

which covers most of the subject matters regulated by the WTO ADA. ❶ Following Regulation 2002 were a series of relevant provisional rules and stipulations on each specific implementing measure. ❷ With this regulation became effective, Regulation 1997 was replaced.

In 2004, the Foreign Trade Law, as the basis for both Regulation 1997

---

❶ Regulation 2002 consisted of six chapters and 59 articles. Chapter II dealt with dumping and injury (Article 3 to 12); Chapter III dealt with antidumping investigation (Article 13 to 27); and Chapter IV dealt with antidumping measures (Article 28 to 47); Chapter V dealt with duration and review of antidumping duties and price undertakings (Article 48 to 52).

❷ The relevant provisions rule and stipulations on each specific implementing measure include:

Provisional Rules on Public Hearing in Antidumping Investigations;

Provisional Rules on Initiation of Antidumping Investigations;

Provisional Rules on Questionnaire in Antidumping Investigations;

Provisional Rules on Sampling in Antidumping Investigations;

Provisional Rules on Disclosure of Information in Antidumping Investigation;

Provisional Rules on On-the-Spot Verification in Antidumping Investigations;

Provisional Rules on Access to Non-Confidential Information in Antidumping Investigations;

Provisional Rules on Price Undertakings in Antidumping Investigation;

Provisional Rules on New Shipper Review in Antidumping Investigations;

Provisional Rules on Refund of Antidumping Duty;

Provisional Rules on Interim Review of Dumping and Dumping Margin;

Provisional Rules on the Procedures for Adjusting Product Scope in Antidumping Investigation;

Rules on Public Hearing with regard to Investigations of Injury to Industry;

Rules on Investigations and Determinations of Industry Injury for Antidumping;

Rules on Investigations of Industry Injury for Antidumping;

Provisions on Certain Questions Concerning the Hearing and Handling of International Trade Administrative Cases;

Provisions on Certain Issues Concerning the Applicability of Laws in the Hearing and Handling of Antidumping Administrative Cases.

and Regulation 2002, was revised. Meanwhile, Regulation 2002 was also revised (Regulation 2004). Regulation 2004 basically uses the same language as its predecessors. It reflects in institutional changes in antidumping investigating authorities, as well as some substantive changes like taking the "public interest" into consideration. [1] This is the current version of Antidumping Regulation in China. Accordingly, the current effective antidumping rules in China including Chinese Foreign Trade Law 2004, Regulation 2004, and a series of relevant provisional rules and stipulations.

6.2.2 Legislative Goal of Antidumping Regulation

With the revision of antidumping regulations in China, the legislative goal has also literally changed to some extent. Article 1 of Regu lation 1997 stated that its goal was to maintain foreign trade order, fair competition, and to protect domestic industry. [2]

Later on, both Regulation 2002 and Regulation 2004 in their Article 1 respectively stated that the specific goal of Chinese antidumping regulation is to maintain foreign trade order and fair competition. [3]

6.2.3 Requirements on "International Dumping"

In China, antidumping is usually said to deal with "international dumping". Faithfully conforming to the WTO ADA, the basic criterion for condemning dumping in China is similar to many other countries, including price calculation, injury, as well as the causation between the two.

---

[1] Junji Nakagawa ed., *Antidumping Laws and Practices of the New Users*, Cambridge Univ. Press, 2007, p. 33.

[2] Regulation 1997, Article 1.

[3] Regulation 2002, Article 1.

6.2.4 Features of Antidumping Cases in China

As to the practical application of antidumping measures, China initiated its first antidumping investigation on 10 December 1997 against imports of newsprint from Canada, Korea and the U. S. Up till now, China has already initiated and rendered final determinations to antidumping actions towards fifty products. Of these fifty cases, twelve cases were initiated under Regulation 1997, fifteen cases were under Regulation 2002, and twenty-three cases were under the current Regulation 2004. The trend of increase can be noticed through these fluctuations.

One notable characteristic of Chinese antidumping cases is that intermediate chemical products have occupied an overwhelming majori ty of the products investigated (thirty-eight out of fifty cases). Two reasons for the concentration of antidumping investigations on chemical products have been pointed out. [1]

The first reason is that, China significantly lowered the tariffs of chemical products when it acceded to the WTO. The tenth five - year plan in 2001 promised to nurturing and development of such industries as the steel, petrochemical, chemical and synthetic fiber industries, and stated that Chinese government would actively made use of antidumping measures to achieve this goal. [2]

The second reason is due to the peculiar characteristics of chemical industry. Chemical products, particularly such general-purpose products, are subject to price fluctuation in international markets when their international market prices go down, their export prices to China

---

[1] Junji Nakagawa ed., *Antidumping Laws and Practices of the New Users*, Cambridge Univ. Press, 2007, p. 71.

[2] *Ibid.*

also go down, which makes the initiation of antidumping investigation easily acceptable. Besides, as the chemical industry is an upstream industry with fewer products categories, it is relatively easy to specify the product scope subject to investigation. [1]

6. 3 Competition Practice in China

6. 3. 1 Development of Competition Legislation

Competition law is a comparatively new field in China. It was not until 1970s, when China decided to transform planned economy into market economy, that there was a need for competition law to regulate the market. Soon after the reform objective "Establishment of Socia list Market Economic System" was determined in 14th National Congress of Communist Party of China in October, 1992, the Standing Committee of the National People's Congress has passed the Law of the People's Republic of China against Unfair Competition (Chinese Unfair Competition Law) in September, 1993, which is the first Chinese competition law. [2]

Chinese Unfair Competition Law is mainly concerned with unfair competitive conducts in the market, such as unfair counterfeiting a registered trademark[3], infringing upon trade secrets[4], fabricating or spreading false information[5] etc. Besides, because antimonopoly law

---

[1] Junji Nakagawa ed., *Antidumping Laws and Practices of the New Users*, Cambridge Univ. Press, 2007, p. 72.

[2] Chinese Unfair Competition Law was adopted at the third meeting of the Standing Committee of the Eighth National People's Congress on September 2, 1993 and promulgated by Order No. 10 of the President of the People's Republic of China on September 2, 1993.

[3] Chinese Unfair Competition Law, Article 5.

[4] Chinese Unfair Competition Law, Article 10.

[5] Chinese Unfair Competition Law, Article 14.

was not enacted during that time, according to the practical needs, some unfair conducts of restrictive competition that are supposed to be dealt with by antimonopoly law, such as predatory dumping❶, monopoly abuse by public utility enterprises❷ or governments❸, have been set forth in this law. ❹

Followed is a series of other laws such as Law of the People's Republic of China on Product Quality 1993, Law of the People's Republic of China on the Protection of Consumer Rights and Interests 1993, Price Law of the Peoples Republic of China 1997 (Chinese Price Law), and Foreign Trade Law of the People's Republic of China 2004 etc., all of which either supplement or combined with Chinese Unfair Competition Law, with the same purpose to safeguard the healthy development of socialist market economy.

As the core of competition system, Chinese Antimonopoly Law has just been published in 2007. ❺ Actually, the draft work of this law started at nearly the same time as the law against unfair competition. However, due to the immature of the relevant remarket conditions, it was not until recently that it has been enacted. During the legislation of the first competition law in 1993, when China was still at the beginning of market economy, most of the domestic economy was still controlled or monopolized by nation. Since it was rather hard in

---

❶ Chinese Unfair Competition Law, Article 11.

❷ Chinese Unfair Competition Law, Article 6.

❸ Chinese Unfair Competition Law, Article 7.

❹ 安建主编、全国人民代表大会常务委员会法制工作委员会编:《中华人民共和国反垄断法释义》,法律出版社 2007 年版,第 11 ~ 12 页。

❺ Chinese Antimonopoly Law was just adopted at the 29th session of the Tenth National People's Congress on August 30, 2007, and will be taken in effect on August 1, 2008.

reality to prohibit monopoly, competition law at that time mainly focused on the conducts of unfair competition, most of which are likely to be commited by small or medium companies. ❶

The draft of Chinese Antimonopoly Law had been under discussion for quite a long while. It was not until 2007 has it been published. Similar to other countries, Chinese Antimonopoly Law also regulates on three main kinds of restraining competition conducts, including monopoly agreement❷, abuse of a dominant market position❸, concentration. ❹Apart from that, abuse of administrative power is also an important section therein. ❺

6.3.2 Legislative Goals of Competition Law

The aforementioned two competition laws comprise the basic competition system in China. The specific goal of each law has been stipulated in Article 1 respectively. As to Chinese Unfair Competition Law, it is formulated with a view to safeguarding the healthy development of socialist market economy, encouraging and protecting fair competition, repressing unfair competition acts, and protecting the lawful rights and interests of business operators and consumers. ❻

As to Chinese Antimonopoly Law, it is enacted for the purpose of preventing and restraining monopolistic conducts, protecting fair competition in the market, enhancing economic efficiency, safeguarding

---

❶ 黄勇:"反垄断法出台法律定位与法律协调决定成败",载《法制日报》2007 年 9 月 2 日,第 012 版, http://www.legaldaily.com.cn/0705/2007-09/02/content_692323.htm, last visited September 18, 2011.

❷ Chinese Antimonopoly Law, Chapter II.

❸ Chinese Antimonopoly Law, Chapter III.

❹ Chinese Antimonopoly Law, Chapter IV.

❺ Chinese Antimonopoly Law, Chapter V.

❻ Chinese Unfair Competition Law, Article 1.

the interests of consumers and social public interest, promoting the healthy development of the socialist market economy. ❶

Under the same category of promoting healthy development of socialist market economy and protecting fair competition, the law against unfair competition is more concerned with unfair competition and protecting defined competitors, whereas antimonopoly law cares more about restrictive competition and protecting competitive process. ❷ Similar to other countries, the three basic common competition principles, including protecting competitive process, enhancing economic efficiency, as well as safeguarding the interests of consumers, have been also clearly stated in Chinese antimonopoly law.

6. 3. 3 Requirements of "Domestic Dumping"

6. 3. 3. 1 Competition Rules on "Domestic Dumping"

As discussed in Chapter IV, for all of the major countries, includ ing the U. S. and the EU, predatory dumping or pricing is regulated under the section of abuse of monopoly power. Even in those countries like Germany, Japan that have the law against unfair competition and the antimonopoly law as well, predatory dumping is only

---

❶ Chinese Antimonopoly Law, Article 1.

❷ 安建主编、全国人民代表大会常务委员会法制工作委员会编:《中华人民共和国反垄断法释义》,法律出版社 2007 年版,第 11 ~12 页。

addressed in the latter one.[1] However, in China, predatory

---

[1] *See*, e. g., Japan has both "Unfair Competition Prevention Act" and "Act on Prohibition of Private Monopolization and Maintenance of Fair Trade". However, predatory pricing is addressed only under the latter one. To be more specific, Artilce 19 of Act on Prohibition of Private Monopolization and Maintenance of Fair Trade stipulates that: "No entrepreneur shall employ unfair trade practices." And Artilce 2 (9) interpretates that, the term "unfair trade practices" as used in this Act means any act falling under any of following items, which tends to impede fair competition and which is designated by the Fair Trade Commission: (i) Unjustly treat other entrepreneurs in a discriminatory manner; (ii) Dealing with unjust consideration; (iii) Unjustly inducing or coercing customers of a competitor to deal with oneself; (iv) Dealing with another party on such conditions as will unjustly restrict the business activities of the said party; (v) Dealing with another party by unjust use of one's bargaining position; (vi) Unjustly interfering with a transaction between an entrepreneur in competition with it in Japan with oneself or a corporation of which oneself is a stockholder or an officer and another transaction counterparty; or, in case such entrepreneur is a corporation, unjustly inducing, instigating, or coercing a stockholder or an director of such corporation to act against the interests of such corporation.

The English Translation of "Unfair Competition Prevention Act" is available at: http://www. cas. go. jp/jp/seisaku/hourei/data/ucpa. pdf, last visited May 7, 2009.

The English Translation of "Act on Prohibition of Private Monopolization and Maintenance of Fair Trade" is available at: http://www. cas. go. jp/jp/seisaku/hourei/data/pmm_2. pdf, last visited May 7, 2009.

See also, in Germany, there are also "The New German Act Against Unfair Competition" and "Act against Restraints on Competition", predatory pricing is also only dealt with under the latter. Section 20 (4) of Act against Restraints on Competition stipulates that: "Undertakings with superior market power in relation to small and medium-sized competitors shall not use their market power directly or indirectly to hinder such competitors in an unfair manner. An unfair hindrance within the meaning of sentence 1 exists in particular if an undertaking offers goods or services not merely occasionally below its cost price, unless there is an objective justification for this."

The English Translation of "The New German Act Against Unfair Competition" is available at: http://www. iuscomp. org/gla/literature/heidenreich. htm, last visited May 7, 2009.

The English Translation of "Act against Restraints on Competition" is available at: http://www. iuscomp. org/gla/statutes/GWB. htm#19, last visited May 7, 2009.

dumping, or predatory price discrimination, is usually called as "domestic dumping". Due to its peculiar legislative development, domestic dumping that should be regulated only under antimonopoly law has currently been subjected to both Chinese Unfair Competition Law and Chinese Antimonopoly Law. Moreover, as a price conduct, it is also stipulated in Chinese Price Law. Accordingly, there are three sets of rules dealing with the issue of low-price selling in China.

The first one is under Chinese Unfair Competition Law. In the Chapter Two of this law, which is "Acts of Unfair Competition", Article 11 stipulates that, a business operator shall not, for the purpose of pushing out their competitors, sell their commodities at prices lower than costs. Any of the following shall not be deemed as an unfair competition act: Ⅰ. Selling perishables or live commodities; Ⅱ. Disposing of commodities near expiration of their validity duration or those kept too long in stock; Ⅲ. Seasonal sales; or Ⅳ. Selling commodities at a reduced pricc for the purpose of clearing off debts, change of business or suspension of operation. [1]

The second one is under Chinese Price Law. According to Article 14 of Chapter Two "Price Acts of the Operators", low-price selling might be considered as unfair price conduct in two circumstances: one is lower-than-the-cost price in Term 2, and the other is price

[1] 英文译本出自中华人民共和国全国人民代表大会网站(英文版),http://www.npc.gov.cn/englishnpc/Law/2007-12/12/content_1383803.htm, last visited September 18, 2011.

discrimination towards other operators in Term 5.[1] The application of the two terms has been specified in two provisions, i. e. , Provisions

---

[1] Chinese Price Law, Article 14: The manager may not commit any of the following illegitimate acts in pricing: (1) colluding with others to manipulate the market price, thus harming the lawful rights and interests of other managers or consumers; (2) besides disposing of perishable, seasonal and overstocked commodities at reduced prices according to law, dumping commodities at prices lower than production cost in order to drive out rivals or monopolize the market, thus disrupting normal production and operational order and impairing the interests of the State or the lawful rights and interests of other managers; (3) fabricating and spreading information about price hikes and forcing up prices, thus stimulating excessive commodity price hikes; (4) using false or misleading prices to deceive consumers or other managers into transacting a deal with him; (5) while providing the same commodities or services, employing price discrimination against other managers with equal transaction conditions; (6) forcing up or forcing down prices in disguised form by raising or lowering grades when purchasing or selling commodities or providing services; (7) making exorbitant profits in violation of the provisions of laws and regulations; or (8) other illegitimate acts in pricing prohibited by laws and administrative rules and regulations. 英文译本出自中华人民共和国全国人民代表大会网站(英文版), http://www.npc.gov.cn/englishnpc/Law/2007-12/11/content_1383577.htm, last visited September 18, 2011.

on Preventing the Conduct of Low-Price Dumping 1999❶, as well as

---

❶ In terms of Provisions on Preventing the Conduct of Low-Price Dumping of 1999, according to Article 1 of this provision, in accordance with the Price Law of the People's Republic of China, the purpose of this regulation is to prevent the acts of low-price dumping to promote an open, fair and legitimate price competition, to protect national interests as well as the legal rights and interests of the operators and consumers.

This regulation has provided a comparatively specific criterion regarding what the "cost", "below the cost", or "below-the-cost dumping" refers to. Article 4 has defined two kinds of "cost": Cost of production and cost of operation. Cost of production refers to manufacture cost plus period expense (consisted by management expense, finance expense as well as sale expense). Cost of operation includes merchandise procurement cost and circulation expense (consisted by operation expense, management expense as well as finance expense).

As to "below the cost", according to Article 5, it means the operator sales the commodities below the reasonable individual cost. On the conditions that the individual cost can not be identified, the relevant governmental authority shall decide according to the average cost of the whole industry of the commodities as well as the floating scope.

While according to Article 2, the so-called "low-price dumping" refers to dumping at the lower-than-the-cost price and disrupting the normal production and management order to the detriment of national interests or the lawful rights and interests of other operators for the purpose of squeezing out other competitors or of sole occupancy of the market other than the disposal of the commodities at reduced prices in accordance with the law.

In article 6, it is pointed out that "the disposal of the commodities at reduced prices in accordance with the law" refers to five situations, including: (1) Selling those commodities which are kept too long in stock; (2) Disposing of commodities out of or near the expiration of the season; (3) Disposing of commodities near the expiration of their guarantee period or validity duration; (4) Perishables or live commodities near the expiration of their guarantee period; (5) Selling commodities at a reduced price for the purpose of clearing off debts, bankruptcy, change of business or suspension of operation.

In article 7, it is pointed out that the "low-price dumping" in Article 2 generally refers to 8 situations, including (1) The price at which the manufacturer sells the commodities is lower than the cost of production, or the price at which the operator sells the commodities is lower than the cost of merchandise procurement cost; (2) To make the price below the relevant cost by the means of substituting high-quality, high-level commodities for low-quality, low-level ones; (3) To make the price below the relevant cost by the means of discount, subsidy, and so on; (4) To make the price below the relevant cost by the means of unequal exchange of materials; (5) To make the price below the relevant cost by the means of paying-a-debt-in-kind Assets; (6) To make the price below the relevant cost by the means of more sales, but less or no invoices; (7) To make the price below the relevant cost by the means of larger quantities, quantity sales and so on; (8) To make the price below the relevant cost by the means of lowering the bidding price in a bid.

本规定由笔者翻译。

Interim Provisions on Preventing the Acts of Price Monopoly 2003 respectively. [1]

The third one is under the latest Chinese Antimonopoly Law. The issue of low-price selling is regulated in the Article 17 of Chapter Three "Abuse of a Dominant Market Position". According to this

---

[1] Be noticed that Interim Provisions on Preventing the Acts of Price Monopoly of 2003 has been out of force right after the completion of this book. The author decided to keep the discussion of such part. As to Interim Provisions on Preventing the Acts of Price Monopoly of 2003, according to Article 1, in accordance with the Price Law of the People's Republic of China, the purpose of this regulation is to prevent acts of price monopoly, to promote fair competition and to protect the legal rights and interests of the operators and consumers. Therefore, the conduct of price discrimination has been addressed as the conduct of such operators as having the market predomination.

It is stipulated in Article 2 and Article 3 that the "acts of price monopoly" refers to the acts that by means of collusion or abuse of the market predominance, the operators control the market prices, disturb the normal production and operation order, impair the legal rights and interests of the other operators and consumers, or harm the interests of the public. While "the determination of market predominance" shall be mainly based on the market shares of the operators in the relevant markets, the substitutability of the commodities and difficulty of the new competitors to enter into the market.

And thereafter the conduct of price discrimination shall be taken as anti-competitive and punishable in light of two circumstances according to Article 7 and Article 8. Article 7 stipulates that: "No business operator may rely on the market predominance to dump commodities at the price lower than the costs for the purposes of supplanting and impairing their competitors; or to make the actual sales prices lower the costs of the commodities themselves by means of lowering the prices under the disguises of kickbacks, subsidies and donations." Article 8 regulates that: "No operator may, when providing same commodities or services, rely on its market predominance to treat the same transaction objects differently in the aspect of transaction price."

Several special provisions concerned with low-price selling in special industry have be regulated according to the basic requirements of the above two provisions. Such as Provisions on Preventing the Unfair Price Conduct of Dumping Industrial Goods of 1998.

该英文译本出自北大法宝网站, http://www.lawinfochina.com/display.aspx? lib = law & id = 2936, last visited September 18, 2011.

article, low-price selling is deemed to be unfair price conduct in two circumstances: One is price below cost in Term 2, and the other is applying dissimilar prices to equivalent counterparties in Term 6. ❶

6.3.3.2 Terminology: "Dumping" and "Price Discrimination"

According to the above introduction, the first thing that must be made clear is the terminology. Most countries do not use the term "dumping" in domestic competition laws, whereas China does. Therefore, it needs to distinguish between two kinds of dumping: one is "international dumping", referring to antidumping law; the other one is "domestic dumping", referring to competition law. ❷

In China, the term "dumping" has separate meaning from the term "price discrimination". "Domestic dumping" refers to selling below

---

❶ Chinese Antimonopoly Law, Article 17: Undertakings holding dominant market positions are prohibited from doing the following by abusing their dominant market positions: (1) selling commodities at unfairly high prices or buying commodities at unfairly low prices; (2) without justifiable reasons, selling commodities at prices below cost; (3) without justifiable reasons, refusing to enter into transactions with their trading counterparts; (4) without justifiable reasons, allowing their trading counterparts to make transactions exclusively with themselves or with the undertakings designated by them; (5) without justifiable reasons, conducting tie - in sale of commodities or adding other unreasonable trading conditions to transactions; (6) without justifiable reasons, applying differential prices and other transaction terms among their trading counterparts who are on an equal footing; or (7) other acts of abuse of dominant market positions confirmed as such by the authority for enforcement of the Antimonopoly Law under the State Council. For the purposes of this Law, dominant market position means a market position held by undertakings that are capable of controlling the prices or quantities of commodities or other transaction terms in a relevant market, or preventing or exerting an influence on the access of other undertakings to the market. 英文译本出自中华人民共和国全国人民代表大会网站(英文版), http://www.npc.gov.cn/englishnpc/Law/2009-02/20/content_1471587.htm, last visited September 18, 2011.

❷ 李书田:"论国际反倾销与国内反低价倾销的差异性",载《价格与市场》2006年第9期,第37~39页。

the cost. Only dumping as proved to be "predatory dumping" or "predatory pricing' is condemned under the law. For instance, Article 11 of Chinese Unfair Competition Law is widely accepted to refer to low-price dumping. Here "dumping" shall be condemned as long as it is proved to be selling goods at prices lower than costs for the purpose of pushing out their competitors. Similarly, Term 2, Article 14 of Chinese Price Law, as well as Provisions on Preventing the Conduct of Low-Price Dumping and Article 7 of the Interim Provisions on Preventing the Acts of Price Monopoly, all use the term "dumping" to refer to lower-than-the-cost price, and condemn dumping for the purpose of squeezing out other competitors or of sole occupancy of the market. Chinese antimonopoly law does not use the term "dumping" to refer to below-cost selling. Instead, it uses "selling commodities at prices below-cost without legitimate reasons" to express similar meanings.

As to the term "price discrimination", it has been addressed by both price law and antimonopoly Law, but not by the law against unfair competition. Term 5, Article 14 of Chinese Price Law, forbids the operators from committing the unfair "price discrimination", which is to discriminate in terms of prices same kinds of merchandises or services offered by certain business operators under same trading conditions. Article 8 of Interim Provisions on Preventing the Acts of Price Monopoly regulates that no operator may, when providing same commodities or services, rely on its market predominance to treat the same transaction objects differently in the aspect of transaction price. Term 6, Article 17 of Chinese antimonopoly law stipulates that undertakings of a dominant market position shall not abuse their dominant market positions to apply dissimilar prices or other transaction terms to equivalent counterparties.

Price discrimination has not been well addressed in China. All of the above rules are too abstract with no specific criteria or guidance. Only Interpretation of Price Law of China 1998 and Interpretation of Chinese Antimonopoly Law 2007 give a similar but very brief interpretation. [1] Consequently, there are seldom cases on price discrimination in practice. Scholars have kept on learning the relevant economic theories and transplanting the relevant practices of the U. S. and the EU to improve it.

Through examining the above Interpretations, the practical cases as well as the discussions of the scholars, and combining with the two-level competition aformentioned, it is found that "price discrimination" in China focused mainly on the secondary-line competition rather than the primary-line competition. [2] In the Interpretation of Price Law of China 1998, it explains that: "Generally speaking, price discrimina-

---

[1] 全国人大法工委、国家计委编:《中华人民共和国价格法释义》,http://wenku. baidu. com/view/c6a5442b3169a4517723a3fe. html, last visited September 18, 2011; 安建主编、全国人民代表大会常务委员会法制工作委员会编:《中华人民共和国反垄断法释义》,法律出版社 2007 年版,第 48 ~ 52 页。

[2] As already analyzed in Chapter III of this book, in economic consideration price discrimination can be either pro-competitive or anti-competitive, while the problem is to identify those situations where it may prove anticompetitive. For this purpose, it is necessary to distinguish between two levels of competition. The first one is the primary-line competition, that is, competition between the discriminating monopolist and his rivals in the same line of business; and the second one is the secondary-line competition, that is, competition between the discriminating monopolist's customers (who may, for instance, be retailers) and their business rivals. For the primary-line competition, there can be no presumption that price discrimination is injurious, and price discrimination can only be considered as anti-competitive in the extreme case, that is, when it is a predatory pricing. The consideration of competitive effects of price discrimination is even more complicated in the secondary-line competition. This basic viewpoint of price discrimination has been accepted both in the U. S. and the EU.

tion means that the operators have no legitimate reasons but treat the counterparties unequally on price with identical trading conditions in providing identical commodities or services. Such as granting Company A at quantity price while not granting Company B; or granting changes of price for Company A but not for Company B; or offering different prices because A is a local company while B is not. Price discrimination makes counterparties at unfair position which has an effect of restraining competition and thereby hinders the fair competition. Therefore, it has been regulated in the antitrust law of almost all of the countries in the world." ❶ Similar statement can also be found in the Interpretation of Chinese Antimonopoly Law 2007, which forbids the operators that have dominant market position to conduct price discrimination towards the counterparties with identical trading conditions. ❷

Regarding the few cases on price discrimination, none of them care about the anti-competitive effect to the competition between the discriminating actor and his rivals in the same line of business. Instead, they mainly discuss on the competition between the discriminating actor's customers and their business rivals, such as *the Ticket Price of Mountain Emei Case*❸, or *the Ticket Price of Siboyuan Case*. ❹

---

❶ 该部分译文由笔者翻译。

❷ 该部分译文由笔者翻译。

❸ "全国首例风景区门票价格地域歧视案开庭",载《兰州晨报》2002 年 10 月 14 日,第 A15 版, http://lzcb.gansudaily.com.cn/system/2002/10/14/000027694.shtml, last visited September 18, 2011.

❹ "'内外有别'昆明世博园'价格歧视'惹争议",载《人民日报》2007 年 7 月 14 日,第 05 版, http://culture.people.com.cn/GB/22219/4591296.html, last visited September 18, 2011.

And also, the academic attention has also been paid only to the secondary-line competition. The scholars are concerned with whether the object of price discrimination should include the final consumers or only the operators, and there are no discussions on the separate criteria of the primary-line competition and the second-line competition. ❶

To sum up, in China the focus of "price discrimination" is on the conductor of price discrimination and its customer or its transactional counterparties, rather than on the actor of price discrimination and its rivals. In other words, it is not interested in the cases where "one price lower than the other" would injure competitors. Accordingly, the term "price discrimination" in Chinese competition rules mainly deals with price discrimination in the secondary-line competition, whereas the term "dumping" is virtually applied in the primary-line competition thereof. Since antidumping law connects with competition law only in the primary-line competition, "dumping" instead of "price discrimination" will be within examination in the following discussion.

6. 3. 3. 3 Similarities and Differences with Other Countries

Compared the rules of "dumping" in China with the other major countries, there exist some similarities and differences. As to the simi larity, low-price selling is not considered as anti-competitive or hurtful unless it is proved to be a predatory dumping. This conforms to economic theories and similar to most of the other major countries.

In terms of the differences, there are two major points. The first

---

❶ 祈玉军:"关于价格歧视的几点思考",载《价格理论与实践》2002 年第 9 期,第 32 ~ 33 页;肖伟志:"应对竞争的抗辩:美国和欧共体反价格歧视法的比较与借鉴",载《河北法学》2005 年第 7 期,第 124 ~ 129 页。

one relates to the legislation of predatory dumping. Dumping is prescribecd not only in competition law, but also provided in price law. The price law of 1997 and the relevant provisions do not merely reite rate what has already been regulated in competition rules, but act as the supplementary or interpretation thereto. ❶ They not only specified the rules on predatory dumping for the early Chinese Unfair Competition law, but also filled the vacancy prior to the enactment of Chinese Antimonopoly Law. The second point links with the criterion for condemning predatory dumping. Unlike most of the other countries where there exists only one set of criterion, in China there are two sets of criterion. This will be discussed in the following part.

6. 3. 3. 4 Two Sets of Criterion of "Domestic Dumping"

According to Chinese officers, with the enactment of Chinese Antimonopoly Law, the relevant amendments towards harmonizing Chinese Unfair Competition Law and Chinese Antimonopoly Law have been carried on, and the basic principle of the amendments is to delete all of the overlap parts in the previous Chinese Unfair Competition Law. However, as to the overlap issue of predatory pricing, up till now, there still lacks a common understanding. ❷

---

❶ Basically speaking, similar as most of the other countries, the purpose of the price law in China is to standardize the price acts from a macro perspective, including giving play to the role of price in the rational allocation of resources, stabilizing the overall price level of the market, and promoting the sound development of the socialist market economy. While the difference is that, the price law of China also needs to protect the lawful rights and interests of the consumers and operators from a micro perspective, that is, to regulate the actual unfair price conducts and predatory dumping is one of them.

❷ Email from Ma Zhengping, Office Worker, *the Commission for Legal Affairs under the Standing Committee of the National People's Congress*, to Bi Ying, LL. D. Candidate, Kyushu University, Apr. 24, 2008. (on file with the author)

Regarding this issue, there are two groups of opinions. One group views that as predatory dumping can be taken as either an unfair competition conduct or a restraining competition conduct, it should be regulated in both laws. ❶ The other group argues that with the enactment of Chinese Antimonopoly Law, such conducts as administrative monopoly, predatory dumping and so on should be regulated only under the antimonopoly law rather than unfair competition law. ❷

This book tends to consider that there exist two sets of Criterion in China at present due to three reasons. The first one is from the perspective of the purpose of each law. As mentioned above, the unfair competition law is more concerned with the negative effects to special competitors, while antimonopoly law cares about restraining competition conducts usually conducted by those big companies as having market dominant positions. Even if predatory pricing should be subject only to antimonopoly law, it was currently subject to both laws due to the particular legislative development in China, which means the specific requirements might be different due to the different focuses of the two sets of rules.

The second one is from the perspective of the specific rules in each law. According to Article 11 of Chinese Unfair Competition Law, it will be taken as an act of unfair competition if a business operator sell their commodities at prices lower than costs for the purpose of pushing

---

❶ 王晓晔:"反垄断法与反不正当竞争法的异同",载新浪博客 2007 年 7 月 11 日, http://blog. sina. com. cn/s/blog_4da7948501000kmw. html, last visited September 11, 2011.

❷ 黄勇:"反垄断法出台法律定位与法律协调决定成败",载《法制日报》2007 年 9 月 2 日, 第 012 版, http://www. legaldaily. com. cn/0705/2007 - 09/02/content_692323. htm, last visited September 11, 2011.

out their competitors, rather than for the purpose of selling perishables or live commodities; disposing of commodities near expiration of their validity duration or those kept too long in stock; Seasonal sales; or selling commodities at a reduced price for the purpose of clearing off debts, change of business or suspension of operation.

According to Term 2, Article 17 of Chinese Antimonopoly Law, it will be taken as an act of abusing the dominant market position so as to restrain the competition if undertakings of a dominant market position sell commodities at prices below cost without legitimate reasons. It has been further explained in the interpretation of Chinese Antimonopoly Law 2007 that this term refers to the conduct of predatory pricing. The dominant company continuously sells commodities at price below cost in order to squeez the competitors out of the market, prohibit the new entry of companies, as well as successfully monopolize the market. The cost of this price is very high, but the dominant company is anticipating the future profit exceed the current lost. Here the legitimate reasons include selling live commodities; disposing of commodities near expiration of their validity duration or those kept too long in stock, or Seasonal sales. [1]

By comparison, it is found that the requirements such as selling commodities at prices below cost, the monopoly purpose, and without reasonable exemptions, have been similar in both laws, but the major difference is that the former law does not require the dominant market power whereas the latter does.

The third one is from the perspective of the relevant provisions of

---

[1] 安建主编、全国人民代表大会常务委员会法制工作委员会编:《中华人民共和国反垄断法释义》,法律出版社 2007 年版,第 48 ~52 页。

Chinese Price Law. As introduced above, there are two kinds of provisions governing predatory dumping. One is Provisions on Preventing the Conduct of Low-Price Dumping of 1999, which resembles and specifies the rules under Chinese Unfair Competition Law; the other one is Interim Provisions on Preventing the Acts of Price Monopoly of 2003, which fills a vacancy at that time the rules under Chinese Antimonopoly Law and requires the dominant position.

For the above three reasons, this book tends to consider that, although the progressing revision work might end up in subjecting predatory dumping only to antimonopoly law in future, which is consistent with the common practice of the other major countries, currently there are two different sets of criterion on predatory dumping in China. One is under Chinese Unfair Competition Law, and the other is under Chinese Antimonopoly Law.

6. 3. 3. 5 Criterion I under Chinese Unfair Competition Law

The first criterion on predatory dumping according to Chinese Unfair Competition Law, and specified by Provisions on Preventing the Conduct of Low-Price Dumping. The Interpretation of Price Law of China 1998 stated that there are basically three key points for the determination of a predatory dumping or a predatory pricing, which has already been widely accepted in China. [1]

The first one is the means, to examine whether the selling is at a price below the cost. That how to calculate the cost has been specifically regulated in Provisions on Preventing the Conduct of Low-Price Dumping. Article 4 has defined two kinds of "cost": cost of

---

[1] 全国人大法工委、国家计委编:《中华人民共和国价格法释义》, http://wenku. baidu. com/view/c6a5442b3169a4517723a3fe. html, last visited September 18, 2011.

production and cost of operation. Cost of production refers to manufacture cost plus period expense (consisted by management expense, finance expense as well as sale expense). Cost of operation includes merchandise procurement cost and circulation expense (consisted by ope ration expense, management expense as well as finance expense). ❶

As to "below the cost", according to Article 5, it means the operator sales the commodities below the reasonable individual cost. In cases where the individual cost can not be identified, the relevant governmental authority shall decide according to the average cost of the whole industry of the commodities as well as the floating scope.

Besides, since the cost calculation is a crucial issue in punishing a predatory dumping, Article 7 of Provisions exemplifies 8 situations which may give birth to a below-cost selling. ❷

The second one is the purpose, to examine whether it is for squeezing out other competitors or of sole occupancy of the market. For instance, in order to open the local market for its newly established

---

❶ Provisions on Preventing the Conduct of Low-Price Dumping of 1999, Ariticle 4.

❷ According to Provisions on Preventing the Conduct of Low-Price Dumping of 1999, Ariticle 5, those situations includes: (1) The price at which the manufacturer sells the commodities is lower than the cost of production, or the price at which the operator sells the commodities is lower than the cost of merchandise procurement cost; (2) To make the price below the relevant cost by the means of substituting high-quality, high-level commodities for low-quality, low-level ones; (3) To make the price below the relevant cost by the means of discount, subsidy, and so on; (4) To make the price below the relevant cost by the means of unequal exchange of materials; (5) To make the price below the relevant cost by the means of paying-a-debt-in-kind Assets; (6) To make the price below the relevant cost by the means of more sales, but less or no invoices; (7) To make the price below the relevant cost by the means of larger quantities, quantity sales and so on; (8) To make the price below the relevant cost by the means of lowering the bidding price in a bid. 该规定由笔者翻译。

branch, by the means of lowering the price at large scale, the operator tries to squeeze out the other competitors and then monopolize this local market. ❶

Even though there do exist the case of which the purpose is obvious or comparatively easy to prove, it is without doubt that the examination of the subjective "purpose" is very hard and involving much discretion. ❷ Therefore, some exemptions of purposes, such as the disposal of such commodities as fresh and living commodities, seasonal commodities and overstocked commodities at reduced prices in accordance with law, have been provided as defense. This has also been specified in Article 6 of Provisions on Preventing the Conduct of Low-Price Dumping. ❸

---

❶ 全国人大法工委、国家计委编:《中华人民共和国价格法释义》, http://wenku.baidu.com/view/c6a5442b3169a4517723a3fe.html, last visited September 18, 2011.

❷ In practice, it is quite hard to directly confirm the predatory purpose, only in very few circumstances. For example, one of the 5 Classic Illegal-Price-Conduct Cases is about one company trying to dump beers in the market of Shangdong Province, 2007. The relevant administrative authority in charge of the investigation has confirmed the purpose of "sole occupancy of the market", mainly based on the statements of the company staff, which pointed out that the company has set "occupying the market through low price" strategy as early as the setup period. "价格研究报告——不正当价格违法行为典型案例", http://www.gswj.gov.cn/detail.asp? LMID = 4&ID = 5544&Class = 1156&FN = Qkwz, last visited September 18, 2011.

❸ Provisions on Preventing the Conduct of Low-Price Dumping, Artilce 6, the disposal of the commodities at reduced prices in accordance with the law refers to five situations, including: (1) Selling those commodities which are kept too long in stock; (2) Disposing of commodities out of or near the expiration of the season; (3) Disposing of commodities near the expiration of their guarantee period or validity duration; (4) Perishables or live commodities near the expiration of their guarantee period; (5) Selling commodities at a reduced price for the purpose of clearing off debts, bankruptcy, change of business or suspension of operation. 该规定由笔者翻译。

The third one is the injury, to see whether the predatory dumping has disrupted the normal production and management order to the detriment of national interests or the lawful rights and interests of other operators. Such as incurring the malignant low-price competition, hindering or threatening the establishment, existence or development of the other competitors, or bringing about the loss of tax revenue and so on.

Compared to cost calculation, prove of injury is relevantly easier. In practice, as long as the above two conditions are satisfied, the injury is probably deemed to exist. As long as the conduct of unfair competition can be proved, it can be taken as violation. [1]

The above three-step criterion in the interpretation has been applied in the cases. Like in the first trial of the case of *Food & Oil Supply Company vs. Food Storage storehouse*, the court judged that the defendant has conducted a predatory dumping and injured the plaintiff

---

[1] This can be indicated from the Answers to Some Questions of Judging Unfair Competition Cases, the High Court of Beijing (Interim). The14th question is "whether the conduct of unfair competition must result in injury", while the court is the opinion that the conduct of unfair competition is such conduct as disrupting the normal social economic order, and injuring the lawful rights and interests of the other operators to trade and compete under equal conditions. Therefore, generally speaking, as long as the conduct of unfair competition can be proved, it can be taken as violation. 北京市高级人民法院《关于审理反不正当竞争案件几个问题的解答(试行)》, http://www.qinquanfa.cn/471w.html, last visited September 18, 2011.

by examining the evidence from the three aspects. ❶ First of all, it referred to the parties in this case. The court decided that the competition relation has existed between the plaintiff and the defendant. Secondly, the court took the view that the defendant sold the red grain at a price lower than the cost, for the purpose of squeezing out the other competitors, and injured the plaintiff. Thirdly, the court ensured that there were no exemptions such as seasonal commodities or overstocked commodities in this case, which was the strongest argument of the defendant. ❷

6. 3. 3. 6 Criterion II under Chinese Antimonopoly Law

The second criterion on predatory dumping is provided under Chinese Antimonopoly Law. The Interpretation of Antimonopoly Law specified that there are basically three key points in deciding a conduct of abusing dominant market. ❸

The first one is market power, which is the major difference from the above criterion. Before investigating the conduct of predatory pricing, dominant position should be decided first. Chinese Antimonopoly Law provides two approaches. One is regulated in Article 18,

---

❶ Food & Oil Supply Company (Chaoyang City, Liaoning Province) vs. Food Storage storehouse (Yibin City, Sicuan Province), No. 523 First Trial of Economic Case, Cuiping Local People's Court (1998). This Case has later on been appealed by the defendant, *See* Food & Oil Supply Company (Chaoyang City, Liaoning Province) vs. Food Storage storehouse (Yibin City, Sicuan Province), No. 121 Final Trial of Economic Case, Yibing Intermediate People's Court (2000).

❷ Food & Oil Supply Company (Chaoyang City, Liaoning Province) vs. Food Storage storehouse (Yibin City, Sicuan Province), No. 523 First Trial of Economic Case, Cuiping Local People's Court (1998).

❸ 安建主编、全国人民代表大会常务委员会法制工作委员会编:《中华人民共和国反垄断法释义》,法律出版社 2007 年版,第 48 ~52 页。

which refers to such factors as market share, competition situation, ability to control the sales markets or the raw material purchasing markets, financial status and technical conditions, the degree of dependence, entry to relevant market and so on, to determine the dominant market position. [1]

The other one is provided in Article 19. [2] In order to save enforcement costs and conduct an efficient supervision, Chinese antimonopoly law, referring to the experiences of Germany and Korea, provides a way to presume dominant market position via calculating the relevant

---

[1] According to Chinese Antimonopoly Law, Article 18, The dominant market position of an undertaking shall be determined on the basis of the following factors: (1) its share on a relevant market and the competitiveness on the market; (2) its ability to control the sales market or the purchasing marker for raw and semi-finished materials; (3) its financial strength and technical conditions; (4) the extent to which other business mangers depend on it in transactions ; (5) the difficulty that other undertakings find in entering a relevant market; and (6) other factors related to the determination of the dominant market position held by an undertaking. 英文译本出自中华人民共和国全国人民代表大会网站(英文版), http://www.npc.gov.cn/englishnpc/Law/2009-02/20/content_1471587.htm , last visited September 18, 2011.

[2] Chinese Antimonopoly Law, Article 19 stipulates that, the conclusion that an undertaking holds a dominant market position may be deduced from any one of the following circumstances: (1) the market share of one undertaking accounts for half of the total in a relevant market; (2) the joint market share of two undertakings accounts for two-thirds of the total, in a relevant market; or (3) the joint market share of three undertakings accounts for three-fourths of the total in a relevant market. Under the circumstance specified in Subparagraph (2) or (3) of the preceding paragraph, if the market share of one of the undertakings is less than one-tenths of the total, the undertakings shall not be considered to have a dominant market position. Where an undertaking that is considered to hold a dominant market position has evidence to the contrary, he shall not be considered to hold a dominant market position. 英文译本出自中华人民共和国全国人民代表大会网站(英文版), http://www.npc.gov.cn/englishnpc/Law/2009-02/20/content_1471587.htm , last visited September 18, 2011.

market share. ❶

The presumptive approach under Article 19 is an efficient way of examination hence open to disprovement by the defendants, whereas Article 18 is a comprehensive way to determine dominant market position. ❷

The second one is that the purpose of the conduct is to maintain or reinforce its dominant position. In terms of the conduct of predatory pricing, Interpretation of Chinese Antimonopoly Law further interpreted that the dominant company continuously sells commodities at price below cost in order to squeez the competitors out of the market, prohibits the new entry of companies, and successfully monopolizes the market. ❸

Although the cost of this predatory behavior is very high, the dominant company can anticipate that the future profit exceeds the current lost. ❹ The below-cost selling will not be condemned on the condition that there are legitimate reasons for doing so, include selling live commodities; disposing of commodities near expiration of their validity duration or those kept too long in stock, or seasonal sales. ❺ Regarding this point, the examination required under unfair law and that under antimonopoly law are similar to each other.

The third one is the conduct should have the effects of restraining

---

❶ 安建主编、全国人民代表大会常务委员会法制工作委员会编:《中华人民共和国反垄断法释义》,法律出版社 2007 年版,第 184 ~ 185 页。

❷ "反垄断法有关'滥用'的解读——访《反垄断法》立法专家小组成员黄勇教授",载《工商行政管理》2007 年第 18 期,第 36 页。

❸ 安建主编、全国人民代表大会常务委员会法制工作委员会编:《中华人民共和国反垄断法释义》,法律出版社 2007 年版,第 48 ~ 52 页。

❹ *Ibid.*

❺ *Ibid.*

competition. This is also not strictly required compared with the above two key points. Up till now, there have been no case yet on predatory pricing.

In the following discussion, the criterion under Chinese Unfair Competition Law will be referred to as Criterion I and that under Chinese Antimonopoly Law will be referred to as Criterion II.

6. 4 Linkage between Antidumping and Competition in China

6. 4. 1 Common Legislative Goal and Legal Terminology

Like the other new users, China adopted antidumping rules mainly in accordance with the requirements of WTO. There was no much further examination as to the justification of condemning dumping, let alone a specific discussion of substituting antidumping by competition.[1] Nevertheless, the current close linkage between the two can be indicated from the perspective of legislative goal as well as that of legal terminology.

6. 4. 1. 1 "Fair Competition" and "Maintaining Foreign Trade Order"

In China, reading antidumping rules and competition rules in text

---

[1] Some Chinese scholars in their papers have mentioned the substitution debate, but no much further discussion. 参见莫世健:"试论反倾销法和反不正当竞争法的关系",载《法学家》1999 年第 5 期,第 42 ~ 49 页; 莫世健,"2007 年贸易救济热点问题思考", 2007 - 02 - 06, http://www.cuplfil.com/show.php? ArticleID = 550, last visited September 18, 2011; 彭兴华:"评有关反倾销法的三种方案",载《武汉大学国际法评论》2003 年第 1 期,第 288 ~ 310 页; 邓纲:"刍议反倾销规则并入竞争法体系的几个问题",载《现代法学》2007 年第 5 期,第 122 ~ 127 页;孙雯:"反倾销法与竞争法之冲突与协调",载《河北法学》2006 年第 1 期,第 53 ~ 57 页; 谢海霞:"从竞争法角度看反倾销法律制度",载《河北法学》2004 年第 3 期,第 61 ~ 64 页;张瑞萍:"反倾销法的性质与演进之分析——从 WTO 竞争法设立的角度",载《当代法学》2006 年第 1 期,第 47 ~ 55 页。

literally suggests that both of them are supposed to achieve the common legislative goal.

In terms of competition rules, as aforementioned, the Chinese Unfair Competition Law 1993 is formulated with a view to safeguarding the healthy development of socialist market economy, encouraging and protecting fair competition, repressing unfair competition acts, and protecting the lawful rights and interests of business operators and consumer. The Chinese Antimonopoly Law in 2008 is enacted for the purpose of preventing and restraining monopolistic conducts, protecting fair competition in the market, enhancing economic efficiency, safeguarding the interests of consumers and social public interest, promoting the healthy development of the socialist market economy. The above stipulations show that both of the two competition laws are intended to protect fair competition.

As to antidumping rules, both the Regulation 2002 and the revised version Regulation 2004 are stated as formulated in accordance with the relevant provisions of the Foreign Trade Law of the People's Republic of China to maintain order in foreign trade activities and to safeguard fair competition.

Interestingly, the earliest regulation on antidumping, i. e. Regulation 1997, stated in Article 1 thereof that the main purpose is to maintain the foreign trade order and fair competition and protecting relevant domestic industries. Nonetheless, Regulation 2002, as well as its revised edition Regulation 2004, is stated to maintain order in foreign trade activities and to safeguard fair competition. The words "protecting relevant domestic industries" in the earliest regulation was deleted in purpose to exclude protecting domestic industries as the legislative purpose of antidumping rules, whereas "protecting fair competitive process" was written into law instead. [1]

In addition, putting both of the laws under the basic law, i. e., Foreign Trade Law of the People's Republic of China 2004, also suggested that they serve the same purpose of opening wider to the outside world, developing foreign trade, maintaining foreign trade order, protecting the legitimate rights and interests of foreign trade dealers and promoting the sound development of the socialist market economy. [2]

In this basic law, competition law is categorized in Chapter Six, Foreign Trade Order. Article 32 thereof stipulates that in foreign trade activities, monopolistic behavior in violation of the provisions of the laws and administrative regulations against monopoly is not allowed. Article 33 thereof provides that in foreign trade activities, no one may engage in unfair competition such as selling commodities at unreasonably low prices, and any unfair competition in foreign trade activities shall be dealt with in accordance with the provisions of laws and administrative regulations against unfair competition. [3]

Antidumping law is categorized in Chapter Eight, Foreign Trade Remedies. Article 41 thereof provides that where a product from another country or region is dumped into the domestic market at a price lower than its normal value, thus causing or threatening to cause

---

[1] Email from Ma Xin, Office Worker, *Bureau of Fair Trade for Imports and Exports*, *Ministry of Commerce of the People's Republic of China*, to Bi Ying, LL. D. Candidate, *Kyushu University*, May 14, 2008. (on file with the author)

[2] Foreign Trade Law of the People's Republic of China 2004, Article 1. 参见王继军:"对新《对外贸易法》中反垄断与反不正当竞争条款基本问题的思考",载《美中法律评论》2005 年第 6 期,第 24 ~ 30 页。

[3] Foreign Trade Law of the People's Republic of China 2004, Article 32 – 33.

substantive damage to an established domestic industry, or presenting a substantive impediment to the establishment of a domestic industry, the State may take antidumping measures to eliminate or mitigate such damage, threat of damage, or impediment. ❶

To sum up the above analysis, in China, both antidumping and competition are expected to serve the same goal of maintaining fair competition and the foreign trade in order to safeguard the healthy development of socialist market economy.

6. 4. 1. 2 "Domestic Dumping" and "International Dumping"

Apart from the common legislative goal, as to the regulated conduct of low-price selling, both antidumping and competition laws share the same legal terminology, i. e., dumping. Unlike other countries where dumping is referred to as one kind of international price discrimination, in China "dumping" is used both in antidumping and competition laws.

Because of this, sifuation sometimes it needs to distinguish between two kinds of dumping: one is "international dumping", referring to antidumping law; the other one is "domestic dumping", referring to competition law. ❷ Accordingly in China, most people would get confused about whether you mean international dumping or domestic dumping, when you only mention dumping. This actually indicates the close relation between antidumping and competition in China.

6. 4. 2 Comparison of the Requirements of "Dumping"

As to the substitution debate, based on the survey of the U. S. and the EU, the traditional heavy users, this book in Chapter IV

---

❶ Foreign Trade Law of the People's Republic of China 2004, Article 41.

❷ 李书田:"论国际反倾销与国内反低价倾销的差异性",载《价格与市场》2006年第9期,第37~39页。

attempted to examine it from three perspectives, including comparing and evaluating the basic elements of the two rules on low-price selling repectively, putting the two sets of rules against the background of modern free trade world and analyzing their relationship with the basic trade and competition principles respectively, as well as examining the applicable effects of the practical cases. According to the above examination, this book then argued that putting dumping under competition rules instead of antidumping rules can be less vulnerable to "protectionist abuse". Here the issue is, how about the situation in China, a new user which is unknown to the world? Whether the alleged advantages of competition rules can be also identified in China, especially when Chinese Antimonopoly Law has just been enacted?

In the following three sections, China will be examined in terms of the above three perspectives. This section will deal with the comparison and analysis of basic elements in China first. Similarly, four aspects of basic elements, including objectives, basic substantive rules, basic procedural rules as well as remedies, will be observed.

6. 4. 2. 1 Objectives

From the perspective of objectives, as to Chinese competition rules, both the Chinese Unfair Competition Law and Chinese Antimonopoly Law are concerned about the protection of fair competitive process, redirecting government policies away from the protection of domestic firms. Furthermore, Chinese Antimonopoly law, as the core of competition system, has clearly stated that its objective includes competitive process, economic efficiency as well as consumer welfare. Although up till now there have been no practical cases due to its new enactment, it is considered that following the practice of most of the other developed countries, Chinese antimonopoly rules have more connection with economic basis, and less vulnerable to political or vested interests.

As to antidumping rules, there is no special concern for consumers, let alone economic efficiency. With the strong supporter of the U. S., modern antidumping rules all around the world, including Chinese antidumping rules, are reluctant to economic theories, and therefore easily susceptible to those vested interests. ❶ Examining those fifty cases gives an impression that the Chinese antidumping rules are in large scale influenced by the state-owned producers, or the transformed joint ventures from these original state-owned producers. ❷

6. 4. 2. 2 Basic Substantive Rules

From the perspective of substantive rules, similar to other major countries, there are also four aspects of differences, including the market power, the intent of low price, the calculation of price, and the injury, through comparing the basic substantive rules between competition and antidumping in China.

---

❶ Not only are antidumping laws susceptible to rent-seeking, but producers in most nations are sufficiently concentrated and have sufficient vested interests and resources to lobby government successfully for favourable antidumping policies. Such lobbying has a high chance of success given that politically appealing arguments can be made for protection against unfair foreign competition. On a global basis, the coalition of interests in favour of maintaining and strengthening antidumping laws has grown faster, and has more political power, than the reform and abolition coalition. This does not bode well for any attempts at reform. Antidumping law may reflect such vested interests directly and indirectly. First, legislators may enact antidumping laws that directly favour those with vested interests. Secondly, legislators may confer broad administrative discretions that enable administrative decision-makers to favour those with vested interests. *See* Martyn D. Taylor, *International Competition Law: A New Dimension for the WTO?* Cambridge Univ. Press Inc. 2006, p. 269.

❷ The upper-level industries in China are often powerful national industries, or joint ventures reorganized by those original national industries. Therefore, they have comparatively strong influence on the administrative authorities. 参见刘松涛、栾成好:"2004 中国反倾销案件回顾",载《WTO 经济导刊》2005 年 Z1 期。

As to the Competition rules in China, it is summarized as follows:

Table 1 Competition Rules in China❶

Competition Laws	
Unfair Competition Law & Relevant Provisions and Interpretations	Antimonopoly Law & Relevant Provisions and Interpretations
Aspect I: Market Power	
No Legislative requirement	Article 18: The dominant market position of an undertaking shall be determined on the basis of the following factors (1) its share on a relevant market and the competitiveness on the market (2) its ability to control the sales market or the purchasing marker for raw and semi-finished materials (3) its financial strength and technical conditions (4) the extent to which other business mangers depend on it in transactions (5) the difficulty that other undertakings find in entering a relevant market; and (6) other factors related to the determination of the dominant market position held by an undertaking Article 19: The conclusion that an undertaking holds a dominant market position may be deduced from any one of the following circumstances (1) the market share of one undertaking accounts for half of the total in a relevant market (2) the joint market share of two undertakings accounts for two-thirds of the total, in a relevant market; or (3) the joint market share of three undertakings accounts for three-fourths of the total in a relevant market Under the circumstance specified in Subparagraph (2) or (3) of the preceding paragraph, if the market share of one of the undertakings is less than one-tenths of the total, the undertakings shall not be considered to have a dominant market position Where an undertaking that is considered to hold a dominant market position has evidence to the contrary, he shall not be considered to hold a dominant market position

❶ 反不正当竞争法的英文译本出自中华人民共和国全国人民代表大会网站(英文版), http://www.npc.gov.cn/englishnpc/Law/2007-12/12/content_1383803.htm, last visited September 18, 2011;反垄断法的英文译本出自中华人民共和国全国人民代表大会网站(英文版), http://www.npc.gov.cn/englishnpc/Law/2009-02/20/content_1471587.htm, last visited September 18, 2011;有关规定及释义的英文由笔者翻译。

<table>
<tr><th colspan="2">Aspect II: Intent of Low Price</th></tr>
<tr><td>Article 11: A business operator shall not, for the purpose of pushing out their competitors, sell their commodities at prices lower than costs
Any of the following shall not be deemed as an unfair competition act
(1) Selling perishables or live commodities
(2) Disposing of commodities near expiration of their validity duration or those kept too long in stock
(3) Seasonal sales; or
(4) Selling commodities at a reduced price for the purpose of clearing off debts, change of business or suspension of operation</td><td>Article 17 (2): without justifiable reasons, selling commodities at prices below cost
Interpretation of Chinese Antimonopoly Law 2007 as to Article 17(2)
This term refers to the conduct of predatory pricing. Specifically speaking, the dominant company continuously sells commodities at price below cost in order to repeal the competitors out of the market, prohibit the new entry of companies, as well as successfully monopolize the market. The cost of this price is very high, but the dominant company is anticipating the future profit exceed the current lost. Here the legitimate reasons include selling live commodities; disposing of commodities near expiration of their validity duration or those kept too long in stock, or Seasonal sales</td></tr>
<tr><th colspan="2">Aspect III: Price Calculation</th></tr>
<tr><td colspan="2">Basic Idea: Price below cost

Provisions on Preventing the Conduct of Low-price Dumping
Article 4: There are two kinds of costs, including cost of production and cost of operation. Cost of production and cost of operation. Cost of production refers to manufacture cost plus period expense (consisted by management expense, finance expense as well as sale expense)
Cost of operation includes merchandise procurement cost and circulation expense (consisted by operation expense, management expense as well as finance expense)

Article 5: "below cost" means the operator sales the commodities below the reasonable individual cost
On the conditions that the individual cost can not be identified, the relevant governmental authority shall decide according to the average cost of the whole industry of the commodities as well as the floating scope

Article 7: The conducts of dumping products at price below cost including
(1) The price at which the manufacturer sells the commodities is lower than the cost of production, or the price at which the operator sells the commodities is lower than the cost of merchandise procurement cost
(2) To make the price below the relevant cost by the means of substituting high-quality, high-level commodities for low-quality, low-level ones</td></tr>
</table>

<table>
<tr><th colspan="2">Competition Laws</th></tr>
<tr><th>Unfair Competition Law & Relevant Provisions and Interpretations</th><th>Antimonopoly Law & Relevant Provisions and Interpretations</th></tr>
<tr><td colspan="2">Aspect Ⅲ: Price Calculation</td></tr>
<tr><td colspan="2">(3) To make the price below the relevant cost by the means of discount, subsidy, and so on
(4) To make the price below the relevant cost by the means of unequal exchange of materials
(5) To make the price below the relevant cost by the means of paying-a-debt-in-kind Assets
(6) To make the price below the relevant cost by the means of more sales, but less or no invoices
(7) To make the price below the relevant cost by the means of larger quantities, quantity sales and so on
(8) To make the price below the relevant cost by the means of lowering the bidding price in a bid</td></tr>
<tr><td colspan="2">Aspect Ⅳ: Injury</td></tr>
<tr><td>According to Article 1, injury refers to the situation whether the predatory dumping has injured the healthy development of socialist market economy, fair competition, as well as the lawful rights and interests of business operators and consumers</td><td rowspan="2">According to Article 1, injury refers to the situation whether the predatory pricing has prevented and restrained monopolistic conducts, against protecting fair competition in the market, enhancing economic efficiency, safeguarding the interests of consumers and social public interest, promoting the healthy development of the socialist market economy</td></tr>
<tr><td>According to Interpretation of Chinese Price Law, injury refers to the situation that whether the predatory dumping has disrupted the normal production and management order to the detriment of national interests or the lawful rights and interests of other operators. Such as incurring the malignant low-price competition, hindering or threatening the establishment, existence or development of the other competitors, or bringing about the loss of tax revenue and so on</td></tr>
</table>

As to antidumping rules in China, it is summarized as follows:

Table 2 Antidumping rules in China[1]

Aspects	Antidumping Regulation & Relevant Provisions
Market Power	No Legislative Requirement
Intent of Low Price	No Legislative Requirement
Price Calculation	Basic Idea: the importing price is below the normal value Article 3, 4, 5 (1) "The normal value" of imported products shall be determined in the following ways on the basis of different circumstances ① in case that the products of the same category as that of the imported products have a comparable price in the domestic market of the exporting country (region) in the ordinary course of trade, that comparable price shall be the normal value ② in case that the products of the same category as that of the imported products are not sold on the domestic market of the exporting country (region) in the ordinary course of trade, or the price or quantity of the products of the same category cannot be used as a basis for fair comparison, the normal value shall be the comparable price at which the products of the same category are exported to a proper third country (region) or shall be the production cost of the products of the same category in the country (region) of origin plus reasonable expenses and profits (2) "The export price" of the imported products shall be determined in the following ways according to different circumstances ① in case the imported products have an actual payment price or a payable price, such price shall be the export price ② in case the imported products do not have an export price or its price is not reliable, the price presumed on the basis of the price at which the imported products are re-sold for the first time to an independent buyer shall be regarded as the export price

[1] 英文译本出自中华人民共和国商务部进出口公平贸易局官方网站,http://gpj.mofcom.gov.cn/aarticle/bi/bj/bk/201106/20110607607638.html, last visited September 21, 2011.

Aspects	Antidumping Regulation & Relevant Provisions
Injury	Article 7: "damage" shall refer to the fact that dumping has caused material damage or constitute a threat of material damage to an already established domestic industry, or caused a material impediment to the establishment of a domestic industry Article 8: when determining the damage caused to a domestic industry by dumping, the following items shall be examined (1) the quantity of the dumped imports, including a sharp increase in the absolute quantity of the dumped imports or the quantity as compared with the production or consumption of the domestic products of the same category, or the possibility of a sharp increase in the quantity of the dumped imports (2) the price of the dumped imports, including the price cuts of the dumped imports or the impacts such as great restraint or reduction, etc. to the price of the domestic products of the same category (3) the impacts of the dumped imports upon the relevant economic factors and targets of the domestic industry (4) the production capacity, export capability of the exporting country (region) and the country (region) of origin on the dumped imports as well as the inventory of the investigated products (5) Other factors which cause damage to the domestic industry The threat of material damage shall be determined on the basis of the facts instead of the accusation, presumption or minor possibility When determining the injury caused by dumping to a domestic industry, the determination shall be based on positive evidence, and the injuries caused by factors other than dumping must not be attributed to dumping

I. Market Power.

Comparing the above four basic elements of substantive rules between antidumping and competition in China respectively, regarding the market power, Chinese antidumping rules have neither legislative requirements nor practical attention to it.

In terms of competition rules, there is no fixed examination of the relevant market required by Chinese Unfair Competition Law, but in practice, the economic power or market advantage is usually being taken into consideration. ❶

Relating to the anti-monopoly law, dominant market position is taken as a premise before the further examination of the price and the cost. Similar to other countries, five major factors are required by law in finding dominant market position. According to Article 18, these includes market share in relevant market, and the competition situation of the relevant market; ability to control the sales markets or the raw material purchasing markets; financial status and technical conditions of the business operator; the degree of dependence of other business operator; entry to relevant market by other business operator and so on. Among the above factors, in China, much concern is given to the market share factor, and in Article 19 provides that a dominant position can be presumed first based on the calculation of its market share.

II. Intent of Low Price.

In terms of the intent of low price, Chinese antidumping rules view all kinds of low-price selling as harmful regardless to their subjective purposes. On the contrary, similar to other countries, both competition laws acknowledge that not all types of price discrimination are harmful. Only those with the purpose of pushing out their competitors, or sell at prices lower than costs without legitimate

---

❶ 付红雷:"试论低价倾销行为",载中国人民法院网, http://www.chinacourt.org/html/article/200705/08/245282.shtml, last visited September 18, 2011.

reasons are considered as harmful. There are also four kinds of purposes exempted from punishment, including the disposal of such commodities as fresh and living commodities, seasonal commodities and overstocked commodities.

III. Price Calculation.

In regards to the price calculation, following the requirements of WTO ADA, Chinese antidumping rules also devote many efforts to finding whether the export price is lower than so-called normal value. All of the complicated calculations are trying to find only the price difference, with no attention paid to whether the export price is lower than its cost. By contrast, as to Chinese competition rules, similar to other countries, price calculation is also taken as one of the most important concerns. Both competition laws conform strictly to the price below cost standard, and there are also specific provisions on how to calculate the cost.

Notwithstanding, the current cost calculation test in China is not as specified as that of the U. S., EU, such as short-run cost-based rules, long-term cost-based rules, or the rule-of-reason test etc. It still needs improved and developed. For instance, there are two major problems of the Provisions on Preventing the Conduct of Low-price Dumping. The first one is in cases where an operator sells the commodities, the price should below which cost, cost of operation or cost of merchandise procurement. This issue has not been prescribed in law. ❶

Another one is the justification of applying the average cost of the whole industry, in cases where the individual cost cannot be identified. This is a special test in China. However, the individual cost of each company is quite hard to calculate, let alone the average cost of the whole industry. ❷ Since the cost of a high-efficient company is certainly lower than the average cost of the whole industry, such test also discourages those high-efficient companies and does no good for the healthy competition process. ❸

IV. Injury.

The last basic element is the injury. Chinese antidumping rules emphasize a lot on the injury to competitors, the domestic industries. Besides, although specific factors need to be taken into consideration when deciding whether dumping has caused a "material" damage to a domestic industry, the causation between dumping and injury can be

---

❶ Provisions on Preventing the Conduct of Low-Price Dumping of 1999, Article 4 defines that the cost in "below the cost" refers to two kinds: cost of production and cost of operation. And Cost of operation includes merchandise procurement cost and circulation expense (consisted by operation expense, management expense as well as finance expense), whereas Provisions on Preventing the Conduct of Low-Price Dumping of 1999, Article 7 defines that regards the operator, below cost selling refers to the situation that price is lower than the cost of merchandise procurement. In practical cases, the governmental authority has applied the lower one, namely the cost of merchandise procurement according to the principle of beneficial to the involved party. "价格研究报告——不正当价格违法行为典型案例",载《甘肃价格网》, http://www.gswj.gov.cn/detail.asp? LMID = 4&ID = 5544&Class = 1156&FN = Qkwz, last visited September 18, 2011.

❷ 王晓晔:"低价倾销行为的几点法律思考",载《价格理论与实践》2004 年第 7 期,第 51 页。

❸ *Ibid.*, p. 51.

easily established.

As to Chinese competition rules, similar to other countries, both of the laws put much emphasis on the injury to competitive process instead of competitors, and a direct causation between the low-price selling and the injury should be established in each specific case. In the practical cases, injury is usually decided as existing if the dominant market position, intent, as well as price below cost are all confirmed. This can be indicated from the Answers to Some Questions of Judging Unfair Competition Cases, the High Court of Beijing (Interim). ❶

V. Summary.

Chinese antidumping rules, following the requirement of WTO agreement, are basically similar to other countries, easily abused for protectionists. As to Chinese competition rules, by setting up a series of tests to select and punish only the predatory price discrimination, are more economic justified, stricter, and less vulnerable to protectionists. Nevertheless, more efforts need to be devoted to perfecting Chinese competition rules.

6. 4. 2. 3 Basic Procedural Rules

I. Administrative Authorities.

The administration of antidumping rules in China is similar to the U. S. The authority in charge of price calculation and that of injury determination are separate. Originally, the Ministry of Foreign Trade and Economic Cooperation (MOFTEC) was responsible for the investigation on and determination of dumping, and the State Economic and Trade Commission (SETC) was responsible for the

---

❶ 北京市高级人民法院《关于审理反不正当竞争案件几个问题的解答(试行)》(No. 73 1998), http://www.qinquanfa.cn/471w.html, last visited September 18, 2011.

investigation on and determination of damage. ❶ After the revision of antidumping regulation in 2004, the two Ministries were combined under the Ministry of Commerce of the People's Republic of China (MOFCOM). ❷

With regards to the administration of competition rules in China, the Chinese Unfair Competition Law set forth that supervision and inspection departments at or above the country level may carry out supervision over and inspection of unfair competition acts. ❸ As to antimonopoly law, the Antimonopoly Commission established under the State Council assumes the responsibility for organizing, coordinating,

---

❶ Regulation 2002, Article 3: The term "dumping" shall refer to the entry of imported products into the market of the People's Republic of China, in the ordinary course of trade, with their export price lower than their normal value. The Ministry of Foreign Trade and Economic Cooperation (hereinafter referred to as the MOFTEC) shall be responsible for the investigation on and determination of dumping.)英文译本出自北大法意网站,http://www.lawyee.org/Act/Act_Other_Trans_Display.asp? ChannelID = 1010200&RID = 1860, last visited September 21, 2011.

❷ Regulation 2004, Article 3: The term "dumping" means that an import is introduced, in the ordinary course of trade, into the market of the People's Republic of China at an export price less than its normal value. The Ministry of Commerce shall be responsible for the investigation and determination of dumping. 英文译本出自中华人民共和国商务部进出口公平贸易局官方网站,http://gpj.mofcom.gov.cn/aarticle/bi/bj/bk/201106/20110607607638.html , last visited September 21, 2011.

❸ Law of the People's Republic of China Against Unfair Competition, Article 3: People's governments at various levels shall take measures to repress unfair competition acts and create favourable environment and conditions for fair competition. Administrative departments for industry and commerce of the people's governments at or above the county level shall exercise supervision over and inspection of unfair competition acts; where laws or administrative rules and regulations provide that other departments shall exercise the supervision and inspection, those provisions shall apply. 英文译本出自中华人民共和国全国人民代表大会网站(英文版), http://www.npc.gov.cn/englishnpc/Law/2007 - 12/12/content_1383803.htm, last visited September 18, 2011.

guiding antimonopoly works including the predatory pricing. ❶ Thereunder, three different government agencies are in charge of the enforcement collectively. MOFCOM is responsible for examining any proposed concentration of undertakings. The Fair Trade Bureau under the State Administratoin for Industry and Commerce (SAIC) is in charge of monopoly agreements and abuse of dominant market position. The National Development and Reform Commission (NDRC) will investigate all price-related monopoly cases. ❷ Besides, as a

---

❶ Chinese Antimonopoly Law, Article 9: The State Council shall establish an anti-monopoly commission to be in charge of organizing, coordinating and guiding anti-monopoly work and to perform the following duties:

(1) studying and drafting policies on competition;

(2) organizing investigation and assessment of competition on the market as a whole and publishing assessment reports;

(3) formulating and releasing anti-monopoly guidelines;

(4) coordinating administrative enforcement of the anti-monopoly law; and

(5) other duties as prescribed by the State Council.

The composition of and procedural rules for the anti-monopoly commission shall be specified by the State Council.

Chinese Antimonopoly Law, Article 10: The authorities responsible for enforcement of the Anti-monopoly Law specified by the State Council (hereinafter referred to, in general, as the authority for enforcement of the Anti-monopoly Law under the State Council) shall be in charge of such enforcement in accordance with the provisions of this Law.

The authority for enforcement of the Anti-monopoly Law under the State Council may, in light of the need of work, empower the appropriate departments of the people's governments of provinces, autonomous regions or municipalities directly under the Central Government to take charge of relevant enforcement of the Anti-monopoly Law in accordance with the provisions of this Law.

英文译本出自中华人民共和国中央人民政府网站(英文版), http://www.npc.gov.cn/englishnpc/Law/2009-02/20/content_1471587.htm, last visited September 18, 2011.

❷ Franki Cheung, *An Overview of China's New Anti-monopoly Law and its relevance to foreign investors*, 2009, *See* http://www.deacons.com.hk/eng/knowledge/knowledge_317.htm, last visited September 18, 2011.

conduct of price, the Price departments under the State Council as well as each level of people's governments can also have the power to handle the predatory dumping or pricing. ❶

II. Discretion of Administrative Authorities.

Under the same requirement of WTO ADA, Chinese antidumping rules also leaves administrative decision makers with considerable discretion. The major common discretions as analyzed in Chapter IV can be also identified in the fifty antidumping cases in China. Taking the determination of the normal value for instance, of all the total 347 registered exporters, there are more than 100 exporters, whose normal value is determined according to BIA. ❷ And almost all of the dumping margins that were determined by the rule of BIA are much higher than determined by the other two methods. For instance, in the No. 26 Chloroprene Rubber Case, the normal values of both Denki Kagaku Kogyo Kabushiki Kaisha and Tosoh Corporation are decided based on their home price or constructive cost, and the dumping margin is respectively 2% and 3%, whereas the dumping margin of the other Japanese exporters, decided by rule of BIA, is 151%.

---

❶ Price Law of the People's Republic of China, Article 5: The competent department for pricing under the State Council shall hold unified responsibility for the work of pricing throughout the country. The other relevant departments under the State Council shall, within the scope of their functions and duties, be responsible for the work respectively. The competent departments for pricing under the local people's governments at or above the county level shall be responsible for the work of pricing within their administrative regions. The other relevant departments of the said people's governments shall, within the scope of their functions and duties, be responsible for the work respectively. 英文译本出自中华人民共和国中央人民政府网站(英文版), http://www.npc.gov.cn/englishnpc/Law/2009-02/20/content_1471587.htm, last visited September 18, 2011.

❷ The number of the cases decided by the first way, including partially adjusted, is 200; the number of the cases decided by the second way is 16.

The abuse of discretion can also take other ways. Taking the determination of injury for anther example, a consistent method of examining the various evidences can hardly be found. ❶ Usually, a conclusion is made following a simple and unconvincing description of the changes of the required items, such as the quantity of the dumped imports, the price of the dumped imports, the production capacity etc. Of all the fifty antidumping cases, only four are determined as no injury. Through comparing the reasoning of "no injury" in these four cases with the rest "injury" reasoning, it is doubtful that why the similar evidence can be viewed as no injury in some cases but injury in others. For instance, comparing the investigations of injury between the No. 13 Coated Art Paper Case and the No. 8 L-Lysine monohydrochlouide Case, it is found that similar facts were explained in totally different ways. Such as the changes of revenue and changes of cash, which are used to support "there was injury" in the No. 13 Coated Art Paper Case, are acting as the demonstrations of "there was no injury" in the No. 8 L-Lysine monohydrochlouide Case. ❷

---

❶ In China, when the relevant investigation authorities evaluate on the facts, it usually lacks of a consistent and objective standard. The final decisions are usually made based on simply-exemplied economic indexes without any persuasive analysis, especially when the different economic indexes conflict with each other. 参见刘勇："从法律的视角看我国反倾销实践的不足及完善建议"，载《国际商报》2007 年 6 月 30 日，http://ibdaily. mofcom. gov. cn/show. asp? id = 162730, last visited September 18, 2011.

❷ *See* the No. 8 L-Lysine monohydrochlouide Case, Public Announcement No. 23 in 2002 of Ministry of Foreign Trade and Economic Cooperation of the People's Republic of China, Chinese version available at: http://china. findlaw. cn/fagui/jj/27/157859. html, last visited September 18, 2011; The No. 13 Coated Art Paper Case, Public Announcement No. 35 in 2003 of Ministry of Commerce of the People's Republic of China, Chinese version available at: http://www. cacs. gov. cn/cacs/news/newshow. aspx? str1 = 2&articleId = 38855 , last visited September 18, 2011.

Accordingly, like the other countries, Chinese administrative authorities also have a broad discretion, which opens the gate for protectionist abuse. Nonetheless, it is worth noticing that Chinese antidumping rules have no special stipulation on non-market country. Although "a comparable price sold at a proper third country" is allowed by law, this method has never been used in practice. This is understandable since China has long suffered from being treated as a non-market country and knows well than any other countries the arbitrary operation of non-market country as well as the substitutive price of a third country.

Concerning the discretion of competition authorities, the competition law text indicates that, the objective to protect the interests of consumers and to maintain fair competition instead of individual competitor is relatively definite; the methodological guidelines, which are based on economic theories to selectively punish those unfair below-cost predatory dumping, instead of all kinds of price difference, is also unequivocal.

Nevertheless, the competition rules still need to be improved on certain aspects. Taken the cost calculation as an example, although there are no such broad abused discretion as man-made high dumping margin resulting from applying substitutive price from a third country, or price determined by BIA rules in antidumping cases, in cases where the individual cost can not be identified, the authorities need to calculate the average cost of the whole industry, which might leave some room for discretion.

6. 4. 2. 4 Remedies

I. Remedies in Antidumping Cases.

From the perspective of effectiveness of correction, similar to other countries, in China, the remedies provided in antidumping rules can only raise the price of the dumped good for the duration of the action to compensate the injurers, and it cannot prohibit the unfair behavior itself, or in other words, prevent its reoccurrence effectively. The chief remedy of Chinese antidumping rules is to impose antidumping duty, the amount of which shall not exceed the dumping margin determined in the final adjudication decision. Other measures such as price undertaking are seldom referred to or granted. As a result, the petitioner receives no compensatory damages for an injury caused by the dumped imports, although if the margin of dumping is sufficiently high.

Moreover, in terms of recourse to judicial review, according to Regulation 2004, in cases where any party is not satisfied with the final determination, a decision on whether or not to impose an antidumping duty, retroactive imposition of an antidumping duty, reimbursement of an antidumping duty, imposition of an antidumping duty on new exporters, or the review findings made under Regulation 2004, it may in accordance with the law file a lawsuit in the people's court.[1] Hence, parties in antidumping cases can only refer an administrative suit to a court. In practice, all of the fifty cases ended up

---

[1] Regulation 2004, Article 53: Where any party is not satisfied with a final determination made under Article 25 of these Regulations, or not satisfied with a decision on whether or not to impose an antidumping duty or a decision on retroactive imposition of an antidumping duty, reimbursement of an antidumping duty or imposition of an antidumping duty on new exporters, which is made under Chapter IV of these Regulations, or not satisfied with the review findings made under Chapter V of these Regulations, it may, in accordance with the law, apply for administrative reconsideration or file a lawsuit in the people's court. 英文译本出自中华人民共和国商务部进出口公平贸易局官方网站, http://gpj.mofcom.gov.cn/aarticle/bi/bj/bk/201106/20110607607638.html, last visited September 21, 2011.

in administrative decisions only. None of them was ever resorted to the courts.

II. Remedies in Competition Cases.

The remedies provided under competition rules, aiming at a prohibition of the practice with appropriate penalties if the offense continues, would be the appropriate action. According to Chinese Unfair Competition Law, a business operator whose lawful rights and interests are infringed upon by unfair competition acts may bring a suit in a people's court.[1] Besides, if a party is not satisfied with the administrative decision, it may apply for review, and may bring a suit to a people's court if it is still dissatisfied with the reconsideration decision, or, the party may directly file a suit in a people's court.[2] In practice, as to the "domestic dumping" cases, courts are often

---

[1] Chinese Unfair Competition Law, Article 20: A business operator who violates the provisions of this Law and thus causes damage to the infringed business operators, shall bear the liability of compensation for the damage. If the losses of the infringed business operator are difficult to estimate, the damages shall be the profits derived from the infringement by the infringer during the period of infringement. And the infringer shall also bear the reasonable expense paid by the infringed business operator for investigating the infringer's unfair competition acts violating his lawful rights and interests. A business operator whose lawful rights and interests are infringed upon by unfair competition acts may bring a suit in a people's court. 英文译本出自中华人民共和国全国人民代表大会网站(英文版), http://www.npc.gov.cn/englishnpc/Law/2007-12/12/content_1383803.htm, last visited September 18, 2011.

[2] Chinese Unfair Competition Law, Article 29: In case a party is not satisfied with the punishment decision made by the supervision and inspection department, it may apply for reconsideration to the competent department at the next higher level within 15 days from receipt of the decision; and if the party is still not satisfied with the reconsideration decision, it may bring a suit in a people's court within 15 days from receipt of the decision; and the party may also directly file a suit in a people's court. 英文译本出自中华人民共和国全国人民代表大会网站(英文版), http://www.npc.gov.cn/englishnpc/Law/2007-12/12/content_1383803.htm, last visited September 18, 2011.

resorted to, such as the cases introduced in the above part.

Regarding Chinese Antimonopoly Law, similarly, when the business operator does not accept the decision made by the antimonopoly execution authorities, it shall apply for administrative review first; and if still disagree with the review, it can then file an administrative lawsuit. Except the above kind of administrative decisions, the business operator can apply either for administrative review or resort to administrative lawsuit when it is dissatisfied with the others administrative decisions. ❶ Besides the administrative litigations, the business operator can also be suited to civil courts by individuals. ❷ Criminal responsibility may also be involved depending on the seriousness of the case.

---

❶ Chinese Antimonopoly Law, Article 53: Where an undertaking is dissatisfied with the decision made by the authority for enforcement of the Anti-monopoly Law in accordance with the provisions of Article 28 or 29 of this Law, it may first apply for administrative reconsideration according to law; and if it is dissatisfied with the decision made after administrative reconsideration, it may bring an administrative action before the court according to law. Where an undertaking is dissatisfied with any decision made by the authority for enforcement of the Anti-monopoly Law other than the decisions specified in the preceding paragraph, it may apply for administrative reconsideration or bring an administrative action before the court according to law. 英文译本出自中华人民共和国全国人民代表大会网站(英文版), http://www.npc.gov.cn/englishnpc/Law/2009-02/20/content_1471587.htm, last visited September 18, 2011.

❷ *See*, e.g., on August 1, 2008, the clamiant, Liu Fangrong, sued the defendant, Association of Insurance Industry in Chongqing City, to the civil court of Yuzhong Local People's Court, Chongqing City, for damges caused by the conduct of restritive competition of the defendant. Besides, in September 22, 2008, the clamiant, Li Fangrong, sued the defendant, China Netcom Group, Beijing Branch, to the civil court of Chaoyang Local People's Court, Beijing City, for damages casued by the monopoly of the defendant. 参见袁定波:"反垄断民事诉讼将成为法院新审判领域:引入集团诉讼",载《法制日报》2008 年 10 月 28 日, http://npc.people.com.cn/GB/14957/53051/8240649.html, last visited September 18, 2011.

To sum up, in competition cases, authorities or petitioners can usually refer the case to domestic courts, where judges are entitled to great latitude as to the best form of compensation as long as the remedy is limited to what is necessary to repair the damage, ranging from civil liability, administrative liability, to criminal liability. At the same time, a domestic producers sued in domestic courts also has many more alternatives than the defendant in an antidumping case.

6.4.3 Comparison in the Modern World

6.4.3.1 Conflict with Basic Modern Trade and Competition Principles

This section will continue to discuss the second aspect, the comparison of competition rules and antidumping rules in the modern free trade world, as to the specific situation in China. It is argued in Chapter IV that in terms of the modern trade policy, the first advantage of competition rules over antidumping rules is that, competition rules can avoid seriously undermining the fundamental principles of GATT/WTO system, the modern multilateral world in three aspects, including free trade, non-discrimination, as well as the principle of reciprocity. In terms of the modern competition policy, the second advantage of the competition rules over the antidumping rules is that it can refrain from conflicting with basic competition principles and therefore can avoid the anti-competitive effects in practice, including protection of competitive process in conformity to the economic efficiency; the maximization of the consumer welfare; avoidance of facilitating the collusion between domestic and foreign producers; avoidance of maintaining domestic monopoly power or form domestic cartels; as well as promotion of market integration in bilateral and regional areas.

As to China, following the same basic requirements of WTO ADA, similar to other countries, Chinese antidumping rules are also born as conflicting with the basic trade principles, including free trade, non-discrimination, as well as reciprocal. The emphasis here shall be put on the relation of antidumping rules with the basic competition principles, to examine whether the application of Chinese antidumping rules actually involves many anti-competitive effects in practice, which can be avoided by applying competition rules to dumping.

Linking with each aspect of conflict to Chinese practice, the following four issues will be examined. [1]

Firstly, in order to examine the conflict with the protection of competitive process, the issue of how many antidumping cases have ended up with affirmed antidumping duties or self-constrained price undertaking, can give some indications of the extent to which that antidumping restrained foreign competitors.

Secondly, in terms of the conflict with the maximization of the consumer welfare, the considerations given to the consumers in each of the antidumping actions shall be examined. These includes whether consumers are supporting or against the antidumping investigations, what are the attitudes of the antidumping authorities towards the objections of consumers, and whether there are any cases lifting antidumping duties by taking the consumers' interests into consideration.

Thirdly, as to facilitating the collusion between domestic and foreign producers, that how many antidumping cases have ended up with price undertaking, as well as whether they are facilitating cross-border cartels in China, will be explored.

---

[1] Since the fifth aspect of conflict with the promotion of market integration specially refers to bilateral and regional areas, the discussion of this will be avoided in examination the single country of China.

Fourthly, as to maintaining domestic monopoly power or form domestic cartels, that whether there are antidumping actions facilitating domestic producers to maintain monopoly power or form domestic cartels, will be investigated.

6. 4. 3. 2 Conflict with Protection of Competitive Process

As introduced, current Chinese antidumping regulation has removed "protection of domestic industry" by "protection of fair competition" as its legislative purpose. However, the practical effects of antidumping actions remained to protect domestic competitors through restraining the import of foreign products, rather than to protect competitive process.[1] According to statistics, among all of the fifty cases, from the first newsprint case to the latest Disodium 5'-Inosinate case, only in one case (the No. 25 Nylon 6. 66 Filament Yarn Case[2]) all registered exporters are determined as either no dumping or dumping margin less than 2%. Two cases (the No. 21 MDI Case[3] and the No. 31 Ethylene – Propylene-non-conjugated Diene Rubberzz Case[4]) are terminated due to the withdrawal of the antidumping

---

[1] This will be analyzed in detail in the following 6. 4. 5 part of this chapter.

[2] Public Announcement No. 13 in 2001 of Ministry of Commerce of the People's Republic of China, Chinese version available at: http://gpj. mofcom. gov. cn/aarticle/d/r/u/200504/20050400082373. html, last visited September 18, 2011.

[3] Public Announcement No. 66 in 2003 of Ministry of Commerce of the People's Republic of China, Chinese version available at: http://www. cacs. gov. cn/news/newshow. aspx? strl = 2&articleId = 38862, last visited September 18, 2011.

[4] Public Announcement No. 9 in 2006 of Ministry of Commerce of the People's Republic of China, Chinese version available at: http://www. cacs. gov. cn/news/newshow. aspx? strl = 2&articleId = 38882 , last visited September 18, 2011.

petitioners. And four cases (the No. 7 Polystyrene Case[1], the No. 8 L-Lysine monohydrochlouide Case[2], the No. 39 Butanols Case[3], and the No. 40 Octanol Case[4]) are determined as no injury. Except the above seven cases, the rest forty-three cases have ended up with affirmative final decisions.

Of the rest forty-three antidumping cases, Roughly 292 out of the total registered 415 exporters have gone through the whole antidumping investigation, among which three exporters were decided as the dumping margin is zero; one exporter was decided as the dumping margin is less than 2% , and fifteen exporters were subject to price undertakings. The specific statistics are as follows:

Three exporters were decided as the dumping margin is zero, including one Russian exporter in No. 2 Cold-rolled steel plate case[5], one

---

[1] Public Announcement No. 13 in 2001 of Ministry of Foreign Trade and Economic Cooperation of the People's Republic of China, Chinese version available at: http://www.hflib.gov.cn/law/law/falvfagui2/JJF/FLFG/DWMY/1169.htm ,last visited September 18, 2011.

[2] Public Announcement No. 23 in 2002 of Ministry of Foreign Trade and Economic Cooperation of the People's Republic of China, Chinese version available at: http://law.laweach.com/rule_45758_1.html,last visited September 18,2011.

[3] Public Announcement No. 10 in 2007 of Ministry of Commerce of the People's Republic of China, Chinese version available at: http://www.cacs.gov.cn/news/newshow.aspx? strl =2&articleId =38837,last visited September 18,2011.

[4] Public Announcement No. 4 in 2007 of Ministry of Commerce of the People's Republic of China, Chinese version available at: http://www.cacs.gov.cn/news/newshow.aspx? strl =2&articleId =38836,last visited September 18,2011.

[5] Public Announcement No. 8 in 2000 of Ministry of Foreign Trade and Economic Cooperation of the People's Republic of China, Chinese version available at: http://www.cacs.gov.cn/news/newshow.aspx? strl = 2&articleId = 38842, last visited September 18, 2011.

Korea exporter in No. 17 Cold Rolled Steel Products case[1], and one Korea exporter in No. 35 Polyurethane case.[2]

In the No. 24 Dispersion Unshifted Single-Mode Optical Fiber Case, one exporter was decided as the dumping margin is less than 2% : the American Corning Incorporated was determined that the dumping margin is 1.51%.[3]

There are fifteen exporters, seven in the No. 4 Cold Rolled Stainless Steel Sheet case[4], one in the No. 18 Polyvinyl Chloride case[5], five in the No. 23 Chloroform case[6], and two in the No. 32 Benzofuranol case[7], subject to price undertakings instead of being imposed

---

[1] Public Announcement No. 50 in 2003 of Ministry of Commerce of the People's Republic of China, Chinese version available at: http://www.cacs.gov.cn/news/newshow.aspx? strl =2&articleld =38859 , last visited September 18, 2011.

[2] Public Announcement No. 74 in 2006 of Ministry of Commerce of the People's Republic of China, Chinese version available at: http://www.cacs.gov.cn/news/newshow.aspx? strl =2&articleld =38890, last visited September 18, 2011.

[3] Public Announcement No. 96 in 2004 of Ministry of Commerce of the People's Republic of China, Chinese version available at: http://www.cacs.gov.cn/news/newshow.aspx? strl =2&articleld =38870 , last visited September 18, 2011.

[4] Public Announcement No. 15 in 2000 of Ministry of Foreign Trade and Economic Cooperation of the People's Republic of China, Chinese version available at: http://www.cacs.gov.cn/news/newshow.aspx? strl =2&articleld =38844 , last visited September 18, 2011.

[5] Public Announcement No. 48 in 2003 of Ministry of Commerce of the People's Republic of China, Chinese version available at: http://www.cacs.gov.cn/news/newshow.aspx? strl =2&articleld =38447, last visited September 18, 2011.

[6] Public Announcement No. 81 in 2004 of Ministry of Commerce of the People's Republic of China, Chinese version available at: http://www.cacs.gov.cn/news/newshow.aspx? strl =2&articleld =38868, last visited September 18, 2011.

[7] Public Announcement No. 7 in 2006 of Ministry of Commerce of the People's Republic of China, Chinese version available at: http://www.cacs.gov.cn/news/newshow.aspx? strl =2&articleld =38884, last visited September 18, 2011.

with antidumping duties.

Accordingly, except for the above nineteen registered exporters, 65.8% exporters (273 out of 415) that have gone through the whole antidumping investigation in 86% cases (43 out of 50) were imposed with antidumping duties. These antidumping actions are always followed by a prominent decrease or even cease of the relevant import, which is usually taken as one factor in evaluating the positive effects of antidumping measures in China.[1] This indicates that antidumping actions actually restrained the foreign competition in large proportion, or in other words, the applicative effects of antidumping measure involve much conflict with the protection of competitive process in China.

6.4.3.3 Conflict with Consumer Welfare *

One of the main concerns of modern competition laws and policy is to

---

[1] This will be analyzed in detail in the following 6.4.5 part of this chapter.

* 本部分内容已经发表, Biying, *The Interaction of Trade and Competition Policy in the Globalization Process – A Survey of "Consumer Interest" in Chinese Antidumping Context*, the Journal of World Investment & Trade, Vol. 12, No. 3, June, 2011, pp. 377–397.

safeguard consumer interest.❶ For instance, strongly favored by the Chicago school that argued for a purely economic construction of the law, the U. S. competition policy has a strong orientation towards consumer welfare.❷ As to the EU, Neelie Kroes, the Commissioner for Competition, stated that "defending consumers' interests is at the heart of the Commission's competition policy", which reflected the importance of competition policy to consumers, and the importance of

---

❶ For example, Kennedy stated in his book that "Antitrust law...focuses on the maintenance of open markets, the promotion of competition, and the maximization of consumer welfare." *See* Kevin C. Kennedy, *Competition Law and the World Trade Organization: The Limits of Multilateralism*, Sweet & Maxwell, 2001, p. 235.

Talyor also recognized that: "competition law gives pre-eminence to considerations of economic efficiency... Competition is viewed as a means of disciplining firms, reducing their market power, and thus ensuring that the market forces of supply and demand operate more effectively and efficiently in allocating global resources...Competition law seeks to lessen power imbalances between firms to ensure that all firms have an equal opportunity to compete on their merits. Competition law also prevents producers from using certain business practices to capture additional wealth from consumers... Indeed, competition laws are commonly drafted so as to favour the interests of end consumers over the interests of producers." *See* Martyn D. Taylor, *International Competition Law: A New Dimension for the WTO?* Cambridge Univ. Press Inc. 2006, p. 264.

Roland considered that although consequently it seems to be difficult to define certain objectives for an international competition law agreement, more and more convergence of objectives between countries has been noted within the last decade. Therefore, he deemed that certain common main objectives, such as economic efficiency, market integration and consumer welfare could be defined for an international agreement, while it may be advisable to pursue other minor goals through separate government policies. *See* Roland Weinrauch, *Competition Law in the WTO: the Rationale for a Framework Agreement*, Wien: NWV Neuer Wissenschaftlicher Verlag, 2004, p. 30.

❷ Bork stated in his famous book "The Paradox Antitrust" that: "the argument of this book, of course, is that competition must be understood as the maximization of consumer welfare or, if you prefer, economic efficiency. *See* Robert H. Bork, *The Paradox Antitrust: A Policy at War with Itself*, The Free Press, 1993, p. 427.

consumer welfare when implementing competition policy. [1]

I. "Consumer Interest" in Chinese Antidumping Rules.

Following the example of other major countries, "safeguarding the interests of consumers" is clearly set forth as one of the main purposes of Chinese Antimonopoly Law 2007 in Article 1 thereof. [2] Hence the issue that lies ahead is how "consumer interest" is considered in Chinese antidumping context. There are two sub-issues therein, one is whether Chinese antidumping rules have given any consideration to consumers, and the other is whether Chinese antidumping cases have given any consideration to such. This section deals with the former sub-issue first.

As aforementioned, the current effective antidumping rules in China includes: Chinese Foreign Trade Law 2004, Regulation 2004, as well as a series of relevant provisional rules and stipulations. Focusing on the current Chinese antidumping rules, especially referring to Regulation 2004, there is no mention of "consumer" throughout the entire text. Nevertheless, the consideration may be given to the "consumer" via attributing it to "other interested organizations and parties" hence deemed as one factor of "public interest". For instance, Regulation 2004, Article 19 states that MOFCOM, in charge of antidumping cases, shall publish the decision to initiate an investigation and notify the applicants, the known exporters and importers, the governments of the exporting

---

[1] John Madill and Adrien Mexis, *Consumers at the heart of EU competition policy*, Competition Policy Newsletter, 2009, p. 1, http://ec.europa.eu/competition/publications/cpn/2009_1_7.pdf, last visited September 18, 2011.

[2] Chinese Antimonopoly Law 2007, Article 1: this Law is enacted for the purpose of preventing and restraining monopolistic conducts, protecting fair competition in the market, enhancing economic efficiency, safeguarding the interests of consumers and social public interest, promoting the healthy development of the socialist market economy.

countries (regions) and "other interested organizations and parties". ❶ Article 37 stipulates that if a final determination establishes the existence of dumping and injury caused by dumping to a domestic industry, an antidumping duty may be imposed. Collection of antidumping duty shall conform to the "public interest". ❷

Linked to this, the relevant rights and obligations of interested parties in the antidumping investigation have been specified in Articles 19, 20,

---

❶ Regulation 2004, Article 19: MOFCOM shall publish the decision to initiate an investigation and notify the applicants, the known exporters and importers, the governments of an exporting countries (regions) and other interested organizations and parties (hereinafter collectively referred to as "the interested parties") ...英文译本出自中华人民共和国商务部进出口公平贸易局官方网站, http://gpj.mofcom.gov.cn/aarticle/bi/bj/bk/201106/20110607607638.html, last visited September 21, 2011.

❷ Regulation 2004, Article 37: If a final determination establishes the existence of dumping and injury caused by dumping to a domestic industry, an antidumping duty may be imposed. Collection of antidumping duty shall conform to public interests. 英文译本出自中华人民共和国商务部进出口公平贸易局官方网站, http://gpj.mofcom.gov.cn/aarticle/bi/bj/bk/201106/20110607607638.html, last visited September 21, 2011.

Comparing with the previous Regulation 1997 and Regulation 2002, one of the major differences is the "public interest" clause in the new Regulation 2004. The reason for this is to give considerations to the lower-level industries and the final consumers. 参见国际在线: "新反倾销条例近期正式实施:将更加关注公共利益", http://big5.cri.cn/gate/big5/gb1.chinabroadcast.cn/1827/2004/06/02/521@180554.htm, last visited September 18, 2011.

21, 22, 23 and 25 of Regulation 2004 respectively.[1] Articles 33 and 37 have required both the price undertakings and antidumping duties to

---

[1] The related rules include:

Regulation 2004, Article 20: MOFCOM may conduct investigation and collect information from interested parties by, among others, sending questionnaires, using samples, holding public hearings and making on-the-spot verification. MOFCOM shall provide opportunities for all interested parties concerned to present their views and supporting arguments...

Regulation 2004, Article 21: An interested party shall provide authentic information and relevant documentation to MOFCOM in the process of the investigation. In the event that any interested party does not provide authentic information and relevant documentation, or does not provide necessary information within a reasonable time-limit or significantly impedes the investigation in other ways, MOFCOM may make determinations on the basis of the facts already known and the best information available...

Regulation 2004, Article 22: An interested party may request MOFCOM to treat the information it provided as confidential if it considers that any disclosure of such information would create significantly adverse effects. MOFCOM shall treat the information submitted by the interested party as confidential if they consider that the request for confidentiality is justifiable, and shall require the interested party to provide non-confidential summaries thereof. The confidential information shall not be disclosed without the permission of the interested party submitting it...

Regulation 2004, Article 23: MOFCOM shall allow the applicant and interested parties to have access to the information relevant to the investigation, provided that the information has not been treated as confidential...

Regulation 2004, Article 25: In cases where a preliminary determination on dumping, injury and the causal link between the two is affirmative, MOFCOM shall carry out further investigations on dumping, the margin of dumping, injury and its degree, and, on the basis of their findings, make final determinations respectively. The final determinations shall be published.

Before the final determinations are made, MOFCOM shall inform all known interested parties of the essential facts on which the final determinations are based...

英文译本出自中华人民共和国商务部进出口公平贸易局官方网站, http://gpj.mofcom.gov.cn/aarticle/bi/bj/bk/201106/20110607607638.html, last visited September 21, 2011.

conform to public interest. [1] Accordingly, in China, from the perspective of antidumping rules, consumers can submit relevant information, present their views or supporting arguments in antidumping investigations. And in cases where there is a strong opposition from consumers, price undertakings or antidumping duties might be suspended due to not conformity to public interest. [2]

II. "Consumer Interest" in Chinese Antidumping Cases.

As analyzed in the section above, Chinese antidumping rules have given certain consideration to consumers. The following step is to explore in practice, whether consumers supported or opposed antidumping investigations? Whether the relevant authorities have given any concern to consumers' interests before imposing antidumping duties? Are there any cases lifting antidumping duties by taking consumers' interests into consideration? This section aims to provide an overall examination of such sub-issue.

One notable characteristic of Chinese antidumping cases is that intermediate chemical products have occupied an overwhelming majority of

---

[1] Regulation 2004, Article 33: If considering that price undertakings made by exporters are acceptable and conform to public interest, MOFCOM may decide to suspend or terminate the antidum-ping investigation without applying provisional antidumping measures or imposing antidumping duties. The decision to suspend or terminate the antidumping investigation shall be published by MOFCOM...英文译本出自中华人民共和国商务部进出口公平贸易局官方网站, http://gpj.mofcom.gov.cn/aarticle/bi/bj/bk/201106/20110607607638.html, last visited September 21, 2011.

[2] Besides Regulation 2004, a few regulations concerning the procedures in antidumping investigation, such as disclosure of information, injury investigation, also have "public interest" clause. 参见王以锦:"反倾销中的公共利益问题研究",见《中国反倾销立法与实践十周年征文》, http://gpj.mofcom.gov.cn/aarticle/subject/fqx/subjectaa/200712/20071205305198.html, last visited September 18, 2011.

the products investigated.[1] More than thirty antidumping cases out of fifty are concerned with the downstream chemical producers instead of the final consumers, such as acrylic ester, polystyrene, and phenol etc. Therefore in China, the conflict between domestic producers and consumers is mainly manifested by the conflict between the upper and the lower producers.

For convenience of discussion in the following section, fifty antidumping cases will be divided into three groups according to the different outcomes of investigations, i. e., definitive measures (to impose antidumping duties); price undertaking (to revise the exporting prices or to cease exports to the area at the dumped prices rather than antidumping duties); as well as termination (failing to be proved, or no injury, or no dumping, or the case is withdrawn). Each group shall be investigated respectively.

A. Group I: Cases Subject to Antidumping Duties.

The thirty-nine antidumping cases subject to antidumping duties will be examined first. According to the final administrative decisions of

---

[1] Two reasons for the concentration of antidumping investigations on chemical products could be given. The first reason is that, China significantly lowered the tariffs of chemical products when it acceded to the WTO. The tenth five-year plan in 2001 promised to nurturing and development of such industries as the steel, petrochemical, chemical and synthetic fiber industries, and stated that Chinese government would actively made use of antidumping measures to achieve this goal. The second reason for this is due to the peculiar characteristics of the chemical industry itself. Chemical products, particularly such general-purpose products, are subject to price fluctuation in international markets when their international market prices go down, their export prices to China also go down, which makes the initiation of antidumping investigation easily acceptable. Besides, as the chemical industry is an upstream industry with fewer products categories, it is relatively easy to specify the product scope subject to investigation. *See* Junji Nakagawa ed., *Antidumping Laws And Practices of the New Users*, Cambridge Univ. Press, 2007, pp. 71 – 72.

MOFCOM, the words "opportunities have been provided for the relevant interested parties concerned to present their views and supporting arguments" have appeared in almost all of the decisions. However, only in the following five cases have the objections of consumers been specified, whereas in the rest of the thirty-four cases, neither their views nor supporting arguments have been stated in the final decisions, let alone the reasons for taking or not taking their interests into consideration. Based on this, one can conclude that the impression that consumer interest is not within major concern in the final decisions and hence often ignored.

The No. 22 Monoethanolamine & Diethanolamine Case *

In the No. 22 Monoethanolamine & Diethanolamine Case, the downstream industry of Glyphosate and that of Coconut Diethanol Amide are the main consumers. Both of them were strongly against the antidumping measure. The downstream industry of Glyphosate is of the viewpoint that the domestic output of Monoethanolamine & Diethanolamine is far from enough to satisfy the needs of the downstream industry. The import of Monoethanolamine & Diethanolamine is not the main reason for the injury of domestic industry. Simply for protecting such domestic industry as lags behind whereas totally ignoring the interests of agriculture and farmers, the imposition of antidumping duties is not in conformity to public interest. [1]

Similarly, the downstream industry of Coconut Diethanol Amide stated that the main reason for the downstream producers to import Monoethanolamine & Diethanolamine from abroad is that the domestic

---

* Public Announcement No. 57 in 2004 of Ministry of Foreign Trade and Economic Cooperation of the People's Republic of China, Chinese version available at: http://www.cacs.gov.cn/news/newshow.aspx?str1 =2&articleId =38867, last visited September 18, 2011.

[1] *Ibid.*

production cannot satisfy the needs, either in quality or in quantity. If antidumping duties were imposed on the imported products, the downstream industry might go into crisis, which could result in the market dominance of the downstream products again by the foreign industries. [1]

Neither of the complaints has stopped MOFCOM from taking definitive measures. MOFCOM stated in the final decision that there are three main reasons to reject their viewpoints. Firstly, as to the downstream industry of Glyphosate, the producing method of using Monoethanolamine & Diethanolamine as the raw materials has only occupied 23% of the whole Glyphosate industry, whereas the rest of the 77% adopted another raw material. Therefore the imposition of antidumping duties would not have a big influence on the main industry. [2] Secondly, for those who use Monoethanolamine & Diethanolamine, around 51.3% of the products are processing materials supplied by clients, so the imposition of antidumping duties would not have too much negative influence on them. [3] Thirdly, the fundamental purpose of antidumping is to maintain normal competitive process of Monoethanolamine & Diethanolamine in the Chinese market. Only under a fair and ordered competitive process could the downstream industry make profits. Consequently, imposition of antidumping duties is in conformity with public interest. [4]

---

[1] Public Announcement No. 57 in 2004 of Ministry of Foreign Trade and Economic Cooperation of the People's Republic of China, Chinese version available at: http://www.cacs.gov.cn/news/newshow.aspx? strl =2&articleId =38867, last visited September 18, 2011.

[2] *Ibid.*

[3] *Ibid.*

[4] *Ibid.*

The No. 29 Trichloroethylene case *

In the No. 29 Trichloroethylene case, the downstream industry expressed their objections towards the antidumping measure. Since the domestic output of Trichloroethylene cannot satisfy the needs of downstream industry, the imposition of antidumping duties would injure the interests of us, the downstream industry. ❶ MOFCOM rejected taking their interests into consideration by simply stating that the imposition of antidumping duties is aimed at correcting the unfair trade conduct-low-price dumping. It does not mean completely restraining the import, so as not to have substantial influence on the downstream industry. ❷

*The No. 33 Disodium 5'-inosinate Case***

In the No. 33 Disodium 5'-Inosinate Case, the main viewpoints of the downstream industry include: as the only domestic producer, the output of the applicant cannot satisfy the needs of downstream industry, the imposition of antidumping duties is not in conformity with public interest. ❸ The reasons for MOFCOM to reject are: although the current output of the applicant cannot satisfy the needs of the downstream industry, the antidumping measures only involve those products from Japan and

---

* Public Announcement No. 37 in 2005 of Ministry of Foreign Trade and Economic Cooperation of the People's Republic of China, Chinese version available at: http://www.cacs.gov.cn/news/newshow.aspx? strl = 2&articleId = 38875, last visited September 18, 2011.

❶ *Ibid.*

❷ *Ibid.*

** The full name of this chemical product is Disodium 5'-Inosinate, Disodium 5'-Guanylate and Disodium 5'-Ribonucleotide, hereinafter referred to Disodium 5'-Inosinate for short. *See* Public Announcement No. 24 in 2006 of Ministry of Foreign Trade and Economic Cooperation of the People's Republic of China, Chinese version available at: http://www.cacs.gov.cn/news/newshow.aspx? strl = 2&articleId = 38885, last visited September 18, 2011.

❸ *Ibid.*

Korea. There are still imported products from the other countries, which could fill the vacancy and ensure that neither the import quantity nor domestic price be substantially influenced. ❶

The No. 35 Polyurethane Case *

In the No. 35 Polyurethane Case, the downstream industry feels anxious of the influence of the antidumping investigation on the export of the downstream textile products. ❷ MOFCOM is of the opinion that the domestic production of polyurethane, either the output or assortment or the quality, can satisfy the needs of the downstream industry. ❸

The No. 38 Wear Resistant Overlay Case **

In the No. 38 Wear Resistant Overlay Case, the downstream industry is strongly against the imposition of antidumping duties and applying for the suspension of the antidumping duties immediately. The main reasons are: the quality of the domestic produced Wear Resistant Overlay is lower than that of the imported products, and the quantity of the domestic products cannot satisfy the needs of the downstream industry. Furthermore, the imported products are not the main causation of material injury to the domestic industry, whereas the competition among domestic

❶ Public Announcement No. 24 in 2006 of Ministry of Foreign Trade and Economic Cooperation of the People's Republic of China, Chinese version available at: http://www.cacs.gov.cn/cacs/news/newshow.aspx? strl = 2&articleId = 38885, last visited September 18, 2011.

* Public Announcement No. 74 in 2006 of Ministry of Commerce of the People's Republic of China, Chinese version available at: http://www.cacs.gov.cn/news/newshow.aspx? strl = 2&articleId = 38890, last visited Setember 18, 2011.

❷ *Ibid.*

❸ *Ibid.*

** Public Announcement No. 93 in 2006 of Ministry of Foreign Trade and Economic Cooperation of the People's Republic of China, Chinese version available at: http://www.cacs.gov.cn/news/newshow.aspx? strl = 2&articleId = 38891, last visited September 18, 2011.

producers themselves is.[1] MOFCOM rejected it by stating that anti-dumping is aimed to maintain a normal fair trade order, and that it will not consist of a barrier to the normal import.[2]

Summary

Judging from the viewpoints of consumers in the aforementioned five cases, it can be seen that in China, though the situation is different in each case, the objections of the downstream industries towards anti-dumping measures which restrained the import and brought about the rising price, are commonly shared but totally ignored in the final administrative decisions. Furthermore, the main complaint of the downstream consumers against antidumping actions is more or less the same: since the domestic output cannot satisfy the needs of downstream industry, by restraining the import, the imposition of antidumping duties is likely to have negative effects on the normal operation of the downstream industry, which include lack of raw materials, the addition of an extra-productive cost, less competitiveness than their foreign competitors, higher price for final consumers, etc. This is where antidumping conflicts with

---

[1] Public Announcement No. 93 in 2006 of Ministry of Foreign Trade and Economic Cooperation of the People's Republic of China, Chinese version available at: http://www.cacs.gov.cn/news/newshow.aspx? strl = 2&articleId = 38891, last visited September 18, 2011.

[2] *Ibid.*

the interests of consumers the most in current China. ❶

---

❶ Apart from the above five cases, as to the rest thirty-four cases, though the reactions of the downstream industries towards antidumping measures were ignored in the final administrative decisions, the general negative effects of antidumping actions on them have been detected and brought about an intensive discussion in China. For instance, in the No. 26 Chloroprene Rubber Case, representative of the downstream industry, the secretary-general Gong Beifan of the industry association has strongly against the antidumping investigation. He stated that, there are only two domestic producers of Chloroprene Rubber currently, the total year yield of which is 40000 ton. While the demand of the downstream industry is about 60000 ton to 70000 ton, which means 20000 ton to 30000 ton are depending on imports. Therefore the imposition of antidumping duties would result in the lack of raw material and disrupt the interests the downstream industries. Gong Beifan also pointed out that, using antidumping measures to prevent or limit the imports cannot guarantee the market share of the domestic producers. The correct way is to improve its own technical abilities and raise the quality of their products that can compete with imported products. The situation was much more serious for those downstream industries whose main raw resources are depending on imports. Lu Qiting, the chief director of Kangda Chemical Limited Company, has also complained that the imposition of antidumping duties has forced the company into very difficult position, since 30% to 40% of the raw materials were coming from imports. 参见"反倾销阵营现异音——龚辈凡:我不同意反倾销",中国中小企业大连网, http://www.smedl.gov.cn/main/News_info_detail.asp? info_id=32769, last visited September 18, 2011.

Take the No. 45 Bisphenol - A Case for another example. In the antidumping investigation, Hongcang Electronic Material Limited Company of Guangzhou City, Qihua Chemical Engineering Limited Company of Dalian City, Baling Petroleum Limited Company, Sanmu Corporation Group, Hengyuan Chemical Engineering Limited Company of Huangshan City and so on, representatives of the downstream industries of Bisphenol - A, have provided a host of datum to prove that antidumping investigation has caused material injury to them, including the highly increased cost of the raw material, the issue of unemployment, and threat from their foreign competitors. Due to the strong objection of the downstream industry, the petitioner, Lanxing Company, first withdrew in September 2005. However, it applied for antidumping investigation again in February 2006, and the strong objection of the downstream industry has not prevented MOFCOM from making a definitive decision this time. 参见"我省首次参加进口反倾销听证会",中安在线, http://ah.anhuinews.com/system/2005/02/02/001125322.shtml, last visited September 18, 2011. 宾建成:"中国首次反倾销措施执行效果评估",载《世界经济》2003 年第 9 期,第 38 ~ 43 页; 朱庆华:"中国反倾销公共利益原则的实践",载《中央财经大学学报》2008 年第 2 期,第 58 ~ 62 页;鲍晓华:"中国实施反倾销措施的经济效应分析",载《经济纵横》2004 年第 1 期,第 16 ~ 19 页;刘卫东:"进口反倾销:特点、成效与对策",载《国际经济合作》2005 年第 1 期,第 17 ~ 19 页;金晓晨:"反倾销中公共利益原则的法理分析——从公平正义的角度",载《当代法学》2007 年第 5 期,第 21 ~ 26 页;马向敏、刘富利:"进口反倾销对上下游产业的影响——基于我国造纸业的分析",载《当代经济》2007 年第 12S 期,第 80 ~ 85 页。

In reply to the above complaints, MOFCOM did not deny the existence of this conflict in each case. However, it insisted the imposition of antidumping duties, which included but not limited to: the scale of the influenced downstream industry is not large; the influence is not substantial; the import is still possible from the other countries, etc. Amongst them, the term "fair competition" or "fair trade" has been used more than once. MOFCOM argued that we need to first correct the unfair dumping and rebuild the ordered competitive process, and then downstream industry's interest will be taken into consideration. Such an argument seems persuasive at first glance as it is understandable that unfair practices should be corrected first, but the problem is that the premise of the argument, i. e., all of the dumping practices are unfair or harmful, is still arguable. MOFCOM just simply borrowed the problematic premise of antidumping without further analysis. A deeper examination and a more comprehensive investigation into the cost and benefit of the whole chain of industries and consumers in the long term, might lead to an opposite conclusion that we should not ignore the conflict with consumers' interests.

B. Group II: Cases Subject to Price Undertakings

The second step is to look into these cases subject to price undertaking to examine whether the interests of consumers have been within the main consideration to accept price undertaking rather than impose antidumping duties. In China, price undertakings were accepted only in four cases, including the No. 4 Cold Rolled Stainless Steel Sheet Case, the No. 18 Polyvinyl Chloride Case, No. 23 Chloroform Case, and the

No. 32 Benzofuranol Case. ❶

The No. 4 Cold Rolled Stainless Steel Sheet Case *

In the No. 4 Cold Rolled Stainless Steel Sheet Case, the downstream industry was strongly against the antidumping measures. And in this case the market share of the import is very large: 1995 – 1998: 53.74%; 62.35%; 54.08%; 63.67%. Restraining foreign import might result in lacking of raw materials or putting up the price, which would harm the downstream industry. Under this situation, instead of imposing antidumping duties, the antidumping authorities decided to accept price undertaking with the main exporters. ❷

*The No. 18 Polyvinyl Chloride Case***

In the No. 18 Polyvinyl Chloride Case, there are twenty registered exporters in total, nineteen of which were subject to antidumping duties. Price undertaking was accepted by MOFCOM to apply to only one Russian exporter. ❸ Therefore the application of price undertaking in this

---

❶ According to Regulation 2004, consumers can be taken into consideration as "public interest" in deciding whether to accept price undertaking. Amongst the four cases, the No. 4 case and the No. 18 case were actually initiated before Regulation 2004 taking into effect, when there was no legislative requirement to evaluate "public interest". However, the related information shall be further examined to see their concerns with consumers.

* Public Announcement No. 15 in 2000 of Ministry of Foreign Trade and Economic Cooperation of the People's Republic of China, Chinese version available at: http://www.cacs.gov.cn/news/newshow.aspx?strl=2&articleId=38844, last visited Setember 18, 2011.

❷ This case is said to have a great influence on the downstream industry. 参见"中国不锈钢冷轧薄板反倾销案",中国贸易救济信息网, http://www.cacs.gov.cn/news/newshow.aspx?strl=2&articleId=37844, last visited September 18, 2011.

** Public Announcement No. 48 in 2003 of Ministry of Commerce of the People's Republic of China, Chinese version available at: http://www.cacs.gov.cn/news/newshow.aspx?strl=2&articleId=38447, last visited September 18, 2011.

❸ *Ibid.*

case has not affected the main export and cannot be referred to as in consideration of public interest.

The No. 23 Chloroform Case *

In the final decision of the No. 23 Chloroform Case, the negative effects, including the increase of price and insufficiency of supply, on the downstream industry was taken into consideration by MOFCOM, and price undertakings with five out of seven submitted exporters were accepted in this case, "considering the interests of both parties". [1] The relevant administrative authority, in the final decision, was of the opinion that after taking the interim antidumping measure, the market price of the investigated products has risen to some extent, but the domestic supply is comparatively lacking, which has a certain influence on the downsteam industry. Therefore, taking the interests of both upstream and downstream industries into consideration, accepting price undertaking with five foreign producers is decided. [2]

*The No. 32 Benzofuranol Case***

In the final decision No. 32 Benzofuranol case, it was stated by MOFCOM that, in order to "keep moderate competition" in the domestic market, price undertaking was agreed and signed with the main

---

* Public Announcement No. 81 in 2004 of Ministry of Commerce of the People's Republic of China, Chinese version available at: http://www.cacs.gov.cn/news/newshow.aspx? strl =2&articleld =38868, last visited September 18, 2011.

[1] *Ibid.*

[2] Public Announcement No. 81 in 2004 of Ministry of Commerce of the People's Republic of China, Chinese version available at: http://www.cacs.gov.cn/news/newshow.aspx? strl =2&articleld =38868, last visited September 18, 2011.

** Public Announcement No. 7 in 2006 of Ministry of Commerce of the People's Republic of China, Chinese version available at: http://www.cacs.gov.cn/news/newshow.aspx? strl =2&articleld =38884, last visited September 18, 2011.

exporters in the U. S. FMC company and the Japanese Farm Chemical Company, rather than imposing antidumping duties. In China, the consideration of "public interest" is normally linking with the interests of downstream industries. However in this case, it refers to the competitive condition of the relevant products in the domestic market. ❶ Such an uncommon consideration may relate to the specific characteristics of this case.

Benzofuranol is one of the downstream products of Catechol. In 2002, imported Catechol products were subject to an antidumping investigation and imposed with antidumping duties, the No. 14 Catechol Case, which incurred an upsurge of the prices of Catechol. ❷ The costs of its downstream products were also increased simultaneously, which drove the Benzofuranol industries into a very difficult position. It is only for protecting themselves from the negative effects brought by the upper industries that domestic Benzofuranol industries also petitioned for antidumping investigation. This is usually called cascading contingent protection. ❸ Accordingly, in this case, it is most likely for preventing the occurrence of similar incidents in the chain reaction that MOFCOM decided to accept price undertaking to mitigate the negative effects of imposing antidumping duties. From this viewpoint, the consideration of taking a price undertaking in this Benzofuranol case is also for balancing

---

❶ 朱庆华:"中国反倾销十年",载《国际商报》, http://ibdaily. mofcom. gov. cn/show. asp? id = 175457 , last visited September 18, 2011.

❷ Public Announcement No. 41 in 2003 of Ministry of Commerce of the People's Republic of China, Chinese version available at: http://www. cacs. gov. cn/cacs/news/newshow. aspx? str1 = 2&articleId = 38856, last visited September 18, 2011.

❸ 李玫瑰、连序海、刘艳红:"反倾销措施对下游企业的产业关联和继发性保护影响——以邻苯二酚和呋喃酚案为例",载《金融经济》2006 年第 6 期,第 59 ~ 60 页。

the upper and the lower interests of the industries.

Summary

In China, agreements of price undertakings are seldom agreed or signed between the main exporters and MOFCOM. Up till now, price undertaking measures instead of imposing antidumping duties have been taken in only four out of fifty cases. It is found that three out of the four cases, i. e., the No. 4 Cold Rolled Stainless Steel Sheet Case, the No. 23 Chloroform Case, and the No. 32 Benzofuranol case, price undertakings were accepted by taking the interests of downstream industries into consideration.

C. Group III: Cases Subject to Terminations

The third step is to examine the rest of the seven cases subject to termination, to see whether there are any cases refusing or lifting antidumping duties by taking consumers' interests into consideration. As introduced above, of the seven cases, in one case (the No. 25 Nylon 6.66 Filament Yarn Case), all registered exporters are determined as either no dumping or having a dumping margin less than 2%; two cases (The No. 21 MDI Case and the No. 31 Ethylene-Propylene-non-conjugated Diene Rubber Case) are terminated because of the withdrawal of the antidumping petitioners; the rest of the four cases (the No. 7 Polystyrene Case, the No. 8 L-Lysine monohydrochlouide Case, the No. 39 Butanol Case, and the No. 40 Octanol Case) are determined as no injury.

Commencing from Regulation 2004, there is a possibility to terminate antidumping investigation for the consideration of "public interest", however, there have been no final decisions up till now that refused or lifted antidumping duties directly due to that reason, let alone for the consideration of consumers.❶ How about those "withdrawal", "no dumping" or "no injury" cases? Whether the virtual reason is for the consideration of the downstream industry or not deserves further examination. The investigation indicates that some weight has been given to downstream industries in certain cases.

The No. 21 MDI case *

The No. 21 MDI Case ends up with the petitioner withdrawing from the antidumping investigation. Guo Xingtian, the manager of the petitioner, Yuantai Wanhua Company, explained in a newspaper interview that there are three reasons for withdrawing this antidumping application. The first one is that after the antidumping investigation, the exporters from Japan and Korea have enhanced the price, so the market order has been gradually recovered.❷ The second one is that Yuantai Wanhua Company has already taken the chance of antidumping investigation to quicken its development.❸ The third important reason is

---

❶ Only in the No. 17 Cold Rolled Steel Case, MOFCOM decided to suspend antidumping duties for a while after the affirmed final decision. The reason was not for public interest but because this product was subject to both antidumping and safeguard at that time. Since the relevant safeguard measures have already been taken, the antidumping duties were suspended. Later on, antidumping duties still continued to be imposed after the termination of safeguard measures. 参见朱庆华:"中国反倾销十年",国际商报, http://ibdaily.mofcom.gov.cn/show.asp? id = 175457 http://ibdaily.mofcom.gov.cn/show.asp? id = 175457, last visited September 18, 2011.

* Public Announcement No. 66 in 2003 of Ministry of Commerce of the People's Republic of China, Chinese version available at: http://www.cacs.gov.cn/news/newshow.aspx? strl =2&articleId =38862, last visited September 18, 2011.

❷ "烟台万华起诉撤诉非做秀 反倾销剑术值得思量",载《证券时报》2003 年 12 月 8 日, http://stock.jrj.com.cn/news/2003 - 12 - 08/000000705752.html, last visited September 18, 2011.

❸ *Ibid.*

concerned with the downstream industry. As the only domestic producer, Wanhua's current output cannot satisfy the needs of downstream industry and nearly 70% of domestic output depends on the import. So the imposition of antidumping duties will definitely harm the interests of the downstream industry. This indicates that the interests of consumers have been given some consideration in the terminated antidumping cases.

It is worth noting that during the process of hearing, major representatives of the downstream industries considered that the domestic output cannot satisfy the needs of the downstream industry and antidumping duty would increase the productive cost for them, whereas a few others favored antidumping duties.[1] For those rare proponents, they did not deny the future increase of their cost in the wake of imposing antidumping duties, instead they believed that the current low cost is temporary, which means, it will not last long because once the foreign competitors achieve the monopoly position the price of the raw material will be even higher.[2] However, such an argument incorrectly quoted predatory dumping theories and hence is untenable. In order to condemn predatory dumping, its existence should be proved first. Modern application of antidumping has far deviated from this theoretical basis and thereby cannot achieve this. It is incorrect to simply use part of the predatory dumping theories to support antidumping measures.

---

[1] Material No. 9 of the Hearing of Industry Injury Investigation of MDI, Chinese version available at: http://www.cacs.gov.cn/cacs/news/xiangguanshow.aspx?articleId=39237, last visited September 18, 2011.

[2] Material No. 8 of the Hearing of Industry Injury Investigation of MDI, Chinese version available at: http://www.cacs.gov.cn/cacs/news/xiangguanshow.aspx?articleId=39237, last visited September 18, 2011.

The No. 8 L-Lysine Monohydrochlouide Case *

Apart from the No. 21 MDI "withdrawn" Case, the No. 8 L-Lysine Monohydrochlouide "no injury" case also deserves discussion. The analysis of "no injury" in this case is less persuasive comparing with that of the other three "no injury" cases. According to the requirements under Article 8 of the Antidumping Regulation 2004, MOFCOM normally refers to thirteen kinds of datum, including output of domestic industry, quantity of sales, price of sales, income of sales, profit before tax, market share, terminal inventory, average year salary per person, the rate of unemployment, the rate of operation, the rate of return on

* Public Announcement No. 23 in 2002 of Ministry of Foreign Trade and Economic Cooperation of the People's Republic of China, Chinese version available at: http://www.cacs.gov.cn/news/newshow.aspx? strl = 2&articleId = 38784, last visited September 18, 2011.

investment, net cash flow and the development of domestic industry. [1] According to the different variations of the aforementioned thirteen kinds in each of antidumping cases, the relevant final decisions of the injury will be made. In the other three "no injury" cases, all of the thirteen kinds of datum consistently show that there is no material injury on domestic industry. However, in the No. 8 case, some of the datum like the output of domestic industry, quantity of sales, price of sales, income of sales etc. are first going down then going up, and some of the datum like market share are going down, and even some of the datum

---

[1] Regulation 2004, Article 8: The following factors shall be examined in the determination of injury caused by dumping to a domestic industry:

(1) whether the volume of dumped imports, including the volume of dumped imports either in absolute terms or relative to the production or consumption of a like domestic product, has been increasing significantly, or the possibility of a significant increase in dumped imports;

(2) the effects of dumped imports on prices, including the price undercutting by the dumped imports, or the significant suppressing or depressing effects on the price of a like domestic product, etc.;

(3) the consequent impact of the dumped imports on the relevant economic factors and indices of the domestic industry;

(4) the production capacity or export capacity of the exporting country (region) or the country (region) of origin, and inventories of the product under investigation;

(5) other factors that may cause or have caused injury to a domestic industry.

The determination of threat of material injury shall be based on facts and not merely on allegation, conjecture or remote possibility.

When determining the injury caused by dumping to a domestic industry, the determination shall be based on positive evidence, and the injuries caused by factors other than dumping must not be attributed to dumping.

英文译本出自中华人民共和国商务部进出口公平贸易局官方网站, http://gpj.mofcom.gov.cn/aarticle/bi/bj/bk/201106/20110607607638.html, last visited September 21, 2011.

like profit before tax' the rate of return on investment renegative. ❶ It seems not so convincing to make a "no injury" decision in this case.

A further examination of this case suggested that, the petitioners of this case are quite different from the other cases. The defendants are exporters from the U. S., Korea, and Indonesia. The petitioners are Chuanhua Weizhisu Company and Quanzhou Daquan Company, both of which are joint ventures. ❷ In fact, 70% share of Chuanhua Weizhisu Company is owned by Weizhisu Japanese Company, and one of the main share holders of Quanzhou Daquan Company is Zhengda Thailand Company. ❸ There are actually no domestic Chinese industries involved in this case. Accordingly, in this "Foreigner v. Foreigner" case, MOFCOM gave more concerns to the final consumers of L-Lysine Monohydrochlouide, the farmers. Because once the antidumping duties are imposed, the price will correspondingly raise, which is really a burden for the domestic consumers. This is possibly the real reason for MOFCOM

---

❶ For all of the 13 kinds of datum, it was decided in the final decision that: "output of domestic industry" is first down then up, "quantity of sales" is first down then up, "price of sales" is first down then up, "income of sales" is first down then up, "profits before tax" are minus, "market share" is decreasing, "inventories" is decreasing, "average salary per year" and "unemployment Rate" are not changing very much, "operation rate" is not enough, "rate of return on investment" is negative, "cash flow" is increasing, "development of domestic industry" is not influenced. *See* Public Announcement No. 23 in 2002 of Ministry of Foreign Trade and Economic Cooperation of the People's Republic of China, Chinese version available at: http://www. cacs. gov. cn/news/newshow. aspx? str1 = 2&articleId = 38784, last visited September 18, 2011.

❷ *Ibid.*

❸ 李弘、田莉:"反倾销在全球性竞争中的战略问题——饲料级赖氨酸反倾销案有感",载《中国集体经济》2002 年第 9 期,第 39 页。

to make a less unconvincing "no injury" decision. [1] This case indicates that interests of consumers can be "conditionally" considered by anti-dumping authorities.

Summary

This part conducted a comprehensive investigation into "consumer interest" in Chinese antidumping context which has not been touched upon yet. It concludes in three fold as follows:

(1) Although there is no mention of "consumer" through the whole text of Chinese antidumping rules, consideration may be given to the "consumer" by attributing it to "other interested organizations and parties" and taking it as one factor of "public interest". Accordingly, in antidumping investigations, consumers can submit the relevant information, present their views or supporting arguments, and if there is a strong opposition from consumers, price undertakings or antidumping duties might be suspended due to nonconformity to public interest.

(2) Antidumping cases involve much conflict with the interests of consumers in practice. In China, such conflict has two features. The first one is in the group of consumers. Consumers are mostly the downstream chemical producers instead of the final consumers. The second one is in the content of conflict. The conflict is not only about putting up the price, adding an extra productive cost for the downstream industry, higher price for the final consumers, but also includes that due to that domestic output cannot satisfy the needs of downstream industry, the imposition of antidumping duties result in restraining the import and thereby may cause a lack of the raw materials for the downstream

---

[1] Interview with Soga Takashi, Manage Partner, Soga Uryu &Itoga Law Firm in Tokyo, Japan ,September 13, 2007.

industry.

(3) Chinese antidumping authorities have not given serious consideration to the conflict with consumer interest in antidumping cases. There are no final decisions that refused or lifted antidumping duties due to the reason of public interest, let alone for the interests of consumers. In most cases that imposed antidumping duties, the interests of consumers are not within the main concern in the final decision hence totally ignored. Only in a few cases, MOFCOM did admit the conflict, but using simply and unconvincing arguments to reject that consideration. Besides, agreements of price undertakings are seldom signed between the main exporters and MOFCOM, and only in three out of four cases they are signed for balancing the interests of the upstream and downstream industries. In the "withdrawn", "no dumping" or "no injury" cases, the interests of consumers might be one of the factors or conditionally considered in terminating antidumping measures.

6. 4. 3. 4 Facilitation of Collusion or Cross-border Cartels

As analyzed in Chapter IV, the self-constrained measure allowed by antidumping rules, i. e., price undertaking, is actually taken as restrains of competitive process and forbidden by antitrust law. Price undertaking may conflict with competition policy by facilitating the collusion between domestic and foreign producers. Case studies in the traditional users of antidumping have shown that, most antidumping complaints were actually concluded with price undertakings instead of the imposition of antidumping duties, which may incentivise or force foreign suppliers to legally collude with their domestic competitors to form lawful cross-border cartels. Accordingly, the third issue hereinafter is concerned with price undertaking, to examine in China how many antidumping cases ended up with price undertaking, and whether they facilitated cross-border cartels.

Agreements of price undertakings were seldom agreed or signed between foreign exporters and MOFCOM in China. As analyzed above, up till now, price undertaking measures instead of imposing antidumping duties were taken in only four out of fifty cases, including the No. 4 Cold Rolled Stainless Sheet Case, the No. 18 Polyvinyl Chloride Case, No. 23 Chloroform Case, and the No. 32 Benzofuranol Case.

In the No. 18 Polyvinyl Chloride case, price undertaking was only applied to one Russian exporter (out of twenty registered exporters), and did not affect the main export, so it was impossible to facilitate cross-border cartels. [1] In the No. 4 Cold Rolled Stainless Sheet Case, the No. 23 Chloroform Case and the No. 32 Benzofuranol case, price undertakings were accepted with a purpose to balance the interests of the upper and the lower industries. [2] Currently, there were no other evidences showing that price undertaking facilitates cross-border cartels between domestic and foreign producers in China.

6. 4. 3. 5 Facilitation of Monopoly Power or Domestic Cartels

Through restraining competition from foreign products, antidumping rules assist to either build domestic monopoly power or form domestic cartels. This kind of conflict has been found both in the traditional users and some of the other new users as aforementioned. Regarding China, in the determination of dominant market position, Chinese Antimonopoly Law provides two approahes. One is regulated in Article 18, which is an overall examination of the dominant market position by taking market share, competition situation, ability to control the sales market and the

---

[1] *See* the above analysis "the examination of the cases subject to price undertaking".

[2] *Ibid.*

other factors into consideration. [1] In addition, the antimonopoly law provides in Article 19 a way to presume dominant market position by calculating the relevant market share. [2]

In the examination of the possibility of antidumping facilitating either monopoly power or domestic cartels in China, it is decided to use the efficient criterion in Article 19 thereof to examine each antidumping case. According to Article 19, a dominant market position can be assumed when:

(1) The relevant market share of one undertaking accounts for1/2 or above;

(2) The joint relevant market share of two undertakings accounts for 2/3 or above;

(3) The joint relevant market share of three undertakings accounts for 3/4 or above.

Examination of "Market Power" in 50 Antidumping Cases

Applying the requirements in Article 19 to fifty antidumping cases in China, only seven cases passed the "market share" test. The specific information is shown in the following table:

---

[1] Chinese Antimonopoly Law, Article 18: The dominant market position of an undertaking shall be determined on the basis of the following factors: (1) its share on a relevant market and the competitiveness on the market; (2) its ability to control the sales market or the purchasing marker for raw and semi-finished materials; (3) its financial strength and technical conditions; (4) the extent to which other business mangers depend on it in transactions ; (5) the difficulty that other undertakings find in entering a relevant market; and (6) other factors related to the determination of the dominant market position held by an undertaking. 英文译本出自中华人民共和国中央人民政府网站(英文版), http://www.npc.gov.cn/englishnpc/Law/2009 - 02/20/content_1471587.htm, last visited September 18, 2011.

[2] This will be discussed in detail in the following 6.4.4 part of this chapter.

Table 3 Antidumping Cases under the "Market Share" Test

Number of Petitioners	Case No.	Product Name	The Total Market Share of Foreign Exporters
1. Petitioner (Market Share >1/2)	36	Catechol Case	2001 – 2004: 1.09%, 9.19%, 48.20%, 49.39%
	43	Paper for Electrolytic Capacitor	2003 – 2005: Above 20%
	45	Bisphenol – A	2003 – 2005: Above 40%
	48	Adipic Acid	2005 – 2008: 26.42%, 30.94%, 39.92%, 37.63%
2. Petitioners (Market Share >2/3)	26	Chloroprene Rubber	2000 – 2003: Above 32%
3. Petitioners (Market Share >3/4)	5	Acrylic Ester	1996 – 1999: 18.30%, 23.95%, 31.29%, 28.52%
	11	Acrylic Ester	1998 – 2001: 5.92%, 15.01%, 21.84%, 31.85%

As shown in the above table, the datum of the total market share of foreign exporters can indicate the total market share of the domestic producers. Of all the antidumping cases:

In fourteen cases, there is only one domestic producer. The market share of the domestic producer might be above 50% in four cases out of them, including the No. 36 Catechol Case❶, the No. 43 paper for

❶ Public Announcement No. 32 in 2006 of Ministry of Commerce of the People's Republic of China, Chinese version available at: http://www.cacs.gov.cn/cacs/news/newshow.aspx? str1 =2&articleId =38886, last visited September 18, 2011.

Electrolytic Capacitor Case[1], the No. 45 Bisphenol-A Case[2] and the No. 48 Adipic Acid Case[3];

There are two domestic producers in ten cases, and one out of them, i. e. the No. 26 Chloroprene Rubber Case[4], the market share of the domestic producers might be above 67.7%;

There are three domestic producers in nine cases, and two out of them, i. e. the No. 5 Acrylic Ester Case[5] and the No. 11 Acrylic Ester Case[6], the market share of the domestic producers in certain time periods might be above 75%.

The statistics shown above can give a general impression that,

---

[1] Public Announcement No. 30 in 2007 of Ministry of Commerce of the People's Republic of China, Chinese version available at: http://www.cacs.gov.cn/cacs/news/newshow.aspx? strl =2&articleId =38895, last visited September 18, 2011.

[2] Public Announcement No. 68 in 2007 of Ministry of Commerce of the People's Republic of China, Chinese version available at: http://www.cacs.gov.cn/news/newshow.aspx? strl =2&articleId =38897, last visited September 18, 2011.

[3] Public Announcement No. 78 in 2009 of Ministry of Commerce of the People's Republic of China, Chinese version available at: http://www.cacs.gov.cn/news/newshow.aspx? strl =2&articleId =62083, last visited September 18, 2011.

[4] Public Announcement No. 23 in 2005 of Ministry of Commerce of the People's Republic of China, Chinese version available at: http://www.cacs.gov.cn/news/newshow.aspx? strl =2&articleId =38873, last visited September 18, 2011.

[5] This is the antidumping investigation against Acrylic Ester produced and imported from the U. S. and Japan. Public Announcement No. 5 in 2001 of Ministry of Foreign Trade and Economic Cooperation of the People's Republic of China, Chinese version available at: http://www.cacs.gov.cn/cacs/news/newshow.aspx? strl = 2&articleId = 38845, last visited September 18, 2011.

[6] This is the antidumping investigation against Acrylic Ester produced and imported from Korea, Malaysia, Singapore, and Indonesia. *See* Public Announcement No. 3 in 2003 of Ministry of Commerce of the People's Republic of China, Chinese version available at: http://www.cacs.gov.cn/cacs/news/newshow.aspx? strl = 2&articleId = 38853, last visited September 18, 2011.

purely examined from the condition of the market share, only in a limited number of cases, i. e. 14% (7 out of 50 cases), there are possibilities that antidumping actions may help to maintain monopoly power or form domestic cartels. A further look could be taken into the above fourteen cases.

The No. 5 Acrylic Ester Case & No. 11 Acrylic Ester Case

Taken the No. 5 Acrylic Ester Case and No. 11 Acrylic Ester Case for instance, Gaoqiao Petrochemical Acrylic Acid Factory of Shanghai City, Oriental Chemical Industry Corporation of Beijing City and Jilian (Jilin) Petrochemical Corporation of Jilin Province were the only three domestic producers of Acrylic Ester. According to the statistics, the joined market share of the three in domestic market were above 75% before 1997, and it might be due to competition from foreign imports, it decreased to 68.71% in 1998. In 1999, three of them petitioned for the antidumping investigation against Acrylic Ester produced and imported from the U. S., Germany, and Japan. Antidumping duties were imposed on the imported products both from the U. S. and Japan. [1]

Afterwards, the foreign competition from the U. S. and Japan became not as threatening as previous, and the three domestic producers had successfully acquired a joined market share of around 80% since

---

[1] The antidumping investigation of Germany was ceased because the amount of import from Germany was less than 3% of the total amount. *See* Public Announcement No. 5 in 2001 of Ministry of Foreign Trade and Economic Cooperation of the People's Republic of China, Chinese version available at: http://www.cacs.gov.cn/cacs/news/newshow.aspx?strl=2&articleId=38845, last visited September 18, 2011.

1999. [1] Neverthelss, in 2001, Acrylic Ester started to be imported from Korea, Malaysia, Singapore, and Indonesia in an increasing way, which reduced the high joined market share of three of three to around 68%. [2] Again, three of them petitioned for the antidumping investigation against Acrylic Ester produced and imported from these countries and succeeded in achieving so.

Combined the two cases together, an impression of using antidumping actions to maintain their own market power in domestic market could be got. According the other relevant information, after the two antidumping actions, the import from all abroad were almost stagnated, and the three domestic producers maintain the monopoly power in China. [3] Up till 2003, the price of Acrylic Ester had increased to two to three times that before antidumping actions, causing more than 30 downstream producers going into bankruptcy. [4] There has been an increasing calling for breaking their monopoly power according to antimonopoly law. [5]

---

[1] Public Announcement No. 3 in 2003 of Ministry of Commerce of the People's Republic of China, Chinese version available at: http://www.cacs.gov.cn/cacs/news/newshow.aspx? str1 =2&articleId =38853, last visited September 18, 2011.

[2] *Ibid.*

[3] 陈芳:"中国亟需反垄断法",新浪财经纵横, http://finance.sina.com.cn/review/observe/20050105/11411272263.shtml, last visited September 18, 2011.

[4] *Ibid.*

[5] 参见杜海涛:"垄断不反不行",载《人民日报》2006 年 7 月 3 日, http://finance.people.com.cn/GB/1037/4551567.html, last visited September 18, 2011;杨国民:"垄断——反倾销带来新课题",载《经济日报》2004 年7 月 27 日, http://www.tmchn.com/pinpai/w/7341.htm, last visited September 18, 2011.

The No. 43 Paper for Electrolytic Capacitor Case

Take the No. 43 Paper for Electrolytic Capacitor Case for another example. With equally matched technical abilities, Chinese complaint Kaien Company and Japanese Defense NKK Company, were the only two producers of paper for electrolytic capacitor competing with each other in the current world. ❶

Being the only producer in the Chinese market possessing nearly 80% market share but was still not content yet, Kaien Company petitioned for the antidumping investigation to block their sole competitor NKK Company. After obtaining the final definitive decision of imposing antidumping duties on NKK by MOFCOM successfully, Kaien Company gained quite a long time of a comfortable market environment and a competitive advantage, to strengthen its market power further. In this case, antidumping action is actually playing the role of facilitating monopoly power. Just as the analysts of China International Tending Web stated during providing their comments on Kaien Stock for stock buyers that, the antidumping action had been of great benefits to Kaien Company, since the dominant position of Kaien has become much firmer and it is very helpful for it to invest abroad. ❷

Summary

As analyzed above, most of the antidumping cases in China are dealing with chemical products, of which domestic industries are new or infant, while foreign imports are comparatively more competitive.

---

❶ "凯恩股份(002012):国内电解电容纸的垄断者",雅虎财经, http://biz.cn.yahoo.com/08-03-/124/ppps.html, last visited September 18, 2011.

❷ 张妍:"电解电容纸反倾销初战告捷　我反倾销力度日趋强劲",中国国际招标网, http://demowww.chinabidding.com/zxzx-detail-449412.html, last visited September 18, 2011.

Therefore, it is understandable that the monopoly power of domestic producers petitioning in each antidumping investigation in China is averagely not as strong as that in the other developed countries. However, a further examination shows that antidumping actions did facilitate monopoly in some cases. It is predictable that with the economic development as well as the improvement of competition legislation in China, this conflict with competition policy would become more severe in the future. The above statistics also indicate that since 2006, one domestic company with large market share has started to appear more than preivous.

6. 4. 3. 6 Summary

Apart from the comparison of each basic element under antidumping rules and competition rules, a comparison investigation was also conducted in the modern free trade world. Against this background, competition rules are also found to be able to avoid much conflict with basic modern trade and competition principles, compared with antidumping rules. To examine such argument under Chinese practice, this part put its emphasis on the relationship of antidumping rules with the basic competition principles. Through observing the four aspects of conflict respectively, that whether the application of Chinese antidumping rules involves many anti-competitive effects that can be avoided by applying competition rules to dumping, can be concluded.

In terms of the conflict with the protection of competitive process, 65.8% exporters (273 out of 415) that went through the whole antidumping investigation in 86% cases (43 out of 50) were imposed with antidumping duties, which indicates that antidumping actions actually restrained foreign competition in large proportion.

As to the impact of antidumping measures on consumer welfare, the strong objections were made by consumers in the antidumping investigations. However, Chinese antidumping authorities either ignored the interests of consumers entirely in the decision of imposition of antidumping duties, or provided with very simply and unconvincing arguments to exclude the consideration of consumers' interests. In rarely few cases awarded with price undertakings, or "withdrawn", "no dumping" or "no injury" cases, the interests of consumers might be one of the factors or conditionally considered in terminating antidumping measures.

Price undertaking may conflict with competition policy by facilitating the collusion between domestic and foreign producers. However in China, agreements of price undertakings were seldom agreed or signed between the main exporters and MOFCOM, and there were no other evidence available showing that in these cases price undertaking facilitated cross-border cartels between domestic and foreign producers.

Through restraining the competition from foreign producers, antidumping rules can also facilitate to maintain domestic monopoly power or form domestic cartels. In china, purely examined from the condition of the market share in each of the antidumping cases, it is found that only 14% (7 out of 50) of the antidumping actions might help to maintain monopoly power or form domestic cartels. With the economic development as well as the improvement of competition legislation in China, this conflict with competition policy is very likely to become more severe in the future.

Consequently, similar to the other study results, in China, antidumping actions also involve many anti-competitive effects in practice, including seriously conflicting with the protection of competitive process, consumer welfare, and also tending to facilitate monopoly power in an increasing way.

6.4.4 Antidumping Cases under Competition Requirements

The following part shall dicuss the third perspective of examining the effects of practical antidumping cases in China. As argued in the part above, though in future predatory dumping might be subject only to antimonopoly law, currently there are two different kinds of criterion on predatory dumping in China. One is under Chinese Unfair Competition Law, referred to as Criterion I, and the other is under Chinese Antimonopoly Law, referred to as Criterion II.

Hereinafter we will link these two sets of criterion with antidumping cases, so as to conduct the empirical study of how many antidumping cases would be considered as harmful from the perspective of competition law in China. The answer to this issue can indicate whether there would be less protectionist abuse in practice. Unlike the other countries, there are two sets of criterion of condemning predatory dumping in Chinese competition rules, so we shall divide the investigation into three parts. The first part will deal with the common area of the two sets of criterion, i. e. the price calculation. The second and third parts will subject these antidumping cases to different requirements under Criterion I and Criterion II respectively.

6.4.4.1 "Below-Cost Calculation" under Both Requirements

"Below-Cost" Test under Competition Requirements

In terms of price calculation, the major difference lies in that, competition law step in only when the price is below "cost" whereas antidumping law matters when the price is below "normal value". According to Chinese competition rules and other relevant provisions, there are two kinds of "cost" in the "price below cost", i. e. cost of production and cost of operation. Cost of production and cost of operation. Cost of production refers to manufacture cost plus period expense (consisted by management expense, finance expense as well as sale expense). Cost of operation includes merchandise procurement cost and circulation expense (consisted by operation expense, management expense as well as finance expense).

As to "below the cost", according to Article 5, it means the operator sales the commodities below the reasonable individual cost. On the conditions that the individual cost can not be identified, the relevant governmental authority shall decide according to the average cost of the whole industry of the commodities as well as the floating scope.

"Normal Value" Test under Antidumping Requirements

According to Chinese antidumping regulations, the "normal value" of imported products shall be determined in the following ways on the basis of different circumstances:

(1) in case that the products of the same category as that of the imported products have a comparable price in the domestic market of the exporting country (region) in the ordinary course of trade, that comparable price shall be the normal value;

(2) in case that the products of the same category as that of the imported products are not sold on the domestic market of the exporting country (region) in the ordinary course of trade, or the price or quantity of the products of the same category cannot be used as a basis for fair comparison, the normal value shall be the comparable price at which the products of the same category are exported to a proper third country (region) or shall be the production cost of the products of the same category in the country (region) of origin plus reasonable

expenses and profits. ❶

In practice, the normal value is determined in three different kinds of ways, including:

(1) The normal value will refer to the comparative price in the domestic market of the exporting country under the following situation: the first step is to decide the "in the ordinary course of trade". If during the investigation period, the proportion of the quantity of the products sold in the domestic market of the exporters to that sold in China is more than 5%, it shall be taken as the basis to apply the comparable price. Then the next step is to apply a below-the-cost test. If in the domestic market of the exporters, the proportion of the

---

❶ According to Regulation 2004, Artilce 4:

The normal value of an imported product shall be determined according to the following methods by distinguishing among differing cases:

(1) where there is a comparable price for the like product of the imported product in the ordinary course of trade in the domestic market of the exporting country (region), such comparable price shall be the normal value;

(2) where there are no sales of the like product of the imported product in the ordinary course of trade in the domestic market of the exporting country (region), or the price and the quantity of such sales do not permit a fair comparison, the normal value shall be the comparable price of the like product when exported to an appropriate third country (region) or the cost of production of the like product in the country (region) of origin plus a reasonable amount for expenses and for profits.

In cases where a product is not imported directly from the country (region) of origin, its normal value shall be determined in accordance with Item 1 of the preceding paragraph. However, under the circumstances that the product is merely transshipped through the exporting country, or the product is not produced in the exporting country (region), or there is no comparable price for the said product in the exporting country (region), the price of the like product in the country (region) of origin may be taken as the normal value.

英文译本出自中华人民共和国商务部进出口公平贸易局官方网站，http://gpj.mofcom.gov.cn/aarticle/bi/bj/bk/201106/20110607607638.html, last visited September 21, 2011.

quantity of the products sold in a below-the-cost way to the whole quantity sold is more than 20% , the quantity of below-the-cost products will be excluded when deciding the comparative price. If it is less than 20% , the quantity will be included.

(2) The normal value will refer to the constructed price under the following situation: if the proportion of the quantity of the products sold in the domestic market of the exporters to that sold in China is less than 5% , or if there are no products sold in the domestic market of the exporters, a price will be constructed as the normal value by the production cost of the products plus reasonable expenses and profits. Although on this condition, a comparable price sold at a proper third country is also allowed by law, this method has not yet been used in China.

(3) The normal value will be determined according to the rule of BIA if the provided information is considered as not completed or reliable, or the exporters haven't registered, or registered but not submitted the price materials. ❶

As to the determination of normal value in those fifty antidumping cases, the total number of registered exporters is about 415. ❷ The number of the cases decided by the first way, including partially

---

❶ These three different kinds of ways in determining the normal value can be identified in each final decision of the Chinese antidumping cases.

❷ There are three points in this calculation. First, it excludes two cases, one is no injury, the other one is withdrawn, both of which has no information available about the price calculation; Secondly, in about 9 cases, the importing companies are also included in counting the registered exporters; Thirdly, in about 3 cases, where there exists the situation that the exporters from certain country neither registered nor submitted any documents, the number of the registered exporters from that country will be counted as 0.

adjusted, is 209;[1] the number of the cases decided by the second way is 17; in the rest more than 180 exporters, the normal value is determined according to BIA.

"Below-Cost" Test v. "Normal Value" Test

Compared the "cost" test with the "normal value" test, it can be deduced that "cost" is usually lower than "normal value" in all of the above three kinds of situations. In the first situation where the normal value refers to the comparative price in the domestic market of the exporting country, whereas the major part of those products as sold below the cost over 20% will be excluded from the calculation of normal value. This indicates that the determined comparative price is higher than the "cost".

In the second situation, when the normal value refers to the constructed price, which includes the production cost of the products plus reasonable expenses and profits, hence is clearly higher than the "cost".

The third situation is when the normal value will be determined according to the rule of BIA. Compared with the above two, it goes without saying that this kind involves much more discretion and thereby is back-up to determine the normal value. Morevoer, almost all of

---

[1] Partial adjustment includes for example, for some investigated products, there are different models or types. The quantity proportion of some types sold in the domestic market of the exporters to that sold in China is more than 5%. However, for the other types, the quantity proportion is less than 5%. On this circumstance, for such types as less than 5%, the method of constructed price will be applied for partial adjustment. After that, according to Regulation 2004, Artilce 6, the margin of dumping shall be established on the basis of a comparison of a weighted average normal value with a weighted average of prices of all comparable export transactions or by a comparison of normal value and export price on a transaction-to-transaction basis.

the dumping margins that were determined by the rule of BIA are much higher than those determined by the above two kinds. [1] Correspondingly, the normal value decided under this situation is also higher than the "cost".

The above analysis indicates that if the fifty dumping cases were decided under Chinese competition rules, the scope of condemnation will definitely be narrowed down. In other words, in terms of the price calculation, there will be less harmful dumping cases if they are examined under competition rules in Chinese, either Criterion I or Criterion II.

6. 4. 4. 2 "Intent to Predation" under Criterion I

"Intent to Predation"

In this as well as the next parts, fifty antidumping cases will be investigated under the different requirements of Criterion I and Criterion II respectively. In terms of Criterion I, as analyzed above, besides price calculation, the examination of "intent to predation" is also a key point. There are five types of exemptions, including:

(1) Selling those commodities which are kept too long in stock;

(2) Disposing of commodities out of or near the expiration of the season;

(3) Disposing of commodities near the expiration of their guarantee

---

[1] For example, in the No. 26 Chloroprene Rubber Case, Denki Kagaku Kogyo Kabushiki Kaisha and Tosoh Corporation, both of whom the normal value are decided by the first kind of way, the dumping margin is respectively 2% and 3%. While the dumping margin of the other Japanese exporters, decided by rule of BIA, is 151%. *See* the No. 26 Chloroprene Rubber Case, Public Announcement No. 23 in 2005 of Ministry of Foreign Trade and Economic Cooperation of the People's Republic of China, Chinese version available at: http://www.cacs.gov.cn/news/newshow.aspx? str1 = 2&articleId = 38873, last visited September 18, 2011.

period or validity duration;

(4) Perishables or live commodities near the expiration of their guarantee period;

(5) Selling commodities at a reduced price for the purpose of clearing off debts, bankruptcy, change of business or suspension of operation.

"*Purpose for Dumping*" *Stated in* 50 *Antidumping Cases*

In examination of "intent to predation" under Criterion I, attention shall be paid mainly to two factors in those fifty antidumping cases, i. e. the statement of purpose for dumping as well as the exemption defense. Accoridng to the survey of this book, there existed no examination of the purpose of squeezing out other competitors or of sole occupancy of the market. Under the criterion of antidumping rules, the exemption defense mainly focused on the existence of injury as well as the causation between dumping and injury, whereas the reasons for dumping were seldom claimed, let alone using them for exemption.

Only in eight cases the reasons for dumping have been stated:

In the No. 6 Dichloromethne Case, it stated that the purpose for the large increasing low-price import of Dichloromethne is the market shrivel in those exporting countries due to the forbidden usage by laws; [1]

In the No. 13 Coated Art Paper Case, the defendants attempted to defense themselves by claiming that the main reason for dumping is to maintain their market share with the increasingly expanding domestic

---

[1] The No. 6 Dichloromethne (or Methylenechloride) Case, Public Announcement No. 20 in 2002 of Ministry of Foreign Trade and Economic Cooperation of the People's Republic of China, Chinese version available at: http://www.cofortune.com.cn/moftec_cn/dwmygl/jckspgl_63.html, last visited September 18, 2011.

industry, so their dumping is trying to meet the competition and totally reasonable;❶

In the No. 24 Dispersion Unshifted Single-Mode Optical Fiber Case, it explained that the purpose for the large increasing low-price import is due to the overproduction in those exporting countries;❷

In the No. 27 Hydrazine Hydrate Case, it mentioned that the purpose for the large increasing low-price import is due to the industry shift of the lower products to China;❸

In the No. 37 Polybutylene Terephthalate Resin Case, the purpose for dumping was due to the overproduction in those exporting countries;❹

In the No. 38 Wear Resistant Overlay Case, the reason for dumping was the overproduction in those exporting countries due to the

---

❶ The No. 13 Coated Art Paper Case, Public Announcement No. 35 in 2003 of Ministry of Commerce of the People's Republic of China, Chinese version available at: http://www.cacs.gov.cn/cacs/news/newshow.aspx? strl = 2&articleld = 38855, last visited September 18, 2011.

❷ The No. 24 Dispersion Unshifted Single-Mode Optical Fiber Case, Public Announcement No. 96 in 2004 of Ministry of Commerce of the People's Republic of China, Chinese version available at: http://www.cacs.gov.cn/news/newshow.aspx? strl = 2&articleld = 38870, last visited September 18, 2011.

❸ The No. 27 Hydrazine Hydrate Case, Public Announcement No. 36 in 2005 of Ministry of Foreign Trade and Economic Cooperation of the People's Republic of China, Chinese version available at: http://www.cacs.gov.cn/news/newshow.aspx? strl = 2&articleld = 38874, last visited September 18, 2011.

❹ The No. 37 Polybutylene Terephthalate Resin Case, Public Announcement No. 42 in 2006 of Ministry of Commerce of the People's Republic of China, Chinese version available at: http://www.cacs.gov.cn/news/newshow.aspx? strl = 2&articleld = 38889, last visited September 18, 2011.

substitution of wear resistant overlay by other materials. [1] Similar reason was also provided in both the No. 42 Potato Starch Case and the No. 47 Acetone Case. [2]

Consequently, there are two chief kinds of alleged reasons. One is the overproduction, either due to the forbidden usage, or the substitution or any other accounts; the other one is to enter a new market, like the industry shift.

"Intent to Predation" v. "Purpose for Dumping"

Combined the above alleged reasons with the five types of exemptions, it can be seen that unless the overproduction could be further proved and attributed to either sell those commodities that are kept too long in stock, or aimed at clearing off debts, bankruptcy, change of business or suspension of operation, none of those reasons could be exempted under Criterion I of Chinese competition rules. Moreover, taking the characteristics of targeted products and relevant information avaiable into consideration, it is deduced that the five kinds of exemptions could hardly happen in those antidumping cases.

Accordingly, through applying Criterion I under the Chinese competition rules to those antidumping cases, as well as based on the current available information of antidumping cases, it is concluded that on the premise that in all of the fifty antidumping cases prices were

---

[1] The No. 38 Wear Resistant Overlay Case, Public Announcement No. 93 in 2006 of Ministry of Foreign Trade and Economic Cooperation of the People's Republic of China, Chinese version available at: http://www.cacs.gov.cn/news/newshow.aspx? strl = 2&articleId = 38891, last visited September 18, 2011.

[2] The No. 42 Potato Starch Case, Public Announcement No. 8 in 2007 of Ministry of Commerce of the People's Republic of China, Chinese version available at: http://www.cacs.gov.cn/news/newshow.aspx? strl = 2&articleId = 38893, last visited September 18, 2011.

below cost, there could be no other reasons for exempting from condemnation.

6. 4. 4. 3 "Market Power" under Criterion II [1]

"Market Share" Test

This part shall continue to put the fifty antidumping cases under Criterion II of Chinese competition rules. It intends to conduct an empirical study of China by testing one specific factor, i. e. market share. Applying a "market share" test means to focus on market power, the primary element in the determination of predatory pricing. The essential idea behind this is the consistency with the methodology applied by most scholars. For instance, in her empirical study of antidumping cases in the U. S., Shin focused on the first element (market power) instead of the complicated cost calculation. A cost-based approach to determine the outcome of antidumping investigations was discarded because it did seem to be a practical and implementable strategy. A more readily administrable test for harmful dumping is one that searches the market for structural characteristics that should exist for predation to be a profitable strategy in the long run. [2] Only if these structural characteristics are found to exist should more complicated calculations be made. [3]

Based on this approach, in Shin's studies, first of all, those

---

[1] 本部分内容的主体已发表, Biying, *the Application of a "Market Share" Test to Antidumping Cases in China – Seeking a New Development Model via the Interaction of Trade and Competition*, Manchester Journal of International Economic Law 2011, Vol. 8, pp. 36 – 56.

[2] Hyun Ja Shin, Possible Instances of Predatory Pricing in Recent U. S. Antidumping Cases, in Robert Z. Lawrence, ed., Brookings Trade Forum, Brookings Institution Press, 1998, p. 84.

[3] *Ibid.*, p. 85.

antidumping cases that were simultaneously applied to the exports of several countries could easily be eliminated.❶ This is because, if there are multiple exporters from a single country or exporters from several countries, successful coordination both in bearing the initial losses during the predatory period and in the later recoupment of these losses becomes increasingly difficult in a market where they would all be active.❷ Secondly, after the elimination of the cases under the above circumstances, the concentration of the market and the industries was examined in the remaining antidumping cases.❸ Through completing these steps, Shin then draws conclusions on the possibility of predatory pricing in antidumping cases of the U.S. during a certain period.❹ This kind of test is quite popular and was followed by Messerlin and the other aforementioned scholars in conducting similar studies with respect to other countries.

After having decided to focus on market power to conduct a similar study as Shin's, the next important issue is what kind of specific test should be applied to make it feasible, as there are many factors in evaluating market power. In Shin's empirical study, the Herfindahl index, developed in economics, was applied to examine the market concentration of the U.S. as well as the foreign seller concentration.❺ By contrast, given the specific context of China, it is decided

---

❶ Hyun Ja Shin, Possible Instances of Predatory Pricing in Recent U.S. Antidumping Cases, in Robert Z. Lawrence, ed., Brookings Trade Forum, Brookings Institution Press, 1998, p. 86.

❷ *Ibid.*, pp. 86 – 87.

❸ *Ibid.*, pp. 87 – 89.

❹ *Ibid.*, pp. 94 – 97.

❺ *Ibid.*, pp. 87 – 89.

to introduce apply a "market share" test.

In almost all of the major countries, market share plays an important role in the assessment of market power. [1] More importantly, as shall be further analyzed in the immediately following section, the newly-enacted Chinese Antimonopoly Law even empowers the competition authorities to apply certain presumptions based on market share to determine that a company has dominant market power. For all of

---

[1] Once the relevant product and geographic markets are determined, market share of the firm or firms under review or investigation is determined. Whether a firm enjoys a dominant position in a relevant market depends on its share of that market. Market share, coupled with the ease or difficulty of entry into a market, is used as a surrogate for determining a firm's monopoly power.

In the EU, a 50 percent and sometimes 40 percent market share translates into dominance, especially if the next largest firms lags far behind. The EU takes the view that a dominant position can generally exist when a firm has a market share of 40 – 45 percent, although dominance may exist even if the market share is 20 – 40 percent.

The U. S., unlike the EU, measures market power and its possible increase microeconomically by considering the relevant factor in the specific context. The supreme court has held, however, that monopoly power could be inferred from a market share of 80 percent. Where barriers to market entry are high, other courts have required less market share for a finding of monopoly power. In the U. S., courts consistently find that a market share of less than 70 percent is insufficient to establish dominance, and that a market share of less than 40 percent virtually precludes a finding of monopoly.

In Canada, in the context of a predatory pricing investigation, the Predatory pricing enforcement guidelines issued by the Director of investigation and research in 1992 note that "it is unlikely that an alleged predatory with a market share of less than 35% would have the ability to unilaterally affect pricing." Pursuant to the PPEG, the first step in a predatory pricing claim is to define the relevant product and geographic market. However, it has been observed that: "the PPEG are only guidelines that are not binding on courts. Consequently [sic], the Canadian definition of ... markets in judicially considered predatory pricing cases may not be clearer than in the U. S."

See Kevin C Kennedy, *Competition Law and the World Trade Organization: the Limits of Multilateralism*, London: Sweet & Maxwell, 2001, pp. 229 – 230.

the above reasons, this part decides to apply a "market share" test to China, to examine how many antidumping cases would also be considered as possibly unlawful under competition law, in terms of possessing a dominant market power as necessary precondition for successful predatory practices.

"Market Share" Requirements under the Chinese Antimonopoly Law

The conduct of low-price sale, i. e. predatory pricing, is prohibited under Article 17 (2) of Chinese Antimonopoly Law, where it is defined as one of the instances of the anti-competitive conduct "Abuse of a Dominant Market Position". [1] In this part, the specific competition requirements under the new antimonopoly law shall be applied to

---

[1] According to Chinese Antimonopoly Law, Article 17 (2): Undertakings holding dominant market positions are prohibited from doing the following by abusing their dominant market positions: ... ② without justifiable reasons, selling commodities at prices below cost; ...英文译本出自中华人民共和国全国人民代表大会网站(英文版), http://www.npc.gov.cn/englishnpc/Law/2009 - 02/20/content_1471587.htm, last visited September 18, 2011.

examine antidumping cases. ❶

❶ Actually in China, the low-price sale issue is also addressed in the previous competition rules, including Chinese Unfair Competition Law 1993 and Chinese Price Law 1997. In the Chinese Unfair Competition Law 1993, Article 11: A business operator shall not, for the purpose of pushing out their competitors, sell their commodities at prices lower than costs. Any of the following shall not be deemed as an unfair competition act: (1) selling perishables or live commodities; (2) disposing of commodities near expiration of their validity duration or those kept too long in stock; (3) seasonal sales; or (4) selling commodities at a reduced price for the purpose of clearing off debts, change of business or suspension of operation. 英文译本出自中华人民共和国全国人民代表大会网站(英文版), http://www.npc.gov.cn/englishnpc/Law/2007-12/12/content_1383803.htm, last visited September 18, 2011.

Besides, Chinese Price Law, Article 14 (2) also stipulates that: The manager may not commit any of the following illegitimate acts in pricing: disposing of perishable, seasonal and overstocked commodities at reduced prices according to law, dumping commodities at prices lower than production cost in order to drive out rivals or monopolize the market, thus disrupting normal production and operational order and impairing the interests of the State or the lawful rights and interests of other managers; 英文译本出自中华人民共和国全国人民代表大会网站(英文版), http://www.npc.gov.cn/englishnpc/Law/2007-12/11/content_1383577.htm, last visited September 18, 2011.

According to relevant Chinese officers, with the enactment of Chinese Antimonopoly Law, the relevant amendments towards harmonizing Chinese Unfair Competition Law and Chinese Antimonopoly Law have been carried on, and the basic principle of the amendments is to delete all of the overlap parts in the previous Chinese Unfair Competition Law. However, as to the overlap issue of predatory pricing, up till now, there still lacks a common understanding. *See* Email from Ma Zhengping, Office Worker, *the Commission for Legal Affairs under the Standing Committee of the National People's Congress*, to Bi Ying, LL. D. Candidate, *Kyushu University* (Apr 24, 2008) (on file with the author) In terms of this issue, there are two groups of opinions in China. One group is of the opinion that as predatory dumping can be taken as either an unfair competition conduct or a restraining competition conduct, it has been regulated in both laws. 参见王晓晔:"反垄断法与反不正当竞争法的异同",新浪博客, http://blog.sina.com.cn/s/blog_4da7948501000kmw.html, last visited September 11, 2011. The other group is of the opinion that, with the enactment of Chinese Antimonopoly Law, such conducts as administrative monopoly, predatory dumping and so on should be regulated only under the antimonopoly law other than unfair competition law. 参见黄勇:"反垄断法出台法律定位与法律协调决定成败",载《法制日报》2007年9月2日,第012版, http://www.legaldaily.com.cn/0705/2007-09/02/content_692323.htm, last visited September 18, 2011.

In this paper, from the perspective of the basic principle of the harmonization work, as well as the consistency with the usual practice of most of the other countries, it is decided to only focus on predatory pricing under the new Chinese Antimonopoly Law.

To be more concrete, in terms of the assessment of a dominant market position, As aforementioned, Chinese Antimonopoly Law provides two methods. One is set forth in Article 18, which is an overall examination of dominant market position by taking market share, competition situation, ability to control the sales market and other factors into consideration.❶ Moreover, in order to save enforcement costs and to exercise an efficient supervision, Article 19 of the Chinese Antimonopoly Law, recognizing the important role of market share and referring to the experiences of Germany and Korea, provides a way to presume a dominant market position on the basis of the relevant market share.❷ According to Article 19(1), a business operator may be presumed to have a dominant market position in cases where:

---

❶ Chinese Antimonopoly Law, Article 18: The dominant market position of an undertaking shall be determined on the basis of the following factors: (1) its share on a relevant market and the competitiveness on the market; (2) its ability to control the sales market or the purchasing marker for raw and semi-finished materials; (3) its financial strength and technical conditions; (4) the extent to which other business mangers depend on it in transactions ; (5) the difficulty that other undertakings find in entering a relevant market; and (6) other factors related to the determination of the dominant market position held by an undertaking. 英文译本出自中华人民共和国全国人民代表大会网站(英文版), http://www.npc.gov.cn/englishnpc/Law/2009 - 02/20/content_1471587.htm, last visited September 18, 2011.

❷ Both Korea and Germany apply the similar presumptive method, with the only difference in the specific market share. In order to save the cost to enforce the law as well as to executive an effective supervision over undertakings, China also applies the similar presumptive method, as in Article 19. As long as the undertaking has reached the regulated market share, the relevant administrative authority can conjecture its dominant position, since market share is a very important factor in judging the dominant position. Both the U.S. and the EU have the requirements similar to Article 18, but they do not have the same presumptive method as provided in Article 19. 参见安建主编、全国人民代表大会常务委员会法制工作委员会编:《中华人民共和国反垄断法释义》,法律出版社 2007 年版,第 184 ~ 185 页。

(1) The relevant market share of one undertaking accounts for 1/2 or above;

(2) The joint relevant market share of two undertakings accounts for 2/3 or above;

(3) The joint relevant market share of three undertakings accounts for 3/4 or above. [1]

In light of the above prerequisites, particular attention should be paid to two essential indices in applying a "market share" test to anti-dumping cases. They are:

(1) The number of targeted exporters from targeted countries (how many have registered after filing the case, and/or have submitted required documents). In line with Shin's approach, our focus shall be on those cases involving not more than three exporters. In other words, antidumping cases that deal with more than three countries, or less than three countries but involving more than three exporters, will be taken out of further examination.

(2) The relevant market share of targeted exporters and, in particular, whether it exceeds 1/2, 2/3 or 3/4 under each circumstance. This allows us to identify dumping cases that may also be deemed to be harmful under competition law.

For convenience of discussion in the following part, the fifty anti-dumping cases (1997 – 2010) shall be divided into two groups according to the number of targeted countries. Group I refers to those cases that involve two or more targeted countries, whereas Group II refers to those cases involving only one targeted country. Before moving to the discussion, three limitations need to be mentioned. First,

---

[1] *See* Chinese Antimonopoly Law, Article 19.

it is not the intention to clearly define "market" and check relevant market share in each particular case. In this study, "market" refers to the whole importing country (domestic market of China). Secondly, in cases where there is lack of data or information, the number of exporters shall be presumed to be zero. Lastly, no further investigation shall be conducted into the cases set forth in Article19 (2), which provides that "Under the circumstance specified in Subparagraph (2) or (3) of the preceding paragraph, if the market share of one of the undertakings is less than one-tenths of the total, the undertakings shall not be considered to have a dominant market position."❶

Antidumping Cases Involving Two or More Targeted Countries

Group I shall be dealt with first. Forty out of the fifty antidumping cases involve two or more countries or areas. Among them, thirty-two cases deal with four or more exporters from two or more countries or areas and hence shall be eliminated. The remaining eight cases, which may either deal with two or three exporters from two countries or areas, or three exporters from three countries or area, will be subject to further examination. The eight cases are:

(1) The No. 8 L-Lysine Monohydrochlouide Case.❷

---

❶ 英文译本出自中华人民共和国全国人民代表大会网站(英文版), http://www.npc.gov.cn/englishnpc/Law/2009-02/20/content_1471587.htm, last visited September 18, 2011.

❷ The No. 8 L-Lysine monohydrochlouide Case, Public Announcement No. 23 in 2002 of Ministry of Foreign Trade and Economic Cooperation of the People's Republic of China, Chinese version available at: http://china.findlaw.cn/fagui/jj/27/157859.html, last visited September 18, 2011.

(2) The No. 29 Trichloroethylene from Russia and Japan. ❶

(3) The No. 32 Benzofuranol from Japan, the EU and the U. S.. ❷

(4) The No. 33 Disodium 5'-Inosinate from Japan and Korea. ❸

(5) The No. 36 Catechol from the U. S. and Japan. ❹

(6) The No. 37 Polybutylene Terephthalate Resin from Japan and Taiwan Area. ❺

(7) The No. 38 Wear Resistant Overlay from the U. S. and the EU. ❻

---

❶ The No. 29 Trichloroethylene case, Public Announcement No. 37 in 2005 of Ministry of Foreign Trade and Economic Cooperation of the People's Republic of China, Chinese version available at: http://www. cacs. gov. cn/news/newshow. aspx? strl = 2&articleld = 38875, last visited September 18, 2011.

❷ The No. 32 Benzofuranol case, Public Announcement No. 7 in 2006 of Ministry of Commerce of the People's Republic of China, Chinese version available at: http://www. cacs. gov. cn/news/newshow. aspx? strl = 2&articleld = 38884, last visited September 18, 2011.

❸ The No. 33 Disodium 5'-Inosinate Case, Public Announcement No. 24 in 2006 of Ministry of Foreign Trade and Economic Cooperation of the People's Republic of China, Chinese version available at: http://www. cacs. gov. cn/news/newshow. aspx?strl = 2&articleld = 38885, last visited September 18, 2011.

❹ The No. 36 Catechol Case, Public Announcement No. 32 in 2006 of Ministry of Commerce of the People's Republic of China, Chinese version available at: http://www. cacs. gov. cn/news/newshow. aspx?strl = 2&articleld = 38886, last visited September 18, 2011.

❺ The No. 37 Polybutylene Terephthalate Resin Case, Public Announcement No. 42 in 2006 of Ministry of Commerce of the People's Republic of China, Chinese version available at: http://www. cacs. gov. cn/news/newshow. aspx? strl = 2&articleld = 38889, last visited September 18, 2011.

❻ The No. 38 Wear Resistant Overlay Case, Public Announcement No. 93 in 2006 of Ministry of Foreign Trade and Economic Cooperation of the People's Republic of China, Chinese version available at: http://www. cacs. gov. cn/news/newshow. aspx?strl = 2&articleld = 38891, last visited September 18, 2011.

(8) The No. 41 Nonyl Phenol from India and Taiwan Area. ❶

As to the number of exporters, there are three targeted exporters in six cases (No. 8, 32, 33, 37, 38 and 41❷). As to the remaining two cases (No. 29 and 36), although both of them involve two countries (Japan and Russian in No. 29; Japan and the U. S. in No. 36), there were no exporters from Japan to either register or submit any document. Hence in this study, the number of exporters in the

---

❶ The No. 41 Nonyl Phenol Case, Public Announcement No. 11 in 2007 of Ministry of Commerce of the People's Republic of China, Chinese version available at: http://www.cacs.gov.cn/news/newshow.aspx? strl = 2&articleId = 38894, last visited September 18, 2011.

❷ The No. 8 L-Lysine Monohydrochlouide Case is dealing with three countries, including the U. S., Korea, and Indonesia, it is determined as no injury and there is no information about market share in the preliminary decision. The market share information of the No. 8 case as follows refers to the statistics. 参见李银雁:"中国入世首起反倾销案惊心动魄",载《价格辑刊》2002 年第 3 期,第 35 ~36 页。

In the final decision of the No 38 Wear Resistant Overlay Case, it only mentioned about the changes of market share without pointing out the exact statistics. Besides, there are also no other information sources concerning this point. Due to lack of information on the market share, further examination cannot be done to the No. 38 Wear Resistant Overlay Case.

above two cases shall be presumed as one.[1] To sum up, the eight cases can be divided into two categories: the No. 29 Case and the No. 36 Case, dealing with one exporter shall be subordinated to Article 19(1), Term 1, to see whether "the relevant market share of one business operator accounts for 1/2 or above", whereas the remaining

---

[1] The general information about the number of registered as well as that of submitted exporters within the 8 cases are as follows:

In the No. 8 Case, L-Lysine Monohydrochlouide from the U. S., Korea, and Indonesia:

- Register: 3 - Submit: 3

In the No. 29 Case, Trichloroethylene from Russia and Japan:

- Register: 1 from Russia ("Usoliekhimprom" LLC); 0 from Japan
- Submit: 1 from Russia ("Usoliekhimprom" LLC)

In the No. 32 Case, Benzofuranol from Japan, the EU and the U. S.:

- Register: 1 from Japan (Nichino Co.); 1 from the EU (Borregaard Italia SpA); 1 from the U. S. (FMC Corporation)
- Submit: 1 from the U. S. (FMC Corporation)

In the No. 33 Case, Disodium 5'-Inosinate from Japan and Korea:

- Register: 1 from Japan (Ajinomoto Co.), 2 from Korea (Daesang Co. and CJ Co.)
- Submit: 1 from Korea (Daesang Co.)

In the No. 36 Case, Catechol from the U. S. and Japan:

- Register: 1 from the U. S. (Rhodia Inc.); 0 from Japan
- Submit: 1 from the U. S. (Rhodia Inc.)

In the No. 37 Case, Polybutylene Terephthalate Resin from Japan and Taiwan Area:

- Register: 2 from Japan (Mitsubishi Chemical Corporation and GE Plastics Japan Ltd.); 1 from Taiwan Area (Chang Chun Plastics Co., Ltd)
- Submit: 1 from Taiwan Area (Chang Chun Plastics Co., Ltd)

In the No. 38 Case, Wear Resistant Overlay from the U. S. and the EU:

- Register: 1 from the U. S. (MW Custom Papers LLC), 2 from the EU (Papierfabrik Schoeller & Hoesch GmbH & Co KG and Papeteries de Mauduit Mill)
- Submit: 1 from the U. S. (MW Custom Papers LLC), 1 from the EU (Papierfabrik Schoeller & Hoesch GmbH & Co KG

In the No. 41 Case, Nonyl Phenol from India and Taiwan Area:

- Register: 1 from India (Schenectady Herdillia Limited), 2 from Taiwan Area
- Submit: ditto

four cases involving three exporters will be examined under Article 19 (1), Term 3, to see whether "the joint relevant market share of three business operator accounts for 3/4 or above".

Table The following step is to further examine the market share in each of the eight cases.

Table 4 The Application of the "Market Share" Test to Antidumping case (1)

Exporter	Case	Market Share					
1	No. 29	Year	1999	2000	2001	2002	2003
		Data[1]	24.61	42.23	50.05	47.15	53.85
	No. 36	Year	2001	2002	2003	2004	
		Data	1.09	9.19	48.2	49.39	
3	No. 8	Year	2000				
		Data	63				
	No. 32	Year	2001	2004			
		Data	64.43	84.21			
	No. 33	Year	2002	2003	2004		
		Data	46	61	64		
	No. 37	Year	2001	2004			
		Data	26.78	45.12			
	No. 38	Lack of Data					
	No. 41	Year	2002	2005			
		Data	27.68	49.67			

According to the above statistics, in No. 29 Trichloroethylene case, the market share of 2003 reached 53.85%, which is above

[1] Data (%).

1/2. In the No. 32 Benzofuranol Case, the total market share is increased from 64.43% in 2001 to 84.21% in 2004, which exceeded the requirement of 3/4. Therefore, in the investigation of the cases involving two or more countries, setting aside one case for lack of data (No. 38), only two cases present a risk of market monopolization or anticompetitive effects and thus seem suitable for further investigation.

Antidumping Cases Involving Only One Targeted Country

This part will examine Group II. Ten out of the fifty antidumping cases deal products from one single country or area. Five out of ten cases, involving four or more targeted exporters, are ruled out. ❶ Only the remaining five cases need further examination, including:

(1) The No. 2 Cold-rolled Steel Plate from Russia. ❷

(2) The No. 14 Catechol from the EU. ❸

---

❶ The general information about the number of registered as well as that of submitted exporters within the 10 cases are as follows: It deals with 2 registered and submitted exporters in the No. 2 Cold-rolled Steel Plate Case, the No. 14 Catechol Case, the No. 43 Paper for Electrolytic Capacitor Case, and the No. 44 Sulfamethoxazole Case; It deals with 3 registered and submitted exporters in No. 42 Potato Starch Case; It deals with 7 registered but only 4 submitted exporters in No. 3 Polyester Films Case, 5 registered and submitted exporters in No. 9 Staple Fiber Case, 7 submitted exporters in No. 10 Glycol-modified PET Case, 15 registered but 9 submitted exporters in No. 25 Nylon 6.66 Case, 58 registered but only 1 submitted exporter in No. 49 Certain Iron or Steel Fasteners Case.

❷ The No. 2 Cold-rolled steel plate Case, Public Announcement No. 8 in 2000 of Ministry of Foreign Trade and Economic Cooperation of the People's Republic of China, Chinese version available at: http://www.cacs.gov.cn/news/newshow.aspx? strl = 2&articleId = 38842, last visited September 18, 2011.

❸ The No. 14 Catechol Case, Public Announcement No. 41 in 2003 of Ministry of Commerce of the People's Republic of China, Chinese version available at: http://www.cacs.gov.cn/news/newshow.aspx? strl = 2&articleId = 38856, last visited September 18, 2011.

(3) The No. 42 Potato Starch from the EU. ❶

(4) The No. 43 Paper for Electrolytic Capacitor from Japan. ❷

(5) The No. 44 Sulfamethoxazole from India. ❸

With regard to the number of exporters, special attention needs to be given to the No. 44 Sulfamethoxazole Case. Although two Indian exporters are involved in this case, i. e. Virchow Laboratories Limited and Andhra Organics Limited, the two companies held shares in each other during the investigation. The board of directors was almost identical, and the affiliation was close enough to influence and control the sale as well as the price of the products. ❹ Hence the two companies are considered together as one exporter.

To sum up, the five cases can be divided into three categories: the No. 44 Sulfamethoxazole Case which is deemed to involve only one exporter, shall be subordinated to Article 19(1), Term 1, to examine whether "the relevant market share of one business operator accounts forl/2 or above"; The No. 2 Cold-rolled Steel Plate Case, the No. 14 Catechol Case and the No. 43 Paper for Electrolytic Capacitor Case,

---

❶ The No. 42 Potato Starch Case, Public Announcement No. 8 in 2007 of Ministry of Commerce of the People's Republic of China, Chinese version available at: http://www.cacs.gov.cn/news/newshow.aspx? strl = 2&articleld = 38893, last visited September 18, 2011.

❷ The No. 43 paper for Electrolytic Capacitor Case, Public Announcement No. 30 in 2007 of Ministry of Commerce of the People's Republic of China, Chinese version available at: http://www.cacs.gov.cn/cacs/news/newshow.aspx? strl = 2&articleld = 38895, last visited September 18, 2011.

❸ The No. 44 Sulfamethoxazole Case, Public Announcement No. 48 in 2007 of Ministry of Commerce of the People's Republic of China, Chinese version available at: http://www.cacs.gov.cn/news/newshow.aspx? strl = 2&articleld = 38896, last visited September 18, 2011.

❹ *Ibid.*

which involve two exporters, shall be examined under Article 19(1), Term 2, to assess whether "the relevant market share of one business operator accounts for 2/3 or above"; The No. 42 Potato Starch Case will be submitted to Article 19(1), Term 3, to determine whether "the relevant market share of one business operator accounts for 3/4 or above".

Table The following step is to further examine the market share in each of the five cases.

Table 5 The Application of the "Market Share" Test to Antidumping Case(2)

<table>
<tr><th>Exporter</th><th>Case</th><th colspan="5">Market Share</th></tr>
<tr><td rowspan="2">1</td><td rowspan="2">No. 44</td><td>Year</td><td>2002</td><td>2003</td><td>2004</td><td>2005</td></tr>
<tr><td>Data❶</td><td>16. 85</td><td>23. 26</td><td>37. 85</td><td>57. 53</td></tr>
<tr><td rowspan="5">2</td><td rowspan="2">No. 2</td><td>Year</td><td>1995</td><td>1996</td><td colspan="2">1998</td></tr>
<tr><td>Data</td><td>41</td><td>33. 4</td><td colspan="2">31. 8</td></tr>
<tr><td rowspan="2">No. 14</td><td>Year</td><td>1999</td><td>2000</td><td colspan="2">2001</td></tr>
<tr><td>Data</td><td>75. 98</td><td>80. 19</td><td colspan="2">91. 90</td></tr>
<tr><td>No. 43</td><td>Data</td><td colspan="4">Around 20</td></tr>
<tr><td rowspan="2">3</td><td rowspan="2">No. 42</td><td>Year</td><td>2002</td><td>2003</td><td>2004</td><td>2005</td></tr>
<tr><td>Data</td><td>26. 54</td><td>28. 71</td><td>17. 63</td><td>39. 01</td></tr>
</table>

According to the statistics above, in the No. 44 Sulfamethoxazole Case, the market share of the affiliated two exporters, Virchow Laboratories Limited and Andhra Organics Limited, reached 57. 53% in 2005, which indicates that the two affiliated exporters as a whole can be presumed to have a dominant market position under Term 1. In the

❶ Data (%).

No. 14 Catechol Case, the total market share of the two exporters, i. e. Rhodia Organique SAS Borregaard and Italia SpA, is 75. 98% in 1999, 80. 19% in 2000 and 91. 90% in 2001, which exceeds 2/3. This indicates that the two exporters can be assumed as having a dominant market position under Term 2. Therefore, in the analysis of the cases involving only one country, only two cases can be considered as having the possibilities of abusing a dominant position through low-price selling.

By applying a "market share" test to antidumping cases in China, this part extended the current empirical research, which directly applies competition standards to antidumping cases to one more significant country which has not yet been analyzed. The results indicate that, of all the antidumping cases that have been initiated and in which a final decision was rendered during 1997 to 2010, there are only four out of the fifty (8%) antidumping cases, including the No. 14 Catechol Case, the No. 29 Trichloroethylene case, the No. 32 Benzofuranol Case and the No. 44 Sulfamethoxazole Case, that are candidates for closer examination on predation grounds, and might also be considered as unlawful under Chinese Antimonopoly Law.

6. 4. 4. 4 Summary

According to the above examination, in applying the two sets of competition criterion concerning predatory pricing to those fifty antidumping cases in China, it is found that in terms of the price calculation, similar to most of the other countries, there would definitely be less harmful dumping cases if they were subject to competition rules in Chinese, either Criterion I or Criterion II. Notwithstanding, the difference lies in that the scope of condemnation under Criterion II is even narrower than that under Criterion I.

Through applying Criterion II to those antidumping cases, assuming that in all of the fifty antidumping cases prices were below cost, only 8% (4 out of the 50) might also be considered as harmful. The four cases include the No. 14 Catechol Case, the No. 29 Trichloroethylene case, the No. 32 Benzofuranol Case and the No. 44 Sulfamethoxazole Case. As to Criterion I, it is concluded that on the same premise as prices were below cost, no other reasons could be provided for further exemptions from condemnation. Nevertheless, the whole study result shows that similar to the other countries, the application of competition to antidumping cases could induce less protectionist abuse.

6. 4. 5 Difficulties of Substitution in China

6. 4. 5. 1 Two Strategic Purposes of Antidumping in China

The above section suggested that in China competition rules are basically qualified to be more appropriate than antidumping rules in detecting dumping without being abused by protectionists, even though Chinese Antimonopoly Law is newly published and more efforts need to be done to its perfection. However, in terms of the political reality, in China, antidumping policy is supposed to serve two strategic purposes, which stands out as the current difficulties of substituting it by competition. One is that antidumping is used as retaliation or a threat to prevent or reduce antidumping actions towards China. The other one is to protect infant chemical industries in China.

Purpose I: Prevention of Antidumping Actions towards China.

In fact, many countries had antidumping laws on their books for many years but did not apply them until recently. Bureaucratic limitations account in some countries, but a retaliatory motive is another worrying possibility. [1] An earlier formal test of this motive was provided by Pursa and Skeath (2000). They found some support for a retaliation motive for both traditional and new users of antidumping, and asserted that antidumping users are more likely to target other users of antidumping than those without such enforcement, and that countries are more likely to target exporting countries with a past history of bringing cases against them. Prusa and Skeath called it retaliation or tit-for-tat, meaning that an immediacy of response in order to use retaliation as a means of establishing credibility of threat, or as an effective tit-for-tat mechanism. [2]

Similarly, one of the main strategic purposes in China is to use antidumping as retaliation or a threat to prevent or reduce antidumping actions towards China. As is known to all that ever since the end of 1980s, China has become the number one target of antidumping actions in the world. This has greatly influenced the export of Chinese products. Correspondingly, in order to prevent the abuse of antidumping measures by foreign countries, relevant domestic industries called for the regulation of antidumping in China. [3]

---

[1] Ian Wooton & Maurizio Zanardi, *Trade and Competition Policy: Antidumping versus Anti-trust* , *University of Glasgrow and CEPR Dicussion Paper in Economics*, 2002, pp. 1, 7, http://homepages. strath. ac. uk/ ~ hbs03116/Research/Trade% 20and% 20Competition % 20Policy % 20Final. pdf , last visited May 24, 2009.

[2] *Ibid. See also* Robert M. Feinberg & Kara M. Reynolds, *the Spread of Antidumping Regimes and the Role of Retaliation in Filings*, 2004, pp. 1, 5, http://129. 3. 20. 41/eps/it/papers/0411/0411003. pdf, last visited September 18, 2011.

[3] 朱庆华:"中国反倾销十年",载《国际商报》2007 年 12 月 10 日, http://ibdaily. mofcom. gov. cn/show. asp? id = 175457, http://ibdaily. mofcom. gov. cn/show. asp? id = 175457, last visited September 18, 2011.

Purpose II: Protection of Infant Chemical Industries in China.

In addition to the retaliatory motive, the other chief strategic purpose to use antidumping in China is to protect domestic industries, especially those infant chemical industries. The text of law indicated that from Regulation 2002, antidumping is supposed to protect fair competitive process instead of competitors. However, in practice, this goal is not fulfilled, and antidumping continues to serve as a protective instrument to protect domestic industries.

As to the fifty cases, there are no significant differences in initiating, investigating, adjudicating between these twelve cases under Regulation 1997, and the later thiry-eight cases under Regulation 2002 and 2004. A further examination of the later thirty-eight cases suggested that more than 50% of them (18 out of 38) are purported to protect these infant chemical industries in China. ❶ These industries were still in its initial stages. The scale was relatively small, the technical competence was immature, and the market share was quite low. Correspondingly, in order to facilitate these infant chemical industries, antidumping actions were used to temporarily prevent the foreign competitors, and to gain more time for adjustment and developing chances for these domestic industries. ❷

6. 4. 5. 2 Incapable of Preventing from being Targeted

Retaliation is deemed to be an antidote to the use of antidumping in China and most of the other new heavy users. However, retaliation as an antidote works when large countries threaten small countries. Thus

---

❶ The No. of these cases are 13,14,16,18,19,21,23,24, 28,29, 30,31,34,35, 38,41,45,46.

❷ "'三吉利'反倾销的启示", 新浪财经, http://finance. sina. com. cn/roll/20051218/1123453278. shtml, last visited September 18, 2011.

it is not an option available to all countries. Also retaliation could lead to further proliferation of antidumping. [1] In terms of the practical application of antidumping in China, more than ten years' practice suggests that initiating antidumping measures itself cannot prevent from being targeted by other countries. China maintains the most targeted country in the world.

As introduced above, China enacted the first antidumping rules in 1994 and initiated the first antidumping case in 1997. According to the statistics of WTO, from the year 1995 to June of 2010, China was subject to antidumping measures in 563 cases, including 79 cases by the U. S., 68 by the EU, 105 by India, 53 by Argentina, 55 by Turkey, 18 by South Africa, 30 by Brazil, 16 by Mexico and so on. [2] And the case number per year is 26, 16, 33, 24, 21, 30, 32, 36, 40, 43, 41, 37, 48, 53, 55 and 25. [3] It can be seen from the above statistics that the number of being antidumped by foreign countries has greatly surpassed that in the other historical periods. Furthermore, it increases per year. This shows that initiating antidumping cannot prevent from being targeted by other countries and hence antidumping cannot achieve this strategic purpose for China.

6. 4. 5. 3 Incapable of Protecting Infant Industries

It is understandable that countries should give special consideration to

---

[1] J. Luis Guasch & Sarath Rajapatirana, *Antidumping and Competition Policies in Latin America and Caribbean: Total Strangers or Soul Mates?* 1998, pp. 1, 24, http://www.worldbank.org/html/dec/Publications/Workpapers/WPS1900series/wps1958/wps1958.pdf, last visited September 18, 2011.

[2] The most recent Statistics, *See* http://www.wto.org/english/tratop_e/adp_e/ad_meas_rep_exp_e.xls, last visited September 18, 2011.

[3] The most recent Statistics, *See* http://www.wto.org/english/tratop_e/adp_e/ad_meas_exp_country_e.pdf, last visited September 18, 2011.

certain industries in different stages of their economic development. However, as analyzed in Chapter V, antidumping is not designed or supposed to and thereby cannot act as a controllable protective instrument necessary to achieve free trade in the current multilateral world. Safeguard measure should take charge of the general, direct protection. And also, there is a specific protective measure current existing in GATT aimed at protecting infant industries, which should be the right answer instead of antidumping. Moreover, the effects of antidumping actions in China suggest that they result in many negative or reverse effects in practice. Antidumping cannot achieve a good protection of infant industries.

Direct Protection Measure for Infant Industries: Article 18 *of GATT*

As analyzed in the above chapters, antidumping is not designed to act as a protective instrument. Instead of such broad and indirect measure, a direct protective measure, which directly aims at these infant chemical industries and is in conformity with the basic principles of free trade and fair competition, should be the right answer. For instance, Article 18 of GATT, i. e. governmental assistance to economic development, points out one direct way to deal with infant industry.[1]

The essential idea of this article is to grant developing countries to modify or withdraw a concession included in the appropriate schedule annexed to this agreement[2], or take such measures as may be necessary to prevent, during that period, imports of the product or products concerned from increasing substantially above a normal level[3], in order

---

[1] GATT, Article 18, http://www.wto.org/english/docs_e/legal_e/gatt47_02_e.htm#articleXVIII, last visited May 10, 2009.

[2] *Ibid.* Section A.

[3] GATT, Section C. http://www.wto.org/english/docs_e/legal_e/gatt47_02_e.htm#articleXVIII, last visited May 10, 2009.

to promote the establishment of a particular industry with a view to raising the general standard of living of its people. This article has set up a series of specific substantive requirements as to the country, particular industry, the purpose.[1] Moreover, there are also relevant procedural requirements on negotiation, compensation, retaliation and

---

[1] *Ibid.* Article XVIII Governmental Assistance to Economic Development:

(1) The contracting parties recognize that the attainment of the objectives of this Agreement will be facilitated by the progressive development of their economies, particularly of those contracting parties the economies of which can only support low standards of living and are in the early stages of development.

(2) The contracting parties recognize further that it may be necessary for those contracting parties, in order to implement programmes and policies of economic development designed to raise the general standard of living of their people, to take protective or other measures affecting imports, and that such measures are justified in so far as they facilitate the attainment of the objectives of this Agreement. They agree, therefore, that those contracting parties should enjoy additional facilities to enable them (a) to maintain sufficient flexibility in their tariff structure to be able to grant the tariff protection required for the establishment of a particular industry and (b) to apply quantitative restrictions for balance of payments purposes in a manner which takes full account of the continued high level of demand for imports likely to be generated by their programmes of economic development.

(3) The contracting parties recognize finally that, with those additional facilities which are provided for in Sections A and B of this Article, the provisions of this Agreement would normally be sufficient to enable contracting parties to meet the requirements of their economic development. They agree, however, that there may be circumstances where no measure consistent with those provisions is practicable to permit a contracting party in the process of economic development to grant the governmental assistance required to promote the establishment of particular industries with a view to raising the general standard of living of its people. Special procedures are laid down in Sections C and D of this Article to deal with those cases.

(4) (a) Consequently, a contracting party, the economy of which can only support low standards of living and is in the early stages of development, shall be free to deviate temporarily from the provisions of the other Articles of this Agreement, as provided in Sections A, B and C of this Article. (b) A contracting party, the economy of which is in the process of development, but which does not come within the scope of subparagraph (a) above, may submit applications to the CONTRACTING PARTIES under Section D of this Article.

(5) The contracting parties recognize that the export earnings of contracting parties, the economies of which are of the type described in paragraph 4 (a) and (b) above and which depend on exports of a small number of primary commodities, may be seriously reduced by a decline in the sale of such commodities. Accordingly, when the exports of primary commodities by such a contracting party are seriously affected by measures taken by another contracting party, it may have resort to the consultation provisions of Article XXII of this Agreement.

(6) The CONTRACTING PARTIES shall review annually all measures applied pursuant to the provisions of Sections C and D of this Article.

so on.[1] Such measure is deemed to be a better and more efficient method to assist infant industries than the broad antidumping measure.

Negative Effects of "Protective" Antidumping Cases

Since antidumping is not supposed to act as a protective instrument, it cannot achieve a good protection of the infant industries in practice. Instead, it has brought about many negative or reverse effects. In China, the alleged positive effects of using antidumping to protect certain domestic industries mainly focus on the temporary, individual welfare, whereas the long-term, overall welfare of the whole country draws least attention.

On one hand, the assessment of the effects of antidumping actions is based on the temporary changes soon after antidumping actions. Hence, antidumping actions are considered to be quite effective, since it is very easy to find in most cases the price of the products involved has raised again, the import number of foreign products has greatly decreased, and the market share of domestic industries has

---

[1] *See*, e. g., Section A (b) If agreement is not reached within sixty days after the notification provided for in sub-paragraph (a) above, the contracting party which proposes to modify or withdraw the concession may refer the matter to the CONTRACTING PARTIES which shall promptly examine it. If they find that the contracting party which proposes to modify or withdraw the concession has made every effort to reach an agreement and that the compensatory adjustment offered by it is adequate, that contracting party shall be free to modify or withdraw the concession if, at the same time, it gives effect to the compensatory adjustment. If the CONTRACTING PARTIES do not find that the compensation offered by a contracting party proposing to modify or withdraw the concession is adequate, but find that it has made every reasonable effort to offer adequate compensation, that contracting party shall be free to proceed with such modification or withdrawal. If such action is taken, any other contracting party referred to in sub-paragraph (a) above shall be free to modify or withdraw substantially equivalent concessions initially negotiated with the contracting party which has taken the action. Similar requirements have also been stipulated in Section C.

become larger etc. [1]

On the other hand, such assessment shows great solicitude for the individual welfare of the relevant domestic industries whereas ignores other interested parties. The positive effects of antidumping actions are therefore concluded in that they have created a solid ground for recovery, and propelled the development of the injured industries. [2]

Notwithstanding, the changes of the above indexes are quite obvious soon after restricting the import of foreign products. To conclude antidumping is an efficient protective instrument merely based on such temporary statistics could not hold water. Instead, taken the long-term, overall welfare of the whole country into consideration, four aspects of negative effects of antidumping actions as protective instrument could be detected.

Negative Effect I: Transfer from Import to Direct Investment

The first aspect is that after being restrained by antidumping actions, the targeted foreign producers turned to direct investment, such as setting up solely foreign-owned enterprises or joint ventures, instead of exporting to China. [3] By conducting so, the foreign

---

[1] For example, a tracking investigation of 25 antidumping cases in 2005 has shown that in 17 cases, the imported quantity from the involved foreign countries have declined; in 16 cases, the import price has increased; in 11 cases, the overall prices has increased clearly. "我国实施贸易救济措施效果情况",中国贸易救济信息网, http://www.cacs.gov.cn/cacs/falv/falvshow.aspx? str1 = 4&articleId = 37847, last visited September 18, 2011.

[2] "我国实施贸易救济措施效果情况",中国贸易救济信息网, http://www.cacs.gov.cn/cacs/falv/falvshow.aspx? str1 = 4&articleId = 37847, last visited September 18, 2011; 夏延:"2004 年中国进口反倾销案件评析",载《时代经贸》2004 年第 12 期,第 55 ~ 56 页。

[3] 夏延:"2004 年中国进口反倾销案件评析",载《时代经贸》2004 年第 12 期,第 56 页。

competitors can not only avoid being imposed with antidumping duties, but also directly compete with the domestic industries for the sources and markets. ❶ This also results in rather intenser competition hence severely impairs the protective effects of antidumping actions.

For instance, in the Dispersion Unshifted Single - Mode Optical Fiber Case, the antidumping action was initiated in July, 2003. ❷ Samsung of Korea, one of the defendants, turned to set up Samsung Electronics Hainan Fiberoptics Co. Ltd. in March, 2004. According to relevant statistics, it reached the productive capacity in March, 2005, and the selling price was the lowest in China. Prior to the setup of the company, the domestic productive capacity is around three times that of domestic requirement. The competition became even fiercer afterwards. ❸

Taking the form of joint ventures to enter Chinese market is also quite common in Petrochemical Industry. ❹ For instance, a project of Acrylic Ester in Nanjing set up by BASF and SINOPEC started to produce since 2005, whose productive capacity was said to be equal to the total sum of domestic industry. Japanese Sanyo Chemical and Mitsubishi chemical planned to set up a project of polymers in Nantong,

---

❶ 夏延:"2004 年中国进口反倾销案件评析",载《时代经贸》2004 年第 12 期,第 56 页。

❷ The No. 24 Dispersion Unshifted Single - Mode Optical Fiber Case, Public Announcement No. 96 in 2004 of Ministry of Commerce of the People's Republic of China, Chinese version available at: http://www.cacs.gov.cn/news/newshow.aspx? strl = 2&articleId = 38870, last visited September 18, 2011.

❸ "我国实施贸易救济措施效果情况",中国贸易救济信息网, http://www.cacs.gov.cn/cacs/falv/falvshow.aspx? strl = 4&articleId = 37847, last visited September 18, 2011.

❹ *Ibid.*

which would give a huge impact on domestic industry. ❶ The similar transfer to direct investment was also found in paper manufacturing. ❷ The aformentioned cases suggest that antidumping actions cannot fulfill its protective role, due to its inducement of direct investment. It results in even more competition to domestic industries.

Negative Effect II: Transfer the Place of Origin or *Import from Other Countries*

The second aspect is reflected in that, since antidumping duties are imposed selectively, they cannot restrain the imports from all of the foreign countries. In order to avoid being targeted, foreign producers turn to transfer the place of origin. For those insufficient products, the import is still increased in large scale from other places afterwards. ❸

Regarding the transfer of origin place, Phenol is the case in point. ❹ From February, 2004, antidumping duties were imposed on those Phenols imported from Japan, Korea, the U. S., and Taiwan Area. According to the statistics of Chinese Customs, the import has decreased by 62. 3% from Japan and there are no imports from the U. S. and Korea since then. However, the place of origin has trans-

---

❶ "我国实施贸易救济措施效果情况"，中国贸易救济信息网，http://www.cacs.gov.cn/cacs/falv/falvshow.aspx? str1 = 4&articleId = 37847, last visited September 18, 2011.

❷ 马向敏、刘富利："进口反倾销对上下游产业的影响——基于我国造纸业的分析"，载《当代经济》2007 年第 12S 期，第 80 ~ 85 页。

❸ 夏延："2004 年中国进口反倾销案件评析"，载《时代经贸》2004 年第 12 期，第 58 页。

❹ The No. 20 Phenol Case, Public Announcement No. 2 in 2004 of Ministry of Commerce of the People's Republic of China, Chinese version available at: http://www.cacs.gov.cn/cacs/news/newshow.aspx? str1 =2&articleId =38864, last visited September 18, 2011.

ferred to Germany, the import amount of which reached 33.2% of the total sum.❶

This shift is caused either by the original foreign importers taking the form of assembles, or by new foreign importers taking this opportunity.❷ Antidumping actions have the effects of either transferring the place of origin to others not involved in antidumping duties, or transferring from those imposed with higher dumping margin to those with relatively lower dumping margin.❸ Consequently, it tends to benefit the foreign competitors in those countries that are not imposed with antidumping duties, rather than the domestic competitors.

Mentioning the insufficient products, Caprolactam is the case in point.❹ From June, 2003, antidumping duties were imposed on those Caprolactams from Japan, Belgium, Germany, Netherland, and Russia. Although the imports were restricted from the above countries, the imports from other countries, including Ukraine, Belarus, Mexico, Poland, and India and so on, increased rapidly due to the domestic insufficiency or incapability of producing Caprolactam. The general price of Caprolactam has also rainsed by 15.2%. In this

---

❶ 黄国华:"化工产品反倾销影响实录",载《精细与专用化学品》2004 年第 18 期,第 1 ~3 页。

❷ 夏延:"2004 年中国进口反倾销案件评析",载《时代经贸》2004 年第 12 期,第 56 页。

❸ *Ibid.*

❹ The No. 12 Caprolactam Case, Public Announcement No. 22 in 2003 of Ministry of Commerce of the People's Republic of China, Chinese version available at: http://www.cacs.gov.cn/news/newshow.aspx?strl = 2&articleId = 38854, last visited September 18, 2011.

case, Caprolactams have to be imported to meet domestic needs. ❶ As a consequence, antidumping actions add more cost to the whole country, rather than protecting domestic industries.

Negative Effect III: Disordered Competition within Domestic Competitors

The third aspect lies in the disordered competition within domestic competitors even after restricting the competition from foreign producers. Imposing antidumping duties temporarily brings about more opportunities to seek profits for domestic industries. However, the subsequent blind expansion would result in the increase of productive capacity exceeding that of actual requirement, where the selling price falls sharply hence the domestic industry is landed in dire straits again.

For instance, in the Polyester Films Case❷, soon after the imposition of antidumping duties, there were more than 20 domestic productive lines from the year 2003 to 2005, most of which were invested by new domestic investors. This has lead to a serious overproduction in 2005. ❸Similar situation happened to Glycol-modified

---

❶ 夏延:"2004 年中国进口反倾销案件评析",载《时代经贸》2004 年第 12 期,第 58 页。

❷ The No. 3 Polyester Films Case, Public Announcement No. 7 in 2000 of Ministry of Foreign Trade and Economic Cooperation of the People's Republic of China, Chinese version available at: http://www.cacs.gov.cn/news/newshow.aspx? strl = 2&articleId = 38843, last visited September 18, 2011.

❸ "我国实施贸易救济措施效果情况",中国贸易救济信息网, http://www.cacs.gov.cn/cacs/falv/falvshow.aspx? strl = 4&articleId = 37847, last visited September 18, 2011.

PET. ❶ Some of the enterprises got bogged down in the very difficult position. ❷ The above cases indicate that antidumping actions cannot ensure the development of domestic industries via preventing competition from foreign producers. The maintenance of a healthy competitive process rather than protecting certain competitors should be more effective for the whole welfare.

Negative Effect IV: Harm the Interests of Downstream Industries

The last but the most severe aspect is that the in China antidumping actions by upper-level producers have a great negative impact on those of the lower-level. As introduced above, one notable characteristic of Chinese antidumping cases is that intermediate chemical products have occupied an overwhelming majority of the products investigated. Therefore, the conflict between upper and lower producers is even intenser in China.

In cases where the upper-level products were protected under antidumping law, more costs will be burdened by the lower-level products, and more lower-level products will be imported as well. Correspondingly, it will bring about negative effects on the competitive capability of the lower-level products. Taken the long term, overall welfare of the country into consideration, the costs distributed to the lower-level producers, hence the final consumers in the long term, in

---

❶ The No. 10 Glycol-modified PET Case, Public Announcement No. 4 in 2003 of Ministry of Foreign Trade and Economic Cooperation of the People's Republic of China, Chinese version available at: http://www.cacs.gov.cn/news/newshow.aspx? str1 = 2&articleId = 1081, last visited September 18, 2011.

❷ "我国实施贸易救济措施效果情况", 中国贸易救济信息网, http://www.cacs.gov.cn/cacs/falv/falvshow.aspx? str1 = 4&articleId = 37847, last visited September 18, 2011.

effect exceed the benefits gained by upper-level producers in the short term. Ignoring all of the other interested parties, antidumping cannot measure up to a good protective instrument.

6.4.6 China and the "Substitution" Debate

Regarding China and the "substitution" debate, first of all, similar to the other new users, China adopts antidumping rules mainly in accordance with the requirements of WTO, and there is not much further examination to the justification of condemning dumping, let alone a specific discussion of substituting antidumping by competition. Nevertheless, compared with other countries, the closer linkage between the two can be indicated from the perspective of legislative goal as well as that of legal terminology. In current China, both antidumping and competition undertake the same goal of maintaining fair competition and the foreign trade in order to safeguard the healthy development of socialist market economy. In addition, as to the conduct of low-price selling, both antidumping and competition share the same legal terminology, i.e., dumping.

After confirming that Chinese antidumping rules are aimed to protect fair competition rather than protecting domestic competitors, an overall investigation of whether competition rules are better than antidumping rules in dealing with the conduct of low-price selling in China was conducted. A similar approach to the examination of traditional users in Chapter IV was applied to Chinese practice, to obseve it from three perspectives: comparing the basic elements of the two sets of rules on low-price selling, putting the two sets of rules against the background of modern free trade world to analyze their relationship with the basic trade and competition principles, as well as surveying the effects of antidumping cases.

Compared the basic elements of antidumping rules on dumping with competition rules on predatory price discrimination, including theoretical basis, basic substantive rules, basic procedural rules as well as remedies, it is found that Chinese competition rules are basically qualified to be more efficient than antidumping rules in addressing dumping without being abused for protectionists, though Chinese competition law needs to be improved still.

In addition, competition rules can also avoid much conflict with basic competition principles comparing with antidumping rules. In Chinese practice, antidumping actions involve serious conflict with the consumer welfare, and also tend to facilitate monopoly power in an increasing way.

Moreover, an empirical study has also been conducted by applying the two sets of competition criterion of predatory dumping to those fifty antidumping cases in China. The result showed that similar to most of the other countries in general, there would definitely be less harmful dumping cases if they were subject to competition rules in Chinese, either Criterion I or Criterion II.

Accordingly, in dealing with the conduct of low-price selling, even though Chinese Antimonopoly Law is newly published and more efforts need to be devoted to perfect it, current competition rules are basically qualified to be more appropriate than antidumping rules in detecting predatory dumping, without being abused by protectionists. In other words, Chinese practice also supports for the substitution.

Nevertheless, in terms of the realization of replacing antidumping by competition currently, there also exist political difficulties. In China, antidumping policy is expected to serve two strategic purposes.

One is as retaliation or a threat to prevent or reduce antidumping actions towards China, and the other is to protect domestic industries, especially those infant chemical industries in China. However, more than ten years' practice suggests that initiating antidumping measure cannot prevent from being antidumped, and China maintains to be the most targeted country in the world.

In addition, theoretically speaking, antidumping is not designed as a controllable protective instrument and therefore it is not captable of achieving free trade in the current multilateral world. Safeguard measure should take charge of the general, direct protection, and there is a specific protective measure current existing in GATT aimed at protecting infant industries specially. Such measures should be the right answer instead of antidumping. Practically speaking, the application of antidumping in China showed that it cannot achieve a good protection of the infant industries in practice. The alleged positive effects of antidumping actions merely focus on the temporary, individual welfare. From the perspective of long-term, overall welfare of the whole country, four main aspects of negative effects of antidumping actions as the protective instrument, i. e. transferring from import to direct investment, transferring the place of origin or import from other countries, still disordered competition within domestic competitors, as well as injuring the interests of downstream industries, can be detected.

In terms of the above political difficulties, this book is of the opinion that with the failure of antidumping fulfilling the two strategic purposes draws more attention, as well as the imporvenment of competition, China is likely to combine "domestic dumping" and "international dumping" together, devote itself into harmonizing national competition rules on predatory price discrimination, and join the camp calling for replacing antidumping by the international agreement on predatory price discrimination in near future.

There have been a few discussions among Chinese legal scholars on the substitution debate, and predictably it would spread to more profound research. The relationship between antidumping and competition has drawn an increasing attention in China ever since 2005. [1] Quite a few Chinese scholars favor that antidumping should be gradually revised and improved in accordance with competition policy. [2]

Accordingly, similar to the research in the other new users, the

---

[1] In China this issue has not been given much attention until the 2005 *Vitamin Case*. The general background is that in 2005, several vitamin companies of China were sued to the U. S. court by claiming that they are putting up the prices in the U. S. and therefore violate the antitrust law. This case was drawn much attention for two reasons, the first is that this is the first case that China has been sued by foreign counties as violating antitrust law, and the second reason, which is more important, is that, in 2001, the vitamin industry of China was sued by the U. S. as dumping, in order to avoid antidumping investigation, the export industry decided to raise the price all together, No wonder this has been taken as the evidence of monopoly and therefore violating antitrust law of the U. S. Similarly, another chemical industry of China has also being first "antidumping" then "antitrust". These cases are still on process. Correspondingly, In China before 2005, there are less than 10 papers discussing the relationship between antidumping law and competition law. However, ever since 2006, there are more and more discussions (around 20 papers) in China about the substitution issue.

[2] 王中美:《以反垄断法替代反倾销法的法律研究》,法律出版社2008年版;黄勇:"中国反垄断法:一部注重整体协调的法律",载《中国发展观察》2006年5月31日,http://www.chinado.cn/ReadNews.asp? NewsID = 613, last visited September 18, 2011;彭兴华:"评有关反倾销法的三种方案",载《武汉大学国际法评论》2003年第1期,第288~310页;邓纲:"刍议反倾销规则并入竞争法体系的几个问题",载《现代法学》2007年第5期,第122~127页;孙雯:"反倾销法与竞争法之冲突与协调",载《河北法学》2006年第1期,第53~57页;谢海霞:"从竞争法角度看反倾销法律制度",载《河北法学》2004年第3期,第61~64页;张瑞萍:"反倾销法的性质与演进之分析——从WTO竞争法设立的角度",载《当代法学》2006年第1期,第47~55页。

survey result of China also supports the substitution work in future and more efforts should be made towards the direction of replacing anti-dumping by competition.

Chapter VII Time to Reexamine Dumping: "Trust Antitrust to Dump Antidumping"

The debate of antidumping versus competition is a relatively new but very significant issue. Based on all of the above analysises and examinations from both traditional and new heavy users of antidumping, this book argues for putting the issue of dumping under competition rules instead of antidumping rules. The domestic antidumping rules and the WTO Antidumping Agreement should be finally substituted by the harmonized domestic competition rules and their basic standard, i. e. the international competition agreement on predatory price discrimination, all around the world in future.

The original and supposed goal of antidumping rules should be the same as that of competition rules. In economic theories, efficiency approach favored by most economists, suggests that dumping is one kind of transnational price discrimination, and only predatory dumping is generally recognized as harmful. As to antidumping law, a journey back to its birth time as well as the following evolvement indicate that, originally antidumping was actually part of antitrust law, to deal with the import price discrimination, and it is only for dealing with these foreign conducts more efficiently that antidumping rules were changed and gradually distinctive from antitrust rules. However, neither the change of special rules nor that of legal areas can be the evidence to question the original and supposed justification of antidumping.

In dealing with the same issue of predatory dumping or predatory price discrimination, modern antidumping rules and competition rules have different requirements. Modeled on the U. S. antidumping law, the WTO ADA has provided the basic requirements on dumping for domestic antidumping rules. As to modern competition rules, the investigation into the U. S. and the EU, two basic models followed by most of the other countries, identifies the common basic standard on predatory price discrimination.

Compared the basic elements on predatory dumping of antidumping rules with those on predatory price discrimination of competition rules, the first advantage of competition rules over antidumping rules is that compeititon rules are more meticulous than antidumping rules without being abused for protectionists. Competition rules, setting up the basic goal of protecting competitive process other than the individual competitors, towards the enhancement of consumer and producer welfare via greater economic efficiency, can redirect government policies away from the protection of domestic firms, take the overall welfare of the country into consideration, and hence are less vulnerable to be influenced by those with vested interests, less susceptible to protectionism. Moreover, competition rules are also more selective in their application and are more effective at distinguishing between fair and unfair trade practices. With comparatively clear objective and strict methodological guidelines, the enforcement authorities of competition rules have significantly less discretion. The remedies provided under competition rules, aiming at a prohibition of the practice with appropriate penalties if the offense continues, are also deemed to be more effective.

Putting the two rules against the whole framework of modern free trade world, the second advantage of competition rules over antidumping rules is that competition rules are more consistent with basic modern trade and competition principles, which are becoming more convergent in modern free trade world. Hence, competition rules can be less subject to traditional protectionist than antidumping rules. In terms of the modern trade policy, comparing with antidumping rules, competition rules can avoid seriously undermining the fundamental principles of GATT/WTO system, including free trade, non-discrimination, as well as reciprocity. In terms of the modern competition policy, competition rules can also refrain from conflicting with basic competition principles and therefore can avoid various anti-competitive effects in practice, including protecting competitive process in conformity to the economic efficiency, the maximization of the consumer welfare, avoiding facilitating the collusion between domestic and foreign producers, avoiding maintaining domestic monopoly power or form domestic cartels, and promoting market integration in bilateral and regional areas.

Apart from the above two aspects, the third advantage of competition rules over antidumping rules lies in the practical application. Antidumping rules and competition rules can and do sometimes jointly regulate the common area of international predatory price discrimination, and this overlapping area has been increasingly broadened with the internationalization of competition rules in the modern world. Various empirical studies, especially on the U. S. and the EU, have been achieved. All of them lead to a common conclusion that if competition rules were applied to the antidumping cases, there would be significantly less condemnable dumping, and the number of antidumping cases would be sharply decreased if competition standards were applied. In other words, based on comparatively solid economic theories, devoting a lot to the sophisticated operation of detecting harmful low-price selling, as well as conforming to the basic trade and competition principles, competition rules can practically avoid the proliferation or protectionist abuse to a greater extent.

Correspondingly, based on all of the above arguments, it is considered that putting dumping under competition rules instead of antidumping rules can be more appropriate, in terms of being less vulnerable to protectionist. However, there are also objections against the substitution. It is summarized that there are two major alleged objections. The first one is in respect of antidumping. Scholars are arguing that antidumping law and competition law have totally different goals. Modern antidumping rules are said to be used either for protecting against "unfair trade" or acting as "a quasi safeguard measure", which has nothing to do with predatory dumping. The second major objection is regarding the competition part. Antidumping advocates are pointing out that there is a lack of domestic competition laws to cover predatory price discrimination, and a lack of international agreementfor enforcement.

Concerning the above objections, it is held in this book that neither of them can be taken as the reason to prevent the substitution of antidumping by competition in future. In terms of "alleged different objectives of antidumping", this book argues that neither "unfair trade" nor "quasi safeguard" is the goal of antidumping. On one hand, the alleged arguments for "unfair trade" are deceptive and hypocritical, and the broad "unfair trade" should not be the essential goal of antidumping system. On the other hand, antidumping system is not aimed at such cannot act as a protective mechanism that is controllable and necessary for the modern free trade world. Therefore, the goal of antidumping should remain to deal with predatory price discrimination.

In terms of "problems of competition of its own", it is argued in this book that competition rules are gradually qualified to substitute antidumping. At the domestic level, although competition standards are far from uniform across countries, at least with respect to predatory price discrimination, some consensus has been reached. For developing countries, especially those new heavy users of antidumping, competition laws have been newly established and gradually developed. Following the essential basic requirements of the U. S. and the EU, predatory price discrimination has been addressed in most of them. Furthermore, the fact that there are no effective national rules cannot be used as an excuse to prevent the substitution. The answer to it should be to accelerate the legislation and development of relevant competition rules. At the international level, there are still many difficulties but also prospects for the creation of international competition law. Many efforts have been continuingly made to achieve this final goal. Compared with the other issues within the international competition framework, the consensus on an international agreement in relation to predatory price discrimination can be reached much more easily. Actually, the successful practices of substitution that have been achieved in bilateral and regional areas, such as the EU, the Australia-New Zealand FTA, and the Canada-Chile FTA, may provide some indications for more progresses.

In addition to focusing on the traditional users, the linkage between antidumping and competition in new heavy users has also started to draw more attention. Up till now, a few studies have been done to some of the new users, such as Brazil, India, and South Africa etc. Based on these studies as well as a specific examination of one of the new users, i. e. , China, it is concluded that the new users adopted antidumping rules mainly in accordance with the requirements of WTO, and hence there was no much further or deeper examination as to the justification of condemning dumping. Antidumping laws are currently used for protecting domestic industries and the like, which have nothing to do with predatory dumping. In this book, a general conclusion is that the new users also support the substitution of antidumping by competition in future, and the current legislation and development of relevant competition rules should be accelerated to be more qualified for the substitution in future.

Based on all of the above analyses and examinations from both traditional and new heavy users of antidumping, this book is of the opinion that antidumping rules should be substituted by competition rules in future. Unfortunately, taking the current political reality into consideration, it seems that antidumping is not likely to be abolished soon around the world. In the multilateral world, with the strong support of antidumping by the U. S. , the substitution work has not achieved too much though it is called on by Japan, Korea, Hong Kong, Canada and so on for a long time. Besides, it is predictable that for a while, antidumping rules will remain to be still attractive for domestic protectionists or for other strategic purposes that have nothing to do with condemning dumping. For instance, for some new heavy users, antidumping is currently used for retaliation or a threat to prevent or reduce antidumping actions towards themselves, or for protecting domestic industries. In addition, although competition rules have been established and gradually developed in those developing countries, the current implements remain weak compared with the developed countries.

Nevertheless, at present, some successful practices of substitution have already been achieved and great efforts are being made in both bilateral and regional areas. Various proposals for reforming current antidumping rules in a way to be substituted by competition rules have also been brought up. For instance, setting "Public Interest Clause" as compulsory for antidumping, and giving more considerations to consumers' interests by achiving such; Granting competition authorities certain rights in the process of antidumping investigation, such as deciding the price, examining any anti-competitive factors etc. ; Reforming substantive rules of antidumping by those of competition in dealing with predatory pricing, such as investigating on the market, injury, price calculation etc. [1]

With the negative effects of using antidumping as protective instrument being detected, as well as the domestic competition rules on predatory price discrimination being gradually developed and harmonized, it is

---

[1] *See*, e. g. , Patrick A. Messerlin, *Should Antidumping Rules be Replaced by National or International Competition Rules*, The Swiss Review of International Economic Relations, 1994, Vol. 49, pp. 351 - 371; P. J. Lloyd, Antidumping and Competition Law, in Patrick F. J Macrory *et al.* , eds. , Macrony et al. , eds. , *II The World Trade Organization: Legal, Economic and Political Analysis*, Springer, 2005, pp. 66 - 81; Yusaf H. Akbar, *Global Antitrust: Trade and Competition Linkages*, Ashagate Publishing, 2003, p. 159; Rodney de C. Grey, *the Relationship Between Antidumping Policy and Competition*, Positive Agenda and Future Trade Negotiations, Gcneva, UN , 2000, pp. 413 - 437, http://ctrc. sice. oas. org/geograph/compol/Articles/Grey_AD_1999. doc, last visited September 18, 2011.

believed that an increasing number of countries will join the camp calling for substituting the domestic antidumping rules and the WTO Antidumping Agreement by the harmonized domestic competition rules and the international competition agreement on predatory price discrimination in future.

Conclusion

The debate of antidumping versus competition is a relatively new but very significant issue. In this book, through examining antidumping law, one of the most controversial trade rules, from the perspective of competition law, this book attempts to contribute to the debate of integrating antidumping with competition, or rather, the so-called "substitution" debate. Based on all of the above analyses and examinations from both traditional and new heavy users of antidumping, this book argues for putting the issue of dumping under competition rules instead of antidumping rules. The domestic antidumping rules and the WTO ADA should be finally substituted by the harmonized domestic competition rules and their basic standard, the international competition agreement on predatory price discrimination, all around the world in future.

Antidumping versus competition is an on-going debate. In this book, the final answer to the substitution debate is made based only on the current state practices and researches. Especially as to the examination of those new users, this book is just an attempt calling for more. It is expected that more specific and deeper researches should be continuingly done to more new users and China as well. This book argues for substituting antidumping by competition in future, and it also favors the idea of reforming antidumping rules in a way to be substituted by competition rules in current practical world. Notwithstanding, due to time limitation, this book could not discuss hence provide with a thoughtful idea as to which is the most workable solution or reform proposal that should be carried out, so as to achieve the substitution in future. More research is also needed regarding this aspect.

Appendix
List of Chinese Antidumping Cases (1997 -2010)

NO.	Time Period		Targeted Product
	Initiation	Final Decision	
1	1997. 12. 10	1999. 06. 03	Newsprint
2	1999. 12. 30	2004. 12. 30	Cold-rolled Steel plate
3	1999. 04. 16	2000. 08. 25	Polyester Films
4	1999. 06. 17	2000. 12. 18	Cold Rolled Stainless Steel Sheet
5	1999. 12. 10	2001. 06. 09	Acrylic Ester
6	2000. 12. 20	2002. 07. 03	Dichloromethane
7	2001. 02. 09	2001. 12. 06	Polystyrene
8	2001. 06. 19	2002. 09. 29	L-Lysine Monohydrochlouide
9	2001. 08. 03	2003. 02. 03	Staple Fiber
10	2001. 08. 03	2003. 02. 03	Glycol-modified PET
11	2001. 10. 10	2003. 04. 10	Acrylic Ester
12	2001. 12. 07	2003. 06. 06	Caprolactam
13	2002. 02. 06	2003. 08. 06	Coated Art Paper
14	2002. 03. 01	2003. 08. 27	Catechol
15	2002. 03. 06	2003. 08. 31	Purified Anhydride
16	2002. 03. 19	2003. 09. 09	Styrene Butadiene Rubber

NO.	Time Period		Targeted Product
	Initiation	Final Decision	
17	2002. 03. 23	2003. 09. 23	Cold Rolled Steel Products
18	2002. 03. 29	2003. 09. 29	Polyvinyl Chloride
19	2002. 05. 22	2003. 11. 22	Toluene Diisocyanate
20	2002. 08. 01	2004. 02. 01	Phenol
21	2002. 09. 20	2003. 11. 28	MDI
22	2003. 05. 14	2004. 11. 14	Monoethanolamine& Diethanolamine
23	2003. 05. 30	2004. 11. 30	Chloroform
24	2003. 07. 01	2005. 01. 01	Dispersion Unshifted Single-Mode Optical Fiber
25	2003. 10. 31	2005. 04. 28	Nylon 6. 66 Filament Yarn
26	2003. 11. 10	2005. 05. 10	Chloroprene Rubber
27	2003. 12. 17	2005. 06. 17	Hydrazine Hydrate
28	2004. 03. 21	2005. 09. 30	Unbleached Kraft Liner/Linerboard
29	2004. 04. 16	2005. 07. 22	Trichloroethylene
30	2004. 07. 16	2006. 01. 16	Dimethyl Cyclosiloxane
31	2004. 08. 10	2006. 02. 09	Ethylene-Propylene-non-conjugated Diene Rubber
32	2004. 08. 12	2006. 02. 13	Benzofuranol
33	2004. 11. 12	2006. 05. 12	Disodium 5'-Inosinate
34	2004. 12. 28	2006. 06. 28	Epichlorohydrin
35	2005. 04. 13	2006. 10. 13	Polyurethane
36	2005. 05. 31	2006. 05. 22	Catechol

37	2005. 06. 06	2006. 07. 22	Polybutylene Terephthalate Resin
38	2005. 06. 13	2006. 12. 12	Wear Resistant Overlay
39	2005. 10. 14	2007. 03. 02	Butanol
40	2005. 09. 15	2007. 01. 31	Octanol
41	2005. 12. 29	2007. 03. 28	Nonyl Phenol
42	2006. 02. 06	2007. 02. 05	Potato Starch
43	2006. 04. 18	2007. 04. 17	Paper for Electrolytic Capacitor
44	2006. 06. 16	2007. 06. 15	Sulfamethoxazole
45	2006. 08. 30	2007. 08. 29	Bisphenol-A
46	2006. 11. 22	2007. 11. 21	Methyl Ethyl Ketone
47	2007. 03. 09	2008. 06. 10	Acetone
48	2008. 11. 10	2009. 11. 01	Adipic Acid
49	2008. 12. 29	2010. 06. 28	Certain Iron or Steel Fasteners
50	2009. 03. 24	2010. 09. 21	Disodium 5'-Inosinate

Bibliography

Books:

[1] Akbar, Yusaf H. , *Global Antitrust: Trade and Competition Linkages* , London: Ashagate Publishing, 2003.

[2] Bergh, Roger J. Van den & Camesasca, Peter D. , *European Competition Law and Economics: A Comparative Perspective*, Intersentia-Hart, 2001.

[3] Dale, Richard, *Antidumping Law in a Liberal Trade Order* , London: the Macmillan Press Ltd. , 1980.

[4] Finger, J. Michael & Nogués, Julio J. , *Safeguards and Antidumping in Latin American Trade Liberalization: fighting fire with fire*, Hampshire ; New York : Palgrave, Macmillan Washington, DC : World Bank, 2006.

[5] Graham, Edward M. & Richardson, J. David, Editors, *Global Competition Policy*, the U. S. A: Institute For International Economics , 1997.

[6] Jackson, John H. & Vermulst, Edwin A. , Editors, *Antidumping Law and Practice: a Comparative Study* , American: Harvester Wheatsheaf, 1990.

[7] Jackson, John H. , *the World Trading System: Law and Policy of International Economic Relations* , 2nd Edition, London: Massachusetts Institute of Technology, 1997.

[8] Kennedy, Kevin C. , *Competition Law and the World Trade Organization: The Limits of Multilateralism*, London: Sweet & Maxwell, 2001.

[9] Lawrence, Robert Z. , editor, *Brookings Trade Forum*, Washington, DC: Brookings Institution Press, 1998.

[10] Lindsey, Brink & Ikenson, Daniel J. , *Antidumping Exposed : the Devilish Details of Unfair Trade Law* , Washington, D. C : Cato Institute, 2003.

[11] Macrory, Patrick F. J & Appleton, Arthur E. & Plummer, Michael G. , Editors, *the World Trade Organization: Legal, Economic and Political*

Analysis, Volume II. , Springer,2005.

[12]Marceau, Gabrielle, *Antidumping and Anti-trust Issues in Free-trade Areas*, New York: Oxford University Press Inc. ,1994.

[13]Matsushita, Mitsuo & Schoenbaum, Thomas J. & Mavroidis, Petros C. , *the World Trade Organization: Law, Practice, and Policy* , New York: Oxford University Press,2003.

[14]Mendes, Mario Marques, *Antitrust in a World of Interrelated Economies: the Interplay Between Antitrust and Trade Policies in the U. S. and the EEC* , Etudes Europeennes,1991.

[15]Nakagawa, Junji, Editor, *Antidumping Laws and Practices of The New Users* Great Britain: Cambridge University Press,2007.

[16]Prusa, Thomas John, *International Trade Policies, Incentives and Firm Behavior* , New York & London: Garland Publishing, Inc. ,1990.

[17] Stewart, Terence P. , Editor, *the GATT Uruguay Round: A Negotiating History* (1986 - 1992), *Volume II: Commentary* , Deventer & Boston: Kluwer Law and Taxation Publishers,1993.

[18]Taylor, Martyn, D. , *International Competition Law: A New Dimension for the WTO?* Cambridge: Cambridge University Press Inc. ,2006.

[19]Trebilcock, Michael J. & Howse, Robert, *the Regulation of International Trade*, 2nd Edition, London & New York: Routledge,1999.

[20]Vermulst, Edwin A. , *the WTO Antidumping Agreement* , New York: Oxford University Press Inc. ,2006.

[21]Viner, Jacob, *Dumping: A Problem in International Trade* , Chicago: University of Chicago Press,1923.

[22] Weinrauch, Roland, *Competition Law in the WTO: the Rationale for a Framework Agreement*, Wien: NWV Neuer Wissenschaftlicher Verlag, 2004.

[23]Mastel, Greg, *American Trade Laws After the Uruguay Round* , New York: M. E. Sharpe. Inc. ,1996.

Periodical Materials:

[1]Beckington, Jeffrey S. , Commentary, the World Trade Organization's Dispute

Settlement Resolution in United States – Antidumping Act of 1916, *Vanderbilt Journal of Transnational Law*, 2001, Vol. 34, p. 199.

[2] Bhala, Raj, Rethinking Antidumping Law, *George Washington Journal of International Law and Economics*, 1995, Vol. 29, p. 1.

[3] Chang, Seung Wha, Interaction between Trade and Competition: Why a Multilateral Approach for the United States? *Duke Journal of Comparative & International Law*, 2004, Vol. 14, p. 1.

[4] Cho, Sungjoon, A Dual Catastrophe of Protectionism, *Northwestern Journal of International Law & Business*, 2005, Vol. 25, p. 315.

[5] Comment, The Antidumping Act – Tariff or Antitrust Law? *The Yale Law Journal*, 1965, Vol. 74, p. 707.

[6] Cunningham, Richard O., Part II: Review of Key Substantive Agreements: Panel II E: Antidumping Agreement (AD) and Agreement on Subsidies and Countervailing Measures (SCM): Commentary on the First Five Years of the WTO Antidumping Agreement and Agreement on Subsidies and Countervailing Measures, *Law and Policy in International Business*, 2000, Vol. 31, p. 897.

[7] DiSalvo, Nicole, Note, Let's Dump the 1916 Antidumping Act: Why the 1994 GATT Provides Better Price Protection for U. S. Industries, *Vanderbilt Journal of Transnational Law*, 2004, Vol. 37, p. 791.

[8] Ehrenhaft, Peter D., Is Interface of Antidumping and Antitrust Laws Possible? *George Washington International Law Review*, 2002, Vol. 34, p. 363.

[9] Fandl, Kevin J., Promoting International Business Development While Protecting Domestic Markets: An Analysis of the New Shipper Review Policy of the United States, *Georgetown University Law Center Georgetown Journal of International Law*, 2005, Vol. 36, p. 605.

[10] Gastle, Charles M. & Leach, James, The Need for an Antidumping Market Structure Test in the Context of Free Trade Agreements, *Trustees of Indiana University Indiana International & Comparative Law Review*, 2000, Vol. 11, p. 37.

[11] Gastle, Charles M., the Convergence of International Trade and Competition

Law Through a WTO Market Access Code, *Currents: International Trade Law Journal* ,1999, Vol. 8,p. 3.

[12] Gingerich, Tara, Comment, Why the WTO should Require the Application of the Evidentiary Threshold Requirement in Antidumping Investigations, *American University Law Review* ,1998, Vol. 48,p. 135.

[13] Gunn, Elizabeth L. , Note, Eliminating the Protectionist Free Ride: the Need for Cost Redistribution in Antidumping Cases, *Boston College International & Comparative Law Review Boston College International and Comparative Law Review* ,2005, Vol. 28,p. 165.

[14] Hamilton, Lee D. , Development: US Antidumping Decisions and the WTO Standard of Review: Deference or Disregard? *Chicago Journal of International Law*,2003, Vol. 4,p. 265.

[15] Hawkins, Adam C. , Comment, Antidumping Beyond the GATT 1994: Supporting International Enactment of Legislation Providing Supplemental Remedies, *Trustees of Indiana University Indiana International & Comparative Law Review*,1999, Vol. 10,p. 149.

[16] Hufbauer, Gary, Trade and Antitrust: Is Rapprochement Desirable? Is It Possible? Antitrust and Antidumping: Forever Separate Tables, *New York Law School Law Review*,2003, Vol. 47,p. 141.

[17] Kennedy, Kevin C. , Symposium: Global Trade Issues in the new Millennium: Foreign Direct Investment and Competition Policy at the World Trade Organization, *George Washington International Law Review* ,2001, Vol. 33, p. 585.

[18] Keppler, Dianne M. , Note, The Geneva Steel Co. Decision Raises Concerns in Geneva: Why the 1916 Antidumping Act Violates the WTO Antidumping Agreement, *George Washington University George Washington Journal of International Law Economics*,1999, Vol. 32,p. 293.

[19] King, Jennifer Karen, Note, In Need of Enlightenment: the international Trade Commission' s Misguided Analysis in Sunset Reviews, *William & Mary Law Review* ,2002, Vol. 43,p. 2151.

[20] Klaproth, Jesse, Recent Development: Decision by the Arbitrator – United

States – Continued Dumping and Subsidy Offset Act of 2000: Payback Is for the Byrds Arbitrator Allows Eight Countries to Sanction the United States for Application of the Byrd Amendment, *Tulane Journal of International and Comparative Law*, 2005, Vol. 13, p. 401.

[21] Laroski, Jr., Joseph A., NMES: A Love Story Nonmarket and Market Economy Status Under U. S. Antidumping Law, *Law and Policy in International Business*, 1999, Vol. 30, p. 369.

[22] Leycegui, Beatriz & Cornejo, Mario Ruiz, Trading Remedies to Remedy Trade: the NAFTA Experience, *Southwestern Journal of Law and Trade in the Americas*, 2003/2004, Vol. 10, p. 1.

[23] Lopez, Daniel M., Comment, the Continued Dumping and Subsidy Offset Act of 2000: "Relief" for the U. S. Steel Industry; Trouble for the United States in the WTO, *University of Pennsylvania Journal of International Economic Law*, 2002, Vol. 23, p. 415.

[24] McGee, Robert W., the Case to Repeal the Antidumping Laws, *Northwestern Journal of International Law and Business*, 1993, Vol. 13, p. 491.

[25] Messerlin, Patrick A., Should Antidumping Rules be Replaced by National or International Competition Rules, *the Swiss Review of International Economic Relations*, 1994, Vol. 49, p. 351.

[26] Miller, Andrea, Comment, the United States Antidumping Statutes: Can a Trade Agreement with the United States be Both "Free" and Fair? A Case Study of Chile, *The Catholic University Law Review Catholic University Law Review*, 2005, Vol. 54, p. 627.

[27] Movsesian, Mark L. & Edited by Caron, David D., International Decision: United States – Continued Dumping and Subsidy Offset Act of 2000, *The American Society of International Law American Journal of International Law*, 2004, Vol. 98, p. 150.

[28] Narayanan, Prakash, Injury Investigations in "Material Retardation" Antidumping Cases, *Northwestern Journal of International Law & Business*, 2004, Vol. 25, p. 37.

[29] Ohnesorge, John K. M., States, Industrial Policies and Antidumping

Enforcement in Japan, South Korea and Taiwan, *The Buffalo Journal of International Law* ,1996 - 1997, Vol. 3, p. 289.

[30] Pippin, Kenneth J., Note, An Examination of the Developments in Chapter 19 Antidumping Decisions under the North American Free Trade Agreement (NAFTA): The Implications and Suggestions for Reform for the Next Century Based on the Experience of NAFTA After the First Five Years, *Michigan Journal of International Law* ,1999, Vol. 21, p. 101.

[31] Piskorskim, Patricia H., Note, A Dangerous Discretionary "Duty": US Antidumping Plicy Towards China, *Hofstra Law Review*, 2005, Vol. 34, p. 595.

[32] Ralf Boscheck, The Governance of Global Market Relations: the Case of Substituting Antitrust for Antidumping, *World Competition*, 2001, Vol. 24 (1), p. 53.

[33] Romero, Alicia Cebada, Antidumping, Countervailing Duties, and Safeguard Measures: Comparison between the Agreements of the European Community and European Eastern Countries and NAFTA, *Arizona Board of Regents Arizona Journal of International and Comparative Law* ,1999, Vol. 16, p. 437.

[34] Schutzman, Meredith, Note, Antidumping and the Continued Dumping and Subsidy Offset Act of 2000: A Renewed Debate, *Yeshiva University Cardozo Journal of International and Comparative Law* ,2004, Vol. 11, p. 1069.

[35] Sheppard, Hale E., The Continued Dumping and Subsidy Offset Act (Byrd Amendment): A Defeat Before the WTO May Constitute an Overall Victory for U. S. Trade, *Tulane Journal of International and Comparative Law*, 2002, Vol. 10, p. 121.

[36] Smitherman, Charles W., The Future of Global Competition Governance: Lessons from the Transatlantic, American University International Law Review, 2004, Vol. 19, p. 769.

[37] Stewart, Terence P., U. S.-Japan Economic Disputes: the Role of Antidumping and Countervailing Duty Laws, *Arizona Board of Regents Arizona Journal of International and Comparative Law*, 1999, Vol. 16, p. 689.

[38] Stump, Monica A., Note, the Alarms are Buzzing in Washington: the Antidumping Act of 1916 Returns from Hibernation, *University of Pittsburgh Law Review*, 2002, Vol. 63, p. 645.

[39] Thuesen, Steven, Note, Sustainable Production Agriculture in the Face of Foreign Commodity Dumping: Achieving Effective Antidumping and Countervailing Duty Determinations, *North Dakota Law Review*, 2001, Vol. 77, p. 453.

[40] Waller, Spencer Weber, Bringing Globalism Home: Lessons from Antitrust and Beyond, *Loyola University Chicago Law Journal*, 2000, Vol. 32, p. 113.

[41] Wolff, Alan Wm., Trade and Antitrust: Is Rapprochement Desirable? Is It Possible? The (Notionally) Bridgeable Chasm Between Antitrust and Trade Policy, *New York Law School Law Review*, 2003, Vol. 47, p. 167.

[42] Yocis, David A., Note, Hardened Positions: Guatemala Cement and WTO Review of National Antidumping Determinations, *New York University Law Review*, 2001, Vol. 76, p. 1259.

[43] Yu, Lei, Note, Rule of Law or Rule of Protectionism: Antidumping Practices Toward China and the WTO Dispute Settlement System, *Columbia Journal of Asian Law*, 2002, Vol. 15, p. 293.

[44] Nedumpara, James J., Antidumping Under the GATT/WTO: Fair Prices and Less Than Fair Rules – An Agenda for Reforms, *Indian Journal of International Law*, 2002, Vol. 42, p. 275.

[45] Marsh, Sarah J., Creating Barriers for Foreign Competitions: A Study of the Impact of Antidumping Actions on the Performance of U. S. Firms, *Strategic Management Journal*, 1998, Vol. 19, p. 25.

[46] Tharakan, P. K. M., the Political Economy of Antidumping Undertakings in the European Communities, *European Economic Review*, 1991, Vol. 35, p. 1341.

[47] Zanardi, Maurizio, Antidumping: What are the Numbers to Discuss at Doha? *The World Economy*, 2004, Vol. 27, p. 403.

Internet Sources:

[1] Acton, Jan Paul, On Proposed Antidumping Regulations and Other

Antidumping Issues, *Statement before the Subcommittee on Trade Committee on Ways and Means U. S. House of Representatives* ,1996, available at: http://www. cbo. gov/ftpdocs/47xx/doc4746/1996Doc09. pdf.

[2] Aggarwal, Aradhna, Antidumping Law and Practice: An Indian Perspective, *Indian Council for Research on International Economic Relations*,2002, available at: http://www. icrier. org/pdf/antiDump. pdf.

[3] Aggrawal, Aradhna, the WTO Antidumping Code: Issues for Review in Post – Doha Negotiations, *Working Paper No.* 99 (2003), available at: http:// www. icrier. org/pdf/WP99. pdf.

[4] Banks, Gary, Australia's Antidumping Experience, *Working Papers of World Bank* , 1990, available at: http://www – wds. worldbank. org/external/default/WDSContentServer/IW3P/IB/1990/12/01/000009265_3960930045442/Rendered/PDF/multi0page. pdf.

[5] Barfield, Claude, Antidumping: Time to: (1) Go Back to Basics; And (2) Politicize the Final Outcome; Or (3) Substitute Safeguards for Antidumping Actions, *Paper Prepared for the Centennial of Anti-dumping Legislation and Implementation Symposium*, 2004, available at: http://fordschool. umich. edu/rsie/Conferences/ADSym/Barfield. pdf.

[6] Barral, Welber & Brogini, Gilvan& Lucenti, Krista& Aggarwal, Aradhna& Mccarthy, Colin, the use of Antidumping in Brazil, China, India and South Africa-Rule, Trends and Causes, *Kommerskollegium National Board of Trade*,2005, available at: http://www. tralac. org/pdf/Antidumping_in_4_Developing_Countries. pdf.

[7] Baylis, Kathy & Malhotra, Nisha, Predatory Pricing: The Effect of Antidumping on Domestic Competition Policy, *University of British Columbia Vancouver, BC* ,2006, available at: http://www. econ. ubc. ca/nmalhotra/Research/Predatory% 20Pricing_CEA2. pdf.

[8] Blonigen, Bruce A. & Prusa, Thomas J. , the Cost of Antidumping: the Devil is in the Details ,2003, available at: http://www. uoregon. edu/ ~ bruceb/ADDetails. pdf.

[9] Blonigen, Bruce A. , the Effects of CUSFTA and NAFTA on Antidumping and

Countervailing Duty Activity, *Draft prepared for World Bank Project* ,2002, available at:http://wbln0018. worldbank. org/lac/lacinfoclient. nsf/ 1daa 4610 32291238852 56831005 ce0eb/ 423c4a3e7f187bf485256c3d0071e254/MYM-FILE/Blonigen% 20NAFTA – AD% 20Paper% 20v3. pdf.

[10]Bown, Chad P. & Hoekman, Bernard & Ozden, Caglar, The Pattern of U. S. Antidumping: the Path from Initial Filing to WTO Dispute Settlement, *World Trade Review* ,2003, available at: http://people. brandeis. edu/ ~ cbown/papers/Bown – Hoekman – Ozden. pdf.

[11]Bown, Chad P. & McCulloch, Rachel, the WTO Agreement on Safeguards, 2003, available at: http://people. brandeis. edu/ ~ cbown/papers/ bown_mcculloch_2. pdf.

[12]Bown, Chad P. & McCulloch, Rachel, U. S. Trade Policy toward China: Discrimination and Its Implications ,2005, available at: http://people. brandeis. edu/ ~ cbown/papers/PAFTAD – Bown – McCulloch. pdf.

[13] Bown, Chad P. , the WTO and Antidumping in Developing Countries , 2006, available at: http://people. brandeis. edu/ ~ cbown/papers/AD_developing. pdf.

[14] Bown, Chad P. , the WTO, Safeguards, and Temporary Protection From Imports, *Critical Perspectives on the Global Trading System and the WTO series*,2005, available at: http://people. brandeis. edu/ ~ cbown/papers/ee_safeguards. pdf.

[15]Bown, Chad P. , Why are Safeguards under the WTO so Unpopular? *World Trade Review* ,2001, available at: http://people. brandeis. edu/ ~ cbown/papers/wtr_safeguards. pdf.

[16]Busch, Marc I. & Raciborski, Rafal & Reinhardt, Eric, Does the Rule of Law Matter? The WTO and US Antidumping Investigations, *Department of Political Science Emory University*,2006, available at: http://www. georgetown. edu/users/mlb66/AD. pdf.

[17]Carpenter, Robert, Antidumping and Countervailing Duty Handbook (11th Edition), United States International Trade Commission ,2005, available at: http://www. gslaw. com. cn/chinese/guangsheng/gslaw/04/06. pdf.

[18] Ciuriak, Dan, Antidumping at 100 Years and Counting: A Canadian Perspective, *Prepared* for "*A Centennial of Antidumping Legislation and Implementation*" *Symposium*, 2005, available at: http://www.fordschool.umich.edu/rsie/Conferences/ADSym/Ciuriak.pdf.

[19] De Araujo Jr., José Tavares, Legal and Economic Interfaces between Antidumping and Competition Policy, *CEPAL – SERIE Comercio Internacional*, 2001, available at: http://www.eclac.cl/publicaciones/xml/0/9040/lcl1685i.pdf.

[20] Feinberg, Robert M. & Reynolds, Kara M., The Spread of Antidumping Regimes and the Role of Retaliation in Filings, 2004, available at: http://129.3.20.41/eps/it/papers/0411/0411003.pdf.

[21] Finger, J. Michael & Zlate Andrei, Antidumping: Prospects for Discipline from Doha Negotiations, *Working Papers in Economics*, 2005, available at: http://escholarship.bc.edu/cgi/viewcontent.cgi? article = 1184& context = econ_papers.

[22] Finger, J. Michael & Ng, Francis & Wangchuk, Sonam, Antidumping As Safeguard Policy, *World Bank Working Paper No.* 2730, 2000, available at: http://www.fordschool.umich.edu/rsie/Conferences/CGP/Oct2000 Papers/Finger.pdf.

[23] Finger, J. Michael, Should Developing Countries Introduce Antidumping? available at: www.worldbank.org/INTRANETTRADE/Resources/WBI – Training/MFinger_antidumping_eng.DOC, last visiting on 2007 – 03 – 25.

[24] Francois, Joseph F. & Niels, Gunnar, Political Influence in a New Antidumping Regime, *Tinbergen Institute Discussion Paper*, 2004, available at: http://www.tinbergen.nl/discussionpapers/04011.pdf.

[25] Grey, Rodney de C., the Relationship Between Anti-dumping Policy and Competition, *Positive Agenda and Future Trade Negotiations*, *Geneva*, *UN*, 2000, available at: http://ctrc.sice.oas.org/geograph/compol/Articles/Grey_AD_1999.doc.

[26] Guasch, J. Luis & Rajapatirana, Sarath, Antidumping and Competition Policies in Latin America and Caribbean: Total Strangers or Soul Mates?

1998, available at: http://www. worldbank. org/html/dec/Publications/Workpapers/WPS1900series/wps1958/wps1958. pdf.

[27] Hoekman, Bernard M. & Mavroidis, Petros C., Antitrust-based Remedies and Dumping in International Trade, *Policy Research Working paper No.* 1347, *World Bank*, 1994, available at: http://www - wds. worldbank. org/servlet/WDSContentServer/WDSP/IB/1994/08/01/000009265_3970716141633/Rendered/PDF/multi0page. pdf.

[28] Hoekman, Bernard, Competition policy and Preferential Trade Agreements, *World Bank and Center for Economic Policy Research*, 1998, available at: http://siteresources. worldbank. org/WBI/Resources/wbi37131. pdf.

[29] Hoekman, Bernard, Free Trade and Deep Integration: Antidumping and Antitrust in Regional Agreements, *World Bank Development Research Group International Trade*, 1998, available at: http://www - wds. worldbank. org/servlet/WDSContentServer/WDSP/IB/1998/07/01/000009265 _ 3980928162543/Rendered/PDF/multi0page. pdf.

[30] Holden, Merle, Antidumping: A Reaction to Trade Liberalisation or Anti Competitive? *School of Economics and Management*, *University of Natal Durban*, available at: http://www. essa. org. za/download/papers/004. pdf, last visiting on 2007 - 03 - 18.

[31] Keyser, Philip De, Exploring WTO dispute settlement in US Anti-dumping Act 1916: An easy case? *The Jean Monnet Seminar at Harvard Law School*, 2001, available at: http://www. jeanmonnetprogram. org/papers/01/ 013101. html.

[32] Knorr, Andreas, Antidumping Rules vs. Competition Rules, *Institution for World Economics and International Management*, 2004, available at: http://www. iwim. uni - bremen. de/publikationen/pdf/W031. pdf.

[33] Krishna, Raj, Antidumping in Law and Practice, available at: http://www. sice. oas. org/geograph/antidumping/krishna. pdf, last visiting on 2006 - 10 - 25.

[34] Leipziger, Danny M. & Shin, Hyun Ja, The Demand for Protection: A Look at Antidumping Cases, *Open Economies Review*, 1991, available at: http://www. springerlink. com/content/k55p29450mq78g77/fulltext. pdf.

[35] Lindsey, Brink & Ikenson, Dan, Antidumping 101: the Devilish Details of "Unfair Trade" Law, *Trade Policy Analysis No.* 20, 2002, available at: http://cato.org/pub_display.php? pub_id = 3637&print = Y.

[36] Lindsey, Brink & Ikenson, Dan, Reforming the Antidumping Agreement: A Road Map for WTO Negotiations, *Trade Policy Analysis No.* 21, 2002, available at: http://cato.org/pub_display.php? pub_id = 3636&print = Y.

[37] Lindsey, Brink, The U. S. Antidumping Law: Rhetoric versus Reality, *Trade Policy Analysis No.* 7, 1999, available at: http://www.cato.org/pub_display.php? pub_id = 3650&print = Y.

[38] Lipstein, Robert A., Using Antitrust Principles to Reform Antidumping Law, *Institute for International Economics*, available at: http://www.iie.com/publications/chapters _ preview/56/13ie1664.pdf, last visiting on 2007 - 03 - 21.

[39] Macmillan, Kathleen, Antidumping: Next on the Trade Agenda, *Canadian Business Economics*, 1995, available at: http://www.cabe.ca/cbe/vol3_3/33 - macmillan.pdf.

[40] Mankiw, N. Gregory & Swagel, Phillip L., Antidumping: the Third Rail of Trade Policy, *Foreign Affairs*, 2005, available at: http://www.manitoba-pork.com/admin/docs/FA_V84_N4_-_Antidumping_The_Third_Rail_of_Trade_Policy.pdf.

[41] Maur, Jean - Christophe, Echoing Antidumping Cases: Regulatory Competitors, Imitation and Cascading Protection, *Groupe d'Economie Mondiale & Institut d'Etudes Politiques de Paris*, 1998, available at: http://gem.sciences - po.fr/content/publications/pdf/echogem_maur.pdf.

[42] Mcgee, Robert W. & Yoon, Yeomin, Antidumping the People's Republic of China: Five Cases Studies, *the Dumont Institution for Public Policy Research*, 1998, available at: http://129.3.20.41/eps/it/papers/9805/9805003.html.

[43] Mcgee, Robert W., Application the Antidumping Laws against Latin American Countries: Six Case Studies and Prospects for the Future, *Presented at the* 14*th Conference of the Business Association of Latin American Studies*, 1997,

available at: http://129. 3. 20. 41/eps/it/papers/9805/9805007. html.

[44] McGee, Robert W. , Some Ethical Aspects of Antidumping Laws, *Reason Paper No.* 25, available at: http://www. mises. org/reasonpapers/pdf/25/rp_25_3. pdf, last visiting on 2007 - 03 - 18.

[45] Messerlin, Patrick A. & Reed, Geoffrey, Antidumping Policies in the United States and the European Community, *the Economic Journal* ,1995, Vol. 105, p. 1567, available at: http://www. jstor. org/view/00130133/di983537/ 98p 0621z/1? frame = noframe&userID = 8505f26d @ kyushu - u. ac. jp/ 01cce4405c00501b55c1e&dpi = 3&config = jstor.

[46] Messerlin, Patrick A. , Antidumping Regulations or Procartel Law? The EC Chemical Cases, *International Trade Working Paper* 0397, *World Bank* , 1990, available at: http://www - wds. worldbank. org/servlet/WDSContentServer/WDSP/IB/1990/04/01/000009265_3960929174031/Rendered/PDF/multi0page. pdf.

[47] Messerlin, Patrick A. , China in the World Trade Organization: Antidumping and Safeguards, *World Bank Economic Review* ,2004, Vol. 18, No. 1, available at: http://wber. oxfordjournals. org/cgi/content/abstract/18/1/105.

[48] Messerlin,Patrick A. ,China in the WTO:Antidumping and Safeguards ,2002, available at:http://www. heisummer. ch/pdf/Contingency% 20Protection/ messerlin. pdf.

[49] Messerlin, Patrick A. , Competition Policy and Antidumping Reform: An Exercise in Transition, *Institute for International Economics*, available at: http://www. iie. com/publications/chapters _ preview/66/13iie2350. pdf, last visiting on 2007 - 03 - 21.

[50] Messerlin, Patrick, Antidumping Laws and Developing Countries, *International Economics Department*, *World Bank*, 1988, available at: http://www - wds. worldbank. org/servlet/WDSContentServer/WDSP/IB/1988/06/01/000009265_3960927004905/Rendered/PDF/multi0page. pdf.

[51] Niels, Gunnar, Trade Diversion and Destruction Effects of Antidumping Policy:Empirical Evidence from Mexico,*OXERA and Erasmus University Rotter-*

dam, 2003, available at: http://www.etsg.org/ETSG2003/papers/ niels.pdf.

[52] Niels, Gunnar, What is Antidumping Policy Really About? *Journal of Economic Surveys*, 2002, Vol. 14, No. 4, available at: http://www.blackwell-synergy.com/links/doi/10.1111/1467-6419.00118.

[53] Prusa, Thomas J. & Skeath, Susan, Retaliation as an Explanation for the Proliferation of Antidumping, 2002, available at: http://www.tulane.edu/~dnelson/PolTransConv/Prusa.pdf.

[54] Prusa, Thomas J. & Skeath, Susan, the Economic and Strategic Motives for Antidumping Filings, *NBER Working Paper No.* 8424, 2001, available at: http://www.nber.org/papers/w8424.pdf.

[55] Prusa, Thomas J., The Growing Problem of Antidumping Protection and what it means for Asia-Pacific Region, 2003, available at: http://www.nber.org/~confer/2003/ease14/prusa.pdf.

[56] Ragosta, John A. & Magnus, John R., Antidumping and Antitrust Reform in the NAFTA: Beyond Rhetoric and Mischief, *The Center for Trade Policy and Law Carleton University/ University of Ottawa*, 1996, available at: http://www.dbtrade.com/publications/183619w.pdf.

[57] Reynolds, Kara M. & Su, Yan, Dumping on Agriculture: Case Studies in Antidumping, 2005, available at: http://nw08.american.edu/~reynolds/casestudies.pdf.

[58] Sapir, André, Some Ideas for Reforming the Community Antidumping Instrument, 2006, available at: http://trade.ec.europa.eu/doclib/docs/2006/august/tradoc_129815.pdf.

[59] Seyffarth, Anamelia Soccal, the Link between Competition Policy and Antidumping Policy. *George Washington University*, *School of Business and Public Management*, *Institute of Brazilian Issues Minerva Program*, 2000, available at: http://www.gwu.edu/~ibi/minerva/Fall2000/Anamelia.Seyffarth.pdf.

[60] Vandenbussche, Hylke, How Can Japanese and Central-European Exporters to the EU Avoid Antidumping Duties? 1995, available at: http://www.

econ. kuleuven. be/public/ndbad40/publications/international/World% 20 competition. pdf.

[61] Wolff, Alan Wm., Role of the Antidumping Laws, *Remarks before the Steel Manufacturers Association*, 1995, available at: http://www. dbtrade. com/ publications/181925w. pdf.

[62] Wolff, Alan Wm., the Notionally Bridgeable Chasm Between Antitrust and Trade Policy, *American Antitrust Institute Program on Trade and Antitrust*, 2002, available at: http://scholar. google. com/scholar? hl = zh – CN&lr = &q = info: LKWNjRyDJf4J: scholar. google. com/&output = viewport&pg = 1.

[63] Wooton, Ian & Zanardi, Maurizio, Trade and Competition Policy: Anti-dumping versus Anti-trust. 2002, available at: http://homepages. strath. ac. uk/ ~ hbs03116/Research/Trade% 20and% 20Competition% 20Policy% 20Final. pdf.

[64] Yin, Jason Z., Strategic Response of Antidumping: Case of China, *Social Science Research*, 2003, Vol. 4, available at: http://pirate. shu. edu/ ~ yin-jason/papers/AD% 20in% 20Chinese – SiChuan2 – 03. pdf.

[65] Yoshimatsu, Hidetaka, the political economy of antidumping in Japan, *Journal of the Asia Pacific Economy*, 2001, Vol. 6, available at: http:// taylorandfrancis. metapress. com/media/hhwx2bryqh0kplk3jmfk/contributions/u/9/t/0/u9t0m6fyntb8ctay. pdf.

[66] Zanardi, Maurizio, Antidumping: A Problem in International Trade, 2005, available at: http://papers. ssrn. com/sol3/papers. cfm? abstract_id = 800406#PaperDownload.

[67] Zeng, Hang, Antidumping and Competition: the Case of China, 2005, available at: http://idrinfo. idrc. ca/archive/corpdocs/122054/101924 – 032 – thesis. pdf.

[68] Bhattacharjea, Aditya, Trade and Competition Policy, Working Paper No. 146, *Indian Council For Research on International Economic Relations*, 2004, available at: http://www. icrier. org/pdf/wp146. pdf.

[69] Malhotra, Nisha, Is Antidumping Legislation a Threat to Competition: A Case Study of the U. S. Chemical Industry, *Competitiveness Review*, 2006,

available at: http://www. econ. ubc. ca/nmalhotra/Research/ChemicalIn-dustryCompreview1. pdf.

[70] Kucherepa, Peter, the Internationalization of Competition Policy over Anti-dumping Agreement, *Presented to the Canadian Institute of International Affairs*, available at: http://www. kucherepa. ca/Peter8. 0/trade_files/Dumping% 20Essay% 20(policy). pdf, last visiting on 2009 - 05 - 01.

[71] Hindley, Brian, Antidumping Policy in the EU, *Policy Briefs No.* 3 ,2007, available at: http://www. ecipe. org/publications/ecipe - policy - briefs/antidumping - policy - in - the - eu/pdf.

[72] Vandenbussche, Hylke & Zanardi, Maurizio, The Global Chilling Effects of Antidumping Proliferation ,2006, available at: http://center. uvt. nl/staff/zanardi/ADchillingeffects. pdf.

[73] Ikenson, Daniel, Abuse of Discretion: Time to Fix to Administration of the U. S. Antidumping Law, *Trade Policy Analysis No.* 31 ,2005, available at: http://www. freetrade. org/pubs/pas/tpa - 031. pdf.

[74] CBO Testimony, Statement of Jan Paul Acton on Proposed Antidumping Regulations and Other Antidumping Issues Before the Subcommittee on Trade Committee on Ways and Means, U. S. House of Representatives, 1996, available at: http://www. cbo. gov/ftpdocs/47xx/doc4746/1996 Doc 09. pdf.

[75] Applebaum, Harvey M. , the Interface of the Trade Laws and the Antitrust Laws, *GEOMASON L. REV* ,1998, Vol. 6:3, available at: http://www. cov. com/files/Publication/8f40aa4c - e6bc - 4147 - b97d - 7c580f5760c2/Presentation/PublicationAttachment/d5ae3e54 - b019 - 4b61 - 81c4 - 84d5a4c453c5/oid5991. pdf.

[76] De Araujo Jr. , José Tavares & Macario, Carla & Steinfatt, Karsten, Anti-dumping in the Americas, *A Publication of the Organization of American States Trade Unit* ,2001, available at: http://www. sedi. oas. org/DTTC/TRADE/PUB/STUDIES/subsid/Antidumptav. pdf.

[77] Chu, Tianshu & Prusa, Thomas J. , the Reasons for and the Impact of Antidumping Protection: the Case of People's Republic of China, *Economic*

Series , 2004, available at: http://www. eastwestcenter. org/fileadmin/stored/pdfs/ECONwp069. pdf.

[78] Aussilloux, Vincent & Kobak, Jr, James B. & Sadni-Jallab, Mustapha, Antidumping as Anticompetitive Practice: Evidence from the United-States and the European Community, available at: http://www. ios. neu. edu/iioc2004/papers/s6k3. pdf, last visiting on 2009 - 05 - 01.

[79] Barral, Welber, Antidumping Measures: Prospects for Developing Countries, *IRI/UFSC Working Paper No.* 01/03 ,2003, available at: http://papers. ssrn. com/sol3/cf _ dev/AbsByAuth. cfm? per _ id = 337747 # show373320.

[80] Wellhausen, Marc, the Community Interest Test in Antidumping Proceedings of the European Union, *American University International Law Review* , 2000, available at: http://www. wcl. american. edu/journal/ilr/16/wellhausen. pdf? rd = 1.

[81] Nelson, Douglas, the Political Economy of Antidumping: A Survey, *Prepared for the joint Murphy Institute/ Leverhulme Center GEP Conference on the* 100th *Anniversary of antidumping*, available at: http://www. tulane. edu/ ~ dnelson/PAPERS/ADPEsurvey. pdf, last visiting on 2009 - 05 - 01.

[82] Barthel, Christian, Predatory Pricing Policy under EC and US Law, *Master Thesis*, *Faculty of Law*, *University of Lund* ,2002, available at: http://web2. jur. lu. se/Internet/english/essay/Masterth. nsf/0/3C4189D171765812C1256BC9002B6A18/MYMFile/xsmall. pdf? OpenElement.

[83] Hoekman, Bernard, the WTO: Functions and Basic Principles, available at: http://www. terry. uga. edu/ ~ eornelas/Econ4040/WTO - basics. pdf, last visiting on 2009 - 05 - 01.

[84] Model Law on Competition, *UNCTAD Series on Issues in Competition Law and Policy*, 2000, available at: http://www. unctad. org/en/docs/tdrbpconf5d7. en. pdf.

[85] Draft opening remarks of Mr. Seiichi Kondo Deputy Secretary General Organisation for Economic Co-operation and Development, *Global Forum on Competition*, 2001, available at: http://www. oecd. org/dataoecd/0/32/

2434223. pdf.

[86] Brazil – Peer Review of Competition Law and Policy, OECD, 2005, available at: http://www. oecd. org/dataoecd/12/45/35445196. pdf.

[87] Public Awareness on Competition Law and Policy, *Competition Commission of India B Block*, available at: http://www. competition – commission – india. nic. in/speeches_articles_presentations/Public% 20Awareness% 20on% 20Competition% 20Law. pdf, last visiting on 2009 – 05 – 01.

[88] South Africa – Peer Review of Competition Law and Policy, OECD, 2003, available at: http://www. oecd. org/dataoecd/43/58/34823812. pdf.

Chinese Books & Journals:

[1]王中美. 以反垄断法替代反倾销法的法律研究,北京:法律出版社,2008.

[2]高永富,张玉卿. 国际反倾销法,上海:复旦大学出版社,2001.

[3]尚明编. 反倾销:WTO 规则及中外法律与实践,北京:法律出版社,2003.

[4]宋和平. 反倾销法律制度概论,北京:中国检察出版社,2003.

[5]谢海霞. 从竞争法角度看反倾销法律制度,河北法学,2004,(3).

[6]张瑞萍. 反倾销法的性质与演进之分析:从 WTO 竞争法设立的角度,当代法学,2006,20,(1).

[7]张晓东. 反倾销立法比较研究,北京:法律出版社、中央文献出版社,2000.

[8]张新娟. 反倾销法律的理论与实际,北京:中国社会科学出版社,2003.

[9]王先林. WTO 竞争政策与中国反垄断立法,北京:北京大学出版社,2005.

[10]柴国梁. PET 薄膜反倾销剖析,上海化工,2001(22).

[11]柴国梁. 涤纶短纤维反倾销案简析,上海化工,2001(20).

[12]柴国梁. 简析邻苯二酚反倾销案,上海化工,2002(11).

[13]柴国梁. 聚苯乙烯反倾销案剖析简述,上海化工,2001(16).

[14]柴国梁. 聚酯切片反倾销案剖析,上海化工,2001(18).

[15]邓纲. 刍议反倾销规则并入竞争法体系的几个问题,现代法学,2007(5).

[16]刁海燕. 2006 年化工产品贸易摩擦大事记,国际化工信息,2006(12).

[17]黄勇. 中国反垄断法:一部注重整体协调的法律,中国发展观察,2006

(6).
[18]江林.反垄断法有关“滥用”的解读:访《反垄断法》立法专家小组成员黄勇教授,工商行政管理,2007(18).
[19]李明晶.中国进口反倾销的现状分析及应对策略,经济研究导刊,2006(6).
[20]刘松涛,栾成好.2004 中国反倾销案件回顾,WTO 经济导刊,2005(2).
[21]刘卫东.进口反倾销:特点、成效与对策,国际经济合作,2005(1).
[22]刘勇.我国对外反倾销实践的特点、不足及其完善建议,江苏商论,2006(5).
[23]钱伯章.化工业反倾销案例回顾,化工管理,2006(11).
[24]孙雯.反倾销法与竞争法之冲突与协调,河北法学,2006(1).
[25]滕玉华,彭克强.WTO《反倾销协议》与竞争法冲突分析,商业时代,2004(23).
[26]王衡.WTO 框架下竞争规则研究:现状与未来,社会科学研究,2005(5).
[27]王继军.对新《对外贸易法》中反垄断与反不正当竞争条款基本问题的思考,美中法律评论,2005(6).
[28]王晓晔.低价倾销行为的几点法律思考,价格理论与实践,2004(7).
[29]吴小琛.中国进口反倾销调查和政策重述//中华全国律师协会 WTO 专门委员会 2004 年年会会议手册,2004.
[30]吴学安.一家中国企业应对外国企业倾销三诉三胜:“三吉利”反倾销的启示,经济参考报,2005-12-17(008).
[31]夏廷.2004 年中国进口反倾销案件评析,时代经贸,2004(12).
[32]张振华.反思 2005 年中国反倾销第一案,中国经贸导刊,2005(3).
[33]黄文俊.美国的反垄断法与反倾销法,国际商报,2003(006).
[34]王希勇.贸易公平:我国反倾销立法的宗旨,国际商报,2003(006).
[35]符勇.反倾销法与公平贸易研究,博士学位论文,西南政法大学,2003(8).
[36]林燕萍.与贸易有关的竞争法律问题研究,博士学位论文,华东政法学院,2004(10).
[37]李小明.反垄断法中滥用市场支配地位法律问题研究,博士学位论文,

中国政法大学,2005(4).
[38]尚明. 反垄断法之滥用市场支配地位规则研究,博士学位论文,对外经济贸易大学,2006(4).
[39]游钰. 论反垄断法对掠夺性定价的规制,法学评论,2004(6).
[40]宾建成. 中国首次反倾销措施执行效果评估,世界经济,2003(9).
[41]朱庆华. 中国反倾销公共利益原则的实践,中央财经大学学报,2008(2).
[42]鲍晓华. 中国实施反倾销措施的经济效应分析,经济纵横,2004(1).
[43]金晓晨. 反倾销中公共利益原则的法理分析:从公平正义的视角,当代法学,2007(5).
[44]马向敏,刘富利. 进口反倾销对上下游产业的影响:基于我国造纸业反倾销的分析,当代经济,2007,12(上).
[45]璐瑶,冯宗宪. 进口反倾销调查对外商投资与国内上下游产业链的影响及其对策,国际贸易,2007(9).
[46]李弘,田莉. 反倾销在全球性竞争中的战略问题:饲料级赖氨酸反倾销案有感,中国集体经济,2002(9).
[47]卞耀武. 全国人民代表大会常务委员会法制工作委员会编,中华人民共和国价格法释义,北京:法律出版社,1998.
[48]安建. 全国人民代表大会常务委员会法制工作委员会编,中华人民共和国反垄断法释义,北京:法律出版社,2007.

Chinese Law and Cases:

– Legal Texts:

[1]《中华人民共和国对外贸易法》(1994 年 5 月 12 日第八届全国人民代表大会常务委员会第七次会议通过,2004 年 4 月 6 日第十届全国人民代表大会常务委员会第八次会议修订,并自 2004 年 7 月 1 日起施行。)
[2]《中华人民共和国反倾销和反补贴条例》(1997 年 3 月 25 日国务院颁布,已被废止。)
[3]《中华人民共和国反倾销条例》(2001 年 10 月 31 日国务院第 46 次常务会议通过,自 2002 年 1 月 1 日起施行,根据《国务院关于修改〈中华人民共和国反倾销条例〉的决定》予以修改并自 2004 年 6 月 1 日起施行。)
[4]《中华人民共和国反不正当竞争法》(1993 年 9 月 2 日第八届全国人民

代表大会常务委员会第三次会议于通过,自1993年12月1日起施行。)
[5]《中华人民共和国价格法》(1997年12月29日第八届全国人民代表大会常务委员会第二十九次会议通过,自1998年5月1日起施行。)
[6]《中华人民共和国反垄断法》(2007年8月30日第十届全国人民代表大会常务委员会第二十九次会议通过,自2008年8月1日起施行。)
[7]《制止价格垄断行为暂行规定》(根据《中华人民共和国价格法》,经国家发展改革委主任办公会议讨论通过,自2003年11月1日起施行。)
[8]《关于制止低价倾销行为的规定》(根据《中华人民共和国价格法》,经国家发展计划委员会会议讨论通过,自1999年8月3日起施行。)

- **Final Administrative Decisions on Antidumping Actions**:

The No. 1 Newsprint Case, Public Announcement No. 4 in 1999 of Ministry of Foreign Trade and Economic Cooperation of the People's Republic of China

The No. 2 Cold-rolled steel plate Case, Public Announcement No. 8 in 2000 of Ministry of Foreign Trade and Economic Cooperation of the People's Republic of China

The No. 3 Polyester Films Case, Public Announcement No. 7 in 2000 of Ministry of Foreign Trade and Economic Cooperation of the People's Republic of China

The No. 4 Cold Rolled Stainless Steel Sheet case, Public Announcement No. 15 in 2000 of Ministry of Foreign Trade and Economic Cooperation of the People's Republic of China

The No. 5 Acrylic Ester Case, Public Announcement No. 5 in 2001 of Ministry of Foreign Trade and Economic Cooperation of the People's Republic of China

The No. 6 Dichloromethne (or Methylenechloride) Case, Public Announcement No. 20 in 2002 of Ministry of Foreign Trade and Economic Cooperation of the People's Republic of China

The No. 7 Polystyrene Case, Public Announcement No. 13 in 2001 of Ministry of Foreign Trade and Economic Cooperation of the People's Republic of China

The No. 8 L – Lysine monohydrochlouide Case, Public Announcement No. 23 in 2002 of Ministry of Foreign Trade and Economic Cooperation of the People's Republic of China

The No. 9 Staple Fiber Case, Public Announcement No. 3 in 2003 of Ministry of

Foreign Trade and Economic Cooperation of the People's Republic of China

The No. 10 Glycol-modified PET Case, Public Announcement No. 4 in 2003 of Ministry of Foreign Trade and Economic Cooperation of the People's Republic of China

The No. 11 Acrylic Ester Case, Public Announcement No. 3 in 2003 of Ministry of Commerce of the People's Republic of China

The No. 12 Caprolactam Case, Public Announcement No. 22 in 2003 of Ministry of Commerce of the People's Republic of China

The No. 13 Coated Art Paper Case, Public Announcement No. 35 in 2003 of Ministry of Commerce of the People's Republic of China

The No. 14 Catechol Case, Public Announcement No. 41 in 2003 of Ministry of Commerce of the People's Republic of China

The No. 15 Purified Anhydride Case, Public Announcement No. 40 in 2003 of Ministry of Commerce of the People's Republic of China

The No. 16 Styrene Butadiene Rubber Case, Public Announcement No. 49 in 2003 of Ministry of Commerce of the People's Republic of China

The No. 17 Cold Rolled Steel Products case, Public Announcement No. 50 in 2003 of Ministry of Commerce of the People's Republic of China

The No. 18 Polyvinyl Chloride case, Public Announcement No. 48 in 2003 of Ministry of Commerce of the People's Republic of China

The No. 19 TDI (Toluene Diisocyanate) Case, Public Announcement No. 61 in 2003 of Ministry of Commerce of the People's Republic of China

The No. 20 Phenol Case, Public Announcement No. 2 in 2004 of Ministry of Commerce of the People's Republic of China

The No. 21 MDI Case, Public Announcement No. 66 in 2003 of Ministry of Commerce of the People's Republic of China

The No. 22 Monoethanolamine & Diethanolamine Case, Public Announcement No. 57 in 2004 of Ministry of Foreign Trade and Economic Cooperation of the People's Republic of China

The No. 23 Chloroform case, Public Announcement No. 81 in 2004 of Ministry of Commerce of the People's Republic of China

The No. 24 Dispersion Unshifted Single-Mode Optical Fiber Case, Public Announcement No. 96 in 2004 of Ministry of Commerce of the People's Republic of China

The No. 25 Nylon 6.66 Filament Yarn Case, Public Announcement No. 13 in 2001 of Ministry of Commerce of the People's Republic of China

The No. 26 Chloroprene Rubber Case, Public Announcement No. 23 in 2005 of Ministry of Foreign Trade and Economic Cooperation of the People's Republic of China

The No. 27 Hydrazine Hydrate Case, Public Announcement No. 36 in 2005 of Ministry of Foreign Trade and Economic Cooperation of the People's Republic of China

The No. 28 Unbleached Kraft Liner/Linerboard Case, public Announcement No. 60 in 2005 of Ministry of Foreign Trade and Economic Cooperation of the People's Republic of China

The No. 29 Trichloroethylene case, Public Announcement No. 37 in 2005 of Ministry of Foreign Trade and Economic Cooperation of the People's Republic of China

The No. 30 Cyclic Dimethyl Siloxane Case, Public Announcement No. 123 in 2005 of Ministry of Foreign Trade and Economic Cooperation of the People's Republic of China

The No. 31 Ethylene-Propylene-non-conjugated Diene Rubberzz Case, Public Announcement No. 9 in 2006 of Ministry of Commerce of the People's Republic of China

The No. 32 Benzofuranol case, Public Announcement No. 7 in 2006 of Ministry of Commerce of the People's Republic of China

The No. 33 Disodium 5' – Inosinate Case, Public Announcement No. 24 in 2006 of Ministry of Foreign Trade and Economic Cooperation of the People's Republic of China

The No. 34 Epichlorohydrin Case, Public Announcement No. 44 in 2006 of Ministry of Foreign Trade and Economic Cooperation of the People's Republic of China

The No. 35 Polyurethane case, Public Announcement No. 74 in 2006 of Ministry of Commerce of the People's Republic of China

The No. 36 Catechol Case, Public Announcement No. 32 in 2006 of Ministry of Commerce of the People's Republic of China

The No. 37 Polybutylene Terephthalate Resin Case, Public Announcement No. 42 in 2006 of Ministry of Commerce of the People's Republic of China

The No. 38 Wear Resistant Overlay Case, Public Announcement No. 93 in 2006 of Ministry of Foreign Trade and Economic Cooperation of the People's Republic of China

The No. 39 Butanols Case, Public Announcement No. 10 in 2007 of Ministry of Commerce of the People's Republic of China

The No. 40 Octanol Case, Public Announcement No. 4 in 2007 of Ministry of Commerce of the People's Republic of China

The No. 41 Nonyl Phenol Case, Public Announcement No. 11 in 2007 of Ministry of Commerce of the People's Republic of China

The No. 42 Potato Starch Case, Public Announcement No. 8 in 2007 of Ministry of Commerce of the People's Republic of China

The No. 43 paper for Electrolytic Capacitor Case, Public Announcement No. 30 in 2007 of Ministry of Commerce of the People's Republic of China

The No. 44 Sulfamethoxazole Case, Public Announcement No. 48 in 2007 of Ministry of Commerce of the People's Republic of China

The No. 45 Bisphenol-A Case, Public Announcement No. 68 in 2007 of Ministry of Foreign Trade and Economic Cooperation of the People's Republic of China

The No. 46 Methyl Ethyl Ketone Case, Public Announcement No. 81 in 2007 of Ministry of Foreign Trade and Economic Cooperation of the People's Republic of China

The No. 47 Acetone Case, Public Announcement No. 40 in 2008 of Ministry of Foreign Trade and Economic Cooperation of the People's Republic of China

The No. 48 Adipic Acid Case, Public Announcement No. 78 in 2009 of Ministry of Foreign Trade and Economic Cooperation of the People's Republic of China

The No. 49 Certain Iron or Steel Fasteners Case, Public Announcement No. 40 in

2010 of Ministry of Foreign Trade and Economic Cooperation of the People's Republic of China

The No. 50 Disodium 5'-Inosinate Case, Public Announcement No. 56 in 2010 of Ministry of Foreign Trade and Economic Cooperation of the People's Republic of China

WTO Materials:

- WTO Antidumping Agreement, WTO Members agreed at the Doha Ministerial Conference to launch negotiations in the area of "WTO Rules". These negotiations relate to the following subject matter: the Agreement on Implementation of Article VI of GATT 1994
- WTO Documents: Working Group on the Interaction between Trade and Competition Policy (WGTCP), avialbe at: http://www.wto.org/english/tratop_e/comp_e/wgtcp_docs_e.htm

WT/WGTCP/W/58 (Submission from Mexico, December 1997)

WT/WGTCP/W/51 (Submission from Canada, December 1997)

WT/WGTCP/W/54 (Submission from Mexico, December 1997)

WT/WGTCP/W/56 (Submission from Korea, December 1997)

WT/WGTCP/W/55 (Submission from Argentina, December 1997)

WT/WGTCP/W/53 (Submission from Hong Kong, China, December 1997)

WT/WGTCP/W/47(Submission from New Zealand, November 1997)

WT/WGTCP/W/46 (Submission from Kenya, November 1997)

WT/WGTCP/W/50 (Submission from Hong Kong, China, November 1997)

WT/WGTCP/W/57 (Submission from Canada, December 1997)

WT/WGTCP/W/52 (Submission from Japan, December 1997)

WT/WGTCP/W/32 (Submission from Japan, September 1997)

WT/WGTCP/W/41 (Submission from Pakistan, October 1997)

WT/WGTCP/W/40 (Submission from Turkey, October1997)

WT/WGTCP/W/39 (Communication from Australia, October 1997)

WT/WGTCP/W/38 (Communication from Romania, October 1997)

WT/WGTCP/W/37 (Communication from Korea, October 1997)

WT/WGTCP/W/35 (Communication from the United States, October 1997)

WT/WGTCP/W/43 (Communication from Morocco, October 1997)
WT/WGTCP/W/36 (Communication from Peru, November 1997)
WT/WGTCP/W/48 (Submission from the United States, November 1997)
WT/WGTCP/W/45 (Communication from the European Community and Its Member States, November 1997)
WT/WGTCP/W/25 (Communication from Japan, July 1997)
WT/WGTCP/W/21 (Communication from OECD, July1997)
WT/WGTCP/W/26 (Communication from Hong Kong, China, September 1997)
WT/WGTCP/W/31 (Communication from Norway, September 1997)
WT/WGTCP/W/30 (Communication from New Zealand, September 1997)
WT/WGTCP/W/29 (Communication fromSwitzerland, September 1997)
WT/WGTCP/W/28 (Communication from Singapore, September 1997)
WT/WGTCP/W/27 (Communication from Hungary, September 1997)
WT/WGTCP/W/33 (Communication from ASEAN, September 1997)
WT/WGTCP/W/32 (Communication from Japan, September 1997)
WT/WGTCP/W/42 (Communication from Canada, October 1997)
WT/WGTCP/W/15 (Communication from Hong Kong, June 1997)
WT/WGTCP/W/16 (Communication from Nigeria, July1997)
WT/WGTCP/W/19 (Communication from ASEAN, July1997)
WT/WGTCP/W/18 (Communication from APEC, July1997)
WT/WGTCP/W/23 (Communication from Poland, July1997)
WT/WGTCP/W/22 (Communication from the World Bank, July1997)
WT/WGTCP/W/24 (Communication from India, July1997)
WT/WGTCP/W/1 (Communication from the European Community and Its Member States, June1997)
WT/WGTCP/W/2 (Communication from Switzerland, June 1997)
WT/WGTCP/W/10 (Communication from Pakistan, June 1997)
WT/WGTCP/W/9 (Communication from Egypt, June 1997)
WT/WGTCP/W/8 (Communication from Australia, June 1997)
WT/WGTCP/W/7 (Communication from Canada, June 1997)
WT/WGTCP/W/6 (Communication from the Untied States, June 1997)

WT/WGTCP/W/5 (Communication from the Republic of Korea, June 1997)

WT/WGTCP/W/4 (Communication from Japan, June 1997)

WT/WGTCP/W/3 (Communication from Peru, June 1997)

WT/WGTCP/W/12 (Communication from Norway, June 1997)

WT/WGTCP/W/14 (Communication from Venezuela, June 1997)

WT/WGTCP/W/13 (Proposal by Mexico on Issues to be Analyzed by the Working Group on the Interaction between Trade and Competition Policy, June 1997)

WT/WGTCP/W/197 (Communication from UNCTAD, August 2002)

WT/WGTCP/W/214 (Communication from Switzerland, September 2002)

WT/WGTCP/W/218 (Communication from the United States, November 2002)

WT/WGTCP/W/92 (Communication from Japan, September 1998)

WT/WGTCP/W/98 (Communication from Australia, September 1998)

WT/WGTCP/W/81 (Communication from New Zealand, August 1998)

WT/WGTCP/W/85 (Communication from Hong Kong, China, August 1998)

WT/WGTCP/W/85 (Communication from Hong Kong, China, August 1998)

WT/WGTCP/W/88 (Communication from the United States, August 1998)

WT/WGTCP/W/90 (Communication from the Republic of Korea, September 1998)

WT/WGTCP/W/78 (Communication from the European Community and Its Member States, July 1998)

WT/WGTCP/W/82 (Communication from New Zealand, August 1998)

WT/WGTCP/W/71 (Communication from the Czech Republic, March 1998)

WT/WGTCP/W/82 (Communication from New Zealand, August 1998)

WT/WGTCP/W/74 (Communication from Peru, April 1998)

WT/WGTCP/W/73 (Communication from the Republic of Korea, March 1998)

WT/WGTCP/W/74 (Communication from Peru, April 1998)

WT/WGTCP/W/122 (Communication from Japan, May 1999)

WT/WGTCP/W/123 (Communication from Japan, May 1999)

WT/WGTCP/W/136 (Communication from Mexico, July 1999)

WT/WGTCP/W/154 (Communication from the Republic of Korea, March 2001)

WT/WGTCP/W/163 (Communication from Hong Kong, China, June 2001)

WT/WGTCP/W/197 (Communication from UNCTAD, August 2002)

WT/WGTCP/W/216 (Communication from India, September 2002)

Electronic Databases:

China Trade Remedy Information, available at: http://www.cacs.gov.cn

Bureau of Fair Trade for Imports and Exports, Ministry of Commerce of the People's Republic of China, available at: http://www.mofcom.gov.cn

China Academic Journals on China National Knowledge Infrastructure, available at: http://c50.cnki.net/kns50/

Law Info China, available at: http://www.lawinfochina.com/

World Trade Organization, available at: http://www.wto.org

United States International Trade Commission, available at: http://www.usitc.gov

United States of America Department of Commerce, available at: http://www.commerce.gov/index.htm

European Union, available at: http://europa.eu/index_en.htm

The World Bank, available at: http://www.worldbank.org

OECD (Competition), available at: http://www.oecd.org/topic/0,3373,en_2649_37463_1_1_1_1_37463,00.html